Creating F...
Applications

The Professional Programmer's Guide to FoxPro™ 2.5

George F. Goley IV

PROGRAMMING
SERIES

QUE ®

Creating FoxPro™ Applications
The Professional Programmer's Guide to FoxPro™ 2.5

Copyright © 1993 by Que® Corporation

Library of Congress Catalog No.: 93-83390

ISBN: 1-56529-093-3

96 95 94 93   8 7 6 5 4 3 2 1

Interpretation of the printing code: the rightmost double-digit number is the year of the book's printing; the rightmost single-digit number, the number of the book's printing. For example, a printing code of 93-1 shows that the first printing of the book occurred in 1993.

Trademarks

Publisher
David P. Ewing

Associate Publisher
Rick Ranucci

Operations Manager
Sheila Cunningham

Acquisitions Editors
Sherri Morningstar
Annette Sheldon
Sarah Browning

Dedication

To my sister, Dawn Goley, whose strength makes me humble, whose lifestyle leaves me often envious, and whose courage gives me hope. Thank you for proving to this most cynical of hearts that miracles do happen—they just require people who refuse to quit. Thanks too for sharing a different world with me, I will always be grateful.

To my wife Patty, who, for reasons known only to herself, continues to put up with me. Thank you Patty. This book is complete only because you had faith in me. You'll probably never understand how much that means to me, but I'll keep trying to tell you anyway. I love you Patty.

To my daughter Nessa, who makes the future seem worth the wait. Any world that includes her genius, and heart, and intensity, has to be worth working for, and I think of you every hour Nessa. I love you Nessa.

To my daughter Kelsey, who, with a single run-and-jump hug can erase the memory of even the most painful day. Kelsey, if I could capture one tenth of the warmth of your smile in a book, I'd be the best author on earth. Daddy loves you Kelsey.

Credits

Title Manager
Walter R. Bruce, III

Product Director
Robin Drake

Production Editor
Kezia Endsley

Editors
Andy Saff
Jill Bond

Technical Editors
Susan Graham
Christina Mcdonald

Editorial Assistants
Elizabeth D. Brown
Sally Smith

Production Manager
Corinne Walls

Proofreading/Indexing Coordinator
Joelynn Gifford

Production Analyst
Mary Beth Wakefield

Book Designer
Amy Peppler-Adams

Graphic Image Specialists
Dennis Sheehan
Susan VandeWalle
Jeff Shrum

Production Team
Claudia Bell
Danielle Bird
Julie Brown
Paula Carroll
Heather Kaufman
Bob LaRoche
Wendy Ott
Caroline Roop
Sandra Shay
Tina Trettin
Michelle Worthington

Indexer
Michael Hughes

Composed in Stone Serif and MCPdigital by Prentice Hall Computer Publishing.

About the Author

George F. Goley IV

George F. Goley IV is the founder of Micro Endeavors Inc., the world's most successful FoxPro training and development firm.

George is also the author of three other database management books entitled *The Dow Jones-Irwin Technical Reference Guide to Microcomputer Database Management Systems, Dynamics of FoxBASE+ Programming,* and *Dynamics of FoxBASE+/Mac Programming,* all by Dow Jones-Irwin.

George is a contributing editor and member of the technical advisory board of *Data Based Advisor (DBA)*. George's articles have appeared in *DBA* since 1986, and he has been voted author of the year twice by DBA's readership. His FoxFiles column in *DBA* was the first Fox column published in a major trade publication, and he published the first reviews of FoxBase+, FoxPro, and many other software packages. His articles appeared in *DBA, FoxTalk, Popular Computing, Byte,* various DataPro research publications, and *Small Business Computing*.

Mr. Goley and Ms. Melissa Dunn co-developed the Micro Endeavors PC database benchmark suite that was published in the *Data Based Advisor*. These benchmarks are still in use by vendors and users alike to determine the relative performance of PC databases.

Mr. Goley has been a featured speaker at all four U.S. Fox Developers conferences, where his performance sessions are *standing room only*. In addition, the author made presentations at Microsoft's German Developers conference, at symposiums, as well as countless user groups around the world.

As a developer, Mr. Goley has worked on some of the world's largest and most successful FoxPro applications, including the Mobil Mariner project. As a trainer, Mr. Goley personally has trained more than 1,000 FoxPro programmers in locations all around the world. His CompuServe address is 71140,3527.

Contributing Authors

Michael L. Brachman, Ph.D.

Mike is Senior Systems Analyst at Micro Endeavors, having been employed there since 1989. Mike has been programming since 1967 in a variety of languages including ML, Assembler, FORTRAN, BASIC, SNOBOL, C, and dBASE. He has been programming in FoxPro almost exclusively since his start at Micro Endeavors.

Mike does applications development in FoxPro for Fortune-500 companies including J. P. Morgan, Marriott Corporation, Rhone-Poulenc Rorer, Envirite, Coopers & Lybrand, and Mobil Oil. He has trained hundreds in FoxPro at the aforementioned as well as at Chase Manahattan Bank, Koch Industries, Glaxo, and many other sites. Mike was a featured speaker at the last two FoxPro Developers' Conferences.

Mike has had articles published in *Data Based Advisor, FoxPro Advisor, FoxTalk, Dr. Dobb's Journal, Science, Chemistry, Journal of the Acoustical Society of America, Brain Research*, and *Hearing Research and Biological Cybernetics*. He received his bachelor's degree in Science from the University of Michigan in 1974 and a Ph.D. in Sensory Science from Syracuse University in 1980. Married, he has two children and two cats. Mike can be reached on CompuServe at 71045,1217.

Dr. Brachman wrote or contributed significantly to Chapters 16, 17, and 18, covering Windows, FoxPro's API, OLE, and DDE topics.

Melissa W. Dunn, MA

Melissa W. Dunn, MA, has been writing Xbase applications for over 12 years. In 1990, Melissa joined the Micro Endeavors staff where she has continued to develop applications for such firms as Mobil Oil. As one of the MEI trainers, Melissa provides FoxPro training around the world.

Melissa is the author of the course materials used in the Microsoft University intermediate and advanced FoxPro training courses. She both wrote and appeared in the Micro Endeavors FoxPro 2.0 Video Training Series—Non-Programmers Edition.

Melissa's articles on FoxPro and SQL appear in the *Data Based Advisor.* Her book on FoxPro 2.0 and SQL is published by Pinnacle Publishing. Melissa was also a featured speaker at the 1992 Microsoft Developer's Conference.

Ms. Dunn received her BA in Political Science from the University of Kentucky, where she also earned an MA in Sociology. She can be reached on CompuServe (CIS:70511,2756).

Melissa wrote or contributed significantly to Chapters 10, 11, and 21, covering SQL, the Report Writer, and cross-platform issues.

Bruce Troutman

Bruce Troutman specializes in large system development and contributed to Chapter 22, "Team Programming." He is the primary author of the Disaster Management System for the Exxon Oil Spill, The Quality Control System for Boise Cascade, and the Accounting System for Mobil's Mariner Project.

Bruce is a native Atlantan, a graduate of Georgia Tech, and currently is a seminar leader for FoxPro and Access courses. His CompuServe address is 71332,3535.

Acknowledgments

Creating FoxPro Applications was written by four people. So, I would first like to thank my co-authors: Dr. Michael Brachman, Melissa Dunn, and Bruce Troutman for their efforts. All three of these outstanding individuals worked overtime to make this book better. Mike and Melissa in particular made personal and professional sacrifices to make this book better, and I am eternally grateful.

At the same time he contributed Chapters 16, 17, and 18 covering Windows fonts and styles, FoxPro's API, and FoxPro's OLE and DDE implementations, Mike Brachman was also responsible for delivering no fewer than four development projects to different clients. Thank you Mike. Without your talent and mastery of C, Windows, and OLE/ DDE, *Creating FoxPro Applications* would be much less than it is.

At the same time she contributed Chapters 10, 11, and 21, covering SQL, the Report Writer, and cross-platform issues, Melissa Dunn was writing 800 pages of course material for the Microsoft University/Micro Endeavors FoxPro training courses. In addition, Melissa was on the road teaching several of our FoxPro classes. Thank you Melissa. If not for your talent, your skill, your all-nighters, and your mastery of SQL, *Creating FoxPro Applications* would be much less than it is.

At the same time he contributed Chapter 22 covering Team Programming, Bruce Troutman was working feverishly to complete another milestone for the Mariner project at Mobil Oil. In addition, Bruce was busily learning and writing about Access. Thank you Bruce. Without your intimate knowledge of team programming dynamics, *Creating FoxPro Applications* would be much less than it is.

As I was spending all my time writing this book, and stealing additional Micro Endeavors resources at the same time, my partner found a way to continue Micro Endeavors' unbelievable rate of growth. Ed Martini has been the perfect business partner for almost 10 years, and *Creating FoxPro Applications* could not have been written without him. Thank you Ed. Without you, there would be no Micro Endeavors.

I would also like to thank Susan Graham for doing an excellent technical edit of the book, and for providing an always honest opinion of my ideas for the book. When I needed a reality check, Susan was always available. Susan even obtained the help of fellow Microsoft employees Matt Pohle and Chris Capossela, who assisted with the technical edit. Thank you Matt. Thank you Chris.

A special thank you to Micro Endeavors administrative staff members Holly Paul, Ileen Martini, Mary Kulsik, and Liz Lagana for their forbearance, support, and professionalism in handling the extra work that *Creating FoxPro Applications* added to their already daunting workloads.

Thanks to Micro Endeavors trainer, author, and developer Rich Wolf, who contributed ideas to several chapters in the book, at the same time he wrote the Access training materials for the Microsoft University/Micro Endeavors training courses.

Thanks to Lisa Slater for her support and insights during the early stages of the book. Lisa is an industry expert I am proud to call my friend, and someone on whom I can always count for an honest opinion.

Thanks to Dave Fulton, Janet Walker, Eric Christenson, Bill Ferguson, Amy Fulton, Chris Williams, Rick Waddell, and the many other members of Fox Software who built the best database product anywhere, and who have been an invaluable source of information and support over the years. Thanks also to Richard McAniff, Morris Sim, Michael Mee, and the many other members of the Microsoft-FoxPro team who have helped make the best DBMS even better.

I would like to thank Rick Ranucci, Walt Bruce, Robin Drake, and all the other fine people at Que who allowed me to write the book you hold. *Creating FoxPro Applications* is a very different book for Que, and it took courage to try something new. Thanks very much folks for your trust, your support, and your skill.

Finally, to my family, who put up with my absence, my distractedness, and my inattentiveness for several months while I completed this book, thank you. Thank you Nessa. Thank you Kelsey. Thank you Patty. Thank you all for your hugs, and your love. I love you too.

Overview

Table of Contents

11 The Report Writer 211

12 The BROWSE Command 237

13 Multiuser Discussions 261

16 Beautifying Windows   369

17 The C Connection   381

Foreword

It is a great pleasure to see George return to writing about FoxPro.

As I recall, George wrote the first book on Fox products. His books on FoxBASE+ and FoxBASE+/Mac helped establish Fox Software as a company, and also helped a great number of our customers learn and use FoxBASE. I have known George a long time, I consider him a personal friend, and I'm gratified and pleased that he has taken up the pen again.

One of the strengths of FoxPro is that it can be used by beginners as well as professional programmers. In contrast to many books on FoxPro, however, George aims *Creating FoxPro Applications* squarely at high-level, experienced developers. George has long been a preeminent FoxPro programmer and teacher and it is clear that he hasn't been reticent in sharing the techniques he has developed.

One aspect I particularly like about *Creating FoxPro Applications* is its emphasis on developing a programming methodology in addition to teaching simple "tips and tricks."

As applications become more elaborate and more central to the businesses that use them, one of the most important things a developer can do is work out a methodology for designing, developing, and testing applications. In my view, this is far more important than mere mastery of a programming language. George's book does the best job I've seen at outlining a solid, workable approach to developing mission-critical applications. I recommend it strongly for this reason alone.

In addition, George has done a fine job of explaining the more advanced aspects of FoxPro development—multiuser programming, event-driven programming, SQL development, the Library Construction Kit application program interface, and DDE commands. His book provides an advanced discussion of all these topics. His discussion of performance issues is, of course, right on target as well.

I think this book will rapidly become an essential reference for every professional FoxPro developer. I'm glad George wrote it, and I think you will be too.

David L. Fulton

Vice President and Database Architect

Microsoft Corporation

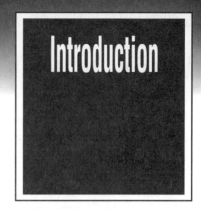
Introduction

Introduction and Answers to Obvious Questions

Welcome to *Creating FoxPro Applications.* Because you took the time (and spent the money) to purchase this book, I assume that you have an interest in creating FoxPro 2.5 applications.

More than that, I assume that your current job requires you to develop FoxPro applications, or that you wish to begin a job that requires you to develop FoxPro applications. In other words, you are, or want to be, a professional FoxPro programmer.

This book is, therefore, *not* about using FoxPro interactively. It is not about using other peoples' applications. It is not even about creating pieces of applications.

Creating FoxPro Applications is a book about creating complete, multiuser, FoxPro 2.5 for Windows and FoxPro 2.5 for DOS applications. The book features both a methodology and a group of techniques and routines that make it possible for you to write important FoxPro applications.

Why Did I Write It This Way?

In my initial attempt at this book, I spent the first 30 pages or so outlining methodologies, explaining file formats, listing naming conventions, and generally preparing you for the work of creating an application. As I wrote however, I couldn't shake the feeling that something was wrong.

The book's message was being lost in the explanations of the details. As I wrote and rewrote the same pages over and over again, it finally occurred to me that I was violating one of the basic principles of training programmers.

After digging around the office a little, I found a brochure for one of Micro Endeavors' earliest training classes. There, in big bold letters, was the principle I had trampled in a stampede of figures, tables, and witticisms. It read, *"Programmers learn how to program by writing programs!"*

In our training classes, programmers type code, lay out screens, paint reports, build menus, and test all of the above in real-time. Further, readers of my previous books unanimously point to the example code as the most valuable portion of the book.

Slowly, it became clear that this book needed to concentrate on demonstrating the development of an application, rather than on defining the development process in an abstract way. So—in an effort to remain focused on the central theme of applications development—the book you hold in your hands contains a great deal less prose, and a great deal more code, than I originally intended.

I hope you find the resultant mix of examples and explanations enjoyable and profitable. I also hope that you will let me know how you feel about the book. You can leave me e-mail on CompuServe at ID 71140,3527.

How Should You Read This Book?

If you are new to FoxPro programming, I suggest that you work your way through the first eight chapters of the book. This effort includes the creation of databases, programs, screens, menus, and reports. More importantly, these chapters introduce you to a methodology that you can follow when writing your own applications.

If you are an experienced FoxPro 2.0 developer, you might want to browse through the first eight chapters of the book, paying close attention to the code listings. Although you may not need the practice that comes with writing applications, I hope you will find many of the techniques valuable. For that reason, I have made a special effort to ensure that the comments in the code listings are extensive.

Chapters 9 through 22 are designed as reference material. As a result, they can be reviewed or studied in any order. If you are an advanced developer, I think Chapter 13, "Multiuser Discussions," Chapter 14, "Event-Driven Programming," and Chapter 15, "Performance" will be of particular interest.

Why Am I Writing This Book?

I am writing in the totally selfless hope that this book will engender goodwill among all the nations of the earth, help clean the environment, and lead to the development of inexpensive solar power.

Ok, ok.

I am really writing this book to make people aware of Micro Endeavors' FoxPro training classes. Not the most altruistic motivation I admit, but an honest one. We have trained more than 3,000 FoxPro programmers at Micro Endeavors, and most of them have asked for a book to take back to the office. Well folks, here's the book I promised. Enjoy.

What Is Expected of the Reader?

I expect that you can handle the FoxPro interface. I expect that you do not need any assistance with moving windows, clicking the mouse, resizing windows, using the text editor, and so on.

I expect that you are willing to write programs. FoxPro is a programming language that has many tools and features for reducing programming effort. In spite of those tools and features however, FoxPro is still a programming language, and programming is still required.

I expect that you know what a database is. I expect that you know what an index is, and how FoxPro 2.5 implements indexes.

I expect that you have a basic understanding of relational databases. For example, the reasons behind maintaining separate databases for invoice headers and invoice line items should be well known to you.

I expect that you can grasp the functionality of DO WHILE, IF...ENDIF, FOR...ENDFOR, and DO CASE...CASE...ENDCASE programming constructs without help from me. I expect that you understand memory variables, data types, and parameter passing.

I expect that you have installed a copy of FoxPro 2.5 for Windows and/or a copy of FoxPro 2.5 for DOS on your computer. I further expect that you can use DOS and/or Windows to create subdirectories, copy files, delete files, and perform other house-keeping chores.

New Ideas

During the course of our discussions, I will suggest several techniques that you won't find in other FoxPro books. Indeed, several of the techniques seem to challenge recommendations made in FoxPro's manuals.

In particular, the Micro Endeavors methods for handling *foundation reads* and *snippets* are in conflict with what some programmers consider "standard" FoxPro programming practice. In these cases, you have every right to ask, "Why should I do it your way, George?"

Why Should You Do It My Way?

The following are *not* good reasons to adopt a programming technique:

1. The author writes well.

2. The author has written lots of other books.

3. The author has a long standing reputation in the industry.

4. The author is a good public speaker.

5. The technique conforms to the current programming fad.

In fact, the acceptable reasons to adopt a programming technique are

1. The technique improves programmer productivity by reducing the amount of code required to perform an action, by reducing debugging effort, or by increasing the maintainability of the application.

2. The technique improves the functionality of the application by increasing performance, by increasing the ease with which users can perform an activity, or by adding a useful feature to the application.

3. The technique is familiar to a majority of programmers who will be working on the project, and/or the technique is easily learned by professional programmers.

But George, How do I know if your techniques qualify?

Micro Endeavors uses the techniques in this book daily on some of the largest, and most critical, FoxPro applications in the world. Further, the more than 3,000 students who have attended our seminars use these techniques daily to develop mission-critical applications at the largest companies in the world. As a result, you can be assured that the techniques covered in this book improve programmer productivity and increase application functionality.

Micro Endeavors has trained more FoxPro programmers than any other training or consulting company in the world. Further, Microsoft University has chosen Micro Endeavors to be the exclusive provider of FoxPro course materials to Microsoft Approved FoxPro trainers worldwide. In other words, if you take a Microsoft Approved FoxPro training class, you will be learning the techniques that are outlined in this book. As a result, you can be assured that the techniques in this book are widely used and easily learned.

What Conventions Are Used?

To get the most out of this book, you should know how it is designed. New terms and emphasized words are presented in *italicized text* and are defined on first reference. Pay close attention to italicized text.

Functions, commands, parameters, and the like are set in monospace text; for example, the BROWSE command.

Placeholder variables, such as the word <column name> in AVG<column name>, are in angle brackets. They indicate that you should enter the appropriate name in place of the placeholder.

All code listings are in monospace text as follows:

```
PROCEDURE vcontrol
* Processes push button selections.
PARAMETERS control
DO CASE
  CASE UPPER(control)=="EXIT"
    CLEAR READ
  CASE UPPER(m.control)=="MENU"
```

Code listing *changes* (from previous lists) or special places of interest in code are indicated by monospace bold, as shown:

```
PROCEDURE vcontrol
* Processes push button selections.
PARAMETERS control
  CASE UPPER(control)=="NEXT"
    DO tsskip WITH 1
    SCATTER MEMVAR MEMO
    SHOW GETS
  CASE UPPER(control)=="PREVIOUS"
    DO tsskip WITH -1
    SCATTER MEMVAR MEMO
    SHOW GETS
DO CASE
  CASE UPPER(control)=="EXIT"
    CLEAR READ
  CASE UPPER(m.control)=="MENU"
```

Other visual pointers found in this book include:

Caution: Caution boxes that warn you of problem areas, including possible cases in which you might introduce bugs into your program or crash your system.

and

Note: Note boxes that provide you with extraneous information. Many times, this information helps speed your learning process and provides you with shortcuts in FoxPro. Other times, it simply reminds you of information important enough to be mentioned twice.

and

Tip: Tip boxes that help you learn special tricks from the masters!

All these conventions are used simply to help arrange the material in a logical manner, thus helping you quickly find the information you need.

What About the Disk?

The disk that accompanies this book contains the completed time sheet application, the databases associated with that application, and all the library routines referenced in the book. If you install the entire disk, you will discover all the programs listed in the book, and quite a few more.

However, to allow you to work along with the book if you like, I have included four extra subdirectories for the application. Although you will perform most of your work in the \BOOK\PRG, \BOOK\DBF, \BOOK\MNX, and \BOOK\SCX subdirectories, the finished version of the time sheet application is installed in the \BOOK\PRG2, \BOOK\MNX2, \BOOK\DBF2, and \BOOK\SCX2 subdirectories of your disk.

If, instead of working along with the book, you want to work through the finished application, just copy the content of the \BOOK\PRG2 subdirectory to \BOOK\PRG, and do the same for the \BOOK\MNX2, \BOOK\SCX2, and \BOOK\DBF2 sub-directories of your disk.

Please feel free to include these programs in your applications. Please feel free to modify these programs as needed. There is no royalty fee associated with the use of the programs found in this book, nor is there a requirement to "credit" me in your applications. (*Note:* If you wish, you can credit Micro Endeavors and George Goley if you include the library routines in your application.)

The programs in this book are copyrighted. So, you can't copy them and give them away. You can't put them on bulletin boards. You can't sell them. (*Note:* You can sell an application of your own design and implementation that includes some or all of the routines, provided that application does not consist largely of the programs found in this book.) Finally, you can't include them in your articles and books without permission.

Final Thoughts

I am a FoxPro programmer, and have been for several years. I wrote this book with the idea that you are also a FoxPro programmer. As a result, I've tried to write a book that is conversational, rather than didactic.

We do a hard thing, we programmers, so I've tried to treat our problems, and the associated solutions, with the proper respect. However, like you, I know that programming is not without humor. (Just remember the last time you tried to identify the *any* key for a user who was befuddled by the Press any key... message.)

Indeed, one of the most important lessons I ever learned about programming was not to take anything too seriously. So, I took the liberty of using some sections of the book to poke fun at myself, at some of the myths of FoxPro programming, and at society in general. I hope you don't mind.

On a similar topic, I am fully aware that programming is not a religion. This book therefore is not entitled "FoxPro: The Goley Method," or "The One True FoxPro," or "Proper FoxPro Programming," or any other title that implies that there is only one correct to write FoxPro applications. Frankly, if there were only one right way to write FoxPro programs, I'd stop programming.

So, I don't expect you to slavishly follow every suggestion I make in this book. On the contrary, I hope you think about every suggestion in the book. If you do, by the end of the eighth chapter, you should have a good idea of why I developed the Micro Endeavors methodology, even if you choose to improve on it for your own use. By the end of the book, you should have a solution, or the start of a solution, for most of your FoxPro programming challenges.

Goal for the Book

As a FoxPro programmer, you are expected to be part artist, part scientist, part mathematician, part psychiatrist, part mind-reader, and part magician. In short, you've got a tough job. I hope this book helps you meet your own expectations of yourself as a programmer, because, in the end, that's the best any of us can hope for.

Preparing To Build an Application

The first seven chapters of this book are designed to race you through the creation of a fairly simple, multifile, multiuser, FoxPro for Windows database application. Along the way you learn much about the FoxPro language. More importantly, you learn a series of steps that you can follow, long after you've read this book for the last time, to develop your own applications.

Readers of my other books have reported best results when they worked their way through the development of applications. Therefore, I wrote the first seven chapters in a way that enables you to type along and paint along with me as I create programs, menus, screens, and reports.

If you are an experienced FoxPro developer, you might prefer simply to browse through these chapters, looking for ideas and code that might be valuable to your current development projects. This is perfectly acceptable, especially given that all the programs listed in this chapter also appear on the source code disk that comes with the book. However, you can gain maximum understanding of the techniques in this chapter by working through the exercises.

As you read the first seven chapters, you probably will wonder whether there is another way of implementing some portion of the sample application. As I was writing, I felt the need to discuss alternative methods for implementing some portions of the application. However, because I use only one solution at a time when developing actual applications, I chose only one solution for each problem in these first seven chapters. Subsequent chapters explore some of the more intriguing alternatives to the solutions chosen in this first chapter.

This chapter presents the steps necessary to set up a working environment for an application. These steps include not only FoxPro programs but operating system settings as well.

By the end of this chapter, you should have an idea how to set up your system to begin work on an application.

Beginnings (Creating the Subdirectory Structure)

To create the time sheet program, you must first create a place to work, such as the subdirectory structure shown in Figure 1.1.

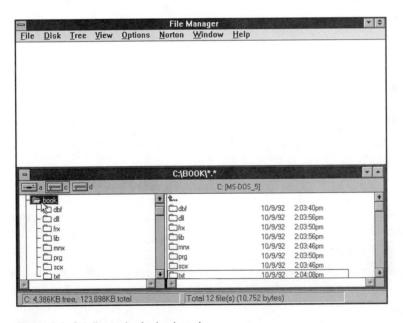

Figure 1.1. Subdirectories for book work.

The reason for creating so many subdirectories for a single application is simple. DOS slows down substantially when it has too many files in a subdirectory. Because FoxPro goes through DOS to access files, FoxPro also is substantially slowed when there are too many files in a subdirectory.

FoxPro includes a text editor, a Screen Builder, a Menu Builder, a Report Writer, and a query generator. It also includes a Project Builder to put all this together, and each of these tools creates many DOS files. Placing all these files in the same subdirectory results in the performance degradation associated with having too many files in the same subdirectory.

The subdirectory structure in Figure 1.1 addresses this problem by placing the files for each of FoxPro's power tools in a separate subdirectory. The subdirectories under \BOOK are named for the type of files they contain.

The first task is to generate a brief statement of purpose for the time sheet application. Because you are developing the application in FoxPro, put the statement of purpose in a place easily accessible from within FoxPro. After you start FoxPro, issue the following commands:

```
SET DEFAULT TO C:\BOOK
MODIFY FILE txt\tsovervw.txt
```

Now that you've found the FoxPro text editor, spend a few seconds entering the following bit of poetry in the \BOOK\TXT\TSOVERVW.TXT file:

```
The time sheet program will gather time sheet information
from employees for the purposes of billing clients, improving
estimates, paying "piece work" employees, and rewarding
outstanding employee contributions. In addition, employees
will be able to identify time wasting activities by reviewing
daily activities.
```

Okay, maybe it's not Robert Frost, but it'll do for now. Wondering why the file was named TSOVERVW.TXT rather than something simple like OVERVIEW.TXT? The *ts* preface at the beginning of the file name indicates that this file belongs to the time sheet tracking system. All the file names associated with the time sheet tracking system include the *ts* preface. This convention facilitates backups, global file searches, and global compiles.

The use of a file name preface is one of several *naming conventions* used throughout this book. If you want to see all of the naming conventions in one place, you can turn to Chapter 9, "Micro Endeavors Naming Conventions."

The purpose of the system overview in TSOVERVW.TXT is to remind you of the most important goals of the system. As development progresses, you use this information to decide which features are necessary and which features you can postpone or omit to meet deadlines.

Overcoming Inertia

When faced with their first (or one hundred and first) FoxPro application, developers are frequently unsure what their first step should be. Should you design the databases first? Should you create a project first? Should you attack the most difficult portion of the application first? Should you work on the log-in procedure first? Should you perform the religious ceremony of your choice first?

The first thing to do is to create a system overview like the one in TSOVERVW.TXT. Second, create a menu system that contains entries for all the major functions in the application. This gives you an opportunity to design the application at the same time as you write a piece of code that proves useful to the finished application.

Establishing a Setup Program

The next step in your applications design is to create a menu. Before doing so, however, you might want to create a setup program to make life a little easier. After all, you don't want to have to precede each of the file names in the application with fully qualified path names. Nor do you want to start each FoxPro session by issuing the SET DEFAULT command in the command window. To address both problems, create a program called TSSETUP.PRG by using the following command:

```
modi comm prg\tssetup
```

You also can use the system menus to create a new program file. To do so, you first select the New... option from the File menu, shown in Figure 1.2. In the subsequent dialog, shown in Figure 1.3, you select the Program radio button. You can then edit the file, as shown in Figure 1.4. Finally, when you save the file, as shown in Figure 1.5, you select the appropriate subdirectory and type the file name, as shown in Figure 1.6. Figures 1.2 through 1.6 demonstrate this rather tedious exercise.

 Note: I don't dislike menus. I don't dislike pointing devices. I don't love to type. I do like to accomplish tasks quickly however, so I prefer to type a single command, rather than select one menu option, and respond to two dialogs. Therefore, this book frequently asks you to issue commands to accomplish tasks that you can also accomplish by using menus and dialogs. This should save you time and keep the focus on the tasks rather than the mechanisms by which those tasks are accomplished. However, feel free to use menus and dialogs.

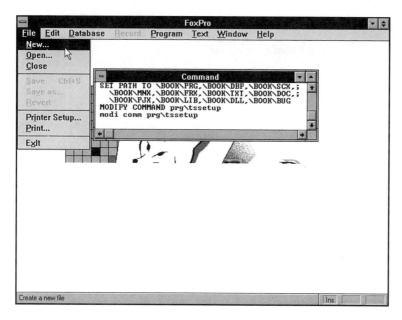

Figure 1.2. The File menu pad.

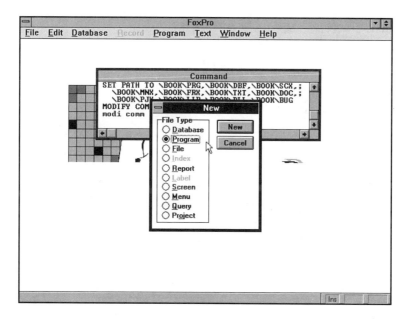

Figure 1.3. The File Type dialog.

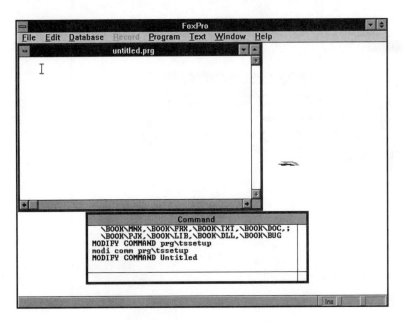

Figure 1.4. Using menus to create a new file—editing the "untitled" file.

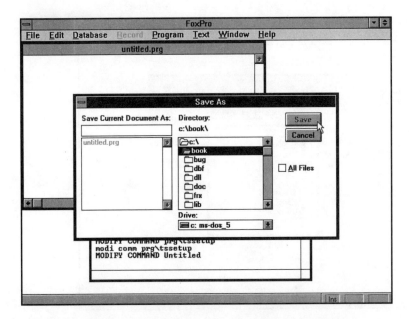

Figure 1.5. Using menus to create a new file—saving the "untitled" file.

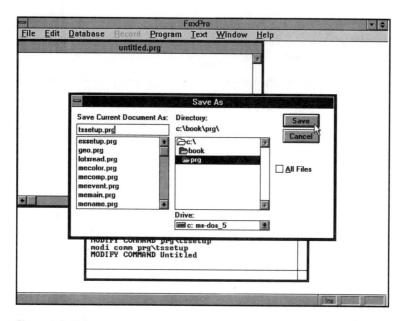

Figure 1.6. Using menus to create a new file—assigning a directory and file name.

After creating the TSSETUP.PRG file, enter the following code:

```
* tssetup.prg
* Sets environment for working with the
* time sheet application
SET DEFAULT TO \book  && drive with book directory
* Make FoxPro look for files in the right places
SET PATH TO \book\lib,\book\prg,\book\dbf,;
\book\scx,\book\mnx,;
\book\frx,\book\txt,\book\doc,\book\dll
SET EXCLUSIVE OFF  && Share databases
SET CLOCK STATUS  && put clock in status bar
SET SAFETY OFF && don't ask before overwriting files
SET TALK OFF && Don't echo results of activities to screen
SET DELETED ON && Ignore deleted records
* Make FoxPro use the FoxFont,7 point font for
* the main screen. All window coordinates will be
* based on the SCREEN font. By forcing the application
* to always use the same font, we help ensure
* that our windows will line up the same way each
* time the application is run.
MODIFY WINDOW SCREEN FONT "Foxfont",7 NOCLOSE
* Eof tssetup.prg
```

When you are finished, close and save the file by pressing Ctrl+W or by choosing the Close option of the File menu, or by choosing the Close option of the window control for the TSSETUP.PRG window.

 Note: No, I don't repeat all of these options every time you have to save a file. Because it doesn't matter how you save the file, I'll just direct you to save and close files. You can decide on the dialogs or keypress issue yourself.

You might wonder why you should choose to use FoxFont,7 as the base font for your application. FoxFont is nonproportional font, and not particularly attractive. However, because FoxFont,7 is a nonproportional font, and because it works in all windows resolutions, the font makes life easier when you must align windows and objects. You will almost certainly decide to use other fonts in your applications, but stick with FoxFont,7 for most of the time sheet application.

You will expand on the TSSETUP.PRG program later. For now, the program serves the purposes of establishing a search path for files and establishing a few rudimentary environmental settings. Because you want these purposes served each time you enter FoxPro, you must direct FoxPro to run this program each time you begin work on the time sheet program.

In the DOS environment, if the FoxPro directory were in the path, you would create in the FoxPro directory a batch file containing the following commands:

```
REM timeshee.bat
REM Time sheet batch file
FoxproX c:\book\prg\tssetup
```

In the Windows environment, you must create a program item for the TSSETUP.PRG program in the FoxPro program group. First, open the FoxPro for Windows program group. Next, choose the New... option from the File menu pad. Then, select the Program Item radio button in the New Program Object dialog. Finally, fill in the Program Item Properties dialog, as shown in Figure 1.7. Here is the full command line for the Program Item Properties dialog:

```
d:\foxprow\foxprow c:\book\prg\tssetup
```

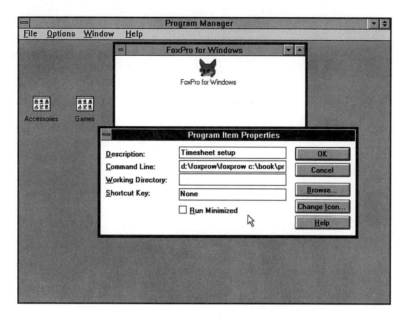

Figure 1.7. The program item for the time sheet setup.

To use this setup for the time sheet application, simply double-click the time sheet icon in the FoxPro for Windows group.

Now, you should be ready to begin working on the application of your choice.

CHAPTER
2

Menus and Databases

In this chapter we create the main menu for our time sheet application and explore FoxPro's menu builder. In addition, we create databases and indexes in which the data for the time sheet application will reside.

By the end of the chapter, you should feel comfortable in creating menus, control programs to process those menus, and databases. In addition, you should understand some of the naming conventions that we use throughout the rest of the book.

Building a Menu

In an effort to jump-start our development process, I am going to lead you through the creation of a fairly primitive menu system. Don't worry, the complexity of our application increases appreciably later in this book.

FoxPro menus are built by issuing a series of FoxPro commands. These commands can be typed into program files, or they can be generated by one of FoxPro's four power tools, the *Menu Builder*. Because our goal is to get a sample application up and running ASAP, we use the Menu Builder.

We use the Menu Builder not because it is a faster way to create menus, because it might not be, but rather because using the Menu Builder shields us from the need to understand FoxPro's verbose menuing syntax.

In standard FoxPro menu systems, *menus* have *pads* which have *popups* which have *bars*. You can implement other kinds of menus (stand-alone popups are among the most useful), but the following discussion focuses on the system pull-down menus created by the Menu Builder.

In Figure 2.1, the Time and Text pads reside in the system menu. The Timesheet popup that we create in this chapter is the list of options that appears beneath the Time pad. The Clients, Projects, Time Sheets, Reports, and Quit prompts are bars residing in the Timesheet popup.

We can create the menu shown in Figure 2.1 by typing the following program "by hand":

```
* tsmenu1.prg
* Hand-coded main menu system
SET SYSMENU TO  && "empty" the system menu
SET SYSMENU AUTOMATIC  && enable the system menu during READs
* Create the Pad
DEFINE PAD timesheet OF _msysmenu PROMPT ;
  "\<Time" KEY alt+t
* Attach a popup to the Pad
ON PAD timesheet OF _msysmenu ACTIVATE POPUP timesheet
* Create the popup
DEFINE POPUP timesheet
* Fill the popup with bars
DEFINE BAR 1 OF timesheet PROMPT "\<Clients"
DEFINE BAR 2 OF timesheet PROMPT "\<Projects"
DEFINE BAR 3 OF timesheet PROMPT "\<Time Sheets"
DEFINE BAR 4 OF timesheet PROMPT "\<Reports"
DEFINE BAR 5 OF timesheet PROMPT "\<Quit"
* Define a command to execute when any of the
* bars on the timesheet popup is selected
ON SELECTION POPUP timesheet DO tsdo WITH PROMPT()
* eof tsmenu1.prg
```

However, the Menu Builder enables us to create the same menu without ever entering the text editor. If you have not already done so, issue the following command:

```
modi menu mnx\tsmenu
```

Now create a pad by filling in the prompt as I have done in Figure 2.2.

For reasons that become clear later, we want to provide our own name for the Timesheet pad. To accomplish this, select the Options check box. In the resulting Prompt Options dialog, select the Pad Name check box. The Pad Name dialog appears, as shown in Figure 2.3. Type the name timesheet and press Enter or choose OK.

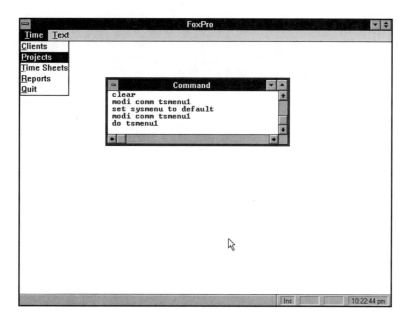

Figure 2.1. The menu for the time sheet program.

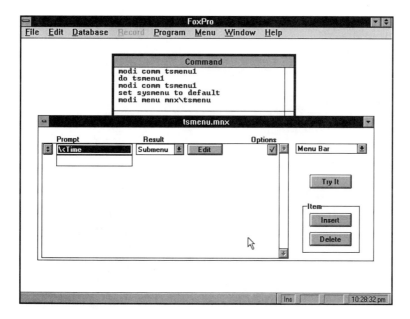

Figure 2.2. Creating the Time pad.

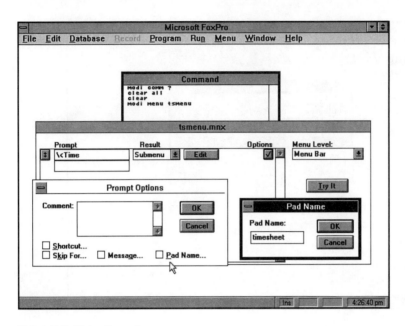

Figure 2.3. Giving the pad a name.

Next, we create a hot key shortcut for this pad by selecting the Shortcut check box, as I have done in Figure 2.4.

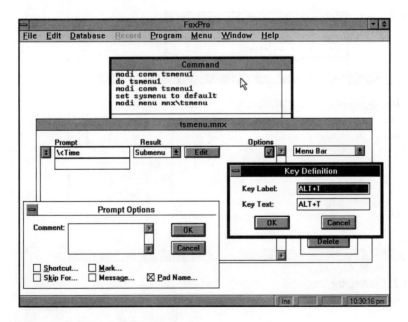

Figure 2.4. Giving the pad a shortcut key.

After closing the Prompt Options dialog, you will want to provide the Time pad with some bars. To do this, press the Create push button that has appeared next to the Time pad. This leads you to the dialog shown in Figure 2.5. Go ahead and provide the appropriate prompts as shown in the figure.

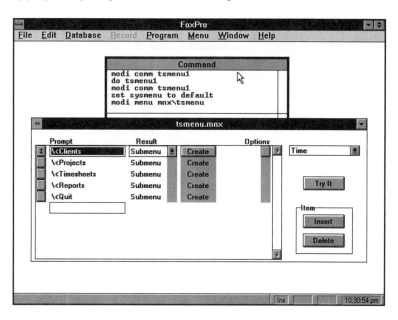

Figure 2.5. Providing bars for the popup.

We are almost finished. However, we still need to tell FoxPro what to do when a user chooses an option from the menu. Further, because I may want to manipulate the time sheet menu programmatically in future programs, I'll need to change the name of the popup to `timesheet`. To accomplish these goals, I choose Time Options... from the Menu pad as shown in Figure 2.6, then complete the popup dialog as shown in Figure 2.7. Please complete your popup dialog to match that in Figure 2.7.

At the beginning of this section, I told you that FoxPro implements menus by executing a series of commands. In fact, I even wrote a hand-coded version of the menu system to demonstrate a command series.

So what? So, our effort to build a menu by using the Menu Builder isn't complete until you generate some source code. You accomplish this by selecting the Generate option of the Program pad and responding to the Generate Menu dialog shown in Figure 2.8.

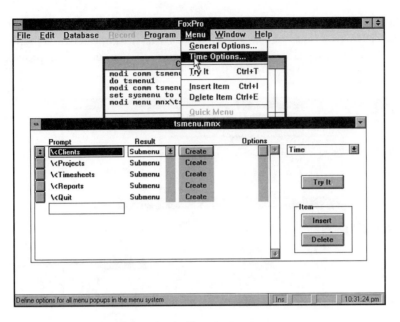

Figure 2.6. Accessing options for the Timesheet popup.

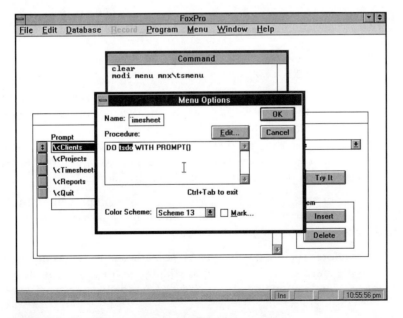

Figure 2.7. Providing an activity for the Timesheet popup.

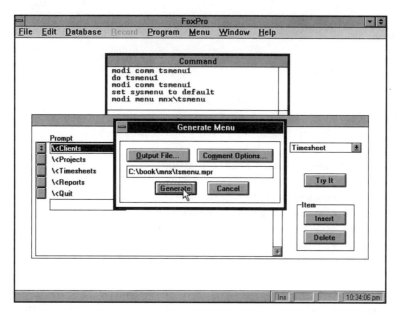

Figure 2.8. Generating a program for the menu system.

This dialog leads to the generation of an .MPR file like the following:

```
***********************************************************
*          *
*          * 09/11/92          TSMENU.MPR          22:34:20
*          *
***********************************************************
*          *
*          * Author's Name
*          *
*          * Copyright (c) 1992 Company Name
*          * Address
*          * City,     Zip
*          *
*          * Description:
*   * This program was automatically generated by GENMENU.
*          *
*          *                    Menu Definition
*          *
***********************************************************
*
```

continues

```
SET SYSMENU TO

SET SYSMENU AUTOMATIC

DEFINE PAD timesheet OF _MSYSMENU PROMPT "\<Time" ;
  COLOR SCHEME 13 KEY ALT+T, "ALT+T"
ON PAD timesheet OF _MSYSMENU ACTIVATE POPUP timesheet

DEFINE POPUP timesheet MARGIN RELATIVE SHADOW ;
  COLOR SCHEME 13
DEFINE BAR 1 OF timesheet PROMPT "\<Clients"
DEFINE BAR 2 OF timesheet PROMPT "\<Projects"
DEFINE BAR 3 OF timesheet PROMPT "\<Timesheets"
DEFINE BAR 4 OF timesheet PROMPT "\<Reports"
DEFINE BAR 5 OF timesheet PROMPT "\<Quit"
ON SELECTION POPUP timesheet DO tsdo WITH PROMPT()
```

Well, the generated code looks like the hand-coded code, so which is better? Even though using the Menu Builder takes longer, I usually use it. Why? For the following reasons:

- Using the Menu Builder doesn't take much longer.

- The volume of typing required for FoxPro's verbose menuing syntax often leads to errors.

- Showing users the Menu Builder's generated code is easier than showing them a .PRG file.

Getting Control of the Situation

Building the menu is one thing, but connecting the selection of a menu option to an activity is another thing altogether. To accomplish this, we need a control program. We create the PRG\TSMAIN.PRG program as follows:

```
* tsmain.prg
* Main control program for the time sheet
* application.
** Save the current state of the menu system
PUSH MENU _MSYSMENU
** set the environment
DO tssetup
** establish a control variable
PUBLIC kaction
```

```
kaction=""
** establish the menu system
DO tsmenu.mpr
** Create an event loop
DO WHILE .T.
  DO CASE
    CASE UPPER(kaction)="CLIENT"
      kaction=""
      DO tsclient
    CASE UPPER(kaction)="PROJECT"
      kaction=""
      DO tsproj
    CASE UPPER(kaction)="TIME"
      kaction=""
      DO tstime
    CASE UPPER(kaction)="QUIT"
      EXIT
    OTHERWISE
      ** wait for the user to select an option
      READ VALID .T.
  ENDCASE && what action was chosen
ENDDO && Do forever
** Put the menu system back the way we found it
POP MENU _MSYSMENU
* eof tsmain.prg
```

At this point we have created a menu to present to the user and an event loop to process the user's selections. We also have told FoxPro how to hook these two objects together. The following command from the TSMENU.MPR directs FoxPro to perform the TSDO program whenever a bar is selected from the Timesheet popup:

```
ON SELECTION POPUP timesheet DO tsdo WITH PROMPT()
```

Menu Builder generated this line of code because we included the DO tsdo WITH PROMPT() command in the Menu Builder under Menu Options, remember?

The obvious question now is, "When can the user select a bar from the Timesheet menu, and thereby execute the TSDO program?" The user can select a menu bar when he or she is engaged in a wait state caused by one of the following commands:

```
READ

BROWSE

ACTIVATE MENU

MODIFY
```

The function of the TSDO.PRG program must be to exit the current wait state and assign a value to the kaction variable. When the wait state is exited, control is returned to the TSMAIN.PRG program, where the DO WHILE .T. and DO CASE structures determine the next session and act accordingly.

Here is the code for the TSDO.PRG program:

```
* tsdo.prg
* Called when user selects an option from the menu.
* Sample: DO tsdo WITH PROMPT()
PARAMETERS p_prompt
* Put the prompt of the selected option into the
* kaction variable. The kaction variable is tested
* by the event loop in tsmain.
kaction=p_prompt
* exit the current read
CLEAR READ
RETURN
* eof tsdo.prg
```

Running the Application

Later, we will have to enhance TSDO.PRG to accommodate BROWSE and MODIFY sessions, but this version fulfills our basic requirements. To test our application, we can create a few "stub" programs. The following is a sample for the client data entry session:

```
* tsclient.prg
* client data entry
* currently just a "stub" for the tsmain program
DEFINE WINDOW tsclient FROM 1,0 TO 5,50 ;
  FONT "FoxFont",9  TITLE "Client Data Entry"
ACTIVATE WINDOW tsclient
@ 1,1 SAY "Stub"
@ 1,COL()+1 GET m.l_stub DEFAULT SPACE(10)
   READ CYCLE
RELEASE WINDOW tsclient
RETURN .T.
* eof tsclient.prg
```

Use the Save As option of the File menu to save TSCLIENT.PRG as TSPROJ.PRG and TSTIME.PRG. (Remember, all .PRG files belong in the \BOOK\PRG subdirectory!) At this point, you have a functional, albeit useless, application. Take a minute to DO tsmain and select each of the menu options on the Time pad.

Using an Alternative TSMAIN.PRG Program

The TSMAIN.PRG program that we have used thus far includes a DO CASE structure that references every session in the application. As we add more sessions to the application, we will expand the entries in the TSMENU.MPR, with a corresponding increase in the number of CASE statements in TSMAIN.PRG. Some programmers find this verbose and prefer a structure like the following:

```
DO WHILE .T.
  IF EMPTY(kaction)
    READ VALID .T.
  ELSE
    DO (kaction)
  ENDIF
ENDDO
```

This approach requires that the programmer place the name of the program to be performed in the kaction variable. I prefer the approach demonstrated in TSMAIN.PRG because it allows the programmer to see, in one place, all the sessions that comprise the application.

Creating Databases

Now that we have listed several of the important activities of the application, it is time to create the databases that will hold the information required to carry out these activities. We need at least the databases listed in Table 2.1.

Table 2.1. Fundamental Databases.

Database File (.DBF)	Description
TSCLIENT.DBF	Client database. One record per client.
TSPROJ.DBF	Project database. One record per project per client. Each project is related to a single client.
TSTIME.DBF	Time sheet entry database. One record per time sheet entry. Each record is related to a record in the TSWEEK.DBF. Each record is also related to a single record in the project file. Each record is also related to a single record in the employee file.
TSEMPL.DBF	Employee database. One record per employee.
TSWEEK.DBF	One record per employee per week worked.

Adding Features to the Menu System— the First Enhancement Request

At this early stage of the development cycle, it is common to adjust the design of the application frequently. In the preceding list of databases, notice that there is no session assigned to employee file maintenance. This omission gives us an opportunity to practice adding features to an existing system, so we'll take some time to enhance the TSMENU menu and the TSMAIN program. See Figure 2.9 for the enhancement to the menu system. After you regenerate the TSMENU.MPR, add the following CASE to the DO CASE in TSMAIN.PRG:

```
CASE UPPER(kaction)="EMPLOYEE"
  kaction=""
  DO tsempl
```

You can repeat this process whenever you want to add a session or activity to your application. With the skeleton of our system in place, it's time to move on to the preliminary design of our databases.

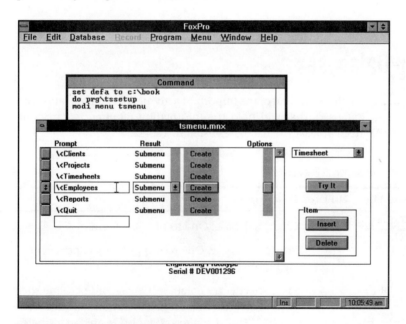

Figure 2.9. Adding an Employee option.

Filling in the Database Structures

At this stage of the design process, we are aware of some of the many fields that will be required to hold information for the Timesheet application. You can create these databases interactively by using the CREATE command, by selecting the New option of the File pad, or by executing the following program:

```
* tsempty.prg
* builds EMPTY tables FOR timesheet PROGRAM
IF NOT FILE("\book\dbf\TSEMPL.DBF")
  CREATE TABLE \book\dbf\TSEMPL (;
    EM_EMPID   C(7),;
    EM_FIRST   C(20),;
    EM_LAST    C(20),;
    EM_MIDDLE  C(1))
  INDEX ON EM_EMPID  TAG em_empid
ENDIF FILE does NOT already exist

IF NOT FILE("\book\dbf\TSCLIENT.DBF")
  CREATE TABLE \book\dbf\TSCLIENT (;
    CL_CLID    C(7),;
    CL_COMPANY C(40),;
    CL_ADDR1   C(30),;
    CL_ADDR2   C(30),;
    CL_CITY    C(30),;
    CL_STATE   C(2),;
    CL_ZIP     C(10),;
    CL_NXTPROJ N(4,0))
  INDEX ON CL_CLID  TAG cl_clid
  INDEX ON UPPER(CL_COMPANY)  TAG cl_company
ENDIF FILE does NOT already exist

IF NOT FILE("\book\dbf\TSPROJ.DBF")
  CREATE TABLE \book\dbf\TSPROJ (;
    PJ_PROJID  C(4),;
    PJ_NAME    C(40),;
    PJ_CLID    C(7),;
    PJ_TYPE    C(10),;
    PJ_DESC    M(10))
  INDEX ON PJ_CLID  TAG pj_clid
  INDEX ON PJ_CLID+PJ_PROJID  TAG clproj
ENDIF FILE does NOT already exist
```

continues

```
IF NOT FILE("\book\dbf\TSTIME.DBF")
  CREATE TABLE \book\dbf\TSTIME (;
    TI_EMPID   C(7),;
    TI_PROJID  C(4),;
    TI_WEEK    D(8),;
    TI_CLID    C(7),;
    TI_NOTES   M(10),;
    TI_ACTION  C(10),;
    TI_HOURS   N(7,2),;
    TI_TIME    C(4),;
    TI_DAY     N(1,0))
  INDEX ON TI_EMPID  TAG ti_empid
  INDEX ON TI_WEEK   TAG ti_week
  INDEX ON TI_CLID   TAG ti_clid
  INDEX ON ti_empid+dtos(ti_week)+str(ti_day,1)+ti_time  TAG empdte
ENDIF FILE does NOT already exist

IF NOT FILE("\book\dbf\TSWEEK.DBF")
  CREATE TABLE \book\dbf\TSWEEK (;
    WK_DATE    D(8),;
    WK_EMPID   C(7),;
    WK_NOTE    M(10))
  INDEX ON wk_date   TAG wk_date
  INDEX ON wk_empid  TAG wk_empid
  INDEX ON wk_empid+dtos(wk_date)  TAG empdte
ENDIF FILE does NOT already exist

* EOF tsempty.prg
```

Don't let the preceding program dissuade you from creating databases and index tags interactively. Indeed, I frequently CREATE .DBFs and use INDEX ON in the command window to create index tags. However, this program is the most efficient way for me to present the data structures to you.

Observations and Field Names

So far, we have at best a bare-bones data design. At this point in the development cycle, however, this is all the database design we need to support the activities I have identified. As we identify new activities and clarify existing activities, I fully expect to enhance this primitive database design.

In addition, you may have noticed that all the field names in all the databases start with a two-character identifier, followed by an underscore. This is another Micro Endeavors naming convention.

Here are Micro Endeavors' rules for naming fields:

- All fields in the same database start with the same two-character identifier and underscore.

- Each database's two-character identifier is unique in the application. As a result, all field names in the application are unique. (*Note:* History files can have the same data structure as the "live" databases they archive. Other exceptions can facilitate updating and importing/exporting.)

- Common fields have the same name across databases, except for the first three characters of the field name; for example, `tsempl.em_empid` and `tstime.ti_empid`.

The following are the advantages of this approach:

- You can execute `SCATTER` and `GATHER` commands without fear of `GATHER`ing memory variables into the current work area that were `SCATTER`ed from another database.

- `SQL SELECT` commands usually do not require the inclusion of file name aliases when listing field names. As a result, you can include more fields in a single `SQL SELECT` command.

- Field names stand out in source code.

- Field names are easily associated with their databases.

The following are the disadvantages of this naming convention:

- Less space is available for providing "meaningful" field names. In essence, the programmer has only seven characters in which to provide a descriptive field name.

- FoxPro's RQBE won't be able to "guess" the relations between databases because this naming convention prevents the occurrence of common field names among databases.

- Import and export to other databases may be impaired because many other databases *require* duplicate field names to establish relationships among tables.

I feel that the advantages of using Micro Endeavors' naming conventions outweigh the disadvantages. Understand, however, that these naming conventions are not requirements of FoxPro, but simply good ideas.

CHAPTER

3

Clients Session

This chapter focuses on the creation of your first READ session. This focus exposes you to the following:

- The creation of a screen with FoxPro's Screen Builder

- The inclusion of push buttons on screens

- The attachment of programs to push buttons

- The proper use of snippets

- The value of the Project Manager

- A method for safely handling menu hits during a READ session

By the end of this chapter you should know how to build a screen, how to provide the user with activities in the screen, how to generate screens using Project Manager, and how to incorporate a screen with the rest of your application.

Our First Session: Clients

At this point in most applications, I try to identify the application's most important data entry sessions. In so doing, I hope to work out the application's most important and difficult design issues.

However, my primary goal for the time sheet application is to help you understand FoxPro applications development. So, I'm going to pick a simple data entry screen first, with the understanding that we will get to the more complicated data entry items shortly.

There isn't much point in keeping track of our time if no one is going to pay us for it. To keep track of those kindly folk who pay us for our time, we create a data entry screen to acquire information about our clients. This activity includes the following steps:

1. Open the client database.

2. Establish memory variables for use by the client data entry screen.

3. Execute a screen (.SPR) file that contains window definitions, @...SAY commands, @...GET commands, and a series of push buttons.

4. Create a procedure to be executed when one of the client push buttons is selected.

We want to create a general-purpose design that we can use over and over again for data entry screens. Our requirements for this particular data entry screen include the capability to:

- Add a new client

- Delete an existing client

- Edit an existing client

- Move Next and Previous through client records

- Select a client from a list

- Operate in a multiuser environment

Our initial effort is modest, including only the capability to display the current client record and the capability to exit from the client data entry screen. So that we can start by displaying a record, we have to "cheat" and input a few records by hand by issuing the following commands in the Command window:

```
CLOSE DATA
USE tsclient
APPEND
```

The APPEND command starts an interactive data entry session. To continue, please create the three records shown in Figure 3.1.

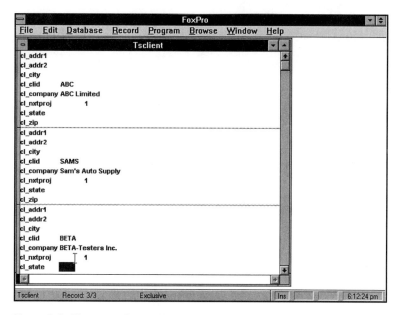

Figure 3.1. Client records to add interactively by using the *APPEND* command.

Now that we have a few sample records to play with, we need to create two files. One is the TSCLIENT.PRG file. The TSCLIENT.PRG file contains the setup code to support the Windows, SAYs, and GETs that are defined in our other file, TSCLIENT.SPR.

We already know how to create a .PRG file, so let's modify the "stub" version of TSCLIENT.PRG as I have in the following code listing. Please note that we make substantial enhancements to this program before we complete the application.

```
* tsclient.prg
* client data entry
* first version. Includes only the capabilities to display
* the current client, and to exit.

* Declare local variables
PRIVATE ALL LIKE l_*
PRIVATE m.control
* Open the client database, if it is not already open
l_wasclient=.T.
IF NOT USED("tsclient")
  l_wasclient=.F.
  USE tsclient IN SELECT(1) AGAIN
ENDIF
```

continues

```
* Make the client work area the current work area, and
* make the client id order the master order.
SELECT tsclient
SET ORDER TO cl_clid

IF EOF()
  * Try to place us on a record if we are sitting at eof
  GO TOP
ENDIF


* Create memory variables from the current tsclient record
SCATTER MEMVAR MEMO
m.control=""  && push button variable

* Run the Window, SAY, READ and GET code:
DO tsclient.spr

IF NOT m.l_wasclient AND USED('tsclient')
  USE IN tsclient
ENDIF
RETURN .T.


PROCEDURE vcontrol
* processes push button selections
PARAMETERS control
DO CASE
  CASE UPPER(control)=="EXIT"
    CLEAR READ
  OTHERWISE
    WAIT WINDOW m.control+" has not been assigned an action...yet!"
ENDCASE
RETURN .T.



* eof tsclient.prg
```

When we provide the user with more actions on this data entry screen, we will return to TSCLIENT.PRG and add code to the vcontrol procedure. Now, however, we need to create the .SPR file referenced in TSCLIENT.PRG. To create the .SPR file, issue the following commands in the Command window:

```
CLOSE DATA
USE tsclient
MODIFY SCREEN scx\tsclient
```

Welcome to FoxPro's Screen Builder. With this handy tool we paint a data entry screen. When we finish, we ask FoxPro to generate some FoxPro code that enables the user to enter data and select activities.

As I mentioned earlier, the .SPR file that results from this Screen Builder session include a window definition. Let's supply the information for that definition by selecting the Layout... option of the Screen pad. Selecting the Layout... option leads you to a dialog such as the one shown in Figure 3.2. Give the window the title Client Data Entry and name the window TSCLIENT. To direct FoxPro to center the window, select the Center check box.

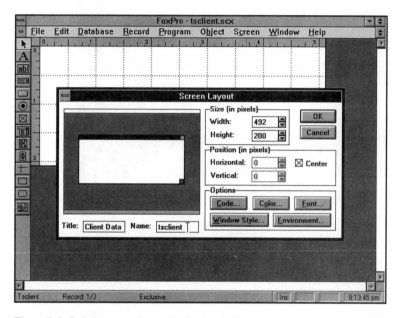

Figure 3.2. Defining a window in the Screen Builder.

After you OK the Layout dialog, select the Quick Screen... option of the Screen pad to open the Quick Screen dialog. Select the vertical layout and the Memory Variables check box, as shown in Figure 3.3.

We need to make the following changes to the Quick Screen that FoxPro produces:

1. Move the client ID and company name fields and labels to the top of the screen.

2. Remove the `cl_nxtproj` label and field from the screen.

3. Move the `cu_zip` field and label onto the same line as the `cu_state` field and label.

4. Resequence the GET objects by selecting the **Object Order** option of the Screen pad, and selecting the By Row push button of the Object Order dialog, as shown in Figure 3.4.

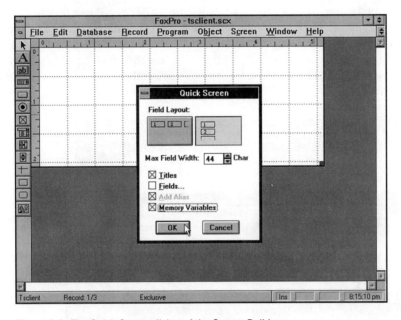

Figure 3.3. The Quick Screen dialog of the Screen Builder.

The Object Order dialog specifies the sequence of GETs in the generated data entry screen. The sequence in which the GETs are established determines the TABbing order that users experience as they tab from GET to GET.

Next, we need to create some push buttons so that users can select an activity while they work on the client data entry screen. You create these push buttons as follows:

1. Select the push button tool from the tool bar.

2. Position the push button cursor near the lower-left corner of the screen.

3. Click the mouse.

4. Respond to the Push Button dialog as shown in Figure 3.5.

Don't OK the dialog yet, however. Simply placing the button on the screen does not attach any programs to the selection of that button. To attach a program to a push button, we must select the **Valid...** push button of the Push Button dialog and respond as shown in Figure 3.6.

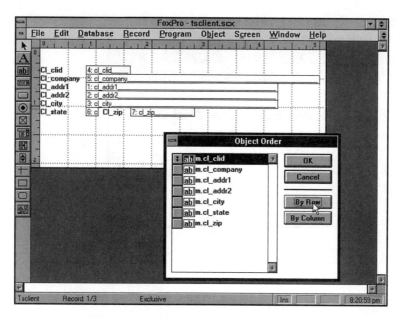

Figure 3.4. The Object Order dialog of the Screen Builder.

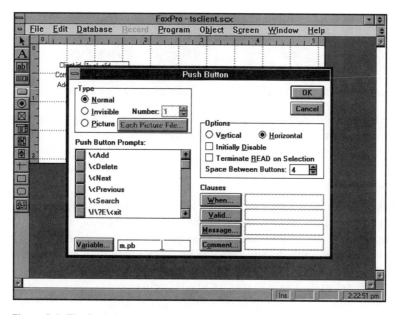

Figure 3.5. The Push Button dialog of the Screen Builder.

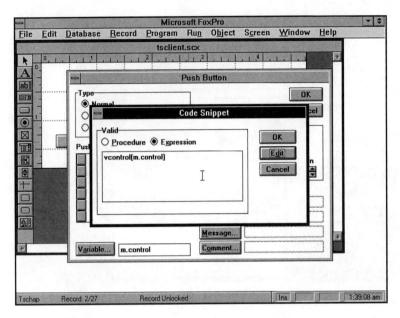

Figure 3.6. Attaching a program to the selection of a push button.

Note: For this process to work, you must select the Expression radio button. I'll explain the difference between the Procedure and Expression radio buttons later in this chapter. For now, make sure you have the Expression radio button selected.

After you OK the Valid clause dialog and OK the Push Button dialog, you will want to resize and reposition the push buttons so that they fit in the window. You will also want to protect the `cl_clid` field from any user changes. To prevent the user from changing the content of this field, double-click the `cl_clid` field and select the Initially Disable Field check box.

Finally, you will want to use the content of your screen to generate the TSCLIENT.SPR file. To accomplish this, choose the Generate option of the Program menu. When FoxPro asks whether you want to save your changes, respond Yes. When asked whether you want to save the environment, respond No. When presented with the Generate Screen dialog, select the More >> push button. This leads you to the dialog box shown in Figure 3.7. Deselect the Open Files and Close Files check boxes. When you select the Generate push button on the Generate Screen dialog, FoxPro generates the source code necessary to present the user with a screen like the one you have described in this Screen Builder session. When FoxPro finishes generating the code, close the TSCLIENT.SCX window.

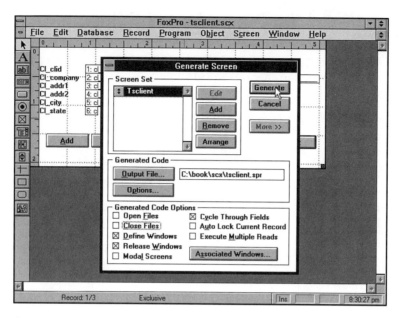

Figure 3.7. The "extended" Generate Screen dialog.

From the Command window, DO TSMAIN and select the Clients option of the Time pad. You should see a screen like the one shown in Figure 3.8.

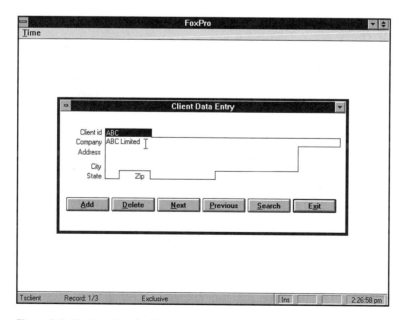

Figure 3.8. First try at a client data entry screen.

A Deep Breath and the Proper Use of Snippets

If you followed the previous section steadfastly, you may feel a little like a swimmer who swam the last lap underwater—you made it to the wall, but you had your head down all the way, and you didn't see much.

Well, take a deep breath and let me catch you up on some of what you may have missed. First, data entry screens in FoxPro usually include push buttons through which users can select actions. Because actions require programs, FoxPro programmers attach programs to the valid clauses of push buttons. When the user selects one of these push buttons, the expression named in the push button's valid clause is evaluated.

In this case, we have elected to reference a *user-defined function* (UDF) named vcontrol in the valid clause of our m.control push button. When the user selects one of these push buttons, FoxPro looks for a procedure named vcontrol. Happily, we have included just such a procedure in the TSCLIENT.PRG file. Further, we have passed the value of the m.control variable to the vcontrol() UDF. All that is left is for the vcontrol() UDF to use a DO CASE structure to test the value that is passed and then execute the appropriate commands.

This use of push buttons, valid clauses, and procedures is the standard method of controlling data entry screens. However, many programmers place their source code in the screen object rather than in a separate .PRG file.

Using Snippets

Take another look at Figure 3.6. Where we have selected the Expression radio button, some programmers would select the Procedure radio button. Further, where we have simply referenced the UDF vcontrol(), some programmers would include all the code we placed in the vcontrol procedure.

Microsoft calls these blocks of code *snippets,* and FoxPro's documentation suggests that we place most of our screen code in snippets. It is not impossible for Microsoft to improve their handling of snippets to the point where the use of snippets will indeed be the best way to develop applications. For now, however, I prefer that we use snippets as *expressions* to reference UDFs, for the following reasons:

- When an error occurs in a snippet, the programmer must cancel the program, open the screen, find the snippet, make the correction, regenerate the screen or screen set, and test for the bug. If an error occurs in a .PRG, FoxPro is nice enough to place the programmer in the text editor, positioned on the offend-ing line of code. Further, no regeneration is needed. By placing code in a .PRG, the programmer saves at *least* 30 to 90 seconds per bug.

- Large volumes of snippet code can slow down generation of screen sets on those occasions when the programmer needs to make changes to the screen layout.

- Too much snippet code can lead to `out of memory` errors during screen generation.

- Code stored in snippets is difficult to document.

- By placing all the control code for a screen in one .PRG, we make it much easier to perform global search and replace operations for that screen.

- By separating the control code in the .PRG from the display code in the .SPR, we make it easier to maintain displays for multiple hardware platforms.

- Compile-time errors are not trapped in snippets, but are trapped in .PRGs.

Given these compelling arguments, why would anyone want to put code in snippets? These are the most commonly cited reasons:

- Programmers who did not write the application but are required to maintain the application will know where to look for the source code associated with a screen or screen object, if that code is stored directly in the snippet of the screen object.

- Placing source code in snippets makes FoxPro appear more "object-like" to some programmers.

When it became obvious to me that placing code in snippets was too cumbersome for substantial development efforts, the one thing I lamented was the loss of an intuitive connection between a screen object and its associated source code. Fortunately, Dr. Mike Brachman, Melissa Dunn, and Bruce Troutman of Micro Endeavors provided the following solutions:

- The .PRG and the .SPR have the same name. In the case of our time sheet program, the TSCLIENT.PRG has the control code for the TSCLIENT.SPR.

- The valid clause for a screen object has the same name as the screen object, preceded by the letter *v*. For example, the `m.control` push button references the `vcontrol()` UDF.

- The `WHEN` clause for a screen object has the same name as the screen object, preceded by the letter *w*. For example, a `WHEN` clause for the `m.cu_state` GET would reference the `wcu_state()` UDF.

- The `READ WHEN`, `READ VALID`, `READ SHOW`, `READ DEACTIVATE`, and `READ ACTIVATE` clauses reference UDFs named `readwhen`, `readvali`, `readshow`, `readdeac`, and `readacti`, respectively.

By separating the control code from the display code, we create an efficient environment for developing, debugging, and enhancing our application. By utilizing the aforementioned naming conventions, we make it easy for programmers to find the code associated with a given screen or object. Experience has taught us that this is indeed the best of both worlds.

The Screen Generation Process

You may be curious about the process FoxPro undertakes when you ask it to generate a screen. The content of the TSCLIENT screen that we created is stored in a plain FoxPro database named TSCLIENT.SCX. When we choose to generate the TSCLIENT program, FoxPro executes a standard FoxPro program named GENSCRN.PRG.

The GENSCRN.PRG program uses the information stored in the TSCLIENT.SCX database to create a text file named TSCLIENT.SPR. This .SPR file contains commands for creating windows, issuing SAYs, issuing GETs, and beginning a READ CYCLE.

Because you know how to use FoxPro databases and write FoxPro programs, you can create your own GENSCRN.PRG program to generate screen code. This program can provide substantial flexibility in the screen generation process. Indeed, you can make a screen generator that prompts the developer for information required to complete an entire application! If you do so, however, you must be prepared to update your personal GENSCRN.PRG whenever Microsoft changes the format of the .SCX file, and whenever Microsoft changes the parts of the language associated with windows, SAYs, GETs, and READs.

In modifying GENSCRN.PRG, some developers attempt to increase the amount of work performed by the resulting .SPR file. I prefer to limit the functionality of the .SPR file to the definition and maintenance of a screen's appearance. This includes colors, sizes, locations, and shapes of objects.

The code associated with these objects is always stored in an associated .PRG file. Because GENSCRN.PRG does a fine job of generating code that affects the appearance of screens and objects, we choose to leave the GENSCRN.PRG program as it is.

Using the Project Manager

When we generated the TSCLIENT.SPR, you may have wondered whether there was some way to save the generator options that we selected. After all, we don't look forward to clicking two push buttons and two check boxes every time we want to generate a screen.

Unfortunately, there is no way to save generator options with an individual screen. However, there are alternative solutions to the problem.

First, we can use the keyboard rather than the mouse to select the generator directives. In this case, we would type **o** for More>>, **c** to deselect the Close Files check box, **f** to deselect the Open Files check box, and Ctrl+W to generate the screen.

This solution is workable, but not optimal. After all, we may want different options for different screens, and we don't want to have to remember which screens have which options. Further, when we begin to create screen sets that contain multiple windows, we will need to save the arrangement of those windows.

Fortunately, there is a solution that addresses all our needs, albeit at the cost of some efficiency. The Project Manager gives us a place to keep all our generator options.

Let's create our first project by entering the following:

```
MODIFY PROJECT ts
```

The ultimate goal of using Project Manager is to build a single file containing all the programs necessary to run an application. At this point, though, we are more interested in Project Manager's capacity to assist us in developing applications that contain multiple screens, programs, menus, and reports.

Project Manager enables us to add, edit, and delete files to and from a project. However, we don't want to type in the names of all the files we have already created. Fortunately, the Project Manager is smart enough to help. Simply select the Add push button.

Next, select the TSMAIN.PRG program from the \BOOK\PRG subdirectory. Then select the Build... push button, which takes you to the Build dialog. Select the Rebuild All check box and the Rebuild Project radio button. Finally, select the OK push button.

FoxPro will now find all the programs and UDFs referenced in TSMAIN.PRG and in the programs called by TSMAIN.PRG. Further, FoxPro recompiles those programs and regenerates menus and screens.

If FoxPro can't find a file, it prompts you for the location of the file. If a file does not exist, the Project Manager generates an error log entry, but continues to build the rest of the project.

When the build is completed, you should see a Project Manager screen like the one shown in Figure 3.9.

Now, to ensure that the TSCLIENT screen set has the proper generation options selected, double-click or select the TSCLIENT screen set entry. The Edit Screen Set dialog that results is the same as the generator dialog we have seen before, except that our selections are saved in the TS.PJX file for future "generations." (I couldn't resist.)

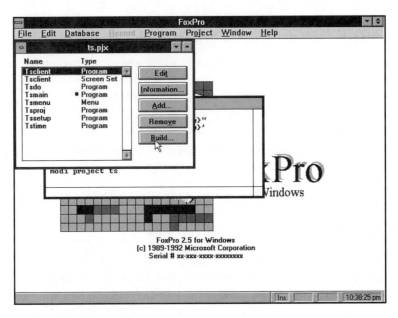

Figure 3.9. A freshly built project.

Note: There is one other difference between the Edit Screen dialog and the Generate Screen dialog: The Edit Screen dialog has no Generate button! When you make a change to a screen or an Edit Screen dialog, you must rebuild the project.

However, you don't have to rebuild the entire project. If you do not choose the Rebuild All check box in the rebuild dialog, the Project Manager regenerates and recompiles only those files that have changed since they were last generated and compiled!

Even though the Project Manager does this rebuild quickly, rebuilding takes longer than modifying the screen, program, or menu directly. In most applications, this slight inefficiency is tolerable, given Project Manager's capability of storing generator options, especially as they apply to multi-window screen sets.

If, like me, you are too impatient to wait even 20 extra seconds from the time you make a change in the Screen Builder until the time you can test the resultant .SPR code, feel free to regenerate screens without the assistance of Project Manager. For example, when working on a particularly complex screen for long periods of time, I frequently eschew the use of Project Manager until I have completed "most" of the screen's functionality.

Taming Rogue Menu Selections

At this point in the application, we have provided some simple access to very simple screens through the use of our `ON SELECTION POPUP timesheet DO tsdo WITH PROMPT()` command. This admirably accomplishes our goals of setting the `kaction` variable to the value of the menu option chosen and exiting the current `READ`. However, this simplistic approach poses certain problems in real-world applications.

In the real world, there will be times when we do not want users to be able to exit the current `READ` session just by selecting a menu option. Other times we will want users to verify that they in fact do want to end their `READ` session before we allow a menu selection to exit a `READ` session. And at other times we will want the act of choosing a menu selection to automatically save (or abort) changes in the current editing session before moving to a newly identified activity.

The root of the problem is that the TSDO.PRG program uses the `CLEAR READ` command to exit the current `READ` session. This unilateral approach gives us no opportunity to test for any of the conditions mentioned in the preceding paragraph. The following adjustment to TSDO.PRG helps solve this problem:

```
* tsdo.prg
* Called when user selects an option from the menu.
* Sample: DO tsdo WITH PROMPT()
PARAMETERS p_prompt
* Put the prompt of the selected option into the
* kaction variable. The kaction variable is tested
* by the event loop in tsmain.
kaction=p_prompt
* exit the current READ
DO vcontrol WITH "MENU"
RETURN
* eof tsdo.prg
```

Now, instead of simply exiting the current `READ` session, the act of selecting a menu option makes a call to the `vcontrol` procedure, passing the value `"MENU"` as a parameter. It is up to the `vcontrol` procedure to decide what to do with the information that the user has selected a menu option.

In most cases, we simply include code such as the following in the `vcontrol` procedure for the current `READ` session:

```
PROCEDURE vcontrol
PARAMETERS control
DO CASE
  CASE UPPER(m.control)="MENU"
    ACTIVATE WINDOW tsclient
    CLEAR READ
```

49

This code has the same effect as if TSDO.PRG had issued the CLEAR READ. However, we may want the vcontrol program to ask users whether they want to leave this wonderful session before allowing the exit:

```
PROCEDURE vcontrol
PARAMETERS control
DO CASE
  CASE UPPER(m.control)="MENU"
    IF l3msg("Ready to leave?","Yes;No")="Yes"
      ACTIVATE WINDOW tsclient
      CLEAR READ
    ELSE
      DO l3msg WITH "Then finish up quickly!"
    ENDIF
```

What happens if the READ session doesn't include a vcontrol procedure in its .PRG file? You get fired, that's what happens.

Actually, FoxPro just generates an error message when it can't find the vcontrol procedure. In other words, make sure every READ session .PRG file has a vcontrol procedure in it. Just in case you forget, however, you can include the following code at the end of the TSMAIN.PRG program:

```
PROCEDURE vcontrol
PARAMETERS p_control
CLEAR READ
RETURN .T.
```

Now, if you forget to include a vcontrol procedure in one of your READ sessions, FoxPro searches the program calling tree until it finds this copy of vcontrol() in the TSMAIN.PRG program.

More Clients

In this chapter we put the finishing touches on our client data entry screen by adding options to search, skip, add, edit, and delete clients. Along the way, we will discuss FoxPro's multiuser locking procedures, methods for enforcing referential integrity, modal and modeless screens, and the READ SHOW clause.

By the end of this chapter, you should be able to create a multiuser, single file data entry screen in FoxPro, create lookups, and provide modal dialogs to the user when necessary.

Next and Previous

That's enough of a break. Let's get back to work. We need to add some functionality to our client maintenance screen. We will start with something simple so that we can concentrate on the approach rather than the specific activities.

All we want our first functionality to do is to enable the user to move to the next or previous record. This action requires several lines of code. Because almost every data entry screen we write will require this functionality, we may as well write a small library routine to accomplish these tasks. Place the following simple code in \BOOK \LIB\TSSKIP.PRG:

```
* tsskip.prg
* Skip forward or backward in a file
```

continues

```
PARAMETERS p_qty
IF p_qty<0
  * wants to move back
  IF NOT BOF()
    ** not already beyond top of file
    SKIP p_qty
    IF BOF()
      ** the move placed him at bof()
      ** so... move him to last record
      ?? CHR(7)
      GO BOTTOM
    ENDIF was on first record
  ENDIF was already at bof()
ELSE
  ** wants to move forward
  IF NOT EOF()
    ** not already at eof()
    SKIP p_qty
    IF EOF()
      ** move placed him at eof()
      ** so... move him to first record
      ?? CHR(7)
      GO TOP
    ENDIF
  ENDIF
ENDIF
RETURN .T.
```

This program is a fairly primitive version of the more sophisticated L3SKIP.PRG program, which we will see later. For now, however, this simple routine allows us to make the following adjustments in TSCLIENT.PRG (the bold face type indicates the changes):

```
PROCEDURE vcontrol
* processes push button selections
PARAMETERS control
DO CASE
  CASE UPPER(control)=="NEXT"
    DO tsskip WITH 1
    SCATTER MEMVAR MEMO
    SHOW GETS
  CASE UPPER(control)=="PREVIOUS"
    DO tsskip WITH -1
    SCATTER MEMVAR MEMO
```

```
    SHOW GETS
  CASE UPPER(control)=="EXIT"
    CLEAR READ
  CASE UPPER(m.control)=="MENU"
    ACTIVATE WINDOW tsclient
    CLEAR READ
  OTHERWISE
    WAIT WINDOW m.control+" has not been assigned an action...yet!"
ENDCASE
RETURN .T.
```

Notice that we had to adjust only the vcontrol procedure to accommodate our change. Indeed, all activities associated with this screen will be initiated in the vcontrol procedure.

We have to issue the SCATTER MEMVAR MEMO commands to update the contents of the memory variables that are displayed on the screen. We issue the SHOW GETS commands to update the screen display.

If you explore FoxPro's sample applications, you may see a single SHOW GETS command at the end of a block of push button code like this. This approach reduces the number of lines of code in the procedure, but it poses problems when a particular activity must control the kind of SHOW GETS command issued.

After some experimentation, I have found it best to include the SHOW GETS command with each activity that requires a screen refresh. In this way, I can allow one action to SHOW only a handful of GETs, while another action refreshes only @...SAY commands, while another action refreshes only the GETs in a particular window, while another action uses the SHOW GETS command to refresh all SAYs and all GETs in all windows.

Saving Changes

Currently, our TSCLIENT.PRG program is worse than useless—it's frustrating. After all, any changes the user makes will be reflected in memory variables, but not in the database! So, we need to enhance the program to save changes.

In a single user environment, we could accomplish this simply by issuing a GATHER MEMVAR MEMO command at the beginning of the vcontrol procedure. However, this is a multiuser application, so we must code accordingly.

There are several different ways to approach the simple problem of allowing multiple users to edit different records in the same table at the same time. We just need one solution at a time, however, so we can postpone a full investigation of the problem until later.

Following is the solution for TSCLIENT; if all these conditions are true, you save the user's changes:

- *If* the user changed any fields, and

- *If* the user wants to save those changes, and

- *If* the program can lock the record that has to be changed, and

- *If* the record has not been changed by another user since this user began the edit

If I were you, I would want to ask one or more of the following questions:

- Where do we put the code? At the beginning of the vcontrol procedure.

- How do we know whether the user made changes? We compare memory variables to fields.

- How do we know the user wants to save the changes? We assume that the user wants to save his or her changes unless the user selected the Cancel push button.

- How do we know whether the record was changed by someone else since the user began the edit? We compare an array copy of the record made before the edit to an array copy of the record we make when we are ready to save the record.

This time, our enhancements require changes to both the screen and the program associated with the client data entry screen. The changes to the screen are trivial, so let's do them first.

Open the TSCLIENT screen from the ts project and make the following changes:

1. Double-click the cl_id field and select the Initially Disabled check box.

2. Add the \<Cancel prompt to the control push button.

3. Resize the push buttons to fit on the screen.

4. Erase the field labels that Quick Screen created and create your own, readable, alternatives.

5. Close and save the screen.

6. Rebuild the project.

So much for the easy part. Now we need to make several changes to the TSCLIENT.PRG. Instead of discussing each change individually, I will show you the finished TSCLIENT.PRG with the required changes in bold face type. Here is the code:

```
* tsclient.prg
* client data entry
* Second version. Includes the capability to edit.
```

```
* Declare local variables
PRIVATE ALL LIKE l_*
PRIVATE m.control
* Open the client database, if it is not already open
l_wasclient=.T.
IF NOT USED("tsclient")
  l_wasclient=.F.
  USE tsclient IN SELECT(1) AGAIN
ENDIF

* Make the client work area the current work area, and
* make the client id order the master order.
SELECT tsclient
SET ORDER TO cl_clid

IF EOF()
  * Try to place us on a record if we are sitting at eof
  GO TOP
ENDIF

* Create memory variables from the current tsclient record
SCATTER MEMVAR MEMO
* Make a "before editing" array copy of the record
SCATTER TO l_old MEMO
m.control=""  && push button variable

* Run the Window, SAY, READ and GET code:
DO tsclient.spr

IF NOT m.l_wasclient AND USED('tsclient')
  USE IN tsclient
ENDIF
RETURN .T.

PROCEDURE vcontrol
* processes push button selections
PARAMETERS control
PRIVATE l_xx,l_oldsele
IF UPPER(m.control)="CANCEL"
  ** get a new copy of the record
  SCATTER MEMVAR MEMO
  SCATTER TO l_old MEMO
  RETURN .t.
```

continues

55

```
ENDIF chose to cancel
** save current work area
l_oldsele=SELECT()
SELECT tsclient
IF tschange(@l_old,"tsclient")
  ** something changed, see if we can lock the record
  IF NOT RLOCK()
    DO l3msg WITH "Record locked by another, no changes saved."
  ELSE  && able to lock the record
    ** Make new copy of record in an array
    SCATTER TO l_new MEMO
    ** compare the two arrays
    FOR l_xx=1 TO ALEN(l_new)
      IF l_new(l_xx) <> l_old(l_xx)
        EXIT
      ENDIF
    ENDFOR
    IF l_xx>ALEN(l_new)
      ** record hasn't changed since we started
      ** editing, so we can save this one
      GATHER MEMVAR MEMO
      SCATTER TO l_old MEMO
      ** release our lock on the record
      UNLOCK
    ELSE
      ** release our lock on the record
      UNLOCK
      DO l3msg WITH "Someone changed this client record while "+;
        "you were working. Your changes have not been saved."
    ENDIF no change since we started
  ENDIF could not lock the record
ENDIF memvars don't match the record
DO CASE
  CASE UPPER(control)=="NEXT"
    DO tsskip WITH 1
    SCATTER MEMVAR MEMO
    SCATTER TO l_old MEMO
    SHOW GETS
  CASE UPPER(control)=="PREVIOUS"
    DO tsskip WITH -1
    SCATTER MEMVAR MEMO
    SCATTER TO l_old MEMO
    SHOW GETS
```

```
    CASE UPPER(control)=="EXIT"
      CLEAR READ
    OTHERWISE
      WAIT WINDOW m.control+" has not been assigned an action...yet!"
  ENDCASE
  ** return to work area we started with
  SELECT (l_oldsele)
  RETURN .T.



  * eof tsclient.prg
```

In the vcontrol procedure, we reference a UDF named tschange(). The purpose of this UDF is to determine whether the user has changed any of the on-screen variables. To make this determination, tschange() compares the memory variables, in which the user may have made changes, to the content of the l_old array, which originally contained the same values as the memory variables. (Remember SCATTER TO l_old MEMO and SCATTER MEMVAR MEMO?)

Obviously, this approach is limited to those screens that edit one record from one table at a time. However, there will be plenty of time to explore alternatives in later chapters. Here is the code for TSCHANGE.PRG:

```
* tschange.prg
* returns .t. if the memory variables created with
* SCATTER MEMVAR MEMO don't match the array created
* with SCATTER TO array MEMO
** p_array=array to test
** p_alias=work area to provide field names
PARAMETERS p_array,p_alias
p_alias=IIF(EMPTY(p_alias),ALIAS(),p_alias)
PRIVATE l_xx
FOR l_xx=1 TO FCOUNT(m.p_alias)
  IF NOT EVAL("m."+FIELD(l_xx,m.p_alias))==p_array(l_xx)
    EXIT
  ENDIF field doesn't match record
ENDFOR test all fields in current database
RETURN l_xx<=FCOUNT(m.p_alias)
```

The vcontrol procedure also references a UDF named l3msg(). You can find the code for l3msg() on the source disk. The UDF also appears in print in Chapter 19, "Library Routines."

If you are unfamiliar with some of the techniques in this version of TSCLIENT, you can read more about them, and several other approaches to record locking, in Chapter 13,

"Multiuser Discussions." For now, be assured that this technique works, and we will move on to the matter of deleting records.

Deleting Clients

To delete a record properly in a FoxPro application, we must:

1. SET DELETED ON to tell FoxPro to ignore deleted records.

2. Lock the record to be deleted.

3. Ensure that the record is not referenced in other tables.

4. Use the DELETE command to mark the record for deletion.

5. Move to an undeleted record when we finish deleting the record in question.

Issue the SET DELETED ON command in the TSSETUP program. While DELETED is set ON, almost every command that moves the record pointer skips over deleted records. The only exception to this behavior is the GOTO # command.

In our application, clients have projects. We don't want to delete any client that has active projects, so we want the application to check for the existence of a project record before we delete a client record. To accomplish this, we need to open the project database. The following reprint of the beginning of the TSCLIENT.PRG program uses bold face to indicate changes:

```
* Open the client database, if it is not already open
l_wasclient=.T.
IF NOT USED("tsclient")
  l_wasclient=.F.
  USE tsclient IN SELECT(1) AGAIN
ENDIF

* Open the project database in case we need to delete
* a client.
l_wasproj=.T.
IF NOT USED("tsproj")
  l_wasproj=.F.
  USE tsproj IN SELECT(1) AGAIN
ENDIF
SET ORDER TO clproj IN tsproj

* Make the client work area the current work area, and
* make the client id order the master order.
```

Now that we have all the necessary work areas, it's time to try to delete the record. As you have probably guessed, we will put the necessary code in the DO CASE area of the vcontrol() procedure. Here is the code:

```
CASE UPPER(m.control)=="DELETE"
   SELECT tsclient
   * make sure the user wants to delete
   IF l3msg("Do you want to delete?","\!\<Yes;\?\<No")="Yes"
      * See if we can lock it
      IF NOT RLOCK()
         DO l3msg WITH "Sorry. Someone else is using "+;
            "this record. I can't delete it for you!"
   ELSE
      * We locked it, see if we have any projects
      * for this client.
      IF SEEK(cl_clid,"tsproj")
         UNLOCK && free up this client record
         DO l3msg WITH "You have projects for this "+;
            "client. So...you can't delete it!"
      ELSE
         * since it has no projects, delete this client
         DELETE
         UNLOCK
         * Now, move forward to, hopefully, another
         * client record.
         DO tsskip WITH 1
         SCATTER MEMVAR MEMO
         SCATTER TO l_old MEMO
         SHOW GETS
      ENDIF has projects
   ENDIF could NOT LOCK the client RECORD
ENDIF wants TO DELETE
```

Coping with Empty Tables by Using *READ SHOW*

The ability to delete records implies the ability to bring into existence an annoying predicament: If the user deletes all the clients, or if we send a copy of the application to the user with no records, we must program for the possibility of an empty table. Oh well, at least FoxPro provides a clever mechanism for accomplishing this feat.

Obviously, we could attack the empty table problem in several different ways. Fortunately, we only need one method at a time, and ours will be a simple one. If no records are in the table, we only allow the user to add records or exit the table.

Each time we display the screen to the user, we check to see whether the record pointer is sitting at end-of-file. If it is, disable all the GETS on the screen, including push buttons, and then enable only the Add and Exit push buttons.

Our first task is to find a place to put this enabling and disabling GET code. As it turns out, the READ SHOW clause is evaluated when we enter a READ command and whenever we issue a SHOW GETS or SHOW GETS OFF command. Because we need to issue the SHOW GETS command to update the screen, READ SHOW is the perfect place for our enabling and disabling GET code.

Finding the READ SHOW clause requires some persistence. After you elect to modify the TSCLIENT screen, choose the Screen Layout menu option. Next, choose the Code push button. Then, choose the On Refresh push button. This takes you to the READ SHOW snippet dialog shown in Figure 4.1.

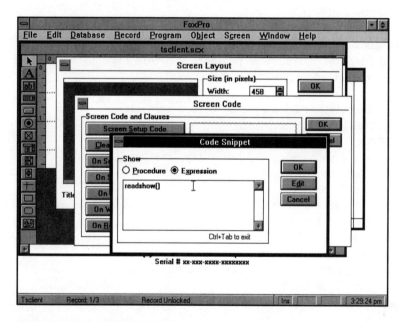

Figure 4.1. The *READ SHOW* snippet.

After you save the changes to the screen and elect to Generate the .SPR file, you need to add the following UDF to the TSCLIENT.PRG program:

```
PROCEDURE readshow
IF EOF('tsclient')
  SHOW GETS DISABLED ONLY
  SHOW GET control,1 ENABLED  && Add
  SHOW GET control,6 ENABLED  && Exit
  ** remember that the current window
  ** is disabled
```

```
    l_wasdisabled=.t.
ELSE
  IF l_wasdisabled
    ** window used to be disabled
    SHOW GETS ENABLED ONLY
    SHOW GET m.cl_clid DISABLED
    l_wasdisabled=.f.
  ENDIF screen used to be disabled
ENDIF at eof in tsclient
* EOP readshow
```

The location of the readshow() procedure within TSCLIENT.PRG is irrelevant, but I always make the readshow() UDF the first procedure following the TSCLIENT cleanup code. Notice the use of the l_wasdisabled variable. We create this variable in the setup code of the TSCLIENT.PRG as follows:

```
* Create memory variables from the current tsclient record
SCATTER MEMVAR MEMO
* Make a "before editing" array copy of the record
SCATTER TO l_old MEMO
m.control=""  && push button variable
m.l_wasdisabled=.f.  && disabled state of screen

* Run the Window, SAY, and GET code:
DO tsclient.spr
```

As it turns out, the l_wasdisabled variable will be helpful when we add our next piece of functionality to the client data entry screen. Obviously, we must add the capability to add clients. Fortunately, adding records is the topic of the very next section in the book.

Adding Clients

Unfortunately, adding a client is not as simple a matter as moving to the next or previous client. In our case, we want the user to be able to create a new client with a unique, user-assigned ID. To accomplish this, we need to check the prospective client ID against the client file to ensure that the prospective ID does not already exist.

First, we need a place to accept the user's prospective ID. We can accomplish this with a simple screen and an equally simple screen control program. All we want the ID screen to do is accept input into a memory variable and present the user with the option to Accept or Cancel. Here is the control program:

```
* tscliena.prg
* Accepts user's "new" id
PRIVATE l_control,l_id
l_id=SPACE(LEN(tsclient.cl_clid))
l_control=""
DO tscliena.spr
IF UPPER(l_control)="ADD" AND NOT EMPTY(l_id)
  RETURN m.l_id
ELSE
  RETURN ""
ENDIF
```

Obviously, the bulk of the work will be done inside TSCLIENA.SPR. We need one text object (New ID), one get field (m.l_id), and one push button (m.l_control). The m.l_id field has a format of !!!!!!!!. Make the m.l_control push button a terminating button (see Figure 4.2). Specify Dialog as the window style, "Please enter an ID" as the title, and TSCLIENA as the window name, and position the window by selecting the Center check box (see Figure 4.3). When you generate the screen (see Figure 4.4), select the Modal Screens option so that the user must respond to the dialog before proceeding.

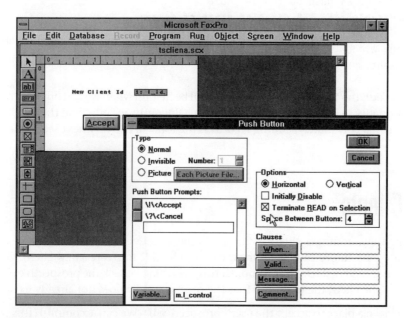

Figure 4.2. Creating a terminating push button.

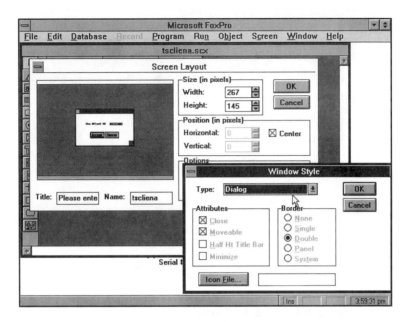

Figure 4.3. Specifying the window's style, title, name, and screen position.

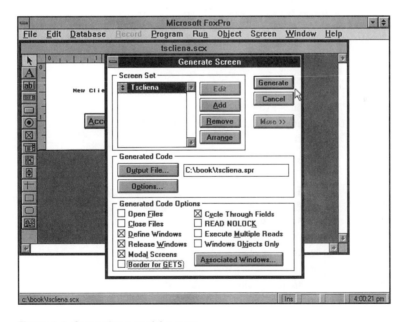

Figure 4.4. Generating a modal screen.

If the user enters a value in the `m.1_id` variable and selects the Accept button, the TSCLIENA program returns the value entered. If the user leaves `m.1_id` empty, or if the user selects the Cancel button, TSCLIENA returns a null string.

As a result, our TSCLIENT program needs code such as the following to determine whether or not the user wants to add a client at this time:

```
CASE UPPER(m.control)=="ADD"
  ** Use tscliena.prg to ask the user for an id
  m.1_newid=tscliena()
  IF NOT EMPTY(m.1_newid)  && he gave us an id to try
    SELECT tsclient
    m.1_currec=RECNO("tsclient") && save our place
    IF FLOCK()
       ** because file is locked, no other user can try to
       ** add the same id at the same time.
       ** Also, the INSERT INTO command is virtually certain
       ** of success, because the FLOCK() will prevent any
       ** other user from applying an flock(), or attempting
       ** to INSERT a record at the same time.
       IF NOT SEEK(m.1_newid,"tsclient")
         ** Id is unique, so add it
         INSERT INTO tsclient (cl_clid) VALUES (m.1_newid)
         SCATTER MEMVAR MEMO
         SCATTER TO 1_old MEMO
         UNLOCK
         * reset the data entry screen
         SHOW GETS
       ELSE && already on file
         * this id already exists, so prepare to edit it
         SCATTER MEMVAR MEMO
         SCATTER TO 1_old MEMO
         UNLOCK
         SHOW GETS
       ENDIF not already on file
       ** Put user in the company name field
       _CUROBJ=OBJNUM(m.cl_company)
    ELSE  && not able to lock the file
      IF BETWEEN(1_currec,1,RECC("tsclient"))
        GOTO 1_currec && go back to record we were on
      ENDIF
      DO 13msg WITH "Sorry. I can't lock the file, so"+;
         " I can't check your id, and I can't add your"+;
         " new record.¦Press [Enter] to retry, or blank"+;
         " field to exit."
```

```
    ENDIF able to lock the file
  ENDIF gave us an id to try
```

If the user gives us a prospective ID to add, we lock the file and then seek that ID. If we don't find the ID, we know it is unique, and we add a new client record. If we find the ID, we allow the user to edit the existing client record.

This example uses an FLOCK() to ensure that two users cannot add the same ID at the same time. Because no other user can obtain an RLOCK() if we have an FLOCK() in place, and because we cannot obtain an FLOCK() while any other user holds an RLOCK() on any record in the table, using FLOCK() is an inferior solution in high-volume systems. However, we don't expect our users to add large numbers of clients daily. So, because this FLOCK() approach is the simplest of several available solutions, we will use it for the TSCLIENT program.

There are many more ways to allow users to add records that feature a user-assigned ID. You can review some of the more effective approaches in Chapter 13, "Multiuser Discussions."

Searching for a Client

Well, we have accomplished almost all our goals for this portion of our application. All that is left is to add some sort of search routine. We want to present users with a scrollable list of available clients, and enable the users to type a few characters of the client ID so they can narrow the search.

There are *many* clever ways of accomplishing this task, most of which include the use of a Browse window, but adding the following code to the vcontrol procedure in TSCLIENT.PRG is probably the simplest:

```
CASE UPPER(m.control)=="SEARCH"
** create a popup from the client table
DEFINE POPUP tsclient FROM 1,0 TO 10,50 ;
PROMPT FIELDS tsclient.cl_clid+;
"¦"+tsclient.cl_company TITLE "Pick a client" ;
IN WINDOW tsclient
** Prepare to exit the popup when the user makes
** a selection
ON SELECTION POPUP tsclient DEACTIVATE POPUP tsclient
l_oldconf=SET('confirm')
** Allow user to type the first few characters of
** the id to narrow the search
SET CONFIRM ON
```

continues

```
** Display and process the popup
ACTIVATE POPUP tsclient REST
** Release the popup
RELEASE POPUP tsclient
** Since we are sitting on a new record,
** put field values into memory variables,
** and refresh the screen
SCATTER MEMVAR MEMO
SCATTER TO l_old MEMO
SHOW GETS
** Put the CONFIRM setting back
** to its previous state
SET CONFIRM &l_oldconf
```

Hey! The client data entry screen is complete! The fact that you can write this portion of the application in a variety of ways, using a variety of techniques, demonstrates the strength of the FoxPro language.

In most cases, this chapter has opted for the simplest technique to provide a given functionality. Later chapters explore alternative methods that enhance or replace the techniques referenced in this section.

CHAPTER 5

Employees and Projects

In this chapter, we leverage the skills we learned in Chapters 1 through 4 to create an employee data entry screen. We take every advantage of the existing TSCLIENT data entry screen to create the TSEMPL data entry screen in minutes, rather than hours.

In addition, we add a project data entry screen to our application that enables the user to add projects for a client. This project data entry screen introduces the BROWSE command.

By the end of this chapter, you will be able to use the TSCLIENT data entry screen as a template for a new single file data entry screen of your own design. You also will be able to add a Browse window to an existing data entry screen. Finally, you will be able to add menus on the fly to the existing menu system.

Employees

Now that we have completed our first single file data entry screen, it should be simple to make another data entry screen that behaves in the same way. Here are the steps you take to create a single file data entry screen for the employee file:

1. Save TSCLIENT.PRG as TSEMPL.PRG.

2. Replace all references of cl_clid with em_empid.

3. Replace all references of cl_* with the em_* equivalent. (In this case, we need to concern ourselves only with the reference to cl_company in the search option).

4. Replace all references of client with empl.

5. Open TSTIME.DBF rather than TSPROJ.DBF. (When you try to delete an employee, make sure that a time sheet record for this employee exists before enabling that deletion.)

6. Replace references of TSCLIENA() with TSEMPLA().

7. From the Command window, USE TSEMPL.DBF.

8. Modify the TSCLIENT screen, and save TSCLIENT.SCX as TSEMPL.SCX. (Remember to save TSEMPL.SCX in the \BOOK\SCX subdirectory.)

9. Select the push button object, then select Copy from the Edit menu.

10. Delete all objects from the screen.

11. Build a quick screen using the memory variable option.

12. Arrange your objects and change the prompts as necessary.

13. To install the push button, select Paste from the Edit menu.

14. Edit the m.em_empid object and mark it as initially disabled.

15. Select the Layout option from the Screen menu, and change the name and title of the window to TSEMPL and Employee Data Entry, respectively.

16. Generate the TSEMPL screen.

17. Modify the TSCLIENA program, save it as BOOK\PRG\TSEMPLA.PRG, and replace all cl_* references with em_*. Replace all references of TSCLIENT with TSEMPL.

18. Modify the TSCLIENA screen and save as \BOOK\PRG\TSEMPLA.SCX.

19. Save and generate the TSEMPLA screen.

That should do it! If you are an experienced programmer, you are probably thinking that this process should be automated. In other words, you should be able to write a FoxPro program that prompts the programmer for a few fields of information and then makes a duplicate of an existing screen, along with any necessary changes.

If you are inclined to use a more object-oriented approach, you may be thinking that the entire single-file data entry process can be rewritten as a general-purpose procedure, to which a few messages can be passed to distinguish between data entry screens.

Both approaches have merit, and we explore some of the possibilities later in this book. For now, we are finished with the single-file data entry screens for our system. Our next task is to create a multifile data entry screen to handle projects.

Projects

Not all of our data entry screens are as easy as the employee and client data entry screens. The project data entry screen in Figure 5.1 can be completed by cloning the client data entry screen, and simply validating that the project be assigned to an existing client.

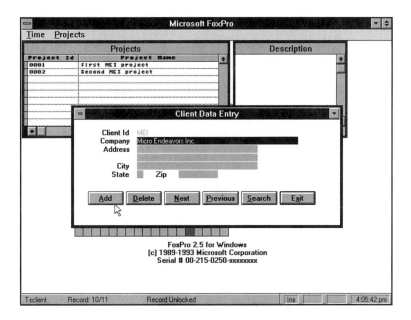

Figure 5.1. Project data entry.

That wouldn't be very much fun however, so we will take a slightly more sophisticated approach, utilizing the Browse window. Here's the plan:

1. Create a TSPROJ.PRG program that will BROWSE KEY NOWAIT in the TSPROJ database.

2. In TSPROJ.PRG, set kaction to "Clients", and return to the TSMAIN program in an attempt to start TSCLIENT.

3. Enhance the TSCLIENT.PRG program to refresh the project Browse window.

4. Enhance the TSCLIENT.PRG program to add a menu pad that will offer project maintenance options like add, delete, and edit.

5. Enhance the TSCLIENT.PRG program to close the TSPROJ Browse window when necessary.

The TSPROJ.PRG program is surprisingly simple. All we have to do is make sure the client and project databases are open, and then issue a single BROWSE command. Here is the code:

```
* tsproj.prg
* project data entry

* Declare local variables
PRIVATE ALL LIKE l_*
PRIVATE m.pb
* Open the client database, if it is not already open
IF NOT USED("tsclient")
  USE tsclient IN SELECT(1) AGAIN
ENDIF


* Open the project database
IF NOT USED("tsproj")
  USE tsproj IN SELECT(1) AGAIN
ENDIF
* Establish the client+project id tag as the
* master order for the project database
SET ORDER TO clproj IN tsproj

IF EOF('tsclient')
   * Try to place us on a client record if
   * we are sitting at eof in the client database
   GO TOP IN tsclient
ENDIF

* Now, put the browse window up containing all projects
* for the current client.

SELECT tsproj
DEFINE WINDOW tsproj AT 0,0 SIZE 15,50 ;
   FLOAT GROW ZOOM MINIMIZE NOMDI SYSTEM FONT "FoxFont",7

BROWSE FIELDS pj_projid:R:H="Project Id",;
  pj_name:H="Project Name" ;
  WINDOW tsproj ;
```

```
   TITLE "Projects" ;
   KEY tsclient.cl_clid ;
   NOWAIT NOMENU NOAPPEND NODELETE ;
   FONT "FoxFont",7

DEFINE WINDOW tsprojds AT 0,52 SIZE 15,27 ;
  FLOAT GROW ZOOM MINIMIZE NOMDI SYSTEM ;
  TITLE "Description" FONT "FoxFont",7

MODIFY MEMO tsproj.pj_desc ;
  WINDOW tsprojds NOWAIT

* Now make the tsclient screen the next action
kaction="CLIENTS"
RETURN .T.
```

If you run this code from the Command window, you notice that the NOWAIT clauses
of the BROWSE and MODIFY MEMO commands allow processing to continue without
starting Browse or modify sessions. In other words, the Command window returns to
the desktop because the TSPROJ.PRG is finished processing. The Browse and MODIFY
MEMO objects, however, are still on-screen, waiting to be used.

When you run TSPROJ.PRG from the TSMAIN program, control returns to TSMAIN
after the Browse and MODIFY MEMO window objects are created. The value of kaction
is "CLIENTS" because the TSPROJ.PRG places "CLIENTS" in kaction before returning. As
a result, TSMAIN.PRG executes the TSCLIENT program immediately after executing the
TSPROJ program.

At this point, we have a Browse window, a MODIFY MEMO window, and the TSCLIENT.SPR
READ CYCLE window on-screen. FoxPro maintains the connection between the Browse
and MODIFY MEMO windows for us, but we have to program the connection between the
READ window and the Browse window.

Our first task is to provide a menu with which the user can add new projects, delete
existing projects, and close the projects window. We will name this menu TSPROJ and
use the Menu Builder to create it. TSPROJ has to produce the following code:

```
DEFINE PAD projects OF _MSYSMENU PROMPT "\<Projects" ;
  COLOR SCHEME 13 KEY ALT+P, "ALT+P";
ON PAD projects OF _MSYSMENU ACTIVATE POPUP projects
DEFINE POPUP projects MARGIN RELATIVE SHADOW COLOR SCHEME 13
DEFINE BAR 1 OF projects PROMPT "\<Add Project"
DEFINE BAR 2 OF projects PROMPT "\<Delete Project"
DEFINE BAR 3 OF projects PROMPT "\<Close Projects"
ON SELECTION POPUP projects do vcontrol with prompt()
```

Place a conditional call to this menu option in the TSCLIENT.PRG program just prior to the execution of TSCLIENT.SPR. The affected portions of TSCLIENT.PRG are printed in bold face in the following code segment:

```
* Make a "before editing" array copy of the record
SCATTER TO l_old MEMO
m.control=""  && push button variable
m.l_wasdisabled=.F.  && disabled state of screen
*# Put the project menu up if the projects window
* has been placed on the screen.
IF WEXIST('projects')
  DO tsproj.mpr
ENDIF
* Run the Window, SAY, and GET code:
DO tsclient.spr
RELEASE PAD projects OF _msysmenu
RELEASE WINDOW projects,tsproj,tsprojds,description
RETURN .T.
```

In essence, when we move to a new record in the TSCLIENT screen, we want the Browse window to display the projects for the new client record. We accomplish this task by issuing the following command:

```
BROWSE KEY tsclient.cl_clid LAST NOWAIT
```

In addition, we want to refresh the project window when we add or delete a project for the current client. To accomplish this task, issue the following command:

```
SHOW WINDOW projects REFRESH SAME
```

You can place these commands individually throughout the TSCLIENT.PRG program whenever the need arises, or you can place them in the READSHOW UDF, which is called when the client record changes. Here is the new version of readshow:

```
PRIVATE l_oldsele
IF EOF('tsclient')
  SHOW GETS disabled ONLY
  SHOW GET control,1 enabled  && Add
  SHOW GET control,6 enabled  && Exit
  ** remember that the current window
  ** is disabled
  l_wasdisabled=.T.
  *# Disable the project menu pad if we aren't
  ** sitting on a valid client record
  SET SKIP OF PAD projects OF _msysmenu .T.
ELSE
```

```
   IF l_wasdisabled
     ** window used to be disabled
     SHOW GETS enabled ONLY
     SHOW GET m.cl_clid disabled
     l_wasdisabled=.F.
   ENDIF screen used to be disabled
   *#
   IF WEXIST('projects')
     ** If the projects window exists, make sure
     ** we display projects for the current client
     ** only.
     l_oldsele=SELECT()
     SELECT tsproj
     IF tsclient.cl_clid <> tsproj.pj_clid
       SEEK tsclient.cl_clid
       BROWSE KEY tsclient.cl_clid LAST NOWAIT
     ELSE
       SHOW WINDOW projects REFRESH SAME
     ENDIF
     SELECT (l_oldsele)
   ENDIF there is a project window that needs refreshing
ENDIF at eof in tsclient
* EOP readshow
```

Adding a Project

Because the TSPROJ menu makes calls to the VCONTROL program, we have to expand
the vcontrol procedure to handle adding projects. Here is the code to do so:

```
CASE UPPER(m.control)=="ADD PROJECT"
   IF NOT EOF('tsclient') AND RLOCK('tsclient')
     SELECT tsclient
     IF cl_nxtproj<=9998
       IF cl_nxtproj<=0
         REPLACE cl_nxtproj WITH 1
         SCATTER MEMVAR MEMO
         SCATTER TO l_old MEMO
       ENDIF started with 0
       SELECT tsproj
       SCATTER MEMVAR MEMO BLANK
       m.pj_clid=tsclient.cl_clid
       m.pj_projid=TRANSFORM(tsclient.cl_nxtproj,"@L ####")
```

continues

73

```
      IF l3insert ()
        SHOW WINDOW projects REFRESH SAME
        SELECT tsclient
        REPLACE cl_nxtproj WITH cl_nxtproj+1
        SCATTER MEMVAR MEMO
        SCATTER TO l_old
        UNLOCK IN tsclient
      ELSE && failed to add proj record
        UNLOCK IN tsclient
        DO l3msg WITH "Could not add a record to the project "+;
          "file."
      ENDIF able to add project record
    ELSE && no more project numbers available
      UNLOCK IN tsclient
      DO l3msg WITH "No more project numbers available "+;
        "for this client."
    ENDIF room to increment the project counter
  ELSE && no client record, or client not lockable
    DO l3msg WITH "I can't lock the current client. "+;
      "So, I can't add a project for you right now."
  ENDIF able to lock client record
```

Adding a project record is slightly different from adding a client record. For one thing, the user does not assign the project ID. Instead, the system assigns the project ID by obtaining the next available ID from the client record. To ensure that no two users can add the same project to the same client simultaneously, the program first attempts to lock the client record before adding the project record.

 Note: Notice the use of the l3insert function to add the project record. This library routine simply attempts to add a record to current work area using the INSERT INTO command. It only returns False if the attempt fails for some reason. In this case, it is unlikely to fail because projects are added to the database infrequently.

Notice that we only update the cl_nxtproj field if the l3insert() succeeds. After the successful addition of the new project, we issue a SCATTER MEMVAR and a SCATTER TO command to refresh the tsclient memory variables. After all, we just changed one of the fields in the database, and we don't want our tschange() function to report incorrectly that the user changed a value in the tsclient record. In fact, our addition of a new project caused the change in the tsclient record.

To show the user that his or her efforts have not been in vain, we include a SHOW WINDOW projects REFRESH SAME command to showcase our effort.

Deleting a Project

Well, we can add a project record, so now we need some method for deleting a project record. All we need do is add the following code to the vcontrol procedure:

```
CASE UPPER(m.control)=="DELETE PROJECT"
  IF tsproj.pj_clid=tsclient.cl_clid AND RLOCK('tsproj')
    IF l3msg("Do you want to delete the "+TRIM(tsproj.pj_name)+;
        " project?","\<Yes;\!\?\<No")="Yes"
      l_wastime=.T.
      IF !USED('tstime')
        USE tstime IN SELE(1) AGAIN
        l_wastime=.F.
      ENDIF
      SET ORDER TO clproj IN tstime
      IF NOT SEEK(tsproj.pj_clid+tsproj.pj_projid,'tstime')
        * go ahead and delete the project
        SELECT tsproj
        DELETE
        SKIP
        IF EOF() OR tsclient.cl_clid<>tsproj.pj_clid
          SEEK tsclient.cl_clid
          BROWSE KEY tsclient.cl_clid LAST NOWAIT
        ELSE && still on a project for the current client
          SHOW WINDOW projects REFRESH SAME
        ENDIF deleted the last project for this client
      ENDIF did not find any time sheets for this project
    ENDIF wants to delete this project
  ENDIF able to lock this project
```

Deleting a project is easier than adding one. We simply need to be able to lock the client record, lock the project record, and make sure there are no time sheets for this project before we delete the project. After deleting the project, we need to refresh the project Browse window, just in case we have deleted the last project for this client.

Closing the Project Screen

Closing the project portion of our multifile data entry screen is simple. The option already is in the TSPROJ menu; now all we have to do is add the following code to the vcontrol procedure:

```
CASE UPPER(m.control)=="MENU"
  ACTIVATE WINDOW tsclient
  CLEAR READ
CASE UPPER(m.control)=="CLOSE PROJECTS"
  RELEASE WINDOW tsproj,projects,tsprojds,description
  RELEASE PAD projects OF _msysmenu
  ACTIVATE WINDOW tsclient
```

The RELEASing of windows and pads when the user selects Close Projects from the TSPROJ menu is straightforward. But you may be wondering why I chose to reprint the "MENU" case here.

 Tip: Notice that when the user makes a selection from the Time pad, (which calls the TSDO program and stores the prompt of the menu option to `kaction` and calls `vcontrol` with "MENU"), I have elected to issue an `ACTIVATE WINDOW tsclient` command before `CLEAR READ`, because in this screen, the user's cursor may reside *in* a Browse or `MODIFY MEMO` window when he or she selects an option from the Time pad.

If I issued a CLEAR READ command while the user resided in a Browse or MODIFY MEMO window, I would not exit the current READ CYCLE session until the user selects the TSCLIENT window! Therefore, I select the TSCLIENT window for the user. This activity is required when the intention of a CLEAR READ command is to exit from the current READ CYCLE session immediately.

Accessing the Project Window

We can add a project, delete a project, and close the project window, but you are probably thinking that I have omitted the fairly important option of editing a project. Even worse, nothing in the code enables the user explicitly to access the project Browse window.

Happily, FoxPro will help us with both concerns. First, the user can access the project window simply by clicking the mouse on that window. What if the user doesn't have a mouse? BUY ONE! Do this with money from your own pocket if necessary, but make sure that your user has a mouse hooked up on his or her system. The aggravation involved in making all actions in a system available by both mouse and keyboard is far greater than any possible remuneration derived from such an effort.

Ok, Ok. Maybe all your users are *rodentially challenged* (a term I first heard used by Lisa Slater to mean that your users not only hate mice, they won't use them even if they are attached to the system). The following command places the user in the projects window when he or she presses the F9 function key:

```
ON KEY LABEL F9 ACTIVATE WINDOW projects
```

Don't forget to reset the function key when you exit the TSCLIENT program—then find some new users.

Editing a Project Record

Because there seems to be no explicit code to lock or edit a project record, I have chosen to rely on FoxPro's implicit record-locking scheme when the user attempts to change a record in the Browse or MODIFY MEMO windows. When the user tries to change a record in the Browse or MODIFY MEMO window, FoxPro attempts to lock the current Browse window record automatically.

This record remains locked until the user moves to another record in the Browse window, or until the user selects another window. If the lock attempt fails, an error is generated that can be trapped by a simple error-trapping routine. (For more information about sample error routines, refer to Chapter 13, "Multiuser Discussions.")

Because you rarely change the name or description of a project, it is unlikely that there will be any contention for these project records. Chapter 13, "Multiuser Discussions," discusses more active locking schemes. In addition, the next module of the application includes an even more sophisticated multifile data entry screen.

Time Sheets

In this chapter, we will begin the creation of a multifile, multiuser, multi-window, data entry screen. Referential integrity, event handling, record locking, multi-window screen sets, and fully integrated Browse windows are among the topics discussed in this and the following chapters.

You don't learn how to add, edit, or delete records in this chapter (that will come in the next chapter), but you do learn how to link data in multiple windows so actions taken in one window are accurately reflected in related windows. You also learn how to combine multiple windows in the same screen set. You learn how to incorporate intelligent Browse windows into your screens, and how to use most of the available READ clauses to handle window events.

Perhaps most importantly, you learn how to plan for all the events that can occur in a multi-window data entry screen. The design demonstrated in this chapter helps to ensure that your complicated programs don't become "write-only" applications that no one, not even you, can maintain.

Sizing Up the Time Sheets Data Entry Screen

In most applications, you encounter at least one *multifile* data entry screen. These screens frequently require the input of multiple *child* records for a single *parent* record. Common examples include line items for an invoice, phone calls from the same client, expenses for a project, student registrations for the same class, and time sheet entries for a given week of a given employee.

Every parent-child data entry screen presents its own challenges; however, most parent-child data, entry screens also share certain attributes. The time sheet data entry screen shown in Figure 6.1 gives us an opportunity to explore the most common challenges of parent-child, data entry screens.

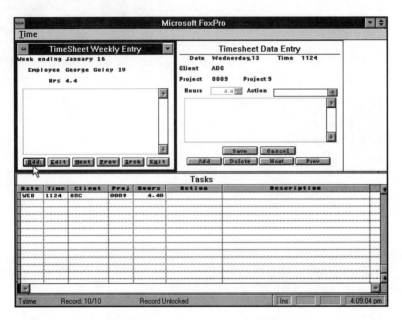

Figure 6.1. A time sheet entry.

In this case, we want users to input one week's worth of time sheet entries to the same screen. The screen gives the user the opportunity to add, edit, and delete time sheet entries and weeks. The *week* record is the parent record in this screen, and the individual time sheet entries associated with that week record are the child records.

The Timesheet Weekly Entry window processes changes to the parent record, and the Timesheet Data Entry window and the Tasks windows provide access to the child records. The Tasks window is read-only, forcing all updates to time sheet records to take place in the Timesheet Data Entry window.

Plan of Attack

The TSTIME1.PRG program that controls the three window screen set includes more than 530 lines of code. Between you and me, the idea of just printing those 530-plus lines of code crossed my mind more than once. There is more to the implementation of a complicated screen, however, than source code. So, let's discuss an approach you can apply to all your sophisticated screen projects. These are the steps I followed to create the time sheet data entry screen:

1. Determine the locking scheme and "modality" of the screen.

2. Write code in the controlling program to open all the affected databases, and then run the controlling program.

3. Use the Screen Builder to lay out all the GET windows. Include all the GET fields, push buttons, popup menus, and so on, that are required.

4. Include all the required necessary field-level WHEN and VALID clause references, but don't write any code yet. Be sure that all event-triggering objects (such as push buttons) reference the vcontrol() UDF.

5. Also include references to UDFs for READ WHEN, READ VALID, READ SHOW, READ DEACTIVATE, and READ ACTIVATE events.

6. Use the Project Manager to arrange the windows, and set generation defaults.

7. Generate the .SPR.

8. Modify the controlling .PRG to include stubs for all the UDFs referenced in the .SPR.

9. In vcontrol(), include CASE statements for every event that can occur during this session. These include a CASE for every push button, a CASE for a menu hit, and CASEs to handle user movement from window to window.

10. In the controlling .PRG, create a stub procedure for each CASE in the vcontrol procedure. Include an ACTIVATE WINDOW and CLEAR READ command in the exit CASE, so that you can exit from this screen set during preliminary testing.

11. Create individual procedures for each Browse window that you want to add to your application. Include the window definition in these procedures.

12. Run the controlling .PRG and then rearrange and redefine windows as necessary.

13. With the look of the screen now well-established, you can begin to add functionality to your screens by filling the stubs found in the controlling program. I suggest that you handle any Next, Previous, or Search options first, your Edit options next, and then handle your Delete options. Finally, handle your Add options. Test each option as you implement it.

Determining the Locking Scheme and Modality of the Screen

Unlike our single file data entry screens, I have included an Edit button on the time sheet data entry screen. Until the user selects the Edit button, all on-screen information is read-only. This approach reduces programming effort and ensures that users make changes only when they intend to make changes.

In many parent-child data entry screens, it is necessary to treat changes, deletions, and additions to the child records as a single transaction. When we add line items to an invoice, for example, we typically wait until we have entered all the line items in a temporary table before we post any of the line items to the "live" line items table.

In our case, however, it is acceptable to treat each time sheet record as an individual transaction. The user, therefore, can abort changes to only one time sheet record at a time. To put it another way, this data entry screen doesn't offer users the option of aborting changes made to all time sheet actions.

We will discuss the "batch" update process in Chapter 13, "Multiuser Discussions." But now it's time to work on the time sheet data entry screen.

Opening DBFs and Creating *mvars* for Time Sheet Data Entry

The name of our time sheet data entry screen will be TSTIME. The control program is therefore named TSTIME.PRG, and the screen names begin with TSTIME.

The design of this data entry session calls for multiple time sheet entries for a single week/employee combination. The session assumes that the currently selected employee is the employee for which time sheet entry should take place.

How does the user select the current employee? The user can select the current employee through the Employee option of the main menu. The TSEMPL program leaves the record pointer in the TSEMPL.DBF sitting on an employee record.

So, in addition to opening the databases, TSTIME.PRG has to store the ID of the current employee in a memory variable. Here is the required code so far:

```
* tstime.prg
* Time data entry

* Declare local variables
PRIVATE ALL LIKE l_*
```

```
PRIVATE m.control,m.control1,m.control2,m.timeemp,m.browwhen
STORE "" TO m.control,m.control1,m.control2
** Try to open the databases and get an employee ID.
IF NOT tstimeopen()
  RETURN .F.
ENDIF couldn't get an employee id
m.timeemp=tsempl.em_empid
** Look for a week record for this employee.
SELECT tsweek
IF SEEK(m.timeemp)
  SCATTER MEMVAR MEMO
  SCATTER TO l_oldwk MEMO
ELSE
  SCATTER MEMVAR MEMO BLANK
  SCATTER TO l_oldwk MEMO BLANK
ENDIF
** Look for the first time sheet record for this
** date/employee.
SELECT tstime
IF SEEK(m.timeemp+DTOS(m.wk_date))
  SCATTER MEMVAR MEMO
  SCATTER TO l_oldti MEMO
ELSE
  SCATTER MEMVAR MEMO BLANK
  SCATTER TO l_oldti MEMO BLANK
ENDIF
** Load an array with values for the action
** popup. Usually, we would SELECT these
** values from a table into an array.
DIME ktsactions(3)
ktsactions(1)="Program"
ktsactions(2)="Train"
ktsactions(3)="Work"
m.browwhen=.F.
STORE "" TO m.control,m.control1,m.control2
l_editmode=.F.
Return .T.
PROCEDURE tstimeopen
* Open the employee database, and ensure that
* we have a valid employee ID.
IF NOT USED("tsempl")
  USE tsempl IN SELE(1) AGAIN
ENDIF
SELECT tsempl
```

continues

```
SET ORDER TO em_empid
IF EOF()
  GOTO TOP
ENDIF at eof now
IF EOF("tsempl")  && still at eof!
  DO l3msg WITH "You must enter at least one employee!"
  RETURN .F.
ENDIF no employee records

* Open the client database, if it is not already open.
IF NOT USED("tsclient")
  USE tsclient IN SELECT(1) AGAIN
ENDIF
SET ORDER TO cl_clid IN tsclient

* Open the project database.
IF NOT USED("tsproj")
  USE tsproj IN SELECT(1) AGAIN
ENDIF
SET ORDER TO clproj IN tsproj

* Open the time sheet database.
IF NOT USED("tstime")
  USE tstime IN SELECT(1) AGAIN
ENDIF
SELECT tstime
* Use the date + employee + line number index.
SET ORDER TO empdte IN tstime

* Open the date database.
IF NOT USED("tsweek")
  USE tsweek IN SELECT(1) AGAIN
ENDIF
SET ORDER TO empdte IN tsweek
RETURN .T.
```

This version of TSTIME.PRG does a nice job of opening the databases needed to create the screens you see at the top of Figure 6.1. Now we need to build the screens.

Building the TimeSheet Weekly Entry Window

TSTIMEWK is the name of the TimeSheet Weekly Entry window. Figure 6.2 shows the completed screen with size and font information as well. The first three fields on the screen are SAY objects.

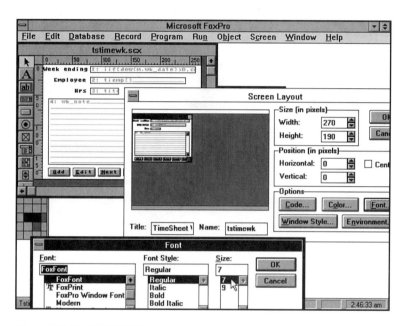

Figure 6.2. The TSTIMEWK screen.

Here are the SAY expressions, with picture clauses:

1. `IIF(DOW(m.wk_date)>0,CMONTH(m.wk_date)+`
   `    " "+LTRIM(STR(DAY(m.wk_date))),"")`

2. `tiemp()`

3. `titothrs() picture "@BZ ###.#"`

Notice that an Output or SAY object can be a UDF. Figure 6.3 illustrates the creation of the `titothrs()` UDF SAY object.

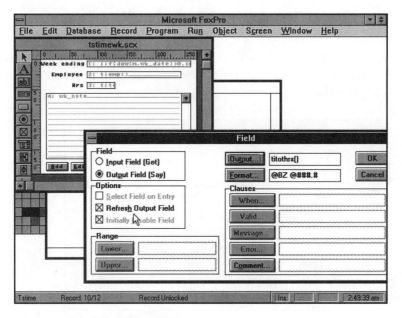

Figure 6.3. The *titothrs( )* UDF *SAY* object.

As usual, the memory variable for the push button on the TSTIMEWK screen is `m.control`. Because we will have many events that call the `vcontrol()` UDF, however, we need to adjust the valid clause for the `m.control` push button. You can see this adjustment in Figure 6.4.

Finally, we need to include READ clause UDFs to support several events. Figure 6.5 shows the necessary code options for this screen. Notice that these READ clause UDFs affect all the windows in this screen set, not just the TSTIMEWK window.

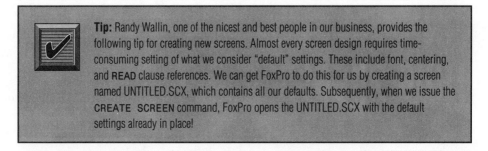

Tip: Randy Wallin, one of the nicest and best people in our business, provides the following tip for creating new screens. Almost every screen design requires time-consuming setting of what we consider "default" settings. These include font, centering, and READ clause references. We can get FoxPro to do this for us by creating a screen named UNTITLED.SCX, which contains all our defaults. Subsequently, when we issue the CREATE SCREEN command, FoxPro opens the UNTITLED.SCX with the default settings already in place!

Before we move to the TSTIME screen, notice that the only entry field on-screen, `m.wk_notes`, is disabled. This is in keeping with our decision to force the user to select Edit before allowing changes to any portion of the screen. At this point, we can save the TSTIMEWK screen, but there is no point in generating the .SPR until both the screens are complete and arranged.

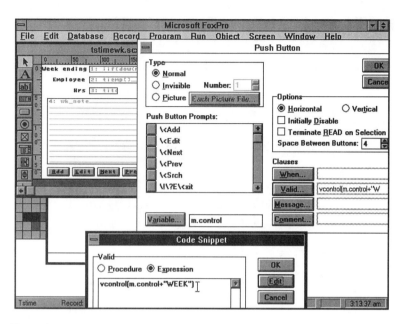

Figure 6.4. The control for TSTIMEWK.SPR.

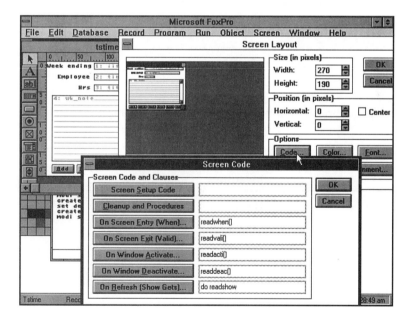

Figure 6.5. The *READ* clause UDFs for TSTIMEWK.

Building the Timesheet Data Entry Window

TSTIME is the name of the Timesheet Data Entry window. Figure 6.6 shows the completed screen, with a list of objects in order.

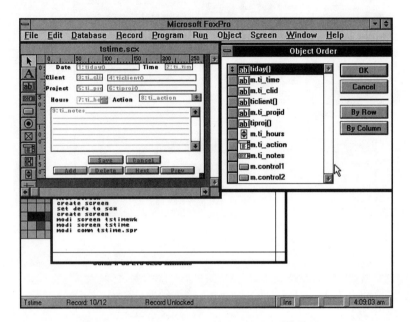

Figure 6.6. The TSTIME screen.

Table 6.1 includes a brief description of each of the screen objects.

Table 6.1. The TSTIME screen objects.

Screen Object	Meaning
tiday() && SAY	Day of week
m.ti_time && SAY	Time started
m.ti_clid && SAY	Client ID
ticlient() && SAY	Client name
m.ti_projid && SAY	Project ID

88

Screen Object	Meaning
tiproj() && SAY	Project name
m.ti_hours &&	Spinner hours
m.ti_action && ktsactions	ARRAY popup
m.ti_notes &&	Text edit region of notes
m.control1 &&	Save/Cancel push button
m.control2 &&	Push button two

The screen is 275 pixels high and 190 pixels wide, with a default font of "Foxfont",7. Once again, all GET objects on-screen are disabled to conform with our decision to force the user to choose Edit before allowing changes.

Because we already included READ clause UDF references in the TSTIMEWK screen, we don't need to include READ clause UDF references in the TSTIME screen. We do need to include valid clauses for both push buttons, however. Here is the expression we need to include in each:

```
m.control1 VALID vcontrol(m.control1+"TIME")
m.control2 VALID vcontrol(m.control2+"TIME")
```

At this point, you probably can't wait to see some results of our effort. To accomplish this, however, we need to use the Project Manager so we can arrange the windows permanently. Figures 6.7 through 6.10 demonstrate the following activities:

1. To add a new screen set to application, use the Add option of the Project Manager.

2. To add a second screen to this screen set, choose Add in the Edit Screen Set dialog box.

3. Use the Arrange option of the Edit Screen Set dialog to arrange our two windows.

4. Use the More option of the Edit Screen Set dialog to establish generator settings.

When these steps are completed, we use the build option of the Project Manager to build the TSTIME.SPR file. The TSTIME.SPR positions both the TSTIMEWK window and the TSTIME window on-screen with all their screen objects.

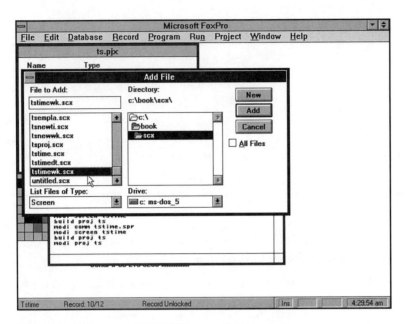

Figure 6.7. Adding a new TSTIMEWK screen to the project.

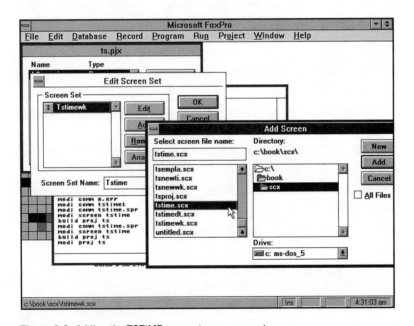

Figure 6.8. Adding the TSTIME screen to a screen set.

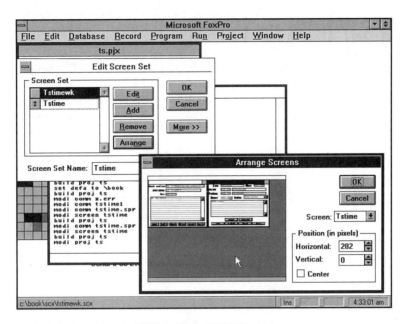

Figure 6.9. Arranging the TSTIMEWK and TSTIME windows.

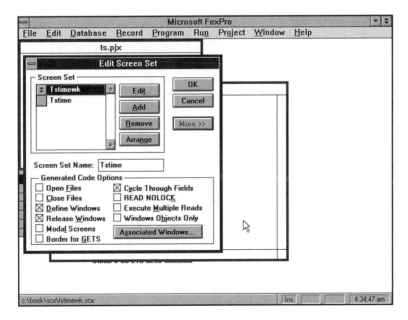

Figure 6.10. Establishing generator settings for TSTIME.SPR.

Stubs and *SAY* UDFs for TSTIME

At this point in the process we need to put stubs into the TSTIME.PRG program so that the TSTIME.SPR program runs without error. In addition, I am going to cheat a little on your behalf by providing the completed SAY UDF procedures. Under normal circumstances, I would make these return sample values until I had completed the design of the screens.

Here are the procedures you need to add to your existing TSTIME.PRG program:

```
PROCEDURE readshow
** Called when program issues SHOW GETS, or SHOW GETS OFF.
RETURN .T.


PROCEDURE readwhen
* Triggered first time into the read cycle.
RETURN .T.


PROCEDURE readdeac
** Triggered when user exits a GET window.
RETURN .F.


PROCEDURE readacti
** Called when user enters a GET window.
RETURN .T.


PROCEDURE readvali
** Called when read is cancelled.
RETURN .T.


PROCEDURE vcontrol
* Processes push button selections.
PARAMETERS control
PRIVATE l_xx,l_oldsele,l_control
l_control=UPPER(ALLTRIM(m.control))
l_oldsele=SELECT()
DO CASE
  CASE l_control=="EXITWEEK" && Exit pb
    CLEAR READ
  OTHERWISE  && Undefined event
    DO l3msg WITH l_control+" is undefined."
ENDCASE
** Return to work area we started with.
SELECT (l_oldsele)
```

```
RETURN .T.
* EOP control

PROCEDURE tiproj
* Displays name of project.
IF ((NOT EMPTY(m.ti_clid)) AND NOT EMPTY(m.ti_projid)) AND ;
   SEEK(m.ti_clid+m.ti_projid,"tsproj")
  ** m.ti_clid+m.ti_projid references an existing project.
  RETURN tsproj.pj_name
ELSE
  ** m.ti_clid or m.ti_projid is probably empty, because
  ** they do not reference an existing project.
  RETURN PADR("Unknown Project",LEN(tsproj.pj_name))
ENDIF

PROCEDURE tiemp
** Returns the employee name for the tstimewk window.
RETURN TRIM(tsempl.em_first)+" "+TRIM(tsempl.em_last)

PROCEDURE titothrs
** Calculates total hours for this week for this
** employee.
PRIVATE l_tothrs
** Note that the SQL SELECT command does not reposition
** the record pointer in TSTIME.DBF. This feature
** obviates the need to save and reset our place.
SELECT SUM(ti_hours) FROM tstime WHERE ;
  ti_empid+DTOS(ti_week)=m.timeemp+DTOS(m.wk_date) ;
  INTO ARRAY l_tothrs
IF _TALLY=0
  ** _TALLY returns the number of rows in the
  ** result. If _TALLY is 0, there are no hours
  ** for this employee in this week. Further, the
  ** l_tothrs array will not be created.
  RETURN 0
ELSE
  ** Notice that we can reference the first element
  ** of an array by not using an element number!
  RETURN l_tothrs
ENDIF

PROCEDURE ticlient
** Return the client company name for the
** tstime window.
```

continues

```
PRIVATE l_client
IF SEEK(m.ti_clid,"tsclient")
  RETURN tsclient.cl_company
ELSE
  RETURN ""
ENDIF

PROCEDURE tiday
** Return the day of this time sheet as
** CDOW() + DAY(), e.g. "Monday, 13".
RETURN IIF(BETWEEN(DOW(m.ti_week-7+m.ti_day),1,7),;
  CDOW(m.ti_week-7+m.ti_day)+","+;
  LTRIM(STR(DAY(m.ti_week-7+m.ti_day))),"")
```

In addition, you have to include code to call the .SPR program. This code belongs at the end of the TSTIME procedure, as follows:

```
STORE "" TO m.control,m.control1,m.control2
l_editmode=.F.
* Run the Window, SAY, and GET code:
DO tstime.spr
RELEASE WINDOW tasks,tstime1
RETURN .T.
```

Be sure that your readdeac() procedure returns .F.; otherwise, FoxPro will end the READ CYCLE session every time the user moves to a new window. The other interesting procedure here is the titothrs() UDF. This procedure uses a SQL SELECT command every time you issue a SHOW GETS or SHOW GETS OFF command to recalculate the number of hours listed on the time sheet of the current week.

The alternative to the titothrs() UDF is to include a wk_tothrs field in the TSWEEK database. That field would be updated each time a time sheet record was added, edited, or deleted. The wk_tothrs approach results in faster screen refreshes; however, it also requires additional code in the data entry process. In addition, if you post a time sheet record without a corresponding update of the wk_tothrs field (which can happen in a power failure or application crash), additional code is required to reset the wk_tothrs field in all TSWEEK records.

As it happens, FoxPro 2.5 can perform this kind of SQL SELECT query so quickly that the titothrs() solution is not noticeably slower than the wk_tothrs solution until several hundred records appear for the same week. Even then, the difference in performance is tolerable.

Note: Unless I need to see running totals immediately, or unless those running totals consist of contributions from thousands of records, I prefer recalculating values to the maintenance of running total fields.

At this point, you should be able to run your TSTIME.PRG program, giving you an opportunity to check for typographical errors in screens and in the TSTIME.PRG program.

The Events of the Year!

Our next step is to identify every event that can occur during the time sheet data entry session. These include each of the push buttons, a menu selection, moving from window to window, and moving from record to record in the Browse window. To facilitate program maintenance, we process all these events in a single DO CASE structure in the vcontrol procedure. Here is the code:

```
PROCEDURE vcontrol
* Processes push button selections.
PARAMETERS control
PRIVATE l_xx,l_oldsele,l_control
l_control=UPPER(ALLTRIM(m.control))
l_oldsele=SELECT()
DO CASE
  CASE l_control=="MENU" AND ;
      UPPER(WONTOP())=="TSTIMEWK" && Menu hit in week window
    DO tstimesw
    DO tstimest
    CLEAR READ
  CASE l_control=="MENU" AND ;
      UPPER(WONTOP())=="TSTIME" && Menu hit in time window
    DO tstimest
    DO tstimesw
    CLEAR READ
  CASE l_control=="MENU" && Menu hit in browse window
    ACTIVATE WINDOW tstimewk
    CLEAR READ
  CASE l_control=="WINDOWWEEK" && Leaving week window
    DO tstimesw
  CASE l_control=="WINDOWTIME" && Leaving time sheet window
    DO tstimest
```

continues

```
      CASE l_control=="BROWSE" && Moved to a new record in the browse
        DO tstimesh
      CASE l_control=="CANCELWEEK"  && Cancel pb in week window
        DO tstimecw
        UNLOCK IN tsweek
        UNLOCK IN tstime
        DO tstimenoedit
      CASE l_control=="CANCELTIME" && Cancel pb in time window
        DO tstimect
      CASE l_control=="SAVEWEEK" && Save pb in week window
        DO tstimesw
        UNLOCK IN tsweek
        UNLOCK IN tstime
        DO tstimenoedit
      CASE l_control=="SAVETIME" && Save pb in time window
        DO tstimest
      CASE l_control=="NEXTWEEK" && Next pb in week window
        DO tstimenw
      CASE l_control=="NEXTTIME" && Next pb in time window
        DO tstiment
      CASE l_control=="PREVWEEK" && Previous pb in week window
        DO tstimepw
      CASE l_control=="PREVTIME" && Previous pb in week window
        DO tstimept
      CASE l_control=="SRCHWEEK" && Search pb
        DO tstimesr
      CASE l_control=="EDITWEEK" && Edit pb
        DO tstimeed
      CASE l_control=="ADDWEEK" && Add pb in week window
        DO tstimeaw
      CASE l_control=="ADDTIME" && Add pb in time window
        DO tstimeat
      CASE l_control=="DELETETIME" && Delete pb
        DO tstimedt
      CASE l_control=="EXITWEEK" && Exit pb
        ACTIVATE WINDOW tstimewk
        CLEAR READ
      OTHERWISE  && Undefined event
        DO l3msg WITH l_control+" is undefined."
    ENDCASE
    ** Return to work area we started with.
    SELECT (l_oldsele)
    RETURN .T.
    * EOP control
```

In earlier data entry screens, we placed the code for each CASE in the vcontrol procedure. In this case, we want to be able to see all the events in one place. To do this, we placed the code for each of the CASEs in a separate procedure.

You can create your own stub programs to handle each CASE, but you still have more work to do to handle the events. We directed each of the push buttons on the screens to call vcontrol() when selected. We directed the menu system to DO vcontrol WITH "MENU" when the user makes a menu selection. However, we haven't done anything to trigger vcontrol() when the user moves to a new record in the Browse window, and we haven't done anything to trigger vcontrol() when we move to a new window.

We will deal with the BROWSE event when we build our Browse windows. In the meantime, we can handle the user's movement from window to window by placing the following code in TSTIME.PRG:

```
PROCEDURE readdeac
** Triggered when user exits a GET window.
IF WLAST()="TSWEEK"
  ** User is leaving the week window.
  DO vcontrol WITH "windowweek"
ELSE
  ** User is leaving the time window.
  DO vcontrol WITH "windowtime"
ENDIF
RETURN .F.
```

Now when the user exits the TSTIME or TSTIMEWK window, vcontrol() is called.

Incorporating a Browse Window in Time Sheet Entry

The BROWSE command gives us an opportunity to present a formatted, scrollable, resizable, and boundless list of time sheet records for this week. Indeed, I wrote one version of this data entry session that consisted of nothing but a single Browse window.

The BROWSE command may be the most powerful command in the FoxPro language— it also can be the most frustrating. The BROWSE command is so intriguing that I have dedicated an entire chapter (Chapter 12, "The BROWSE Command") to its use. For now, however, we need only learn how to incorporate a Browse window that can display all the time sheet records for this week.

The first step to creating the Browse window is to define a window for the Browse window to mimic. This seems simple enough; however, for the following reasons, I cannot hard code the location or size of the window:

- The size of the FoxPro window might change in Windows.

- The size of the screen might change in DOS.

- I might change the size and/or location of the TSTIMEWK window.

In any of these cases, I want the Browse window to adapt, providing the best possible size to view the greatest possible number of time sheets for the current week. Our first challenge is to find a place to put the Browse window definition code. Because we don't know the size and location of the TSTIMEWK window until we perform the TSTIME.SPR, we have to define our window *inside* the READ CYCLE.

The READ WHEN clause fits the bill perfectly. READ WHEN is evaluated when FoxPro first encounters the READ CYCLE command. Because the .SPR file DEFINEs the TSTIMEWK and TSTIME windows before the READ CYCLE command is executed, the READ WHEN event is the perfect time to line up the Browse window.

Include the following code in TSTIME.PRG:

```
PROCEDURE readwhen
* Triggered first time into the read cycle.
IF SROWS()<=WLROW("tstimewk")+WROW("tstimewk")+3
  ** Expand the FoxPro window sufficiently to support
  ** the browse window.
  ZOOM WINDOW SCREEN NORM SIZE ;
    WLROW("tstimewk")+WROW("tstimewk")+20,SCOLS()
ENDIF
DO tstimebr
RETURN .T.
```

The readwhen() UDF first checks to make sure that the FoxPro window is large enough to hold all the time sheet data entry sessions. If the FoxPro window is not large enough, readwhen() enlarges it. Next, readwhen() calls the TSTIMEBR procedure to define and animate the Browse window. Add the following code to TSTIME.PRG:

```
PROCEDURE tstimebr
** Build the browse window.
* Create a window in which to browse time sheets.
DEFINE WINDOW tstime1 AT WLROW("tstimewk")+WROW("tstimewk")+3,;
  WLCOL("tstimewk") SIZE ;
  SROW()-WROW("tstimewk")-WLROW("tstimewk")-6, ;
  SCOLS() ;
  FLOAT GROW ZOOM MINIMIZE FONT WFONT(1,""),;
```

```
     WFONT(2,"") STYLE WFONT(3,"")
* Put the browse window up.
m.browwhen=.T.  && Don't refresh the tstimewk window
BROWSE WINDOW tstime1 ;
   KEY m.timeemp+DTOS(m.wk_date) ;
   FIELDS ;
   calc1=SUBSTR("SUNMONTUEWEDTHUFRISAT",;
   MAX(1,MIN(ti_day,7))*3-2,3):H="Date",;
   ti_time:H="Time",;
   ti_clid:H="Client",;
   ti_projid:H="Proj",;
   ti_hours:H="Hours",;
   ti_action:H="Action",;
   calc2=MLINE(ti_notes,1):H="Description":35 ;
   NOWAIT NOMENU NOAPPEND NODELETE NOMODIFY ;
   WHEN m.browwhen OR NOT vcontrol("BROWSE") TITLE "Tasks" ;
   FONT WFONT(1,"tstime"),WFONT(2,"tstime") ;
   STYLE WFONT(3,"tstime")
m.browwhen=.F.
RETURN .T.
```

The window definition uses FoxPro's window functions to place the new Browse window just below the TSTIMEWK window and to size the Browse window to take advantage of all available screen space.

The BROWSE command has several interesting aspects. The BROWSE KEY m.timeemp+DTOS(m.wk_date) portion of the command ensures that only time sheet records pertaining to the current employee and week appear.

The calc1 calculated field shows the day for the time sheet entry. The calc2 calculated field shows the first line of the ti_notes field. The NOWAIT clause causes processing to continue after the Browse window is painted. In other words, the Browse window is placed on-screen, but the user is not placed in the Browse window.

The WHEN m.browwhen OR NOT vcontrol("BROWSE") clause causes FoxPro to call the vcontrol() UDF every time the user moves to a record in the Browse window, unless the m.browwhen variable is False.

We include the vcontrol("BROWSE") argument to force FoxPro to call vcontrol() when the user moves to another record in the Browse window. If we do not include the m.browwhen argument, however, vcontrol() also is called when the program issues the BROWSE NOWAIT or subsequent BROWSE NOWAIT command. The result is a "double" painting of the TSTIME window, which can create an annoying flicker and delays in FoxPro for Windows.

Bracketing all `BROWSE NOWAIT` commands with `m.browwhen=.T.` and `m.browwhen=.F.` ensures that `vcontrol()` is called only by the Browse window when the user actually moves to a new record in the Browse window.

Moving to the Next Week and Previous Week

Moving to the next and previous record in the employee and client data entry screens is a simple matter of a `SKIP` and a `SHOW GETS`. Moving to the next and previous week in the Timesheet Data Entry Session is a bit more complicated.

One reason the latter is more complicated is because of our need to refresh three windows instead of one. On the other hand, because the Next and Previous buttons are available only when the user is not editing, we don't need to check for changes before moving. Because we need to refresh different windows under different circumstances, I have broken the refresh routine into two separate routines.

Following is the `CASE` code in `vcontrol`. (Note that nw stands for Next Week and pw stands for Previous Week.)

```
CASE l_control=="NEXTWEEK"  && Next pb in week window
    DO tstimenw
CASE l_control=="PREVWEEK"  && Previous pb in week window
    DO tstimepw
```

Here are the TSTIMEPW and TSTIMENW procedures:

```
PROCEDURE tstimenw
* Move forward to next week.
SELECT tsweek
IF NOT EOF()
  SKIP
ENDIF
DO tsweeksh
DO tstimesh
RETURN .T.


PROCEDURE tstimepw
* Previous week
SELECT tsweek
IF NOT BOF()
  SKIP -1
ENDIFDO tsweeksh
DO tstimesh
RETURN .T.
```

100

After moving to a new week record, we call both refresh routines because all three windows will need refreshing. Notice that we did not use 13skip to ensure that the user doesn't move beyond the end or beginning of the file. This is handled by the TSWEEKSH routine, as follows:

```
PROCEDURE tsweeksh
** Refresh display of week window.
PRIVATE l_oldsele
l_oldsele=SELECT()
SELECT tsweek
IF EOF("tsweek") OR wk_empid > m.timeemp
  ** If you are at eof, or if you have moved to a
  ** week record for a new employee, find the
  ** first week record for the current employee.
  SEEK m.timeemp
ELSE
  IF BOF("tsweek") OR wk_empid < m.timeemp
    ** If you are at bof, or you have moved to a
    ** week record for a previous employee,
    ** find the last week record for the
    ** current employee.
    SET ORDER TO empdte DESC
    SEEK m.timeemp
    SET ORDER TO empdte ASCENDING
  ENDIF
ENDIF
IF EOF("tsweek") OR wk_empid <> m.timeemp
  ** No week records available for the current
  ** employee, so show blanks.
  SCATTER MEMVAR MEMO BLANK
  SCATTER TO l_oldwk MEMO BLANK
  SHOW GETS DISABLE WINDOW tstimewk
  SHOW GET m.control,1 ENABLE && Add
  SHOW GET m.control,6 ENABLE && Exit
ELSE
  ** Obtain and display new values.
  SCATTER MEMVAR MEMO
  SCATTER TO l_oldwk MEMO
  IF m.l_editmode
    ** Enable all objects on the tstimewk window,
    ** except the control push button, which is
    ** already enabled.
```

continues

```
      ** Believe it or not, this loop is faster than
      ** a SHOW GETS ENABLE because it does not
      ** force a refresh of the push button!
      FOR l_xx=1 TO OBJNUM(m.control)-1
        SHOW OBJECT (l_xx) ENABLE
      ENDFOR
    ELSE
      ** Disable all objects on the tstimewk window,
      ** except the control push button.
      FOR l_xx=1 TO OBJNUM(m.control)-1
        SHOW OBJECT (l_xx) DISABLE
      ENDFOR
    ENDIF
ENDIF no timesheet records on file
** Refresh any "Refreshing" SAYs in the tstimewk window
SHOW GETS OFF WINDOW tstimewk
SELECT (l_oldsele)
RETURN .T.
```

The use of a FOR...ENDFOR loop in place of a single SHOW GETS command highlights an important aspect of Windows programming. Windows takes a long time to display objects on-screen. On some hardware, this poor performance results in an annoying screen flicker. Therefore, especially on slower hardware, the programmer needs to write extra code so objects do not reappear unnecessarily.

This becomes even more important when the objects appearing are bitmapped graphics. (I will demonstrate the use of .BMP files as push buttons in Chapter 21, "Cross-Platform Issues.") Avoiding unnecessary object redisplay is much less important in the DOS version of FoxPro 2.5.

After you refresh the TSTIMEWK window, you need to refresh both the time sheet windows. Here is the code for the TSTIMESH procedure:

```
PROCEDURE tstimesh
** Redisplay time sheet records for the current
** employee and week.
PRIVATE l_oldsele
l_oldsele=SELECT()
SELECT tstime
IF ti_empid+DTOS(ti_week)<>m.timeemp+DTOS(m.wk_date)
  ** Current time sheet record does not belong to
  ** the current employee and week.
  m.browwhen=.T.
  ** Find the first record for this employee/week.
```

```
      SEEK m.timeemp+DTOS(m.wk_date)
      ** Reset the browse window to include only records
      ** for the current employee/week.
      BROWSE KEY m.timeemp+DTOS(m.wk_date) LAST NOWAIT
      m.browwhen=.F.
ELSE
      ** You are sitting on a time sheet record that belongs
      ** to the current employee/week.
      IF UPPER(WONTOP())<>"TASKS"
        ** You are not in the browse window, so refresh
        ** the records that are already in the Browse window.
        SHOW WINDOW tasks REFRESH SAME
      ENDIF not in the browse right now
ENDIF
SELECT tstime
IF EOF("tstime") OR ;
   ti_empid+DTOS(ti_week)<>m.timeemp+DTOS(m.wk_date)
   ** No time sheet records for this employee/week.
   SCATTER MEMVAR MEMO BLANK
   SCATTER TO l_oldti BLANK MEMO
   SHOW GETS WINDOW tstime DISABLE
   IF m.l_editmode
     SHOW GET m.control2,1 ENABLE && Add button
   ENDIF editing
ELSE
   ** Obtain and display info for the current time
   ** sheet record.
   SCATTER MEMVAR MEMO
   SCATTER TO l_oldti MEMO
   IF m.l_editmode
     SHOW GETS WINDOW tstime ENABLE
   ELSE
     SHOW GETS WINDOW tstime DISABLE
   ENDIF editing
ENDIF not sitting on a good timesheet record
SELECT (l_oldsele)
RETURN .T.
```

At this point, you might want to add a few records to the TSWEEK and TSTIME databases interactively so you can test the Next and Previous buttons of the TSTIMEWK window.

Searching for Weeks

Because searching for a week involves most of the same activities as moving to the Next and Previous week, we will do the search routine next. Here is the vcontrol case:

```
CASE l_control=="SRCHWEEK" && Search pb
   DO tstimesr
```

Here is the TSTIMESR procedure:

```
PROCEDURE tstimesr
* Search for a particular week.
PRIVATE l_oldconf,m.abortpick
** Open the tsweek database again to use as a lookup
** file.
USE tsweek AGAIN IN SELECT(1) ORDER empdte ;
   ALIAS tstimesr
SELECT tstimesr
** Goto the current tsweek record in the tstimesr
** work area.
IF BETWEEN(RECNO('tsweek'),1,RECCOUNT('tsweek'))
   GOTO RECNO('tsweek')
ENDIF
** Make a window in which to browse.
DEFINE WINDOW tstimesr IN WINDOW tstimewk ;
   AT 0,0 SIZE ;
   WROWS('tstimewk')-2,WCOLS('tstimewk')
PUSH KEY CLEAR && Save current OKL assignments
** "Arm" the Enter key and right mouse button to
** "select" the current record from the
** browse pick list.
ON KEY LABEL enter KEYBOARD "{ctrl+w}" PLAIN
ON KEY LABEL rightmouse KEYBOARD "{ctrl+w}" PLAIN
** "Arm" the Esc key to abort the selection.
ON KEY LABEL ESCAPE DO tstimesr1
m.abortpick=.F.
** Prevent any menu selections
SET SKIP OF MENU _msysmenu .T.
** Present user with a Browse window of week records
** for the current employee.
BROWSE KEY m.timeemp FIELDS ;
   calc1=CMONTH(wk_date)+;
   ","+STR(DAY(wk_date),2):15:H="Date",;
   calc2=MLINE(wk_note,1):H="Notes" ;
```

```
    WINDOW tstimesr TITLE "Choose a Week" ;
    NOMENU NOMODIFY NOAPPEND NODELETE
RELEASE WINDOW tstimesr
POP KEY  && restore previous OKL settings
SELECT tsweek
IF NOT m.abortpick
  IF BETWEEN(RECNO('tstimesr'),1,RECCOUNT('tstimesr'))
    GOTO RECNO('tstimesr')
  ENDIF
ENDIF did not hit escape
USE IN tstimesr  && close tstimesr area
DO tsweeksh
DO tstimesh
SET SKIP OF MENU _msysmenu .F. && Allow menu selections again
RETURN .T.

PROCEDURE tstimesr1
** Exits browse without selecting.
m.abortpick=.T. && set abort flag
KEYBOARD "{ctrl+w}" PLAIN && exit browse
RETURN .T.
```

Our previous search routines made use of the DEFINE POPUP command to construct a pick list of entries from a database. In this case, however, we want the user to select from a list of weeks for the current employee only. We also want the weeks to appear in order, by date.

When the following conditions are in place, the DEFINE POPUP solution is unacceptably slow:

- The .DBF is large, including more than a few thousand records. (TSWEEK.DBF can be very large, depending on the number of employees and the amount of history retained in the file.)

- The values must be presented in indexed order. (We want the weeks to appear in date order.)

- A filter condition exists. (We want to see records only for the current employee.)

Fortunately, under these conditions, the BROWSE KEY command is much faster than the DEFINE POPUP command. Before we can browse, however, we have to ensure that the database is in the proper order and positioned on the appropriate record.

Rather than use the TSWEEK database for the search directly, I have chosen to consume one of the 225 work areas to USE the TSWEEK database AGAIN under the tstimesr ALIAS. This allows me to establish the empdte index as the master index in TSTIMESR without worrying about saving and reestablishing the current master index in TSWEEK. Furthermore, I know that I can move around in the TSTIMESR work area without worrying about any impact on the current record-pointer in the TSWEEK database.

You can apply this technique of using the same file in multiple work areas to many standard activities. In general, the technique reduces code normally required to save and restore the "state" of a database.

Arming the Browse Search

The next topic of interest in this routine is the code used to prepare the keyboard and the desktop for the coming of the Browse window. In essence, we remap three keypresses to enable the user to select a new week or abort the selection process. Here is that code:

```
PUSH KEY CLEAR && Save current OKL assignments
** "Arm" the Enter key and right mouse button to
** "select" the current record from the
** browse pick list.
ON KEY LABEL enter KEYBOARD "{ctrl+w}" PLAIN
ON KEY LABEL rightmouse KEYBOARD "{ctrl+w}" PLAIN
** "Arm" the Esc key to abort the selection.
ON KEY LABEL ESCAPE DO tstimesr1
m.abortpick=.F.
** Prevent any menu selections.
SET SKIP OF MENU _msysmenu .T.
```

In general, when we want to use a Browse window as a pick list, we "arm" one or more hot keys to select the current record from the Browse window. Pressing Ctrl-W closes the Browse window and leaves the user positioned on the current record in the database being BROWSEd.

Tip: When you redirect the Enter key with an ON KEY LABEL command, you may find yourself unable to issue any commands in the Command window if your program *abends* (from *ab*normal *end*) before you can reset the Enter key. If this happens, press Shift-Enter to issue a command in the Command window. For example, you might enter the command ON KEY LABEL Enter, followed by the Shift-Enter keys.

In addition to enabling the user to select a new week for review, we also want the user to be able to abort the search process. To accomplish this, we arm the Esc key to DO tstimesr1. The tstimesr1 procedure simply sets the m.abortpick variable to True and kills the Browse window.

As a result, the program can test the value of m.abortpick to see whether the user chose to abort the selection process. If the user aborts the selection process, the program redisplays the current record. If the user selects a new week, the program displays the values associated with that new week.

After determining whether the user aborted and repositioning the TSWEEK record pointer accordingly, the TSTIMESR procedure must clean up any window definitions, menu changes, and hot key reassignments.

Final Thoughts

Well, the easy part is over. We have successfully implemented the Next, Previous, and Search routines for the Timesheet Data Entry Program. We have accomplished more than just the implementation of the movement options, however. We have also developed the tstimesh and tsweeksh routines that will be used by many other routines. Further, we have developed a very good first guess at the screen layout.

At this point, I would make sure that my prospective client had a good look at the application. However, because I've already completed the entire application, you and I can move on to the editing of the time sheet data.

CHAPTER
7

Updating Time Sheets

In this chapter we make our time sheet program useful. We provide the application with the capability to add and edit weekly time sheet information, including the capability to add, edit, and delete individual time sheet entries.

To accomplish these goals, we will learn about the following:

- Locking multiple records in multiple files

- Updating Browse windows when values are changed in READ windows

- Refreshing READ windows when users move to new records in Browse windows

- Saving values when users move from window to window

- Adding children in a parent-child relationship

In addition, we will learn how to use scrollable lists to update displays dynamically as users move from item to item in the list. We also will learn how to change the content of scrollable lists, radio buttons, and push buttons on the fly.

In short, this is the fun stuff. Enjoy!

The Edit Push Button

The Edit push button on the TSTIMEWK window should enable all the editable GETs on both READ windows and generally allow the user to edit parent (week) record information. In addition, selecting the Edit button should provide the user opportunities to add, edit, and delete the children (time sheet entries) of this parent.

The vcontrol() CASE statement looks like this:

```
CASE l_control=="EDITWEEK" && Edit pb
  DO tstimeed
```

Including an Edit button on the screen is a design decision. We have decided to require the user to press a key before editing can begin. This requirement allows us to make several valuable assumptions when coding the other activities in the time sheet data entry screen.

First, you may have noticed that the Next, Previous, and Search options make no provision for saving changes. We can safely assume that there are no changes to save because the Edit activity disables the Next, Previous, Delete, Search, Add, and Exit push buttons. Therefore, the only time these push buttons will be selected is when the user is *not* editing.

Second, because the user chose to Edit, we will assume that she means to save any changes made during the edit session. By default, therefore, we will save any changes made by the user.

In fact, we won't even bother to ask about saving changes. Instead, whenever the user makes a selection that requires a choice between preserving and discarding those changes, we will simply save those changes. Only if the user specifically chooses to cancel his or her changes will we abort changes to the week record.

Here is the code for the edit procedure:

```
PROCEDURE tstimeed
* Edit a weekly timesheet
* Try to lock the weekly time sheet record
IF RLOCK('tsweek')
  SELECT tstime
  l_oldtime=RECNO()
  ** Try to lock all of the time sheet records
  ** for this employee for this week
  SEEK m.timeemp+DTOS(tsweek.wk_date)
  SCAN WHILE ti_empid=m.timeemp AND ;
      ti_week=tsweek.wk_date AND ;
```

```
      RLOCK()
   ENDSCAN
   IF ti_empid=m.timeemp AND ti_week=tsweek.wk_date
      * didn't lock them all!!!

      UNLOCK IN tstime
      UNLOCK IN tsweek
      l_editmode=.F.
      DO l3msg WITH "I couldn't lock all of your records."
   ELSE
      l_editmode=.T.
      ** Reset tstimewk push button so that
      ** the user can only save or cancel.
      SHOW GET m.control,1 PROMPT "\!\<Save"
      SHOW GET m.control,2 PROMPT "\?\<Cancel"
      SHOW GET m.control,3 DISABLE
      SHOW GET m.control,4 DISABLE
      SHOW GET m.control,5 DISABLE
      SHOW GET m.control,6 DISABLE
   ENDIF
   IF BETWEEN(l_oldtime,1,RECC('tstime'))
      SELECT tstime
      GOTO l_oldtime
   ENDIF
ENDIF able to lock the week record
** Refresh the screen. If the lock was successful
** GETs will be enabled by the tsweeksh and
** tstimesh programs
DO tsweeksh
DO tstimesh
RETURN .T.
```

The tstimeed procedure manifests another design decision. When editing records, we can choose between passive or active locking schemes. In the earlier data entry screens, we chose the passive or "lock only when you need to write" approach to saving changes. The tstimeed procedure demonstrates the active locking scheme, which calls for all records associated with this screen to be locked when the user selects the Edit option.

This approach ensures that all information presented to the user is current. It also ensures that the program saves any changes the user makes. Because any procedure that writes changes to records can do so without first checking for a record lock, the active locking approach reduces coding.

Some programmers argue that the active record locking approach prevents other users from editing any records that are locked by the current user. Further, if the current user goes to lunch, or goes on vacation, these records remain locked until he or she returns.

In Chapter 13, "Multiuser Discussions," we will explore a passive locking scheme for multifile data entry screens such as the time sheet session. That chapter also explores some of the solutions to the "out to lunch" problem posed by the active locking scheme.

Whether we choose to lock all members of this family of records when the user selects the Edit option (as we did in TSTIME), or choose to lock all members of this family of records only when the user saves changes (as we did in TSEMPL and TSCLIENT), the technique for locking multiple records in multiple files is the same.

First, we lock the parent record. Next, we find the first child record for this parent and SCAN WHILE parent.id=child.id AND RLOCK(). At the end of this SCAN loop, we check to see whether we are still sitting on a child record for this parent. If we are, the RLOCK() function failed to lock one of the children.

If we failed to lock one of the children, we unlock the parent and all the other children, and tell the user that he or she cannot edit this family of time sheet entries at this time. If we succeeded in locking the parent and all its children, we set the m.l_editmode variable to True and refresh the screen displays.

The tstimesh and tsweeksh procedures that we use to refresh the windows both use the status of the m.l_editmode variable to determine which GETs to enable or disable. As a result, after selecting the Edit option, the user is presented with a screen like the one shown in Figure 7.1. If you compare the screen in Figure 6.1 to the screen in Figure 7.1, you will see the following differences:

- The only push button options available in the TSTIMEWK window are Save and Cancel.

- All the push buttons are now enabled in the TSTIME window.

- The hours spinner and the action popup are enabled in the TSTIME window.

- The comment text box is enabled in the TSTIMEWK window.

The ability to edit the current time sheet family of records presents the user with a plethora of additional activities. Because we will be saving any changes before executing most of these activities, we next turn our attention to the save routines.

112

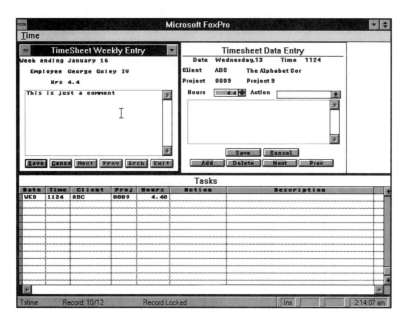

Figure 7.1. Time sheet session in Edit mode.

The Save Routine for the Week Record

When users press the Save button in the TSTIMEWK window, they save any changes made to the TSTIMEWK window and end the Edit session. Here is the vcontrol() CASE statement:

```
CASE l_control=="SAVEWEEK"  && Save pb in week window
  DO tstimesw
  UNLOCK IN tsweek
  UNLOCK IN tstime
  DO tstimenoedit
```

Here is the tstimesw procedure:

```
PROCEDURE tstimesw
* save week info
IF l_editmode
  ** we are editing, so there might be something to save
  SELECT tsweek
```

continues

113

```
   IF tschange(@l_oldwk,"tsweek")
     ** Since the record was locked by the edit option,
     ** we can just save it
     GATHER MEMVAR MEMO
     SCATTER TO l_oldwk MEMO
   ENDIF something changed in this week record
ENDIF editing
RETURN .T.
```

The tstimesw procedure checks the value of m.l_editmode in case any of the activities call the procedure while the user is not editing. To avoid updating a record that has not been changed, the procedure checks the tschange() state of the memvars associated with the TSWEEK database.

Notice that we call the tstimenoedit procedure in the vcontrol() CASE structure. Here is the code (followed by some explanation):

```
PROCEDURE tstimenoedit
** Set the screens into "read-only" or
** NOedit mode. Disable all gets, then
** reset and enable the push buttons in
** the tsweek window.
SHOW GETS disabled ONLY
SHOW GET m.control,1 PROMPT "\<Add"
SHOW GET m.control,2 PROMPT "\<Edit"
SHOW GET m.control,3 ENABLE
SHOW GET m.control,4 ENABLE
SHOW GET m.control,5 ENABLE
SHOW GET m.control,6 ENABLE
l_editmode=.F.
RETURN .T.
```

Why didn't we put the reference to tstimenoedit in the tstimesw procedure? Because sometimes we will want simply to save changes to the TSWEEK record *without* exiting the Edit mode. By separating the two procedures, we can save the TSWEEK record when we move to another window in the screen set.

Notice how simple the save routine is? This simplicity is due in part to the Edit mode approach we have taken. After all, we don't have to worry about record locking at Save time, because that was already handled when the user selected the Edit option.

The Save Routine for Time Records

The user can also change TSTIME records, so we need a save routine for time sheet records. Here is the vcontrol() CASE:

```
CASE l_control=="SAVETIME" && Save pb in time window
  DO tstimest
```

Here is the tstimest procedure:

```
PROCEDURE tstimest
* save time info
IF tschange(@l_oldti,"tstime")
  SELECT tstime
  GATHER MEMVAR MEMO
  SCATTER TO l_oldti MEMO
  ** Refresh the Browse window
  SHOW WINDOW tasks REFRESH SAME
  SHOW GETS OFF
ENDIF
RETURN .T.
```

This rather unobtrusive block of code saves changes made in memory variables to the current TSTIME record. The only item of interest in this procedure is the command SHOW WINDOW tasks REFRESH SAME. This command updates the Browse window with the current values of all records displayed in the Browse window. If the current TSTIME record does not appear in the tasks Browse window, the Browse window is redrawn to include this TSTIME record.

The next section answers the question, "What if the user changes a value in a GET and then uses the mouse to change windows?"

Changing Windows

The good news is, FoxPro 2.5 enables users to move between multiple windows simply by clicking the mouse. The bad news is, FoxPro 2.5 enables users to move between multiple windows simply by clicking the mouse.

What if the user changes a value in a GET and then uses the mouse to change windows? When the user exits a window that contains GETs, FoxPro evaluates the DEACTIVATE clause of the READ CYCLE command. Earlier we used the Screen Layout dialog of the TSTIMEWK screen to include a READ DEACTIVATE clause. That clause references the readdeac() UDF.

In this session, I have decided to save any changes made to the current window whenever the user attempts to exit the current window. Here is the `readdeac` procedure:

```
PROCEDURE readdeac
** Triggered when user exits a GET window
IF WLAST()="TSWEEK"
  ** User is leaving the week window
  DO vcontrol WITH "windowweek"
ELSE
  ** User is leaving the time window
  DO vcontrol WITH "windowtime"
ENDIF
RETURN .F.
```

Notice the use of the WLAST() function to determine which window the user is leaving. Because readdeac() makes a call to the vcontrol() procedure, I suspect that you will be interested in the following vcontrol() code:

```
CASE l_control=="WINDOWWEEK" && Leaving week window
  DO tstimesw
CASE l_control=="WINDOWTIME" && Leaving time sheet window
  DO tstimest
```

Obviously, I could save a little processing time and a bit of code by calling the tstimesw and tstimest procedures directly from the readdeac procedure. However, by forcing all events to go through the vcontrol() procedure, I give future programmers one place to look for activities in the TSTIME program. In other words, although I might decrease runtime performance imperceptibly by issuing a call to vcontrol, I also greatly increase program readability by forcing all events to go through the vcontrol program.

FoxPro provides the READ DEACTIVATE clause to process when the user exits a GET window, and provides the READ ACTIVATE clause to process when the user enters a GET window. While we are working on this screen, we might as well protect against a user inadvertently closing the Browse window. This can occur when the user presses Esc or Ctrl+W while the cursor is sitting in the Browse window.

When the user closes the Browse window, the cursor automatically moves into a GET window. As a result, the READ ACTIVATE clause is triggered when the user closes the Browse window. Because we have already referenced the readacti() UDF in the Screen Layout dialog of the TSTIMEWK window, you can include the following procedure in TSTIME.PRG:

```
PROCEDURE readacti
** Called when user enters a GET window
IF NOT WEXIST("Tasks")
  ** he closed the Browse window, so put it back!
  DO tstimebr
ENDIF
```

Because I was in a contrary mood when I wrote this section of the application, I simply refused to let the user close the Browse window. If the user attempts to do so, the program immediately rebuilds the Browse window with a call to the `tstimebr` procedure.

Why not handle the closing of the Browse window in the READ DEACTIVATE clause, you ask? Because READ DEACTIVATE and READ ACTIVATE do not apply to Browse windows. In other words, when the user exits a Browse window, there is no evaluation of the READ DEACTIVATE clause. Further, when the user enters the Browse window, there is no evaluation of the READ ACTIVATE clause. Life's like that sometimes.

Menu Selections

What happens if the user chooses a menu option while working on the time sheet screen? The first thing that happens is a call to the `tsdo` procedure, as follows:

```
ON SELECTION POPUP timesheet DO tsdo WITH PROMPT()
```

We entered this line of code when we created the TSMENU menu. The TSDO program shows extraordinary civility by calling the `vcontrol()` UDF as follows:

```
* tsdo.prg
* Called when user selects an option from the menu.
* Sample: DO tsdo WITH PROMPT()
PARAMETERS p_prompt
* Put the prompt of the selected option into the
* kaction variable. The kaction variable is tested
* by the event loop in tsmain.
kaction=p_prompt
* exit the current read
DO vcontrol WITH "MENU"
RETURN
* eof tsdo.prg
```

How does TSDO.PRG know which vcontrol program to call? It doesn't "know" anything about which vcontrol procedure will be executed. However, because the vcontrol() procedure found in TSTIME is the first vcontrol procedure FoxPro finds when searching the calling tree, the vcontrol procedure in TSTIME.PRG is the one that will be executed when the user makes a menu selection during the time sheet entry session.

We can choose to do many different things with the information that the user has made a menu selection. In this case, however, we simply choose to save everything and exit the time sheet session.

Here is the code taken from the vcontrol program:

```
CASE l_control=="MENU" AND ;
    UPPER(WONTOP())=="TSTIMEWK" && Menu hit in week window
  DO tstimesw
  DO tstimest
  CLEAR READ
CASE l_control=="MENU" AND ;
    UPPER(WONTOP())=="TSTIME" && Menu hit in time window
  DO tstimest
  DO tstimesw
  CLEAR READ
CASE l_control=="MENU" && Menu hit in Browse window
  ACTIVATE WINDOW tstimewk
  CLEAR READ
```

The TSTIMESW and TSTIMEST windows check the value of m.l_editmode before actually attempting to save anything, so we don't have to worry about writing to the file unnecessarily. However, the actions taken when the user selects a menu option while resting in the Browse window bear close examination.

When we issue a CLEAR READ, FoxPro does not immediately exit the READ CYCLE session and move to the next command. Instead, FoxPro waits until control is returned to the READ CYCLE, and then it exits the READ session. Normally, this is not a problem, because issuing a simple return from the vcontrol UDF usually returns us to the READ CYCLE.

However, if the Browse window is the currently active window, FoxPro does not consider control returned to the READ CYCLE until one of the GET windows becomes the active window. For this reason, we activate one of the GET windows before returning control to the READ CYCLE.

If this concept is confusing, try running the program without the ACTIVATE WINDOW tstimewk command. If you make a menu selection while residing in the Browse window, nothing appears to happen until you click one of the GET windows. Only then does the menu selection take effect.

Moving to the Next and Previous Time Sheet

The options to move to the next and previous time sheet record are handled by the following CASE statements in vcontrol():

```
CASE l_control=="NEXTTIME" && Next pb in time window
   DO tstiment
CASE l_control=="PREVTIME" && Previous pb in week window
   DO tstimept
```

Here are the tstiment and tstimept procedures:

```
PROCEDURE tstiment
* move forward to next entry for this week's time sheets
SELECT tstime
DO tstimest && save this time record
IF NOT EOF()
   SKIP
ENDIF
DO tstimesh
RETURN .T.


PROCEDURE tstimept
* Previous time sheet record for this week
SELECT tstime
DO tstimest && save this time record
IF NOT BOF()
   SKIP -1
ENDIF
DO tstimesh
RETURN .T.
```

As was the case with the next and previous week procedures, the next and previous time sheet procedures depend on the show routine (tstimesh for time sheets) to ensure that only time sheet records for this week and employee are accessible to the user. In other words, tstiment and tstimept move the record pointer and depend on tstimesh to find a valid record if tstiment or tstimept moved to an invalid record.

Moving to a New Record in the Browse Window

Although moving to the next and previous record in the time sheet window is a valuable activity, it's not nearly so sexy as browsing among the time sheets for the current employee and week. Happily, this activity is provided to the programmer virtually free of charge via the BROWSE command. However, this particular data entry screen demands more than even the BROWSE command can provide on its own. This data entry screen demands that the TSTIME window be updated to reflect the current time sheet record whenever the user moves to a new record in the Browse window.

We can accomplish this by including a WHEN clause on the BROWSE command. Here is the BROWSE command from the tstimebr procedure:

```
BROWSE WINDOW tstime1 ;
  KEY m.timeemp+DTOS(m.wk_date) ;
  FIELDS ;
  calc1=SUBSTR("SUNMONTUEWEDTHUFRISAT",;
  MAX(1,MIN(ti_day,7))*3-2,3):H="Date",;
  ti_time:H="Time",;
  ti_clid:H="Client",;
  ti_projid:H="Proj",;
  ti_hours:H="Hours",;
  ti_action:H="Action",;
  calc2=MLINE(ti_notes,1):H="Description":35 ;
  NOWAIT NOMENU NOAPPEND NODELETE NOMODIFY ;
  WHEN m.browwhen OR NOT vcontrol("BROWSE") TITLE "Tasks" ;
  FONT WFONT(1,"tstime"),WFONT(2,"tstime") ;
  STYLE WFONT(3,"tstime")
```

The definitions we apply when we issue the BROWSE command remain in effect when the user moves into the Browse window by clicking the mouse or pressing a hot key. Therefore, when the user moves to a new record in the Browse window, the vcontrol() UDF is called with a "BROWSE" argument.

Here is the vcontrol() code that handles this occurrence:

```
CASE l_control=="BROWSE" && Moved to a new record in the browse
  DO tstimesh
```

Again, we could save a little processing time by calling the tstimesh procedure directly, but we choose to increase readability by calling all activities through the vcontrol program. The tstimesh procedure not only shows the new values in the TSTIME window, but it also creates memory variables for the current time sheet record.

Canceling Changes to the Week Record

When the user of this sample application selects the Cancel push button in the TSTIMEWK window, any changes made to memory variables associated with the TSWEEK database are aborted and the edit mode is ended.

Here is the vcontrol() CASE:

```
CASE l_control=="CANCELWEEK"  && Cancel pb in week window
  DO tstimecw
```

Here is the tstimecw procedure:

```
PROCEDURE tstimecw
* cancel changes to this week record
SELECT tsweek
SCATTER MEMVAR MEMO
SCATTER TO l_oldwk MEMO
UNLOCK IN tsweek
UNLOCK IN tstime
DO tstimenoedit
RETURN .T.
```

Canceling Changes to Time Records

Canceling changes to the current time record aborts changes made to memory variables associated with TSTIME.DBF but does not end the Edit session. Here is the vcontrol() CASE:

```
CASE l_control=="CANCELTIME" && Cancel pb in time window
  DO tstimect
```

Here is the tstimect procedure:

```
PROCEDURE tstimect
* cancel changes to this time record
SELECT tstime
SCATTER MEMVAR MEMO
SCATTER TO l_oldti MEMO
DO tstimesh
RETURN .T.
```

Deleting a Time Record

The following CASE in vcontrol() handles the deletion of the current time sheet record:

```
CASE l_control=="DELETETIME" && Delete pb
  DO tstimedt
```

121

The actual code is trivial, in part because we know the time sheet record in question is already locked. We know this because the Delete push button is available only after the user selects the Edit option. Here is the code for `tstimedt`:

```
PROCEDURE tstimedt
* Delete a time sheet entry
SELECT tstime
DELETE
SKIP
DO tstimesh
RETURN .T.
```

If you are feeling especially generous, you might ask users whether they are sure they want to delete this record. Notice that once again we depend on `tstimesh` to position us on a valid record for this week if, while deleting and skipping in the TSTIME database, we find ourselves positioned on a TSTIME record that belongs to another week or employee.

Adding a Week Record

The following `vcontrol()` CASE statement handles the addition of a week record:

```
CASE l_control=="ADDWEEK" && Add pb in week window
  DO tstimeaw
```

In general terms, the `tstimeaw` procedure enables the user to scroll through a list of valid "week ending" dates. When the user picks one of those dates, the program determines whether that date already exists. If that date already exists for this employee, the program assumes that the user wants to edit that time sheet. If the date does not already exist for this employee, the program attempts to add the new TSWEEK record. Here is the code for `tstimeaw`:

```
PROCEDURE tstimeaw
* Add a new weekly time sheet
PRIVATE l_newweek,l_oldweek,l_oldsele
l_oldsele=SELECT()
SELECT tsweek
l_oldweek=RECNO()
** Call the tsnewwk.prg UDF to ask the user
** for a new week.
```

```
l_newweek=tsnewwk()
IF NOT EMPTY(l_newweek)
  ** He didn't cancel
  IF NOT SEEK(m.timeemp+DTOS(m.l_newweek))
    ** It doesn't already exist
    SCATTER MEMVAR MEMO BLANK
    SCATTER TO l_oldwk MEMO BLANK
    ** Load the key fields with the date the
    ** user selected and the user's id.
    m.wk_empid=m.timeemp
    m.wk_date=l_newweek
    ** Try to insert the record into the tsweek
    ** database
    IF NOT l3insert()
      ** Couldn't add the record. Someone probably has
      ** the file locked.
      DO l3msg WITH "Failed to add your week record."
      IF l_oldweek>0
        GOTO (l_oldweek)
      ENDIF
      l_editmode=.F.
    ELSE
      l_editmode=.T.
      ** Put us in edit mode
      DO tstimeed
    ENDIF not able to add the thing
  ENDIF not a duplicate
  ** Refresh all windows with the newly added or
  ** found time sheet week information
  DO tsweeksh
  DO tstimesh
ENDIF chose not to cancel
SELECT (l_oldsele)
RETURN .T.
```

The tsnewwk() UDF presents the user with a screen like the one shown in Figure 7.2. If tsnewwk() returns a date, we seek the combination of the employee ID and the returned date. If we don't find that combination in the TSWEEK database, we add the record. If we find the record, we do nothing.

Next, whether we added a record or simply found an existing record, we display all the windows in the time sheet session again by calling TSWEEKSH and TSTIMESH.

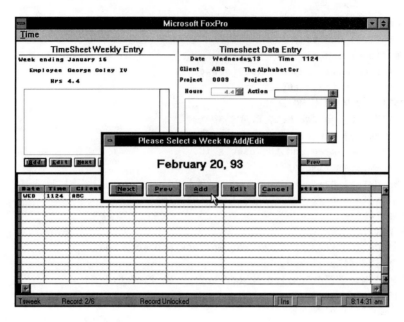

Figure 7.2. Adding a new week.

Note that this particular add routine is not absolutely foolproof. If two users select the same employee and choose to add the same new week record at exactly the same time, the routine might add a duplicate TSWEEK record. Operationally, this should never happen, because each employee is supposed to enter his or her own time sheet. Further, the chances of two users attempting to do this admittedly unusual thing at *exactly* the same time are infinitesimally small. However, if you don't like a solution that potentially can add records to a table with non-unique keys, see Chapter 13, "Multiuser Discussions," for a more foolproof solution.

In the meantime, let's take a brief look at Figure 7.2. While the screen is displaying February 20, 93, the Edit button is disabled. This indicates to the user that there is no time sheet record for this employee for that date. If the user had scrolled to a date that had a time sheet record, the Edit button would be enabled and the Add button would be disabled. Enabling the user to select only those options that are available can make a program easier to use and can reduce coding. Here is the code for the TSNEWWK.PRG program:

```
* tsnewwk.prg
* pick a new week for the time sheet data entry screen
PRIVATE l_thisweek,m.control
USE tsweek AGAIN IN SELE(1) ALIAS tsnewwk ORDER empdte
l_thisweek=IIF(EMPTY(tsweek.wk_date),;
  DATE()-DOW(DATE()),tsweek.wk_date)
m.control=""
```

```
DO tsnewwk.spr
USE IN tsnewwk
RETURN IIF(upper(m.control)="CANCEL",{},m.l_thisweek)

PROCEDURE readwhen
IF SEEK(m.timeemp+DTOS(m.l_thisweek),"tsnewwk")
   SHOW GET m.control,3 DISABLE && add button
   SHOW GET m.control,4 ENABLE && edit button
ELSE
   SHOW GET m.control,3 ENABLE && add button
   SHOW GET m.control,4 DISABLE && edit button
ENDIF

PROCEDURE vcontrol
PARAMETERS m.control
_CUROBJ=_CUROBJ
DO CASE
   CASE UPPER(m.control)=="NEXT"
     l_thisweek=l_thisweek+7
     DO readwhen
     SHOW GETS OFF
   CASE UPPER(m.control)=="PREV"
     l_thisweek=l_thisweek-7
     DO readwhen
     SHOW GETS OFF
   CASE UPPER(m.control)=="ADD"
     CLEAR READ
   CASE UPPER(m.control)=="EDIT"
     CLEAR READ
   CASE UPPER(m.control)=="CANCEL"
     CLEAR READ
ENDCASE
RETURN .T.
```

Notice the use of the TSWEEK database in another work area to preserve the record pointer in the original TSWEEK work area. The TSNEWWK screen is unremarkable except that it is generated with the Modal option selected. By selecting the Modal option of the Generate Screen dialog, we prevent the user from moving to another window or making a menu selection while we are presenting the TSNEWWK screen.

The TSNEWWK screen includes a single SAY object consisting of MDY(l_thisweek) in "MS Sans Serif",14 font. Because different months consume different amounts of screen space, I chose the Center option of the Format dialog for the MDY(l_thisweek) object. Obviously, TSNEWWK also includes a push button and a reference to READWHEN() in the screen layout.

Adding a Time Record

The following vcontrol() CASE code handles the addition of a time sheet record:

```
CASE l_control=="ADDTIME" && Add pb in time window
  DO tstimeat
```

The code for tstimeat closely mirrors the tstimeaw procedure:

```
PROCEDURE tstimeat
* Add a new time sheet record to this week
PRIVATE l_newtime,l_oldtime,l_oldsele
* First try to save the current time sheet record
DO tstimest
* Now try to add a record to this week
l_oldsele=SELECT()
SELECT tstime
l_oldtime=RECNO()  && Save our place
** Make empty values
SCATTER MEMVAR MEMO BLANK
SCATTER TO l_oldti MEMO BLANK
** Preload key values, and defaults
m.ti_week=tsweek.wk_date
m.ti_empid=m.timeemp
m.ti_day=tstime.ti_day
m.ti_time=tstime.ti_time
** Call the tsnewti.prg UDF to ask the user for
** the day, and time of this time sheet record.
IF tsnewti(tsweek.wk_date,m.ti_day,m.ti_time)
  SELECT tstime
  IF NOT SEEK(m.timeemp+DTOS(m.ti_week)+STR(m.ti_day,1)+m.ti_time)
    ** new one
    IF NOT l3insert()
      DO l3msg WITH "Failed to add your time sheet record."
      IF BETWEEN(l_oldtime,1,RECC('tstime'))
        SELECT tstime
        GOTO (l_oldtime)
      ENDIF
    ENDIF failed to add
  ELSE &&
    ** The user picked an existing record.
    WAIT WINDOW "Day and time already exist." NOWAIT
  ENDIF not a duplicate
ELSE && The user canceled this request.
```

```
   ** Go back to the current time sheet record
   IF BETWEEN(l_oldtime,1,RECC('tstime'))
     SELECT tstime
     GOTO (l_oldtime)
   ENDIF
ENDIF asked us to add one
** Show the newly added/found time sheet record
DO tstimesh
** Put the cursor in the hours field.
_CUROBJ=OBJNUM(m.ti_hours)
RETURN .T.
```

The call to the `tsnewti()` UDF produces a screen like the one shown in Figure 7.3. In this screen, we want to capture all the key field information for the new time sheet item. This information should be entered only once and is unavailable for editing later.

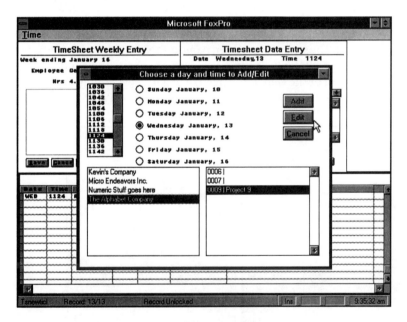

Figure 7.3. Adding a time sheet record for this week.

This particular screen includes three scrollable lists, a group of radio buttons, and a set of push buttons. The scrollable list of valid times of the day is particularly interesting. If the user types in a time that already exists, or if the user scrolls to a time that already exists, the TSNEWTI screen disables the Add push button and enables the Edit push button.

We accomplish this by including a simple WHEN clause on the m.1_time list of valid times. The scrollable list of available companies also makes good use of the WHEN clause.

Movement in the company scrollable list results in a redisplay of the projects scrollable list. In addition, moving to a new company in the company scrollable list automatically makes the most current project the default selection in the project scrollable list.

Finally, the radio button group includes the month and date for each day of the week. Obviously, this information changes depending on the current week. This capability to display different prompts in the radio button group depending on the current week is handled in the READ WHEN clause of the TSNEWTI program.

 Note: Be sure to make the radio buttons on the screen large enough to hold the additional month and date information.

The TSNEWTI window includes several interesting objects, so I have provided Figure 7.4 to help you create the screen. The screen name is TSNEWTI. The window is centered and 426 pixels wide by 310 pixels high. When you generate the window, select the Modal Screens option of the Generate Screen dialog to prevent users from moving to another window or selecting a menu option while the TSNEWTI.SPR is running.

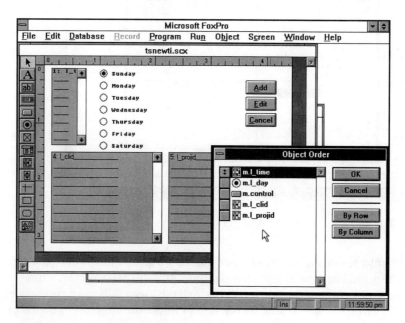

Figure 7.4. The TSNEWTI screen definition.

Here is the code for TSNEWTI.PRG:

```
* tsnewti.prg
* Pick a new time sheet entry
** P_week = Date week ends
** p_day = Day of week
** p_time = time of day as HHMM
PARAMETERS p_week,p_day,p_time
PRIVATE l_time,l_day,allday,m.control,tsnewtipj,l_projid,l_clid
l_projid=""
l_clid=""
l_day=p_day
l_time=1
** Build an array of valid times
DIMENSION allday(240)
FOR l_xx=0 TO 23
  l_hours=PADL(LTRIM(STR(l_xx)),2,'0') && +":"
  FOR l_yy=1 TO 10
    allday(l_xx*10+l_yy)=l_hours+;
      PADL(LTRIM(STR((l_yy-1)*6)),2,'0')
  ENDFOR
ENDFOR
** Open a copy of the tstime database to seek in
IF USED("tsnewti")
  USE IN tsnewti
ENDIF
USE tstime IN SELE(1) AGAIN ALIAS tsnewti ORDER empdte
** Open another copy of the client table
IF USED("tsnewticl")
  USE IN tsnewticl
ENDIF
USE tsclient IN SELE(1) AGAIN ALIAS tsnewticl ORDER cl_company
** Make a popup of valid clients
SELE tsnewticl
DEFINE POPUP tsnewticl PROMPT FIELD tsnewticl.cl_company
l_clid=tsnewticl.cl_company
** Set up the list of projects for the current client record
DIMENSION tsnewtipj(1)
DO loadproj
** Choose the latest project for the current client record
m.l_projid=tsnewtipj(ALEN(tsnewtipj))
** Create an array for the current client
m.control=""
** Call the screen
```

continues

```
DO tsnewti.spr
USE IN tsnewti
USE IN tsnewticl
RETURN UPPER(m.control)<>"CANCEL"

PROCEDURE vcontrol
PARAMETERS m.control
IF UPPER(m.control)!="CANCEL"
  ** If the user didn't cancel, save the selections
  ** in the appropriate m.ti_* variables for use by
  ** the calling procedure.
  m.ti_day=m.l_day
  m.ti_time=allday(m.l_time)
  m.ti_clid=tsnewticl.cl_clid
  m.ti_projid=LEFT(m.l_projid,4)
ENDIF
CLEAR READ
RETURN .T.

PROCEDURE wl_time
** When clause for the time of day scrollable list
** Refresh push buttons with the showbutt procedure.
DO showbutt
RETURN .T.

PROCEDURE wl_day
** When clause for the l_day radio button.
DO showbutt
RETURN .T.

PROCEDURE readwhen
** Set up radio button prompts for the current week.
** Adds date to day prompt.
SHOW GET m.l_day,1 PROMPT "Sunday "+CMONTH(p_week-6)+", "+;
  LTRIM(STR(DAY(p_week-6)))
SHOW GET m.l_day,2 PROMPT "Monday "+CMONTH(p_week-5)+", "+;
  LTRIM(STR(DAY(p_week-5)))
SHOW GET m.l_day,3 PROMPT "Tuesday "+CMONTH(p_week-4)+", "+;
  LTRIM(STR(DAY(p_week-4)))
SHOW GET m.l_day,4 PROMPT "Wednesday "+CMONTH(p_week-3)+", "+;
  LTRIM(STR(DAY(p_week-3)))
SHOW GET m.l_day,5 PROMPT "Thursday "+CMONTH(p_week-2)+", "+;
  LTRIM(STR(DAY(p_week-2)))
```

```
  SHOW GET m.l_day,6 PROMPT "Friday "+CMONTH(p_week-1)+", "+;
    LTRIM(STR(DAY(p_week-1)))
  SHOW GET m.l_day,7 PROMPT "Saturday "+CMONTH(p_week)+", "+;
    LTRIM(STR(DAY(p_week)))
  DO showbutt
  RETURN .T.


  PROCEDURE showbutt
  * Enables Add button if employee+week+day+time does
  * not exist. Otherwise, enables the Edit button.
  IF SEEK(m.timeemp+DTOS(p_week)+STR(l_day,1)+;
    allday(l_time),"tsnewti")
    SHOW GET m.control,1 DISABLE
    SHOW GET m.control,2 ENABLE
  ELSE
    SHOW GET m.control,1 ENABLE
    SHOW GET m.control,2 DISABLE
  ENDIF


  PROCEDURE loadproj
  ** Puts the projects for the currently selected
  ** client into an array.
  PRIVATE l_myclid
  m.l_myclid=tsnewticl.cl_clid
  SELECT pj_projid+" ¦ "+pj_name FROM tsproj ;
    WHERE pj_clid = m.l_myclid ;
    INTO ARRAY tsnewtipj
  IF _TALLY=0
    DIMENSION tsnewtipj(1)
    tsnewtipj="None"
  ENDIF


  PROCEDURE wl_clid
  ** When clause for client scrollable list
  DO loadproj && Load and display project scrollable list
  IF UPPER(tsnewtipj(1))="NONE" AND ALEN(tsnewtipj)=1
    ** If no projects available, disable project
    ** scrollable list.
    m.l_projid=""
    SHOW GET m.l_projid DISABLE
  ELSE
    ** Default to newest project for this client, and
    ** enable scrollable list.
```

continues

```
    m.l_projid=tsnewtipj(ALEN(tsnewtipj))
      SHOW GET m.l_projid ENABLE
ENDIF
RETURN .T.
```

In addition to forcing the user to pick valid values, the TSNEWTI screen demonstrates several powerful concepts. First, we can change the prompts of existing radio buttons and push buttons. (This capability also applies to check boxes.) This capability can be particularly handy when writing applications that must provide prompts in multiple languages.

The screen also demonstrates that we can run a program any time a user moves to a new item in a scrollable list. Finally, the `wl_clid` function demonstrates that we can change the content of a scrollable list, even when that scrollable list is in use.

That's it, there are no more data entry screens for our time sheet tracking program. However, most people consider an application to be only as good as the information it provides. So far, we have concentrated on providing input capabilities to our application. Now it's time to turn our attention to the problem of reports and queries.

Reporting on the Time Sheet Application

This chapter was originally intended to present a handful of reports that would logically be required for our time sheet application, thereby completing our application. However, I had already decided to cover the mechanics of creating queries and reports in separate chapters. How then could I keep you amused, finish the application, and not appear redundant all in the space of one small chapter?

Two pots of coffee, four restarts, three aborted programs, and five CDs later, I had an answer. Because reports in FoxPro 2.5 are most often a combination of a query and a report, I write a front-end for my report system that allows the user to:

- Select multiple reports to be run together in an unattended batch

- Enter a SQL SELECT command

- Direct output to one of eight destinations

- Modify the report form layout

- Add a new report to the application

- Copy, change, and save an existing report

- Perform all the above in a multiuser environment

I hope you have as much fun playing with TSREPO as I had creating it. While you're at it, stay alert for tips on the following subjects:

- Creating scrollable lists that change the content of a screen as the user moves from item to item.

- Storing files in memo fields.

- Using FoxPro's low-level file I/O functions.

- Using macros.

- Creating graphs and cross tabs.

- Creating and erasing temporary files.

- Using cursors to hold pending changes for a master database.

- Directing output of a report to assorted devices.

A Word About Reporting in the 90s

One of the basic requirements of the time sheet application is to provide a weekly report of employee activity by client and by project. This report requires information from the TSWEEK, TSCLIENT, TSEMPL, TSPROJ, and TSTIME databases.

In the days before FoxPro 1.0, Xbase language programmers would hand code this report, using the SEEK, SKIP, DO WHILE .NOT. EOF(), and @...SAY commands to output the results.

With the advent of the FoxPro 1.0 Report Writer, many developers elected to establish relationships between the various databases and then call the Report Writer with a FOR clause to handle the actual printing of the information.

Fortunately, FoxPro 2.0 introduced the SQL SELECT command to the FoxPro language, and report writing will never be the same again. Now, programmers typically issue only two commands to handle a report request.

The first command is a SQL SELECT command that filters, orders, and joins data from multiple tables. The second command is a REPORT FORM command that handles the formatting and printing of the data generated by the SQL SELECT command.

Generating a Weekly Report by Employee, by Client, and by Project

For example, the weekly report by employee, by client, and by project is accomplished with the following lines of code:

```
* tsrpweek.prg
* Report of weekly activity by employee,
* by client, by project
PRIVATE ALL LIKE l_*
SELECT ti_action,ti_notes,ti_hours,ti_time,ti_day,;
  ti_empid,ti_projid,ti_clid,cl_company,;
  pj_name,em_last,em_first,wk_date,wk_note FROM ;
  tsweek,tsclient,tsempl,tsproj,tstime ;
  WHERE ti_empid = em_empid AND ;
  cl_clid=pj_clid AND ;
  pj_clid+pj_projid = ti_clid+ti_projid AND ;
  ti_week=wk_date AND ;
  wk_date={01/23/93} ;
  ORDER BY ti_empid,ti_clid,ti_projid ;
  INTO CURSOR tsrpweek
REPORT FORM tsrpweek
USE IN tsrpweek
RETURN .T.
```

Figure 8.1 shows the TSREPWEEK report definition. Yes, this is my entry in the world's ugliest report contest. However, all the pertinent information is included, along with the appropriate groups and totals.

I am in no way recommending that you create ugly reports. Indeed, Chapter 11, "The Report Writer," includes several very attractive reports. The layout in Figure 8.1 does show the entire report in a single screen shot, however, so we'll trade form for function in this instance.

Providing a Little Flexibility

In its current state, the TSRPWEEK report program was valuable only in the week ending January 23, 1993. Because your client is unlikely to pay you to change the TSRPWEEK program weekly, you need a better solution.

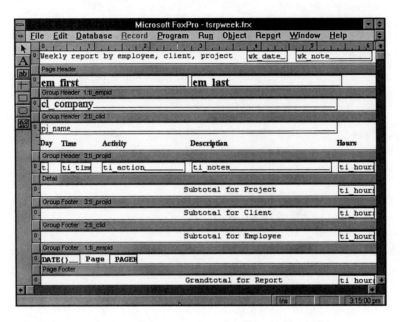

Figure 8.1. Reporting the week by employee, by client, and by project.

Here is a slightly more sophisticated version of TSRPWEEK that users might enjoy:

```
* tsrpweek.prg
* Report of weekly activity by employee
* by client by project
PRIVATE ALL LIKE l_*
* Put a list of valid weeks in a cursor
SELECT DISTINCT wk_date FROM tsweek ;
   ORDER BY wk_date INTO CURSOR tsrpweek
* Create a popup of valid weeks from the cursor
DEFINE POPUP tsrpweek PROMPT FIELD wk_date TITLE "Pick a date"
ON SELECTION POPUP tsrpweek DEACTIVATE POPUP tsrpweek
* Find the current week in the cursor if possible
LOCATE FOR wk_date>=DATE()-DOW(DATE())+7
IF NOT FOUND()
   GO BOTTOM
ENDIF no dates >= this week
* Present the popup to the user
ACTIVATE POPUP tsrpweek REST
RELEASE POPUP tsrpweek
IF READKEY()=12
   USE IN tsrpweek
   RETURN .F.
```

```
ENDIF pressed escape
* Store the user's selection in a memory variable
m.l_week=tsrpweek.wk_date
USE IN tsrpweek
* Perform the filtered join
SELECT ti_action,ti_notes,ti_hours,ti_time,ti_day,;
   ti_empid,ti_projid,ti_clid,cl_company,;
   pj_name,em_last,em_first,wk_date,wk_note FROM ;
   tsweek,tsclient,tsempl,tsproj,tstime ;
   WHERE ti_empid = em_empid AND ;
   cl_clid=pj_clid AND ;
   pj_clid+pj_projid = ti_clid+ti_projid AND ;
   ti_week=m.l_week AND ;
   wk_date=m.l_week ;
   ORDER BY ti_empid,ti_clid,ti_projid ;
   INTO CURSOR tsrpweek
* Use the tsrpweek.frx report on the resultant cursor
REPORT FORM tsrpweek PREVIEW
USE IN tsrpweek
RETURN .T.
```

This approach enables users to pick a different week each time the report is run. As a side benefit, the technique of providing users with a list of weeks from the TSWEEK database ensures that they will pick a valid week.

Contortionism: The Art of Fully Flexible Reporting

The minute users get a taste of flexible reporting, they want control over every aspect of the report process. At least that's what they tell you.

An immutable truth applies to computing in general and report writing in particular: It goes something like this: The more flexible or powerful a program is, the more difficult it is to use. (Remember this the next time you see an advertisement that touts the *power* of a program in the same breath that it extols the program's *ease of use,* and beware.)

In other words, the more choices you give someone, the more difficult it is for that person to make a choice. In the case of reports, because previously selected options often affect currently available options, full flexibility is frequently more than the user can handle.

Even so, users regularly insist on fully flexible reporting solutions, so let's build a fully flexible query/report writer to include in our time sheet application. Our goals were outlined at the beginning of the chapter, and our solution starts with the next topic.

Running Multiple Reports in an Unattended Batch

This part of our report front end is useful in most applications. Our goal is to enable the user to tag as many reports as required from a list of available reports. When the user chooses to run the reports, all the selected reports are processed in order, without input from the user. Our approach calls for the creation of a TSREPO.DBF to hold information about each report available in the system. Here is the structure for TSREPO.DBF:

```
Structure for table:     c:\book\dbf\tsrepo.dbf
Number of data records: 2
Date of last update:     03/09/93
Memo file block size:    64
Field  Field Name  Type        Width    Dec    Index
    1  RP_DESC     Character      30             Asc
    2  RP_FILE     Character     128
    3  RP_FRT      Memo           10
    4  RP_FRX      Memo           10
    5  RP_OUTPUT   Character      10
    6  RP_QUERY    Memo           10
** Total **                     199
```

We will present this database to the user in a data entry screen that includes a scrollable list. Figure 8.2 shows the entire data entry screen, but the scrollable list particularly requires some explanation.

The scrollable list references a popup named TSREPO, which we could create as follows:

```
USE tsrepo ORDER rp_desc
DEFINE POPUP tsrepo PROMPT FIELDS rp_desc
```

However, this popup won't give the user an opportunity to tag reports to be run. There are several solutions to the problem, but the following solution is one I particularly enjoy.

Let's create a memory variable called m.1_pick that contains one space for every record in the report database. For the purposes of our program, each space holds information about one record. We take advantage of record numbers by associating the first space in m.1_pick with the first record in TSREPO, the second space in m.1_pick with the second record in TSREPO, and so on.

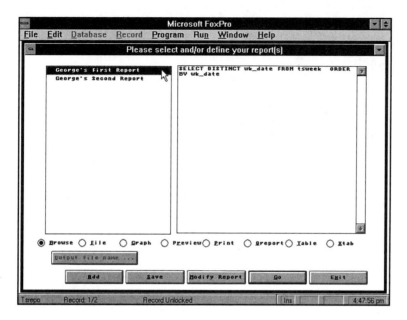

Figure 8.2. The TSREPO front end.

Here then is the setup code for the scrollable list, and for the rest of the data entry screen:

```
* tsrepo.prg
* Allows user to choose one or more time sheet
* reports to run
PRIVATE ALL LIKE l_*
PRIVATE m.control
* Open the file containing report definitions
IF NOT USED("tsrepo")
  USE tsrepo IN SELECT(1) AGAIN
ENDIF
SET ORDER TO rp_desc IN tsrepo
* Create l_pick variable.
* Each character in m.l_pick references a record
* number in tsrepo. For example, the first character in
* m.l_pick refers to record # 1 in tsrepo.dbf.
* If the m.l_pick character associated with a record
* contains a check mark (Chr(251)), this record has been
* selected by the user. If the m.l_pick character does
* not contain the check mark, or if the record number is
* greater than the number of characters in m.l_pick, the
```

continues

```
* user has not selected this tsrepo record.
l_pick=SPACE(RECCOUNT("tsrepo"))
* Create a popup for use as a scrollable list in tsrepo.spr.
DEFINE POPUP tsrepo PROMPT FIELDS ;
   IIF(LEN(l_pick)>=RECNO("tsrepo"),,;
   SUBSTR(l_pick,RECNO("tsrepo"),1)," ")+" "+tsrepo.rp_desc
* Create a cursor to hold temporary changes for reports,
* SQL SELECT, output, and file.
CREATE CURSOR temprepo ;
   (tm_recno N(13,0),,;
   tm_action C(1),,;
   rp_query m(10),,;
   rp_frx m(10),,;
   rp_frt m(10),,;
   rp_output C(10),,;
   rp_file C(128),,;
   rp_desc C(30))
SELECT temprepo
INDEX ON UPPER(rp_desc) TAG rp_desc
INDEX ON tm_recno TAG tm_recno
SELECT tsrepo
SCATTER MEMVAR FIELDS rp_query,rp_output,rp_file,rp_desc MEMO
m.control=""
l_choices=1 && Variable for scrollable list
DO tsrepo.spr
USE IN temprepo
RETURN
```

The popup definition warrants closer examination. The DEFINE POPUP command directs FoxPro to display the content of the character in m.l_pick associated with the record number of the TSREPO record on which the scrollable list resides.

Notice that we have to expand the IIF() condition to ensure that the current TSREPO record number is not longer than the m.l_pick variable. This sad state of affairs could occur if another user adds a record to TSREPO after we create the m.l_pick variable.

This popup definition is useful only if we have some method of toggling the m.l_pick space associated with a given TSREPO record from chr(32) to chr(251) and back. We can do this easily by placing a valid clause on the m.l_choices scrollable list and including the following procedure in TSREPO.PRG:

```
PROCEDURE vl_choices
** Valid clause triggered when user selects a report
** from the scrollable list. Toggles the selected state
** of this report.
```

```
IF LEN(l_pick)<RECNO('tsrepo')
  ** Make m.l_pick long enough
  l_pick=PADR(l_pick,RECNO('tsrepo'))
ENDIF l_pick too short for current tsrepo record
** Toggle this tsrepo record's position in m.l_pick
l_pick=STUFF(l_pick,RECNO('tsrepo'),1,;
  IIF(SUBSTR(l_pick,RECNO('tsrepo'),1)=CHR(251),;
  " ",CHR(251)))
SHOW GET l_choices
_CUROBJ=OBJNUM(l_choices)
RETURN .T.
```

This little piece of code allows the user to toggle the selected state of a report. We could have accomplished this goal by adding a field to the TSREPO database that could be displayed in the DEFINE POPUP and toggled in vl_choices(), but that solution would not work well when two users attempted to run reports at the same time.

We could have used the TEMPREPO cursor we created to include one record for every record in the TSREPO database. In this scenario, the program would toggle a field in the temporary database when the user selected a report. However, this would require that we set a relationship between TSREPO and TEMPREPO, which would result in slower performance.

Finally, we could have used array elements to store the selected state of each report rather than a single memory variable. However, this would consume considerably more memory than the m.l_pick solution, and performance again would be degraded.

All in all, the memory variable with one space per record trick is the best solution. You can use this trick anytime you are certain that less than 65,000 records will exist in the original table.

Tip: If you are willing to sacrifice speed for capacity, you can even enhance this technique to allow the user to tag up to 520,000 records! The trick is to use each bit in the 65,000 character string to represent a single record in the database. Then all you need is a program that can toggle each of those bits and report on the state of any one of those bits. Thanks to Mike Brachman, we have just such a program:

```
* l3bitmp2.prg
* Sets and/or returns the setting of a single bit in a
* character string.
* string = string containing the bits of interest
* offset = bit you want to set/test First bit is 0
* oper = one of the following:
```

continues

141

```
continued
* I = INVERT (TOGGLE)
* N = NEGATE (TOGGLE)
* R = RESET (SET TO 0)
* S = SET (SET TO 1)
* T = TEST
PARAMETER string,offset,oper
* offset 0 -  7 is first byte
* offset 8 - 15 is second byte, etc.
DIMENSION bits[8],two[8]
STORE 0 TO bits
two[1] = 1
two[2] = 2
two[3] = 4
two[4] = 8
two[5] = 16
two[6] = 32
two[7] = 64
two[8] = 128
chrset = INT(offset/8)+1
foxset = MOD(offset,8) + 1 && since FoxPro starts at 1 not 0
CHR = ASC(SUBSTR(string,chrset,1))
FOR i=1 TO 8
  lt = INT(CHR/2)
  bits[i] = CHR - lt*2
  CHR = lt
ENDFOR
DO CASE
  CASE oper = 'S'
    bits[foxset] = 1
  CASE oper = 'R'
    bits[foxset] = 0
  CASE oper = 'I' OR oper = 'N'  && invert or negate
    bits[foxset] = 1 - bits[foxset]
  OTHERWISE  && must be test only
    *
ENDCASE
retval = bits[foxset]
an = 0
FOR i=1 TO 8
  an = an + IIF(bits[i]=1,two[i],0)
```

```
ENDFOR
string = STUFF(string,chrset,1,CHR(an))
RETURN retval
```

Because including the `l3bitmp2()` UDF in the scrollable list slows scrolling noticeably, and because we are not likely to need more than 65,000 reports in our Timesheet program, we won't use the `l3bitmp2()` method of tagging records.

If the capability to select multiple reports to be run in a batch were the only goal of the TSREPO.PRG program, we would need only a procedure such as the following to parse the `m.l_pick` string:

```
SELECT tsrepo
SCAN FOR RECNO('tsrepo')<=LEN(m.l_pick) AND ;
    SUBSTR(m.l_pick,RECNO('tsrepo'),1)=CHR(251)
  DO rp_program
ENDSCAN get all of the marked reports
```

In this scenario, the TSREPO database would include a field containing the name of the program that runs the requested report. We have somewhat loftier goals, however, including the capability to show the query and output information associated with each report. This information should be displayed on the data entry screen as the user scrolls from report to report in the `l_choices` scrollable list. Fortunately, the WHEN clause on a scrollable list is evaluated each time the user moves to a new item in the list. Therefore, we need only reference the following UDF in the `l_choices` WHEN clause:

```
PROCEDURE wl_choices
** When clause on scrollable list.
** Update memory variables and screen display with the
** information associated with this report.
DO tsreposhow
RETURN .T.
```

The `tsreposhow` procedure is responsible for updating memory variables and for refreshing the screen display. Here is the code for `tsreposhow`:

```
PROCEDURE tsreposhow
* Refresh screen using temporary or
* original data
IF SEEK(RECNO('tsrepo'),"temprepo")
   ** There is a temprepo record for this report,
   ** which indicates that changes have been made,
   ** so use the temprepo contents on the screen.
   SELECT temprepo
```

```
ELSE
  SELECT tsrepo
ENDIF
SCATTER MEMVAR FIELDS rp_query,rp_output,rp_file,rp_desc MEMO
SHOW GET m.rp_query
SHOW GET m.rp_output
SHOW GET m.rp_file
RETURN .T.
```

Enabling the User To Make Temporary Changes to Reports

Notice that the tsreposhow procedure might fill the screen variables with values from the TEMPREPO database or with values taken from the TSREPO database. As we will see shortly, every time the user changes the content of a memory variable on the TSREPO.SPR screen, those changes are saved to the TEMPREPO cursor.

By using this approach, we can save the user's changes to multiple reports without actually writing those changes to the TSREPO database. After all, the user may not want to save the changes permanently, or one user may be making changes to a report that another user is running. In either case, we cannot afford to save changes directly to the TSREPO database.

The tsreposhow procedure demonstrates the method for retrieving either the TEMPREPO or TSREPO record as required. Therefore, all that remains is to demonstrate the creation of a TEMPREPO record. The simplest example is in the valid clause of the rp_output radio button. Here is the code:

```
PROCEDURE vrp_output
* output radio button
IF SEEK(RECNO('tsrepo'),"temprepo")
  * use the temp file contents
  SELECT temprepo
ELSE
  SELECT tsrepo
ENDIF
IF m.rp_output<>rp_output && they changed something!
  DO CASE
    CASE UPPER(m.rp_output)="BROWSE"
      SHOW GET m.l_outbutt DISABLE
      m.rp_file=SPACE(128)
    CASE UPPER(m.rp_output)="FILE"
      m.rp_file=PADR(PUTFILE("Name of output text file:",;
        "*.txt","TXT"),128)
```

```
      CASE UPPER(m.rp_output)="GRAPH"
        SHOW GET m.l_outbutt DISABLE
        m.rp_file=SPACE(128)
      CASE UPPER(m.rp_output)="PREVIEW"
        SHOW GET m.l_outbutt DISABLE
        m.rp_file=SPACE(128)
      CASE UPPER(m.rp_output)="PRINT"
        SHOW GET m.l_outbutt DISABLE
        m.rp_file=SPACE(128)
      CASE UPPER(m.rp_output)="QREPORT"
        SHOW GET m.l_outbutt DISABLE
        m.rp_file=SPACE(128)
      CASE UPPER(m.rp_output)="TABLE"
        m.rp_file=PADR(PUTFILE("Name of output table:",;
          SYS(2003)+"\*.DBF","DBF"),128)
      CASE UPPER(m.rp_output)="XTAB"
        m.rp_file=PADR(PUTFILE("Name of output table:",;
          SYS(2003)+"\*.DBF","DBF"),128)
    ENDCASE
    SHOW GETS OFF
    ** Find or create the temprepo record to hold the
    ** changed output device and target file
    IF NOT SEEK(RECNO('tsrepo'),"temprepo")
      DO tsnewtmprepo
    ENDIF no temporary record exists yet
    SELECT temprepo
    REPLACE rp_file WITH m.rp_file,rp_output WITH m.rp_output
ENDIF they changed something
RETURN .T.
```

The vrp_output procedure makes good use of FoxPro's PUTFILE() function to prefill the target file variable if an appropriate radio button is selected. However, the following three lines contain the block of code that deals with the creation of TEMPREPO records:

```
IF NOT SEEK(RECNO('tsrepo'),"temprepo")
  DO tsnewtmprepo
ENDIF no temporary record exists yet
```

The tsnewtmprepo procedure creates a new record in the TEMPREPO cursor containing all the information found in the original TSREPO database, plus the record number of the original TSREPO record. Here is the code:

```
PROCEDURE tsnewtmprepo
* Create a new temporary record to hold pending
* changes for the current tsrepo record.
```

continues

145

```
PRIVATE ALL LIKE rp*
PRIVATE tm_recno
PRIVATE l_oldsele
l_oldsele=SELECT()
SELECT tsrepo
SCATTER MEMVAR MEMO
m.tm_recno=RECNO()
INSERT INTO temprepo FROM MEMVAR
SELECT (l_oldsele)
RETURN .T.
```

Note that `tsnewtmprepo` does not require any multiuser locking efforts because it is a cursor and therefore open EXCLUSIVEly. When the `vrp_output` procedure finishes finding or creating the TEMPREPO record associated with this TSREPO record, it stores the new value for `rp_output` in the `temprepo.rp_output` field.

Changing the Query

Obviously, when we change the content of the query field, we will want to save those changes to a TEMPREPO record as well. We have another requirement for the query field, however.

Because we provide the user with the `rp_output` radio button to designate the target of the SQL SELECT command, we cannot allow the user to include a target clause in the actual query. Here is the valid clause for the `rp_query` field:

```
PROCEDURE vrp_query
* Processes changes made to a query
IF SEEK(RECNO('tsrepo'),"temprepo")
  * use the temp file contents
  SELECT temprepo
ELSE
  SELECT tsrepo
ENDIF
** rip out any semicolons, carriage returns, line feeds
m.rp_query=CHRTRAN(m.rp_query,";"+CHR(13)+CHR(10)," ")
** see if they put a target in
IF " IN "$UPPER(m.rp_query) OR " INTO "$UPPER(m.rp_query)
  ** Rip out the target
  ** If I were feeling generous, I might provide a message
  ** to the user directing him to use the output radio button
  ** to identify a target for the query.
  m.rp_query=tsnotarg(m.rp_query)
```

```
ENDIF has a target
** FInd or create the temprepo record to hold the
** changed query
IF NOT SEEK(RECNO('tsrepo'),"temprepo")
  DO tsnewtmprepo
ENDIF no temporary record exists yet
SELECT temprepo
REPLACE rp_query WITH m.rp_query
RETURN .T.
```

Notice the use of CHRTRAN() to remove CRLF and semicolon characters from the query. Those characters would cause FoxPro to choke later when you attempt to macro-expand the query. Obviously, the tsnotarg() function performs the most of the work in this program, so you might find the following source code interesting:

```
* tsnotarg.prg
* Strips the target from a select command
PARAMETERS p_select
PRIVATE ALL LIKE l_*
l_into=ATC(" into ",p_select)
l_to=ATC(" to ",p_select)
l_retval=m.p_select
l_eos=len(m.p_select)
DO CASE
  CASE l_into>0
    ** Found an into statement
    l_qty=1
    l_start=l_into+1
    DO WHILE SUBSTR(p_select,l_start,1)<>" " and l_start<=l_eos
      l_qty=l_qty+1
      l_start=l_start+1
    ENDDO parse out the into statement
    * look for next word
    DO WHILE SUBSTR(p_select,l_start,1)=" " and l_start<=l_eos
      l_qty=l_qty+1
      l_start=l_start+1
    ENDDO look for next word
    * parse out the into clause (i.e. table, cursor, dbf, etc.)
    DO WHILE SUBSTR(p_select,l_start,1)<>" " and l_start<=l_eos
      l_qty=l_qty+1
      l_start=l_start+1
    ENDDO parse out the into clause
    * look for next word
    DO WHILE SUBSTR(p_select,l_start,1)=" " and l_start<=l_eos
```

continues

147

```
        l_qty=l_qty+1
        l_start=l_start+1
      ENDDO look for next word
      * Parse out the file name
      DO WHILE SUBSTR(p_select,l_start,1)<>" " and l_start<=l_eos
        l_qty=l_qty+1
        l_start=l_start+1
      ENDDO parse out the into clause
      l_retval=stuff(p_select,l_into,l_qty,"")
    CASE l_to>0
      ** Found a to statement
      l_qty=1
      l_start=l_to+1
      DO WHILE SUBSTR(p_select,l_start,1)<>" " and l_start<=l_eos
        l_qty=l_qty+1
        l_start=l_start+1
      ENDDO parse out the to statement
      * look for next word
      DO WHILE SUBSTR(p_select,l_start,1)=" " and l_start<=l_eos
        l_qty=l_qty+1
        l_start=l_start+1
      ENDDO look for next word
      * Parse out the file name
      DO WHILE SUBSTR(p_select,l_start,1)<>" " and l_start<=l_eos
        l_qty=l_qty+1
        l_start=l_start+1
      ENDDO parse out the into clause
      l_retval=stuff(p_select,l_to,l_qty,"")
ENDCASE
RETURN m.l_retval
```

Two items are noteworthy in TSNOTARG. First, in spite of its length, it performs its appointed task very quickly. Second, the STUFF() function is invaluable when working with strings. In this case, TSNOTARG uses STUFF() to replace all the characters beginning at the TO or INTO clause and continuing for the number of characters counted in the l_qty variable.

Changing the Output File Name

Some reports direct their output to a permanent disk file. In those cases, we want our front end system to provide the user with a nice dialog for creating a valid file name. Here is the simple code that is triggered when the user presses the Output File name... push button:

```
PROCEDURE vl_outbutt
** Valid clause for target file push button. Calls PUTFILE()
** to identify a target file for the current report.
DO CASE
  CASE UPPER(m.rp_output)="BROWSE"
    SHOW GET m.l_outbutt DISABLE
    m.rp_file=SPACE(128)
  CASE UPPER(m.rp_output)="FILE"
    m.rp_file=PADR(PUTFILE("Name of output text file:",;
      "*.txt","TXT"),128)
  CASE UPPER(m.rp_output)="GRAPH"
    SHOW GET m.l_outbutt DISABLE
    m.rp_file=SPACE(128)
  CASE UPPER(m.rp_output)="PREVIEW"
    SHOW GET m.l_outbutt DISABLE
    m.rp_file=SPACE(128)
  CASE UPPER(m.rp_output)="PRINT"
    SHOW GET m.l_outbutt DISABLE
    m.rp_file=SPACE(128)
  CASE UPPER(m.rp_output)="QREPORT"
    SHOW GET m.l_outbutt DISABLE
    m.rp_file=SPACE(128)
  CASE UPPER(m.rp_output)="TABLE"
    m.rp_file=PADR(PUTFILE("Name of output table:",;
      SYS(2003)+"\*.DBF","DBF"),128)
  CASE UPPER(m.rp_output)="XTAB"
    m.rp_file=PADR(PUTFILE("Name of output table:",;
      SYS(2003)+"\*.DBF","DBF"),128)
ENDCASE
SHOW GETS OFF
** Find or create a temprepo record to hold the new
** output file value.
IF NOT SEEK(RECNO('tsrepo'),"temprepo")
  DO tsnewtmprepo
ENDIF no temporary record exists yet
SELECT temprepo
REPLACE rp_file WITH m.rp_file
RETURN .T.
```

Changing the Report Format

One of our goals for this program was to enable users to change report definitions on
the fly. This goal poses several challenges. First, two users can't modify the same report

file at the same time. Second, one user can't modify a report while another user is running that report.

Our solution is not to have any report files! That's right, we don't need any TS*.FRX/ .FRT files in the entire application! Instead, we will store the content of any .FRX files in the rp_frx memo field and store the content of the associated .FRT file in the rp_frt memo field. At runtime, we will copy the content of these variables to temporary files and reference the names of those temporary files in the REPORT FORM command.

Listen, don't jump out of any open windows just yet. This procedure is a neat little technique, but it is far from common. Most of Micro Endeavors' applications still use .FRX and .FRT files for reports. However, because external .FRT and .FRX files won't enable us to accomplish our goals for this application, we will continue to explore the "report in a memo field" concept.

As Figure 8.2 shows, one of the buttons on the TSREPO screen invites the user to Modify the Report. Here is the pertinent section from the vcontrol procedure in the TSREPO.PRG program:

```
CASE UPPER(m.control)=="MODIFY REPORT"
   ** Modify the report format (if any) associated with
   ** this report
   DO tsrepomodi
```

Here is the code for the tsrepomodi procedure:

```
PROCEDURE tsrepomodi
* Modifies the report form associated with this report
PRIVATE l_oldrecno,l_query
l_oldrecno=RECNO('tsrepo')
IF SEEK(l_oldrecno,"temprepo")
   * use the temp file contents
   SELECT temprepo
ELSE
   SELECT tsrepo
ENDIF
IF NOT EMPTY(rp_query)
   ** Run the query, to give the user something to work with
   m.l_query=rp_query
   &l_query INTO CURSOR tsrepomo
ENDIF there is a query involved
m.l_temprepo=SYS(2023)+"\"+SYS(3)
IF NOT EMPTY(rp_frx)
   COPY MEMO rp_frx TO (m.l_temprepo+".frx")
   COPY MEMO rp_frt TO (m.l_temprepo+".frt")
ELSE
```

```
   ** make a quick report for them to play with
   CREATE REPORT (m.l_temprepo) FROM (DBF('tsrepomo'))
ENDIF
** Now let them modify the temporary report
MODIFY REPORT (m.l_temprepo)
IF NOT SEEK(l_oldrecno,"temprepo")
   ** Make a temporary record to hold the changes
   DO tsnewtmprepo
ENDIF
SELECT temprepo
IF FILE (m.l_temprepo+".frx")
   ** Put the report form into memo fields in the temprepo
   ** cursor
   APPEND MEMO rp_frx FROM (m.l_temprepo+".frx") OVERWRITE
   APPEND MEMO rp_frt FROM (m.l_temprepo+".frt") OVERWRITE
   ** Clean up
   ERASE (m.l_temprepo+".frx")
   ERASE (m.l_temprepo+".frt")
ENDIF report was created
IF USED("tsrepomo")
   ** erase the cursor we created
   USE IN tsrepomo
ENDIF
RETURN .T.
```

Once again, we store any changes to the TEMPREPO file. In addition, we run the query associated with this report so that the user can work with real field names, and so the user can execute a Page Preview of his or her report. Notice that the report files exist only while the user is modifying the report format. When the user saves or aborts changes, the temporary files are reincorporated into the rp_frx and rp_frt memo fields.

Let's Run Some Reports

Now that we can modify the query, the output, the output file name, and the report form, it is time to actually run the report. Here is the full code for the vcontrol procedure, though we are particularly interested in the "GO" CASE:

```
PROCEDURE vcontrol
** Control program for tsrepo.prg/spr
PARAMETERS control
DO CASE
```

continues

```
      CASE UPPER(m.control)=="ADD"
        ** Add an entirely new report (Not a copy of an existing
        ** report) to the report database
        DO tsrepoad
        SELECT tsrepo
        IF EOF("tsrepo")
          GO TOP
        ENDIF
        ** Refresh the screen
        SHOW GET m.l_choices
        DO tsreposhow
      CASE UPPER(m.control)=="SAVE"
        ** Write pending changes in temprepo to tsrepo
        DO tsreposave
        SELECT tsrepo
        GO TOP
        DO tsreposhow
      CASE UPPER(m.control)=="MODIFY REPORT"
        ** Modify the report format (if any) associated with
        ** this report
        DO tsrepomodi
      CASE UPPER(m.control)=="GO"
        ** Run the reports that were selected
        IF NOT CHR(251)$m.l_pick
          DO l3msg WITH "No reports selected."
        ELSE
          SELECT tsrepo
          SCAN FOR RECNO('tsrepo')<=LEN(m.l_pick) AND ;
              SUBSTR(m.l_pick,RECNO('tsrepo'),1)=CHR(251)
            IF SEEK(RECNO('tsrepo'),"temprepo")
              * use the temp file contents
              SELECT temprepo
            ELSE
              SELECT tsrepo
            ENDIF
            m.l_temprepo=SYS(2023)+"\"+SYS(3)
            IF NOT EMPTY(rp_frx)
              COPY MEMO rp_frx TO (m.l_temprepo+".frx")
              COPY MEMO rp_frt TO (m.l_temprepo+".frt")
            ELSE
              m.l_temprepo=""
            ENDIF
            DO tsrepogo WITH rp_query,m.l_temprepo,rp_output,;
              rp_file
```

```
        ERASE (m.l_temprepo+".frx")
        ERASE (m.l_temprepo+".frt")
     ENDSCAN get all of the marked reports
     SELECT tsrepo
     GO TOP
     DO tsreposhow
   ENDIF no reports selected
 CASE UPPER(m.control)=="EXIT"
   CLEAR READ
 CASE UPPER(m.control)=="MENU"
   ACTIVATE WINDOW tsrepo
   CLEAR READ
ENDCASE
RETURN .T.
```

When the user elects to GO, the vcontrol procedure scans through the TSREPO
database, looking for any record with a corresponding spot in the m.l_pick variable
that is occupied by chr(251). When the procedure finds such a record, it checks
whether a TEMPREPO record is associated with the TSREPO record. If there is an
associated TEMPREPO record, vcontrol uses that record; otherwise the procedure uses
the TSREPO record's contents for the report.

Next, vcontrol copies the contents of the rp_frx and rp_frt fields to a report file for
use by TSREPOGO. When TSREPOGO is finished, vcontrol erases its temporary report
file and looks for another flagged report.

The content of TSREPOGO is of interest, so here's the code:

```
PROCEDURE tsrepogo
* Runs the query/report
PARAMETERS p_query,p_report,p_output,p_file
DO CASE
  CASE UPPER(p_output)="BROWSE"
    * The SELECT will output to a browse
    * automatically, but we don't want it to take over
    * the current window, so send it to a cursor
    * and then browse the cursor
    DEFINE WINDOW tsrpcurs FROM 0,0 TO SROWS(),SCOLS() ;
      ZOOM CLOSE FLOAT GROW TITLE rp_desc
    &p_query. INTO CURSOR tsrpcurs
    BROWSE WINDOW tsrpcurs
    RELEASE WINDOW tsrpcurs
  CASE UPPER(p_output)="FILE"
    * Output result of query to file, then
    * open the file read-only
```

continues

```
        &p_query. TO &p_file NOCONSOLE
      CASE UPPER(p_output)="GRAPH"
        ** Output to a cursor, then call gengraph
        &p_query INTO CURSOR tsrpcurs
        DO (_GENGRAPH)
      CASE UPPER(p_output)="PREVIEW"
        ** Output to a cursor, then call the
        ** report with the preview option
        &p_query INTO CURSOR tsrpcurs
        REPORT FORM (p_report) PREVIEW
      CASE UPPER(p_output)="PRINT"
        ** Output to a cursor, then call the
        ** report with the print option
        &p_query INTO CURSOR tsrpcurs
        REPORT FORM (p_report) TO PRINT NOCONSOLE
      CASE UPPER(p_output)="QREPORT"
        ** Output to a cursor, then create a
        ** quick report from the cursor,
        ** then send the report to the printer
        &p_query INTO CURSOR tsrpcurs
        l_qreport=SYS(2023)+"\"+SYS(3)
        CREATE REPORT (l_qreport) FROM tsrpcurs
        REPORT FORM (l_qreport) TO PRINT NOCONSOLE
        ERASE (l_qreport+".frx")
        ERASE (l_qreport+".frt")
      CASE UPPER(p_output)="TABLE"
        ** Send result of report to designated table
        &p_query INTO TABLE (p_file)
      CASE UPPER(p_output)="XTAB"
        ** Output to a cursor, then call _genxtab
        ** to create a table to contain the results.
        ** This table can be used in subsequent report
        ** runs.
        &p_query INTO CURSOR tsrpcurs
        DO (_GENXTAB) WITH (p_file),.F.
      OTHERWISE
        ** Just browse it
        &p_query. INTO CURSOR tsrpcurs
        DEFINE WINDOW tsrpcurs FROM 0,0 TO SROWS(),SCOLS() ;
          ZOOM CLOSE FLOAT GROW TITLE rp_desc
        BROWSE WINDOW tsrpcurs
        RELEASE WINDOW tsrpcurs
    ENDCASE
```

```
IF USED('tsrpcurs')
  USE IN tsrpcurs
ENDIF
RETURN .T.
```

 Note: Notice the power of the & macro command. In FoxPro 2.5 macros can contain up to 2,048 characters, which is plenty for most queries. Note also the use of the _GENXTAB and _GENGRAPH system variables. These variables contain the names of applications provided with FoxPro. These applications convert data from databases or cursors into cross tab tables or graphs, respectively. Also note the CREATE REPORT FROM command, which enables us to create a Quick Report on the fly, based on the structure of the cursor that results from the query.

Saving the Changes

Occasionally users want to save the changes they make to a report or query. Fortunately, the TSREPO program provides just such a capability. Pressing the Save button on the TSREPO screen triggers the following procedure:

```
PROCEDURE tsreposave
* Save all of the changes made to reports, outputs, queries, etc.
PRIVATE ALL LIKE rp*
* Give them a browse window for actions
DEFINE WINDOW tsreposave AT 0,0 SIZE 15.0,70.0 ;
  TITLE "Press enter when complete" FONT WFONT(1,""),WFONT(2,"")
MOVE WINDOW tsreposave CENTER
** Prepare temprepo cursor for action
SELECT temprepo
SET ORDER TO rp_desc
REPLACE ALL tm_action WITH "O"
** Establish a relationship between the temprepo cursor and
** the tsrepo.dbf file.
USE tsrepo AGAIN IN SELECT(1) ORDER 0 ALIAS tsreposave
SET RELATION TO tm_recno INTO tsreposave
PUSH KEY
ON KEY LABEL enter KEYBOARD "{ctrl+w}"
** Give them a browse of all changed reports, so they can
** determine what to do with each report on an individual
** basis.
```

continues

```
BROWSE FIELDS ;
  rp_desc:R:H="Description":15,;
  t1=IIF(rp_desc<>tsreposave.rp_desc,"Ch"," "):H="Desc",;
  t2=IIF(!rp_frx==tsreposave.rp_frx OR !rp_frt==tsreposave.rp_frt,;
  "Ch"," "):H="Repo",;
  t3=IIF(!rp_query==tsreposave.rp_query,"Ch"," "):H="Qry",;
  t4=IIF(rp_output<>tsreposave.rp_output,"Ch"," "):H="Out",;
  t5=IIF(rp_file<>tsreposave.rp_file,"Ch"," "):H="File",;
  tm_action:H="":1:p="!":v=tm_action$"ICO":F;
  :E="(I)gnore changes, Save as (N)ew report,"+;
  " (O)verwrite existing definitions",;
  t6=IIF(tm_action="I","(I)gnore Changes",;
  IIF(tm_action="N","Save as (N)ew report",;
  "(O)verwrite existing definitions")):H="(O)ver, (N)ew, (I)gnore";
  WINDOW tsreposave NOMENU NOAPPEND NODELETE FREEZE tm_action
POP KEY
RELEASE WINDOW tsreposave
** Close up the relationship between temprepo and the USE AGAIN
** tsrepo.dbf
SELECT temprepo
SET ORDER TO tm_recno
SET RELATION TO
USE IN tsreposave
** Process requests made in the browse window.
IF LASTKEY()<>27 && did not press escape
  IF FLOCK('tsrepo')
    SCAN FOR tm_action="N" OR tm_action="O"
      SCATTER MEMVAR MEMO
      DO CASE
        CASE tm_action="N"
          ** Save the changes as a new report
          INSERT INTO tsrepo FROM MEMVAR
        CASE tm_action="O"
          ** Overwrite the existing report
          SELECT tsrepo
          GOTO (temprepo.tm_recno)
          IF RLOCK()
            GATHER MEMVAR MEMO
          ENDIF
          UNLOCK
      ENDCASE
    ENDSCAN
    ** Clean out the pending changes in the temprepo file.
    SELECT temprepo
```

```
      ZAP
      UNLOCK IN tsrepo
   ENDIF able to lock the tsrepo database
ENDIF did not press escape
```

The `tsreposave` procedure allows users to select which changes should be used to overwrite existing definitions, which changes should be used to create new reports, and which changes should be ignored.

Adding New Reports

Now that we can run existing reports, change existing reports, and save those changes, all in a multiuser environment, all that is left is to enable the user to add new reports to the database. If you were to review the `vcontrol` listing, you would find the following code of interest:

```
CASE UPPER(m.control)=="ADD"
  ** Add an entirely new report (Not a copy of an existing
  ** report) to the report database
  DO tsrepoad
  SELECT tsrepo
  IF EOF("tsrepo")
    GO TOP
  ENDIF
  ** Refresh the screen
  SHOW GET m.1_choices
  DO tsreposhow
```

The TSREPOAD.PRG program contains the interesting parts of this aspect of the application. Figure 8.3 shows the screen presented by TSREPOAD.SPR.

Here is the setup code for TSREPOAD.PRG:

```
* tsrepoad.prg
* Add a report to the report database
PRIVATE ALL LIKE 1_*
PRIVATE m.control
SELECT tsrepo
SCATTER MEMVAR MEMO BLANK
1_qryname=SPACE(128)
1_repname=SPACE(128)
1_query=""
1_report=""
```

continues

```
m.control=""
DO tsrepoad.spr
RETURN UPPER(m.control)="GO"
```

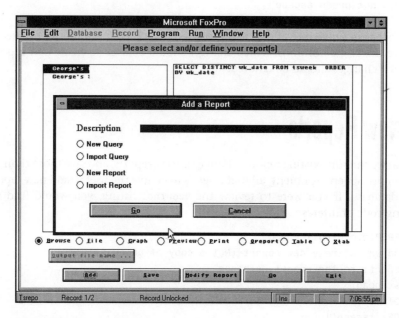

Figure 8.3. Adding a report.

Notice that the TSREPOAD.SPR screen provides options for importing reports and queries from existing files. The report portion of this equation is simple, but the query portion presents a few challenges. First, here's the control code for the push button on the TSREPOAD.SPR, along with the valid clauses for the two radio buttons:

```
PROCEDURE vcontrol
PARAMETERS m.control
DO CASE
  CASE UPPER(m.control)="GO"
    SELECT tsrepo
    IF l3insert()
      ** Able to add the report record
      IF RLOCK()
        ** See if we need to import an existing query
        IF UPPER(m.l_query)="IMPORT QUERY" AND ;
           FILE(TRIM(m.l_qryname))
          REPLACE rp_query WITH getselect(TRIM(m.l_qryname))
```

```
               ENDIF wants to import an existing query
               IF UPPER(m.l_report)="IMPORT REPORT" AND ;
                  FILE(TRIM(m.l_repname))
                 APPEND MEMO rp_frx FROM (TRIM(m.l_repname))
                 APPEND MEMO rp_frt FROM (LEFT(TRIM(m.l_repname),;
                   LEN(TRIM(m.l_repname))-3)+"FRT")
               ENDIF able to lock the report record
               UNLOCK
               CLEAR READ
            ENDIF able to lock the tsrepo record
         ENDIF able to add the record
      CASE UPPER(m.control)="CANCEL"
         CLEAR READ
ENDCASE


PROCEDURE vl_report
IF m.l_report <> "New"
   m.l_repname=PADR(GETFILE("FRX","Choose a report form"),128)
   IF EMPTY(m.l_repname)
     m.l_report="New Report"
     SHOW GET m.l_report
   ENDIF
ELSE
   m.l_repname=SPACE(128)
ENDIF wants an existing report
SHOW GETS OFF
RETURN .T.


PROCEDURE vl_query
IF l_query <>"New"
   m.l_qryname=PADR(GETFILE("QPR;PRG","Choose a query"),128)
   IF EMPTY(m.l_qryname)
     m.l_query="New Query"
     SHOW GET m.l_query
   ENDIF
ELSE
   m.l_qryname=SPACE(128)
ENDIF wants an existing one
SHOW GETS OFF
RETURN .T.
```

Importing the report is handled neatly with two APPEND MEMO commands. Importing
an existing query, however, requires further processing. The getselect() UDF opens

a .PRG or .QPR file, finds the first SQL SELECT command, and returns the entire string of the SQL SELECT command minus any IN or INTO clauses. Here is the code for getselect:

```
PROCEDURE getselect
* Pulls the first SQL SELECT command from a .PRG or .QPR file
PARAMETERS p_file
PRIVATE ALL LIKE l_*
l_selstr=""
IF FILE(m.p_file)
   ** Open the file read-only, and put the number of the file
   ** handle in the l_fh memory variable
   l_fh=FOPEN(m.p_file)
   IF l_fh>0
      ** If l_fh >0, the file was opened successfully
      DO WHILE NOT FEOF(l_fh) && Until I hit EOF in the file
         ** Read until I hit a CRLF, up to 2048 characters max
         ** Note that FGETS() strips off the CRLF
         l_selstr=LTRIM(FGETS(l_fh,2048))
         ** If the line starts with "SELE", it may be a SQL SELECT
         ** command.
         IF UPPER(l_selstr)="SELE"
            ** Read the entire command, by getting lines until
            ** you hit one that does not end in a semicolon
            DO WHILE RIGHT(TRIM(l_selstr),1)=";" AND NOT FEOF(l_fh)
               l_selstr=CHRTRAN(l_selstr,";"," ")
               l_selstr=l_selstr+LTRIM(FGETS(l_fh,2048))
            ENDDO while a ";" continuation is found and not feof()
            ** If there is a FROM clause in the command, it is
            ** a SQL SELECT command, not an Xbase SELECT command.
            IF "FROM"$UPPER(l_selstr)
               ** Strip the target from the SELECT command
               m.l_selstr=tsnotarg(m.l_selstr)
               EXIT && from the master do while not feof()
            ENDIF this is a SELECT command
         ENDIF starts with "SELE"
      ENDDO until end of query file
      ** Close the file handle to this file
      =FCLOSE(l_fh)
   ENDIF able to open the file
ENDIF the file exists
RETURN l_selstr
```

The `getselect()` UDF not only pulls the first `SQL SELECT` command from a .PRG or .QPR, it also nicely demonstrates FoxPro's low-level file I/O functions. Notice that `getselect()` also uses the `tsnotarg()` UDF, which resides in the TSREPO.PRG program.

Closing Thoughts and Potential Enhancements

I designed the TSREPO.PRG program to provide a maximum number of discussion topics, not to provide the ultimate in user-friendliness. As it stands, TSREPO.PRG is an interesting study of scrollable lists, temporary files, batch updates, low-level file I/O, and string manipulation. It is also a good way for programmers to add reports to an existing application. The program is not, however, very user-friendly. It is also not fully bulletproof.

For example, there is no way to change the description of an existing report. Nor is there any way to provide a new description for changed reports that are to be saved as New. I didn't include these simple enhancements because they didn't add to the discussion.

Further, TSREPO requires that users edit `SQL SELECT` commands to change filter conditions. A better approach would be to include additional fields in the TSREPO.DBF for variable names and values. In this scenario, the user could still edit the `SQL SELECT` command, but the data entry screen would also include fields in which the user could enter values for variables referenced in the `SQL SELECT` command.

Also, you could enable the user to access the RQBE by using a push button. Because you already have the `getselect()` procedure, you could easily read the `SQL SELECT` command out of the resultant .QPR file. Of course, the user would need a licensed copy of FoxPro to access the `MODIFY QUERY` command.

Finally, you could write your own RQBE and link in your own data dictionary, to provide the ultimate in user-friendly query and report generation. In Chapter 20, "A Data Dictionary," I add a few more thoughts on this matter.

CHAPTER

9

Micro Endeavors Naming Conventions

When searching for FoxPro programmers to hire, pursue those folks who look like the *before* picture in a tanning salon's before and after ad. (Great programmers would rather code than tan, and most haven't actually seen the sun in several years.)

Of those programmers who pass the no-tan test, look favorably on the nearsighted among them. (Programmers who have worked hard enough to be valuable developers invariably can't see much beyond the 24-inch distance that usually separates their eyes from their monitors.)

Finally, look for the programmer whose code reflects a curious consistency in the naming of files, fields, variables, and procedures. Programmers who demonstrate this peculiar habit have had to maintain code (theirs or someone else's), and they were smart enough to learn the importance of naming similar things similarly.

After hiring dozens of programmers in the last 13 years, I can tell you that the first two indicators mentioned above are funny, sometimes accurate, and lousy ways to screen programmers. Invariably, however, good programmers use good naming conventions. If your candidate does not use some kind of naming conventions, you should probably keep looking.

Because you are reading this book, I assume you are already a good programmer. Therefore, you almost certainly have your own set of naming conventions. However, you might not have a set of naming conventions that is specific to FoxPro. Or, you might be interested in reviewing a set of naming conventions that has proven to be very useful in FoxPro applications written for a wide variety of clients.

So, whether you are looking for a whole new set of naming conventions, or just some ideas to enhance your existing standards, this is the chapter for you.

Note: For the most part, FoxPro is unaffected by your choice of names. (There are exceptions, however, which I will discuss shortly.) Therefore, naming conventions are almost strictly for the benefit of programmers. Further, there is no one right way to name objects in FoxPro. The Micro Endeavors method has much to commend it, but you can be an excellent programmer without using our naming conventions. You cannot, however, be an excellent programmer without using some kind of naming conventions.

For your convenience, Table 9.1 lists all the Micro Endeavors naming conventions. Don't worry, explanations will follow.

Table 9.1. Micro Endeavors naming conventions.

Convention	Explanation
File name prefix	All file names in the same application start with same first two characters.
L3 for library routines	All library routines start with L3.
DBF names = 6 characters	We try to limit all database file names to six characters.
Fields = 2 characters + underscore (_)	All fields in the same database start with the same first two characters plus the underscore character.
Field names are unique	Because each field prefix is unique to each database, all field names are unique.
Common field names from characters 3 through 10	Fields that have the same function in multiple databases share the same name, except for the two-character prefix.
??MAIN	The main program in an application is named ??MAIN.PRG.

Convention	Explanation
Controlling program	For each .SPR file, there is a controlling .PRG file of the same name.
VALID and WHEN UDFs take the name of their GET	V+get_name for VALID clauses, W+get_name for WHEN clauses.
READ UDFs = READ + clause	READACTI(), READSHOW, READDEAC(),READVALI(), READWHEN().
Local variables = L_*	Allows for PRIVATE ALL LIKE L_*.
Global variables = K*	No hiding or releasing K variables.
Parameter variables = P_*	Indicates that this variable may have been passed by reference.
Arrays = A_*	Prevents conflicts with function names.
Popups named after .DBF or .PRG	Prevents duplication of popup names.
Window names same as .SCX	Prevents duplication of window names.
Window of Browse not named after database	Prevents problems with Browse window naming.

Using a Two-Character Prefix for File Names

All file names that belong to the same application start with the same first two characters. For example, all the files in the time sheet application start with TS. This convention facilitates backups, installations, and search and replace operations across multiple programs. This naming convention is mandatory at MEI.

Prefixing Library Routines

The only exception to the two-character prefix rule arises from the use of library routines. Many applications use these procedures, functions, and programs. Therefore, each of these routines start with L3*, LB*, or L2*, depending on which version of the Micro Endeavors library routines are in use.

For maintenance reasons, MEI programmers are not allowed to change library routines. If a programmer wants to alter the behavior of an existing library routine, he or she copies the original to another L3* name and makes adjustments to the copy.

At Micro Endeavors, we do not bind all the library routines into a single procedure file as some programmers do. Keeping each procedure in a separate .PRG makes it easier to quickly review a library routine. After all, it is easier to MODI COMM l3msg than it is to MODI COMM mylib and search for the l3msg routine. In addition, keeping the library routines in separate .PRG files makes it much easier to view the contents of multiple library routines simultaneously.

Naming Database Files

Database files belonging to the same application share the same two-character prefix, followed by four or five characters that describe the database, as in TSTIME.DBF, TSWEEK.DBF, and TSPROJ.DBF. MEI programmers usually try to limit names to a total of six characters so that we can use the last two characters available in DOS file names to name associated database files. For example, the history file associated with the TSTIME.DBF database might be called TSTIME_H.DBF.

If a maintenance screen program is associated with a database, it has the same name as the database. In the time sheet application, for example, the TSEMPL.PRG program handles the maintenance of the TSEMPL.DBF database.

Naming Fields

In MEI applications, fields in the same database all have the same first two characters, followed by an underscore. In case you haven't read the first eight chapters of this book, here is a sample database structure taken from the example application:

```
Structure for table:    c:\book\dbf\tsclient.dbf
Number of data records: 15
Date of last update:    02/19/93
Field   Field Name  Type        Width   Dec   Index
    1   CL_ADDR1    Character      30
    2   CL_ADDR2    Character      30
    3   CL_CITY     Character      30
    4   CL_CLID     Character       7          Asc
    5   CL_COMPANY  Character      40          Asc
    6   CL_NXTPROJ  Numeric         4
    7   CL_STATE    Character       2
    8   CL_ZIP      Character      10
** Total **                      154
```

In addition, each database has a unique first two-character field name prefix. Exceptions are allowed for history and temporary files that have the same structure as their master file counterpart.

Whenever possible, the two-character prefix for the field names should be the same as the third and fourth characters in the database file name. For example, all the fields in the TSCLIENT.DBF begin with cl_.

Common fields in multiple databases have the same name from the third through tenth characters. For example, the client ID field is found as tsclient.cl_clid, tsproj.pj_clid, and tstime.ti_clid in the TSCLIENT.DBF, TSPROJ.DBF, and TSTIME.DBF databases, respectively.

This naming convention yields the following benefits:

- Programmers can tell at a glance that a token is a field name because memory variables are not allowed to use this naming convention. (Variables created with SCATTER MEMVAR are an exception.)

- Because all field names in the application are unique, programmers needn't worry that a SCATTER MEMVAR in one work area will overwrite memory variables created by a SCATTER MEMVAR issued in another database.

- Accordingly, programmers needn't worry that a GATHER MEMVAR will inadvertently pick up memory variables created by SCATTER MEMVARS in other databases.

- STORE or = commands won't inadvertently overwrite variables created with a SCATTER MEMVAR, because variable names that are not created with SCATTER MEMVAR are not allowed to start with two characters and an underscore.

- Because every field name in the application is unique, SQL SELECT commands needn't use alias names to reference fields.

- Field names in source code are easily associated with their databases.

This naming convention is controversial because it has the following disadvantages:

- Less space is available for providing meaningful field names. In essence, you have only seven characters in which to provide a descriptive field name.

- FoxPro's RQBE isn't able to "guess" the relations between the databases, because this naming convention prevents the occurrence of common field names among databases.

- Import and export to other databases may be impaired because many other databases require duplicate field names to establish relationships among tables.

Thirteen years of development indicate that this naming convention's benefits far outweigh its disadvantages. It is a required naming convention at Micro Endeavors.

Naming Program, UDF, and Procedure Files

Program files in the same application share the same two-character file name prefix. Programs associated with a database often share that database name. This is one argument in favor of limiting database names to six characters, in case the developer has multiple programs associated with a single database.

The first program in an application is called ??MAIN.PRG. Programmers can always look for the ??MAIN.PRG program to start their investigation of an application.

For each .SPR program in the application, there is a .PRG file of the same name. The .PRG file is responsible for setting up before, and cleaning up after, the execution of the .SPR. In addition, this controlling .PRG file must contain all the UDFs referenced in the .SPR file.

UDFs that are valid clauses all begin with the letter *v* (for *valid*) and continue with the full name of the GET field from which the UDF is called. For example, a valid clause on the cl_state field would be vcl_state().

UDFs that are WHEN clauses all begin with the letter *w* (for *when*) and continue with the full name of the GET field from which the UDF is called. For example, a WHEN clause on the cl_state field would be wcl_state().

Any UDFs associated with READ CYCLE clauses are named as follows.

Clause	UDF Name
READ ACTIVATE	readacti
READ DEACTIVATE	readdeac
READ SHOW	readshow
READ VALID	readvali
READ WHEN	readwhen

Obviously, because an application has many READ CYCLE commands, you must store these READ clause UDFs in the controlling program for the .SPR file.

Note: The first 10 characters of a procedure name must be unique. However, FoxPro allows the procedure name to be of any length. Therefore, we ensure that the first 10 characters of a procedure name are unique within a .PRG, but we often extend those procedure names to make them more readable.

For example, in the TSTIME.PRG program, we reference the `tstimenoedit` procedure. Even though FoxPro only considers the first 10 characters of the procedure name, the extra two characters are allowed, and render the name more understandable.

Naming Local Variables

At MEI, we name all local variables L_*. In this way, we can issue the following command to ensure that none of our local variables overwrite existing memory variables:

```
PRIVATE ALL LIKE L_*
```

For this reason, variables intended for use across multiple procedures must either be passed as parameters or specifically not named with L_ as a prefix.

Naming Global Variables

Global memory variables are those variables that must be available to all procedures at all times. In order to fulfill this requirement, global variables cannot be passed as parameters by reference; global variables cannot be released; global variables cannot change data types; and global variables cannot be made private.

To help programmers identify global variables, and thereby avoid any of the offensive actions mentioned above, Micro Endeavors programmers begin all global memory variable names with a *K*. Only global memory variables are so named.

Naming Parameter Variables

Variables created with the PARAMETER statement all begin with P_. Often these parameter variables are copied to local variables for manipulation.

Naming Arrays

If an array is created from the content of one or more records in a database, that array usually has the same name as the database. Otherwise, the array name usually starts with the name of the program that created it.

 Caution: Avoid using FoxPro function names as array names. Depending on the context, FoxPro might attempt to evaluate a FoxPro function when the programmer expects FoxPro to perform an action on an array element.

Lately, MEI has been experimenting with the use of A_ as a prefix for all array names. In the future, we will adopt this as a naming convention to avoid confusing array names with procedure names and FoxPro functions.

Naming Popups

Popups based on databases have the same name as the work area from which they were created. Other popups have the name of their .PRG at the beginning of the popup name. This makes it easier to release popups when exiting from a program and, more importantly, makes it easier to avoid accidentally applying the same name to two different popups.

Naming Windows

Windows created in .SPRs have the same name as the .SCX in which the window was defined. Windows that will be used in BROWSE WINDOW clauses *do not* have the same name as the work area that will be BROWSEd. These Browse window templates also do not have the same name as the title of the BROWSE command.

Typically, hand-coded window names include the name of the .PRG in which they were created. This makes it easier to release windows when exiting from a program and, more importantly, makes it easier to avoid accidentally applying the same name to two different windows.

CHAPTER

10

SQL SELECT

Melissa Dunn is the country's foremost expert on FoxPro's SQL (pronounced "se-quel") implementation. Fortunately for me, she works at Micro Endeavors. Fortunately for you, she was somehow able to find time in her schedule to write this chapter. I think you'll like it.

You'll also understand how to take advantage of the power and flexibility of SQL SELECT to reduce your programming effort and increase the performance of your applications. When you combine the lessons of this chapter with the information found in Chapter 11, "The Report Writer," and Chapter 15, "Performance," you'll know how to create the fastest, prettiest, most code-efficient output possible. Enjoy.

Introducing the *SQL SELECT* Command

The SQL SELECT command is FoxPro 2.5's implementation of the query command used in *Structured Query Language* (SQL). Although most often found in client-server DBMS applications, SQL has slowly been appearing as embedded commands in other database products such as FoxPro, dBASE, and Access.

A properly constructed SQL SELECT usually queries tables faster than standard FoxPro procedural code. You can use the result of a SQL SELECT to create reports, BROWSEs, or new tables. The tables created by SQL can be either permanent FoxPro tables (.DBF) or temporary tables (cursor). We will discuss the differences between "real" tables and cursors later in this chapter.

Furthermore, an ANSI/ISO standard defines how SQL SELECT clauses are implemented. This provides the capability to transport queries created in FoxPro to other platforms, including client-server platforms such as ORACLE and SQL Server. As we go along, I will point out those instances in which the FoxPro implementation deviates from the standard. If transportability is a requirement for your application, you should avoid using these "nonstandard" techniques in your queries.

The remainder of this chapter is divided into three sections:

- The "SQL SELECT Basics" section discusses the composition of a "simple" SQL SELECT statement, with a few hints for better performance along the way.

- The "FoxPro 2.5 RQBE and SQL SELECT" section introduces *Relational Query By Example* (RQBE), the FoxPro user interface for building SQL SELECT statements.

- Finally, the "Complex Queries" section discusses complex queries such as self-joins, unions, and subqueries.

Throughout this chapter, I will refer to the SQL SELECT statement simply as SELECT. The term *column* equates to a FoxPro *field,* and the term *row* is equivalent to a *record.* Our terms now agreed upon, let's begin exploring the SELECT statement.

SQL SELECT Basics

The SELECT statement has many components, but only two are required: the FROM clause and the fields list.

The *FROM* Clause

The FROM clause tells SQL where to find the columns in the fields list. If the tables listed are closed, FoxPro will open them *but not close them*. If you don't want to keep the tables open, you will have to close them explicitly.

If the tables are already open, FoxPro will reopen them with the USE...AGAIN command. When a table is reopened in this manner, FoxPro requires the use of another work area but not another file handle. Because there are 225 work areas, it is doubtful that opening tables for SQL use will cause undue stress on the number of available work areas. If you must have the tables open for the application, just open them all at the beginning of the application. It requires significantly less time for SQL to reopen the table than to open the table initially.

The Fields List

The other mandatory requirement to produce a valid query is a fields list. The fields list tells SQL which fields to include in the result. The list immediately follows the SELECT statement and may include any of the following elements:

- The * wildcard
- Any field from a table named in the SELECT
- Any valid FoxPro function
- Any SELECT column function
- Any valid UDF

We'll talk more about SELECT column functions later (see the section "Column Functions"). Elements in the list are separated by commas:

```
SELECT cl_id,cl_company,cl_state ;
FROM tsclient
```

If the columns are *unambiguous* (uniquely named), you don't need to preface the column with the work area: SQL can find them without any further help. If the columns are *ambiguous* (using the same name in more than one table in the FROM clause), FoxPro returns the following error message:

```
<field> ¦ <variable> is not unique and must be qualified
```

To correct this error, you must preface the columns with the work area alias.

If you include a FoxPro function in the field list, you are likely to render your query unreadable to another SQL implementation. However, the power of FoxPro's extensive list of functions is so valuable that we find most developers make full use of FoxPro functions in SELECT field lists.

SQL and User-Defined Functions

As mentioned earlier, FoxPro supports the use of UDFs in the SELECT's field list. Obviously, other implementations of SQL may or may not support user-defined function calls within the SELECT fields list, so transportability can be a problem.

However, there is another, much more important problem with user-defined functions in SQL statements. Because SELECT causes the creation of temporary tables, temporary indexes, and temporary relationships, UDFs cannot depend on the location or existence of table data. In other words, while the SELECT is running, your UDF should not reference data from underlying tables, because those tables may or may not be ordered, filtered, or related in the way your UDF expects.

Another problem with UDF usage leads us smoothly into a discussion of the SQL parser. If you include in the field list a UDF that includes a variable which is updated each pass through the UDF (for example, a counter), you might notice that the variable is always off by one pass. In other words, if your UDF is counting the number of rows whose value for column fld1 is `"X"`, you will find that the variable holding the count is one greater than the actual number of rows in the result. This occurs because of the way in which SQL parses the `SELECT`.

SQL Parser

When you execute a query, FoxPro has a great deal of work to do before it can start the query. First, FoxPro breaks the `SELECT` statement apart, checking for syntax or other runtime errors. Second, FoxPro evaluates all the names and expressions found in the query. For example, FoxPro checks to see whether all the tables listed in the `FROM` clause are available. FoxPro also ensures that all the columns in the fields list exist in one of the `FROM` tables. Then, FoxPro checks to see whether there are any ambiguous column names in the fields list. Finally, FoxPro evaluates any functions or UDFs in the query. When FoxPro evaluates a UDF, the UDF is actually executed. Because this evaluation takes place before any data is actually retrieved, your UDF is executed once too often.

After FoxPro validates the contents of the `SELECT`, the SQL optimizer takes over. The optimizer determines the best way to carry out the query by answering such questions as the following:

- Are any indexes available that can speed up the query?

- Should an index be created on the fly?

- Should the query perform a *join* first and then apply all filters and subfilters, or vice versa?

- Can FoxPro avoid a sequential search through the tables (the slowest way to retrieve data) by creating an intermediate table?

After exploring the possibilities, the optimizer chooses the one that seems best and executes the query.

Field List Keywords and Clauses

The `SELECT` command provides for flexible selection of columns in the field list. The following sections explain the available options.

The *SELECT* Field List Wildcard (*)

The asterisk (*) is one of three SQL wildcards. The * can appear only within the fields list. The meaning of the SQL * is similar to the meaning of the DOS *, because it brings in all the fields for the table, or tables, listed in the FROM clause.

Optionally, you can preface the wildcard with a work area alias. If you choose this option, all the fields from the specified work area appear in the result, along with any other fields named in the fields list. For example:

```
SELECT * FROM tsclient,tsproj ;
WHERE pj_clid = cl_id

SELECT tsclient.*,pj_projid,pj_name ;
FROM tsclient,tsproj ;
WHERE pj_clid = cl_id
```

The first query contains all the fields from both tables. The second query produces a result that contains all the fields in the client table and only the project ID and name from the project table.

The Column-Level Alias (AS)

FoxPro 2.5 provides a way (which does *not* comply with the ANSI/ISO standard) to rename columns in the SELECT result: You can use the AS clause with any or all columns in the fields list. This is extremely useful when you use the result in a BROWSE or report. For example, instead of presenting the user with a BROWSE that has the column headings cl_id and cl_company, we could write the following SELECT:

```
SELECT cl_id AS client, cl_company AS company ;
FROM tsclient
```

The resulting BROWSE would have the column headings of client and company. Column-level aliases cannot exceed 10 characters or include spaces. Because the column alias becomes the column name in the resulting output, we need to follow the naming conventions used when creating a standard FoxPro table.

Preventing Duplication with *DISTINCT*

The last of the field list keywords, DISTINCT, eliminates duplicate rows in the result. For example, if we want a list of all the projects with hours, we might use the hours table with the following SELECT:

```
SELECT DISTINCT ti_projid ;
FROM tshours
```

There is, however, a caveat: All the values for the columns in the fields list must be exactly the same. For instance, if the query included the employee ID as well, and two tasks had different employees for the same client, the result would contain both rows and duplicate client IDs.

When SQL encounters the DISTINCT keyword, it creates an intermediary table that contains all the rows in the set. It then creates a unique index based on the concatenation of all columns in the fields list. SQL then applies the index to the intermediate table and moves into the result only those rows in the index. Hey, presto: no duplicates. However, when the SELECT has a large list of columns, this process can be time consuming.

The rest of the SELECT keywords and clauses are optional. All you need to produce a SQL SELECT result are the fields list and the FROM clause tables list.

Specifying Rows with *WHERE*

We usually don't want to retrieve all rows; rather, we want to retrieve only those rows that satisfy a condition or conditions. To accomplish this, we need to be able to apply a filter to the SELECT. Using the SET FILTER command against a table before executing a SELECT statement has absolutely no effect on the SELECT. External filters are completely ignored. Therefore, the following code still generates a SQL result with all records:

```
USE tsclient
SET FILTER TO UPPER(cl_state) = "PA"
SELECT cl_clid,cl_company,cl_state ;
FROM tsclient
```

To implement conditional retrieval of rows, we need to use the WHERE clause. The WHERE clause limits the query result to those rows that match the condition or conditions. To select only clients in Pennsylvania, use the following code:

```
SELECT cl_clid,cl_company,cl_state ;
FROM tsclient;
WHERE UPPER(cl_state) = "PA"
```

Filters and Subfilters

You can have as many filter conditions as you like within the WHERE clause. If the conditions are connected with the Boolean AND, you create one long filter condition that each row must match exactly:

```
SELECT cl_company,ti_projid ;
FROM tsclient,tstime ;
WHERE ti_clid = cl_clid ;
```

```
AND UPPER(cl_state) = "PA" ;
AND ti_week >= {01/01/91} ;
AND ti_week <= {12/31/91}
```

You can also create subfilters by using the Boolean OR:

```
SELECT cl_company,cl_clid,ti_week ;
FROM tsclient,tstime ;
WHERE ti_clid = cl_clid ;
AND UPPER(cl_state) = "PA" ;
OR (ti_week >= {01/01/91} ;
AND ti_week <= {12/31/91})
```

In the first SELECT, the result includes all companies in Pennsylvania that became clients during 1991. The second SELECT produces a result containing all companies in Pennsylvania, regardless of their starting date, and all companies that became clients during 1991, regardless of the firm's location.

Notice that we have filter conditions on fields that are *not* listed in the fields list (for example, ti_week and cl_state). This is perfectly acceptable because the filter is applied against the source table or tables before the result is built.

Join Conditions

When we have multiple tables involved in a query, we need to include a special type of WHERE condition, called a *join*. A join condition establishes a relationship, whether one-to-one or one-to-many, between two tables listed in the FROM clause.

If the tables are not joined, SQL produces a *Cartesian product,* in which each row in table1 is assumed to be related to all rows in table2, and vice versa. The result contains the product of the rows in all listed tables. For example, if table1 has 10,000 rows and table2 has 200,000 rows, the result contains 2,000,000,000 rows.

 Caution: Because performing a Cartesian product like this is valid, FoxPro does not warn you that you have an improperly joined query. On the other hand, the fact that the query takes 24 hours and consumes five gigabytes of disk space might be a clue. Obviously, you will run out of patience, and disk space, long before a query of this type finishes.

Although you can join any number of tables into a single query, there is a limitation: You cannot have a query in which one table is related to more than one other table as a parent. For instance, in an order entry system, the invoice table (EXORDERS.DBF) is involved in a one-to-many relationship with both the line items (EXLITM.DBF) and the payments (EXPAYMNT.DBF) table. However, you can't generate an aging report (which shows invoices as current, 30, 60, 90, or 90+ days old) with a simple SELECT like this one:

```
SELECT * FROM exorders,expaymnt,exlitms ;
WHERE py_orderno = or_orderno;
AND li_orderno = or_orderno
```

Because SQL matches rows from the many to the one, you get one row in the result for each of the rows in the child with the most records. In this case, you get one row for each matching row in the line items file. Therefore, you get significantly more payment rows than there are payment records. Although this result is interesting, it is far from correct. The "Complex Queries" section later in this chapter looks at ways you can solve this problem.

In addition to the comparison testing conditions (<, >, <=, >=, =, ==, and <>), other search conditions can be used in a WHERE clause, including range, set membership, and pattern matching tests.

Range Tests

The range test uses the BETWEEN keyword to check whether a column value lies between the two specified values. The BETWEEN requires you to list the expression to be evaluated and the low and high ends of the range. The values must all be of comparable data types:

```
SELECT ti_projid ;
FROM tstime ;
WHERE ti_week BETWEEN {01/01/91} AND {12/31/91}
```

Set Membership Tests

Set membership testing compares a column to a list of values. If the current column value is in the target list, the row is included in the result:

```
SELECT cl_company,cl_clid ;
FROM tsclient ;
WHERE UPPER(cl_state) IN("NY","NJ","PA","CA")
```

Note: The section "Subquery Membership and Quantification Testing," later in this chapter, describes the use of IN.

As in all the tests, the values in the list, as well as the data value, must be of comparable data types. Furthermore, listing what the column value *cannot* be is often easier than listing what it can be. Therefore, you might preface the test with the Boolean NOT, as follows:

```
SELECT cl_company,cl_clid, pj_name,pj_projid ;
FROM tsclient,tsproj ;
WHERE pj_clid = cl_clid ;
AND cl_state NOT IN("PA","NJ")
```

Pattern Matching Tests

Occasionally, we don't want to match the expression exactly, perhaps because we aren't sure what exactly the expression should be. Suppose we want a company name but aren't sure of either the spelling or the full name. We would then use the LIKE evaluator. When SQL encounters the LIKE keyword, it compares the column value to the pattern.

Typically, a pattern matching test includes one or both of the following wildcards: the percent sign (%) or the underscore (_).

The % matches any number of characters and can be placed anywhere in the string. This wildcard is especially useful when you need to locate an expression within a memo field:

```
SELECT cl_company,cl_clid, pj_projid,pj_name ;
FROM tsclient,tsproj ;
WHERE pj_clid = cl_clid ;
AND pj_desc LIKE "%FoxPro 2.5 For Windows%"
```

The result of this SELECT includes the company name, client number, and the project identification information for those clients who have the phrase "FoxPro 2.5 For Windows" somewhere in the memo pj_desc.

The other pattern matching wildcard, the _ (underscore), is similar to the DOS ?. It matches any single character. For example, the following SELECT finds any company that is Jacobsen or Jacobson:

```
SELECT cl_company,cl_clid, pj_name, pj_projid ;
FROM tsclient, tsproj ;
WHERE pj_clid = cl_clid ;
AND cl_company LIKE "Jacobs_n"
```

You can use both of the pattern matching wildcards in the same string if required:

```
SELECT cl_company,cl_clid, pj_name, pj_projid ;
FROM tsclient, tsproj ;
WHERE pj_clid = cl_clid ;
AND cl_company LIKE "%Jacobs_n%"
```

The result of this query contains such companies as William Jacobsen Corp., The Jacobson's Family Restaurant, and Jacobsen's.

Finally, there is the little matter of trying to match a pattern that contains one of the wildcards. For instance, suppose you want to find any company that contains a % in its name. The following query just results in a list of all companies:

```
SELECT cl_company,cl_clid, pj_name, pj_projid ;
FROM tsclient, tsproj ;
WHERE pj_clid = cl_clid ;
AND cl_company LIKE "%%%"
```

To ensure that SQL treats a wildcard as a literal, you must use the ESCAPE keyword and any one-character constant. The query for finding any company containing a % should look like this:

```
SELECT cl_company,cl_clid, pj_name, pj_projid ;
FROM tsclient, tsproj ;
WHERE pj_clid = cl_clid ;
AND cl_company LIKE "%/%%" ESCAPE "/"
```

When SQL encounters the ESCAPE keyword, it takes the character string immediately following the keyword and compares it to the pattern. When SQL finds the constant (/), it treats whatever single character precedes the constant as a literal. In this example, SQL treats % as a literal because it precedes the constant.

SQL and Macros

The SELECT statement can handle macros with ease and speed. After all, a macro is expanded only once, and the SELECT statement can then use the expanded value throughout the query. Before the following query, we got the table name and the expression to match from the user:

```
SELECT * ;
FROM (usertable) ;
WHERE cl_company = &username
```

Macros can even be embedded in the pattern matching wildcards:

```
SELECT cl_company,cl_clid,pj_name,pj_projid ;
FROM tsclient, tsproj ;
WHERE pj_clid = cl_clid ;
AND pj_desc LIKE "%&searchstring%"
```

In the preceding query, we let the user enter the character string to match in the memo field (`pj_desc`). The query result contains all companies that have the string in the memo.

SQL and Case Sensitivity

SQL is case-sensitive. To construct queries that return valid answers, therefore, you need to make sure that the case used in the condition (for example, UPPER(`cl_state`)) matches the values in the rows. In other words, if the company names are stored as uppercase, you must make the example uppercase. If the company names are lowercase or mixed case, the following SELECT returns an incomplete result:

```
SELECT cl_company,cl_clid ;
FROM tsclient ;
WHERE cl_company = "ACME"
```

This query returns only those rows with the customer name ACME; entries for which the company name is entered as Acme are not included. The safest way to retrieve character columns is to always use the UPPER() function and enter the example (in this case, ACME) in uppercase as well. Here's the corrected version:

```
SELECT cl_company,cl_clid ;
FROM tsclient ;
WHERE UPPER(cl_company) = "ACME"
```

SQL and Indexes

WHERE conditions use Rushmore and indexes to speed up row retrieval. SQL can use any type of index: structural .CDX (tag), external .CDX, or external .IDX. However, for SQL to use external indexes, you have to open them before running the SELECT, as in the following example:

```
USE file INDEX idxfile,external cdxfile
```

SQL uses Rushmore in the same way as standard procedural code. The filter condition must be optimizable, which means that the filter expression (for example, UPPER(`cl_company`)) must exactly match the expression used to create the index.

Tip: Whether or not you create all required indexes should depend on the application. If the user wants high-performance queries and isn't concerned about data maintenance, create all the appropriate query indexes. However, if data maintenance is more critical than querying, keep the indexes to a minimum and let SQL create what it needs.

Sorting Results with *ORDER BY*

Because the SQL optimizer takes what it considers to be the most efficacious path to the data retrieval, by default, the query results are presented in random order. In fact, you can never count on the result having the rows in the same order.

However, many applications require that the results be sorted by a field or fields. You can accomplish this by using the ORDER BY clause.

The ORDER BY clause can contain as many columns as listed in the fields list:

```
SELECT cl_company,cl_state,cl_clid ;
FROM tsclient ;
WHERE cl_state IN("NY","NJ","PA","CA") ;
ORDER BY cl_state,cl_company
```

In the results from this query, company names are listed in alphabetical order in each state (which also are listed in alphabetical order). By default, the rows are ordered in ascending order (A through Z), but you can specify the optional keyword DESCENDING to create a descending order (Z through A). You can also mix ascending and descending orders:

```
SELECT cl_company,cl_state,cl_clid, pj_name,pj_desc,ti_week ;
FROM tsclient,tsproj,tstime ;
WHERE pj_clid = cl_clid ;
AND ti_projid = pj_projid ;
AND cl_state IN("NY","NJ","PA","CA") ;
ORDER BY cl_state,cl_clid,ti_week DESC
```

This query produces an ascending ordering of rows by state and company, but within each company the project tasks appear in descending start date order. You can mix ascending and descending order because the query result is physically sorted.

Because ordering occurs in the result, the ORDER BY clause cannot include fields that are not in the fields list. After all, it is rather difficult to sort a table on fields that don't exist!

Finally, the ORDER BY allows you to identify columns by their position number in the fields list. For example, the preceding query becomes:

```
SELECT cl_company,cl_state,cl_clid, pj_name,pj_desc,ti_week ;
FROM tsclient,tsproj,tstime ;
WHERE pj_clid = cl_clid ;
AND ti_projid = pj_projid ;
AND cl_state IN("NY","NJ","PA","CA") ;
ORDER BY 2,3,6 DESC
```

This capability to use field position references is extremely useful when we need to order the result on fields that contain user-defined or FoxPro functions (for example, UPPER() and LEFT()).

Column Functions

Among the field list values, you can include any of the five SQL column functions, as listed in Table 10.1.

Table 10.1. The SQL column functions.

Function	Description
AVG(column name)	The mathematical average of the specified column. You can specify only numeric columns.
SUM(column name)	The mathematical sum of the specified column. You can specify only numeric columns.
MIN(column name)	The smallest value for the specified column. You can use numeric, character, or date type columns.
MAX(column name)	The largest value for a column. You can specify numeric, character, or date type columns.
COUNT(column name)	The number of rows in which the column occurs. Because all rows in a relational table have the same columns, COUNT() produces a count based on the filter criteria. Because of this, you can use the * wildcard as the column name rather than a specific column.

Column functions are aggregate functions; that is, they produce a single summary row. The following query, therefore, will give us the total number of hours spent on tasks, regardless of client, project, or employee:

```
SELECT SUM(ti_hours),em_last ;
FROM tstime,tsempl ;
WHERE ti_empid = em_empid
```

Notice that the employee last name (em_last) is completely random, and therefore irrelevant. We'll have to wait for our discussions of the GROUP BY clause to make the em_last field meaningful in a query like this one (see the upcoming section "Subtotaling with GROUP BY").

If you want, you can order the data by a column function. However, unless you use the AS keyword to give the column function an alias, FoxPro generates an unambiguous name to be used in the result table. At times like this, the capability to reference columns by their fields list position number is extremely useful:

```
SELECT SUM(ti_hours),em_last ;
FROM tstime,tsempl ;
WHERE ti_empid = em_empid ;
ORDER BY em_last, 1 DESC
```

Using *DISTINCT* in Column Functions

You can use the DISTINCT keyword in any column function, other than MIN() and MAX(), to eliminate the inclusion of duplicate values:

```
SELECT AVG(DISTINCT ti_hours) ;
FROM tstime
```

This query averages only unique values from the hours column. Remember that you can have only one DISTINCT in the fields list. Therefore, the following query will not run:

```
SELECT DISTINCT AVG(DISTINCT ti_hours),ti_empid
FROM tstime
```

A final note on distinct column functions: the COUNT() function does not allow the use of the * wildcard if the keyword DISTINCT is also included in the COUNT() function (for example, COUNT(DISTINCT *)). To create a distinct COUNT(), you need to specify a column.

Nesting Column Functions

A nested column function looks something like this:

```
SELECT SUM(AVG(ti_hours)), ti_projid ;
FROM tstime ;
GROUP BY ti_projid
```

You might expect the result of this query to be the total average hours spent on each project. However, the actual response from FoxPro is the following error message:

```
AVG.PRG cannot be found
```

The bottom line is that you cannot nest column functions.

Subtotaling with *GROUP BY*

Earlier, we discussed the following query:

```
SELECT SUM(ti_hours),em_last ;
FROM tstime,tsempl ;
WHERE ti_empid = em_empid
```

As noted at the time, this query returns a single row. However, what we really wanted was the total number of hours spent by each employee, or one row per employee, with a subtotal of hours for each employee. To get column functions to return subtotals, we need to use the GROUP BY clause.

The GROUP BY clause literally does just that: it groups the result by whatever columns you specify. For instance, to have the query provide the number of hours for each employee, you change the query as follows:

```
SELECT SUM(ti_hours),em_last ;
FROM tstime,tsempl ;
WHERE ti_empid = em_empid ;
GROUP BY em_empid
```

Notice that we grouped on the employee ID rather than the last name, because names are not necessarily unique whereas the ID is unique. However, we didn't list the employee ID field as one of the result fields. This is quite acceptable, because of the way in which SQL generates a grouped query.

When we request a grouped query, SQL creates an intermediate table that contains all the columns in the fields list as well as the grouping columns (for example, em_empid). At this point, the rows have been filtered by whatever conditions exist in the WHERE clause. SQL now groups the rows according to the GROUP BY criteria, executes the column functions, and places the columns from the fields list into the result. If the grouping column is not in the fields list, it is simply not placed in the result.

However, grouping on a column not listed in the fields list is not recommended. Here is the result of our query:

```
Sum_ti_hou     Em_last

72.20          Goley IV

11.00          Dunn

10.00          Dunn
```

As you can see, without the grouping column (such as em_empid), it becomes difficult to distinguish between groups.

Subtotaling Multiple Grouping Columns

SQL does not limit the number of groups you can include in a GROUP BY clause. For example, we can change our query so that it gives us the number of hours for each employee in each project:

```
SELECT SUM(ti_hours),em_last,em_empid,ti_projid ;
FROM tstime,tsempl ;
WHERE ti_empid = em_empid ;
GROUP BY ti_projid,em_empid
```

However, regardless of the number of grouping columns, you get only a single row for each group combination. The SQL SELECT cannot return multiple subtotals, such as the hours subtotal for employee and the hours subtotal for project. However, you can obtain this type of subtotaling by combining the various FoxPro tools. For instance, you can send the query result to a report form that has data groups for employee and project. The query generates the proper result set, and you can use the Report Writer to give all the appropriate subtotals and totals.

Choosing Between *GROUP BY* and *DISTINCT*

Earlier in this chapter, I mentioned that using the DISTINCT keyword to produce a unique result set could be extremely time consuming, depending on the number of columns in the fields list. A faster way to produce a distinct result is to group the result table on the required column or columns:

```
SELECT ti_clid,ti_week,ti_projid ;
FROM tstime ;
GROUP BY ti_projid
```

This query produces a single row for each project ID—in other words, a complete project list.

Why is the GROUP BY faster than DISTINCT? Because the GROUP BY is required to compare only the columns in the group by list, whereas the DISTINCT clause forces a comparison of all columns in the fields clause.

Using the *HAVING* Clause

Now that we can retrieve subtotals, we face another problem: how do we control, or filter, which groups are included in the result? We can't use the WHERE clause, because that filters the rows in the source tables and what we need is to filter out groups created in the intermediate table.

The HAVING clause allows us to control which groups are passed from the intermediate table to the final result. Although we can use any legitimate column or expression in a HAVING clause, we typically end up including a column function. After all, the only reason we need to use the HAVING clause is that we have included a GROUP BY clause, which means that we have a column function in the fields list:

```
SELECT ti_projid, SUM(ti_hours), ti_empid,;
    TRIM(em_first)+" "+TRIM(em_last) ;
FROM tstime,tsempl ;
WHERE ti_empid = em_empid ;
GROUP BY ti_projid,ti_empid ;
HAVING SUM(ti_hours) > 10
```

This query includes only those projects and employees for which more than 10 hours have been recorded.

The column function, however, need not be the same as the function in the fields list:

```
SELECT ti_projid, SUM(ti_hours), ti_empid,;
    TRIM(em_first)+" "+TRIM(em_last) ;
FROM tstime,tsempl ;
WHERE ti_empid = em_empid ;
GROUP BY ti_projid,ti_empid ;
HAVING AVG(ti_hours) > 10
```

In this query, we are including only those projects for which the average number of hours is more than 10, even though the result contains the total number of hours.

Both the WHERE clause and the HAVING clause provide filters for our queries, but I am often asked which is "better." For maximum performance, use the WHERE clause to filter rows from the source tables and the HAVING clause to filter rows from the intermediate tables.

Tip: A common mistake made by novice SQL SELECT programmers is to use the HAVING clause in a command like the following:

```
SELECT * FROM tsclient HAVING cl_state="NJ"
```

Although this command works, it cannot take advantage of Rushmore and therefore can take hundreds or even thousands of times longer than the following command:

```
SELECT * FROM tsclient WHERE cl_state="NJ"
```

Directing Output

Until now, we have not actually told SQL what to do with the result of the query, so the output has been directed automatically into a temporary table called QUERY, with a BROWSE being issued immediately thereafter.

FoxPro 2.5 allows you to direct the output from a SELECT INTO a CURSOR, DBF/TABLE, or an ARRAY. Each of these options will allow you to use the result in further program processing.

You can also send the query result TO an ASCII FILE or the PRINTER. You can choose an INTO or a TO option, but not both. In fact, if you include both of these directional clauses, SQL gives precedence to the INTO clause.

INTO CURSOR

SELECT cursors are often referred to as "temporary tables," but cursors are not tables. In fact, cursors are often RAM-resident or a "view" of the underlying table(s) that use a filter. Depending on the size of the source table, the size of the result, the amount of available memory, and the SELECT options, the cursor may or may not have a disk presence. In fact, in the case of a filtered query of a single table, FoxPro often reopens the source database in another work area and establishes a filter on that database.

This agility makes output to a cursor faster than output to a table. This agility also leads to some confusion about the possible and proper uses of cursors.

Cursors are designed to be read-only. They are most useful as the basis for read-only Browse windows and as the foundation for reports.

However, because cursors can be created more quickly than tables, and because FoxPro automatically erases any files associated with a cursor when that cursor is closed, many developers try to use cursors for read-write activities.

If you want to accomplish any of the following objectives, I strongly suggest that you direct the result of your query to a table:

- To include the query's result in a future query

- To build indexes on the result of your query for further review

- To change the values stored in the result of your query

- To add the results of your query to another database

Because there seems to be some fascination with the idea of creating cursors that can be indexed, updated, and appended to other databases, I will note that you can force a cursor to enjoy a disk presence by employing one of the following methods:

- Include an AS clause on one of the fields

- Include an expression other than a single field name in the fields list

- Include a GROUP BY or ORDER BY clause

- Include a column function in the fields list

Suppose you are attempting to use the cursor to update another table by using the APPEND FROM command. You have to be very sure that your cursor is a "real" table rather than a filter.

You see, if your cursor is the original table with a filter established, the APPEND FROM command will ignore the filter established by the SELECT command, and append all the records from the source table.

To determine whether you have a filtered or "real" cursor, enter the following after the query has completed:

```
xx = DBF()
```

This stores the name of the underlying table to the variable xx. If xx is the same as the underlying source table, you have a filtered cursor. If a table with the extension .TMP is returned, you have a "real" cursor.

However, you still cannot refer to the work area alias (in this case, the cursor name) when using a command, such as APPEND FROM, that requires the table name. To use a cursor in such commands, you need to do something like this:

```
SELECT * FROM tstime ;
  WHERE ti_week BETWEEN {01/01/92} AND {12/31/92} ;
  INTO CURSOR old ORDER BY ti_week
SELECT history
APPEND FROM (DBF("old"))
```

The use of name expression parentheses is required around the DBF() function to ensure that the underlying table name is passed to the command.

Finally, if you are using cursors in a multiuser environment, be aware of the fact that the values in a "filtered cursor" may change if the underlying table changes. There is a fairly simple explanation: If the cursor is nothing more than a filter placed against a table, any changes to that table which affect the filter also affect the contents of the cursor.

To test this "changing cursor" phenomenon for yourself, try the following:

```
SET DELETED OFF
SELECT cl_company,cl_state ;
FROM tsclient ;
WHERE cl_state = "PA" ;
INTO CURSOR temp
```

189

After checking to make sure that you have a "filtered" cursor, issue the BROWSE command to view the result set. Now go to another workstation and change the filter (WHERE) value for one of the rows visible in the BROWSE.

Back on the original workstation, scroll past the affected row and then scroll back. The row now either appears or disappears, depending on what you did to the filtered field.

You can prevent this behavior by using one of the previously listed methods to force FoxPro to create a temporary table; by placing an FLOCK() on the original table prior to performing the query; or by directing the output of your query to a table rather than to a cursor.

INTO ARRAY

The syntax for creating a resulting array is straightforward:

```
SELECT cl_company,cl_state ;
FROM tsclient ;
WHERE cl_state = "PA" ;
INTO ARRAY temp
```

The resulting array is a standard FoxPro array that you can manipulate by using any of the array functions (ALEN(), ASORT(), and so on).

Tip: There are a couple of caveats to sending the result into an array. First, if no values are in the result set, the array is *not* created. You must verify the existence of the array before executing any code referencing it.

One way to determine the existence of the array is to check the value of the _TALLY system variable after the SELECT has completed. If the value returned equals zero, no values were loaded into the array:

```
IF _TALLY = 0  && no array elements loaded
   ** code to handle a null result set
ENDIF
```

Second, if you aren't sure how large the result will be, you may not want to use the INTO ARRAY option. The maximum number of array elements allowed in FoxPro 2.5 is 65,000. The amount of memory available on the system may also impose a constraint. If you exceed either of these limitations, you get a FoxPro error message.

INTO TABLE/DBF

If you need the result set to be stable and the possibility exists of exceeding the array limitations, you may want to create a permanent table. Or, if you plan to use the query result as part of another query, you need to send the result INTO TABLE. The following code creates a table that satisfies either objective:

```
SELECT cl_company,cl_state ;
FROM tsclient ;
WHERE cl_state = "PA" ;
INTO TABLE temp
```

The INTO TABLE clause creates a standard FoxPro table. You can treat this table as you would any other table in the application. You can add, delete, and edit records, and add tags and external indexes.

Because this is a true FoxPro table, you need to explicitly delete the .DBF and any associated files (such as .CDX, .FPT, or .IDX) when you are finished with the table.

 Caution: If you SET SAFETY OFF, you do not receive any warning that a table already exists with the same name as the INTO TABLE. If your target table name already exists, FoxPro closes the currently open version, *overwrites* it with the result of your query, and reopens the table ready for input. This occurs even if the target table is already open in another work area.

TO

Although most applications require you to send the results into some data-ready format such as a cursor or a table, you have the option of sending the results directly to a printer or an ASCII text file.

FILE

If you want to store the results of a single, or many, queries in a text file, you need only to issue the following SELECT:

```
SELECT cl_company ;
FROM tsclient ;
TO FILE sqlfile.txt ADDITIVE
```

SQL looks for a file called SQLFILE.TXT. If it doesn't find such a file, it creates one. If SQL finds the .TXT file, it adds the result from this query to the bottom of the file. If you want only the information from this query to be stored in the file, don't include the ADDITIVE keyword.

PRINTER

You can send the results from a query directly to a printer with this command:

```
SELECT cl_company ;
FROM tsclient ;
TO PRINTER NOCONSOLE
```

The NOCONSOLE option prevents the query results from being echoed to the screen while the results are being printed on the printer.

FoxPro 2.5 RQBE and *SQL SELECT*

So far, we have covered the basics of writing a SQL SELECT statement. If you find that you are still a bit confused about the components—when they are used and where they should appear in the statement—FoxPro provides training wheels: the RQBE.

The *Relational Query By Example,* or RQBE, is the user interface that creates a query program (.QPR) based on the information entered into the various parts of the interface and interface dialogs. Although the query may not produce the result you want, at least the syntax is always correct.

For the end-user, the RQBE is a great place to create ad hoc queries. For the developer, the RQBE is a great place to learn how to write SQL SELECT statements. However, there are some limitations on the types of queries you can create within the confines of the RQBE. But we'll get to that momentarily.

The main RQBE window contains sections for the FROM clause (tables), the fields list (output fields), the WHERE clause (selection criteria), and the INTO/TO clause (output and name). There are also check boxes for choosing the columns for the fields list, the ORDER BY, GROUP BY, and HAVING. We'll take a quick look at the behavior of each of these sections and dialogs separately.

From (Tables)

The RQBE knows that you need to have at least one table to have a viable query. To make sure that you follow this requirement, the RQBE executes the SELECT FILE dialog and requires that you select a table before the RQBE appears. If tables are already open, the RQBE assumes that you want to use the one located in the current work area. Therefore, when the RQBE appears, that table automatically appears in the Tables section.

If you want to add tables to the query, you simply choose the Add button located below the Tables section. Choosing the Add calls the Select File dialog.

If you choose the Clear button, the RQBE clears all references to the table pointed to in the Tables section. This means that all conditions (column- or group-level), columns, orders, and groups pertaining to this table are permanently removed from the query.

The Fields List ([ ]Fields/Ouput Fields)

The fields list is displayed in the Output Fields section. The order of the fields represents the order in which they will appear in the result. If you want to change the order, you can use the mover bars located to the left. Which fields are included in the Output Fields section is determined first by the RQBE and second by you.

The second requirement for a valid SELECT is the inclusion of at least one column in the fields list. To prevent you from violating this requirement, the RQBE includes all fields from the first table selected in the Tables section. All tables added subsequently will not have any fields added to the fields list by default.

You can choose the fields to include in the fields list by clicking the Fields check box. This action activates the RQBE SELECT FIELDS dialog. Within this dialog you can choose any field from any table included in the query. If you decide you don't want to include a field, you can remove it from the Selected Output list. Mover bars located in the Selected Output area allow you to change the order of the fields without removing and reading them.

The No Duplicates check box adds the DISTINCT clause to the query and the Functions/ Expressions area allows you to choose a SQL column function (by using the Functions popup) or to create your own FoxPro expression.

If you choose to create a SQL column function, the RQBE presents a list of all fields from the currently included tables. However, only those fields with the appropriate data type are enabled for selection. In other words, if you choose to include a SUM(), the RQBE enables only those fields that have a numeric data type.

If you select only three fields, the Cross Tabulate check box becomes enabled. The field order determines the x-axis, y-axis, and the values to be spread between. The capacity to generate cross tabs is not inherent in SQL. Rather, the RQBE generates an additional line of code that immediately precedes the query:

```
DO (_GENXTAB) WITH 'Test1'
```

The results of the query are processed through whatever program is contained in the system variable _GENXTAB. By default, this program is GENXTAB.PRG, which is included with FoxPro 2.5.

The *WHERE* Clause

The SELECTION CRITERIA section represents the join and filter conditions found in the WHERE clause.

Filter Conditions

You can add filter conditions to the SELECT by choosing one of the fields from the popup presented when you click the text area under the FIELD NAME heading. All the fields from all the tables currently in the TABLES section will be listed. You can also use the Expression Builder by choosing <expression ... > from the field listing.

 Tip: If your expression requires the concatenation of more than one field for improved performance, you can combine fields by using the Expression Builder.

The standard evaluators are located in the popup following the Boolean NOT check box.

The text area located under the EXAMPLE heading is where you type the condition that the FIELD NAME column must meet. You can include the use of the wildcards % and _ in the example column if you enclose your expression in quotation marks.

Finally, the check box under the heading UP/LO is used to control for case sensitivity. When the box is checked, the RQBE places the UPPER() function around both the column to be evaluated and the condition that it must meet.

 Note: If you select the UP/LO option, your query will not be Rushmore-optimizable, unless there is a corresponding UPPER() tag or index associated with your database. See Chapter 15, "Performance," for more details.

The Join Condition Dialog

When you click the Add button to add another table to the query, the RQBE immediately presents the RQBE Join Condition dialog. The popup on the left contains all the fields from the newly added table and the popup on the right contains the fields from all the tables already in the query. Your task is to choose the relational key fields from the proper tables. This dialog also includes an UP/LO check box to prevent case-sensitivity errors.

Note: If your tables contain field names that are common to both tables, the RQBE will try to guess the join condition based on the common field name. If the RQBE guesses incorrectly, you can override the RQBE's choice in the Selection Criteria area of the RQBE dialog.

When you choose OK, the RQBE immediately places the join condition in front of any other filter condition. A double-headed arrow in the area located between the mover bar and the FIELD NAME indicates that this is a join. Although the RQBE does its best to ensure a proper SELECT statement, it won't prevent you from deleting this line from the WHERE clause.

ORDER BY

The ORDER BY check box triggers the ORDER BY dialog. You will notice that only those columns that appear in the OUTPUT FIELDS area appear in this section. Again, this conforms to the SQL standard that you can create an order only on fields that exist in the output.

The dialog includes radio buttons that allow you to choose whether you want the order to be ascending or descending, and mover bars that allow you to change the sorting order.

When you have completed the ordering selection, take a look at the OUTPUT FIELDS section. You will notice that the ordering position and direction are indicated by numbers and arrows placed by the appropriate column.

GROUP BY

You use the GROUP BY check box to control the GROUP BY dialog much like you use the ORDER BY check box to control the ORDER BY dialog. Notice that, in accordance with the SQL rules, you can choose from all fields in the query, not just those columns selected for output.

However, if you do choose to group by a column not in the output, you discover that the RQBE places the grouping column into the OUTPUT FIELDS box, indicating that the field will be included in the intermediate table but not in the final result. I would also take this as a subtle suggestion that, if the RQBE is including the field, perhaps you should legitimize that idea and use the SELECT FIELDS dialog to officially include your group by field in the result.

The *HAVING* Clause

The HAVING dialog looks amazingly like the SELECTION CRITERIA (WHERE) section. Of course, we know that the HAVING is nothing more than filter conditions—or a WHERE clause for groups—so this is no surprise.

Output

After you build the basic query (including the output columns, order, groups, conditions, and so on), you are ready to choose what will happen to the query result. Of the five options in the Output popup, TABLE/DBF and CURSOR generate the standard SQL INTO clauses. There is no option for INTO ARRAY.

The BROWSE option, which is the default, creates a cursor and then immediately BROWSEs that work area.

Choosing REPORT/LABEL enables the OPTIONs.. check box. In the RQBE DISPLAY OPTIONS dialog you can select a report or label form, create a Quick Report, or send the result TO FILE or TO PRINTER. These last two options are the standard SQL clauses.

When you choose any option that is not a standard SQL clause, the RQBE adds a line of code that executes your choice. For instance, choosing a Quick Report causes the RQBE to send the result into a cursor and then execute the following lines of code in the query program (.QPR):

```
CREATE REPORT test1.frx FROM Test1 WIDTH 640 COLUMN
REPORT FORM test1.frx PREVIEW
```

Of significant interest in the Output popup is the GRAPH option. Choosing this option executes the GraphWizard.

The *GraphWizard* uses the Microsoft Graph package provided with most Microsoft applications, including FoxPro 2.5. You can store the resulting graph as a general field in a special table associated with this query.

Why Use the RQBE?

Developers may find the RQBE useful in creating an application for several reasons. First, if you don't know how to construct a proper SELECT statement, the RQBE is a great teaching tool. All you have to do is open the See SQL window below the main RQBE window and watch the RQBE construct the query.

This is also a fine way to learn how to include the lines of code necessary to have your program fire the GraphWizard or generate a Quick Report.

You can include the query program created by the RQBE into your own programs simply by calling the query like this:

```
DO myquery.QPR
```

You don't have to cut and paste the RQBE output unless you prefer to include the SELECT statement directly in your code.

Why Not Use the RQBE?

Given that you have a simple interface in which to build queries, why not just use it for all your application queries and not bother to learn how to build your own SQL SELECT statements?

Remember that the RQBE is really designed to be an end-user interface tool. As such, the RQBE is terrific for simple queries or even a self-join, but its overall capabilities are limited. The more you use SELECTs, the more you will find that complex queries are beyond the scope of the RQBE.

Complex Queries

A complex query is any query that requires the use of more than one SELECT statement to determine the final result set. Traditionally, complex queries include subqueries, self-joins, and UNIONs.

Subqueries

A *subquery* is literally a query within a query. You use subqueries when, to produce the final result set, you need the result from another query. The following is an example of a subquery:

```
SELECT cl_company,pj_name,pj_projid ;
FROM tsclient,tstime,tsproj ;
WHERE ti_clid = cl_clid ;
AND pj_projid = ti_projid ;
AND ti_empid = (SELECT em_empid ;
                FROM tsempl ;
                WHERE UPPER(em_last) = "GOLEY") ;
GROUP BY ti_projid
```

In this example, we want a listing of projects for the employee GOLEY. To accomplish this, we need to know the employee ID, because the employee ID, not the name, links the files together.

SQL runs the inner query first to find the employee ID (assume in this case that the employee ID is GFG4). After this query runs, SQL processes the outer query. The subquery in this example is completely "self-contained;" in other words, SQL runs it only once. After determining the result, SQL treats the result as a simple value. The query is now executed as if we had written the following:

```
SELECT cl_company,pj_name,pj_projid ;
FROM tsclient,tstime,tsproj ;
WHERE ti_clid = cl_clid ;
AND pj_projid = ti_projid ;
AND ti_empid = "GFG4" ;
GROUP BY ti_projid
```

Note: This example uses the GROUP BY to eliminate duplicates because there could be more than one time sheet for any given project. Because we are interested in projects, not time sheets, we need to use the DISTINCT keyword or group the time sheets. I opted to group the time sheet rows for better performance.

Because subqueries are used to filter the results of the main query, they appear in the WHERE (record-level filter) or HAVING (group-level filter) clause.

When you use subqueries, however, some restrictions apply:

- The query can contain only a single field name in the fields list. The exception is the use of the * wildcard for an existence test.

- You can use UNION and ORDER BY clauses only in the main query, *not* in a subquery.

- Subqueries must be enclosed within parentheses.

- Comparison, membership, existence, and quantification tests are the only tests that subqueries can use.

- The WHERE clause in the subquery can reference fields from the main query. This is called an *outer reference*.

For example, let's pretend that in the project table we have a field, pj_estime, that contains the estimated amount of time that project would take to complete. Given this example, we would be able to query which projects, if any, were over their estimated time.

To get this result, you could write a query like this:

```
SELECT pj_projid,pj_name ;
FROM tsproj ;
WHERE pj_estime < (SELECT SUM(ti_hours) ;
                   FROM tstime ;
                   WHERE ti_projid = pj_projid)
```

Notice that the main difference between this query and the one at the beginning of this section is that this subquery uses a WHERE clause to reference a field from the main, or outer, query table, whereas the first subquery references a value from its own FROM clause.

The value of ti_projid is taken from the record currently being tested in the main query.

Queries such as this, which are often called *correlated queries,* may take longer to process because each row in the main query has to be "correlated" with the subquery result. In other words, a correlated subquery must be executed for each row in the outer query. In the first example, however, the subquery had to be executed only once and thereafter the result was treated as a constant.

Subquery Membership and Quantification Testing

When doing a membership test, the subquery result presents a list against which the current value in the outer query is compared. For example, the following query results in a list of all clients and projects for which work is being done this month:

```
SELECT cl_company, pj_name ;
FROM tsclient,tsproj ;
WHERE pj_clid = cl_clid ;
AND pj_projid IN(SELECT ti_projid ;
                 FROM tstime ;
                 WHERE ti_week >= {01/01/93} ;
                 AND ti_week <= {01/31/93};
                 GROUP BY ti_projid)
```

When used as a subquery, the IN membership test generates the list of values against which the main query value is checked before including or excluding the row from the result.

Therefore, when you want SQL to compile the list of valid values rather than entering them yourself, you use an IN subquery rather than the simple IN evaluator.

The quantification test is an extension of the membership test which is available only as a subquery. The IN test is a simple comparison to determine whether the outer query value is equal to one of the values in the list. The quantification test expands the membership test to use any of the valid SQL evaluators (<, >, <>, and so on). Quantification tests can take the form of either ANY/SOME or ALL.

ANY/SOME

For the sake of argument, we'll add another field to our project table: pj_status. The status field contains the values "O" for ongoing, "C" for completed, and "H" for on-hold.

Of interest to us are employees whose completed projects took more than the estimated time:

```
SELECT SUM(ti_hours) AS hours,ti_empid,ti_projid ;
FROM tshours;
GROUP BY ti_empid,ti_projid ;
INTO TABLE temp
SELECT TRIM(em_last)+" "+TRIM(em_first);
FROM tsempl,temp ;
WHERE ti_empid = em_empid ;
AND hours < ANY(SELECT pj_estime ;
                FROM tsproj ;
                WHERE pj_projid = ti_projid ;
                AND pj_status = "C") ;
INTO CURSOR tempemp
```

The membership test returns a True value if *any* of the values produced by the subquery match, based on the evaluator in the outer query. Most SQL optimizers cease the comparison as soon as they find one value that matches.

ALL

The ALL returns a True value only if all the values in the subquery list match the outer query evaluator. If so much as one value fails the evaluation, the processing ceases and a False value is returned.

You may have noticed that this query needed two SELECT statements to be completed. To obtain the information that we want, we need to know the total number of hours each employee put into any given project. We need a GROUP BY to obtain this total. However, if we performed the GROUP BY on the query containing the quantification test, the GROUP BY would have occurred *after* the membership test. Consequently, we had to create the comparison values before we could perform the desired query.

Quantification queries are often confusing to read because the evaluator often appears to be the reverse of what you want in the answer. For example, if the query is supposed to return those employees involved in projects that were over the estimated time to complete, the evaluator is a less than (<) rather than a greater than (>) sign.

Remember that SQL processes the inner query first and then makes the comparison. In this example query, for instance, if a project has an estimated time of 320 hours and the employee works 321 total hours, the comparison becomes 320 (estimated hours) < 321 (real hours) which is true. This is also the same as saying that 321 (real hours) > 320 (estimated hours). Always think of the evaluative sign in terms of comparing the result of the inner query to the current value of the outer query, not the other way around.

Finally, note that this quantification test produces a true or false answer rather than a comparison value. This differs from any of the other tests discussed so far.

Subquery Existence Testing

Existence testing is just that: we want to know whether some value for the outer query row exists in the inner query table. For example, we might want to know which clients have not had any work done this year. To find out, we might write a query like the following:

```
SELECT cl_company ;
FROM tsclients ;
WHERE cl_clid NOT EXISTS(SELECT * ;
                    FROM tstime ;
                    WHERE ti_clid = cl_clid ;
                    AND ti_week BETWEEN {01/01/93} ;
                    AND {12/31/93})
```

The existence test works like this: SQL takes the value of the current client ID and performs the inner query to determine whether any rows are between the specified dates. If even one row matches, a True value is returned and the client name is included in the result. If the inner query finds no matches, a False value is returned and the outer query row is excluded from the result.

There are two things you must note about existence tests. First, existence tests are always correlated queries; that is, to perform this test, the inner query must reference a field from the outer query (for example, cl_clid). This makes existence subqueries fairly slow because the inner query must be performed for each row in the outer query. The larger the number of rows that must be evaluated in the outer query, the slower the query.

Second, the existence test is the only subquery that allows you to use the * wildcard instead of requiring that you specify a field name. Because the result is always either a True or False, it doesn't matter which field is specified, so you can use the wildcard. In reality, existence subqueries rarely appear with anything other than the * wildcard.

Finally, although existence subqueries are easy to understand, they are actually never necessary. For instance, the following query produces the same result as the query that includes an existence test:

```
SELECT cl_company ;
FROM tsclient ;
WHERE cl_clid NOT IN(SELECT ti_clid ;
                     FROM tstime ;
                     WHERE ti_week BETWEEN {01/01/93} ;
                     AND {12/31/93})
```

This query actually takes less time to execute because it is not a correlated query. Remember that IN subquery behaves as follows: The inner query is performed first, only once. The result of the inner query is a list of client IDs that have time sheets within the date range. The main query is now executed. Each new client ID is compared to the generated list. If the current value is *not* in the list, the row is included in the result. If the current value *is* in the list, the row is excluded.

Existence tests, then, are merely a specialized form of the standard IN subquery. Generally, the IN is quicker to perform than the existence test, although what the query is testing for may not be as intuitive.

Note: A final note on subqueries: The ANSI/ISO standard does not limit the number of nested subqueries. In fact, you can place as many queries within another query as required to get the proper information into the result. However, FoxPro does set a limit on the number of nested subqueries: none.

In the current implementation of SQL SELECT, all subqueries must exist on the same level as the main query; that is, you can use subqueries as search or filter conditions for the main query only. A subquery cannot use another subquery for one of its filter conditions.

Self-Joins

You use a *self-join* when information in a table must be compared to other information in the same table. There are two typical situations in which this is necessary: when there is a many-to-many relationship and you need to use the resolver table, and when a table holds information that spans time periods.

The time sheet dataset, for example, includes a many-to-many relationship: Employees can be assigned many projects and any given project may have many employees. To unravel this interconnection, we have the hours table (TSTIME), which contains both the employee ID and the project ID. If you want to know which projects are assigned to an employee, you query distinct the employee ID field (ti_empid). If you want to know which employees are working on a project, you query distinct the project ID.

But what if you want to know which projects, if any, two specific employees have worked on, or are working on, together? This requires a subset of two queries. A query of the employee IDs yields *all* the projects with which they are associated, not just the projects they have in common. A self-join allows us to look at the common ground between the employees. The query might look like this:

```
SELECT time1.ti_projid ;
FROM tstime time1,tstime time2 ;
WHERE time1.ti_empid = "GFG4" ;
AND time2.ti_empid = "MWD" ;
AND time1.ti_clid+time1.ti_projid = ;
  time2.ti_clid+time2.ti_projid ;
INTO CURSOR tempsql
```

There is a new construct in this query: *table aliases*. Notice that because you need to use the same table twice, you need some way of telling SQL how to distinguish between the two copies. You can accomplish this by assigning a table alias in the FROM clause.

A table alias is easy to create: You simply name the table (as TSTIME, for example) and then immediately give the alias (TSTIME TIME1, for example). However, after you create a table alias, you must make sure that all columns, including those in the fields list, are prefaced by the appropriate alias (i.e. `time1.ti_clid` or `time2.ti_clid`).

In the preceding query, the subset information is actually obtained by the last filter condition (`time1.ti_clid + time1.ti_projid = time2.ti_clid + time2.ti_projid`). The first two conditions merely get all the projects for both employees. The final condition, however, makes sure that only those rows which have identical project IDs are included in the result.

The second instance in which you usually use self-joins occurs when you must make comparisons to data that spans a time period. Again, you can use the time sheet hours table because it contains information about projects over time.

For example, we might create the following query if we want a list of clients for whom we worked last year but who have not requested any work from us this year:

```
SELECT cl_company ;
FROM tstime time1,tsclient ;
WHERE time1.ti_clid = cl_clid ;
AND time1.ts_week BETWEEN {01/01/92} ;
AND {12/31/92} ;
AND NOT IN(SELECT time2.ti_clid ;
        FROM tstime time2 ;
        WHERE time2.ts_week BETWEEN {01/01/93} ;
        AND {12/31/93})
```

In this query, the self-join actually occurs in the subquery rather than in the main query. Simply stated: You use the time table again in the subquery to generate a list of all client IDs for the current year. The client ID from the current row in the first version of the time table is then compared against the IDs in this list; if no match is found, the client name is placed into the result.

Self-joins are a natural for SQL. After all, SQL always USEs a table AGAIN anyway, so to request that SQL open a table more than once is no effort at all. In fact, self-joins are the only complex query that you can accomplish from the RQBE.

UNIONs

Unlike the other complex queries, UNION is actually a clause on the SELECT statement. A UNION combines information from two or more independent SELECT statements into a single result. Most often, you use a UNION when you need to combine information from unrelated tables.

The UNION clause has an optional keyword, ALL. Unlike the SELECT statement, the UNION assumes that you want the result to contain DISTINCT records—that is, no duplicates. UNIONs therefore perform a DISTINCT operation implicitly. If you want to speed up the UNION, you can use the ALL keyword, which stops the UNION from checking for duplicate records.

Why does the UNION default to DISTINCT? Because of the nature of its operation. When you combine the results from two nonrelated tables, information about the same entity is likely to exist in both tables. For example, if you try to get information about orders, parts, and manufacturers, you would expect to find references to a specific part in all the tables. To eliminate this duplication, you need the DISTINCT.

Like the DISTINCT in the standard SQL fields list, UNIONs slow down when the DISTINCT is assumed. Therefore, if you are sure, based on your knowledge of the application and tables, that there are few or no duplications, the ALL keyword can decrease the execution time.

To run successfully, UNIONs, like subqueries, have rules that you must follow:

- UNIONs may exist only in outer queries; you cannot use them to combine the results of subqueries.

- UNIONed SELECT fields lists must have the same number of fields, datatypes, and characteristics (width and precision), because the SQL must combine the results from all the UNIONed SELECTs into a single result table.

  To accomplish this, SQL uses the fields list from the first SELECT statement as the structure for the result table. If fields are required in the results from subsequent SELECTs, they must be represented in the first SELECT's field list.

The same holds true for subsequent SELECT fields lists. If a field in the first fields list is not in the tables of a following SELECT, the field must still be represented in the fields list of that SELECT.

For example, suppose we have a company with two separate divisions. One division sells car repair services and the other gasoline. Each division has its own order entry table but a shared payments received table. Each wants to send a unified statement to clients who have purchased both gasoline and services. To achieve this, we need to combine the information from the two order entry tables.

Before creating the actual UNION, we will get a list of customers with nonzero balances and the current billing cycle date:

```
SELECT cu_custid,ml_number,ml_baldue ;
FROM excust,exmail ;
WHERE ml_number = cu_number ;
AND ml_baldue <> 0 ;
INTO TABLE idowe
IF !USED("exsyst")
  USE exsyst IN SELECT(1) AGAIN
      ENDIF
mdate = exsyst.sy_billdte
```

Now that we have a list of customers requiring statements, we are ready to use this list as part of the main query:

```
SELECT ml_number AS number, ml_baldue AS baldue,;
    ga_galdel AS gals,ga_deldate AS date,ga_cost AS cost,;
    ga_invoice AS invoice,SPACE(7) AS type,00000.00 AS amount ;
    FROM idowe,exgas ;
    WHERE ga_custid = cu_custid ;
    AND ga_deldate <= mdate ;
    UNION ;
    SELECT ml_number,00000.00,0000.0,py__date,;
      00000.00,SPACE(5),py_type,py_amount ;
      FROM idowe,expay ;
      WHERE py_custid = cu_custid ;
      AND py_date <= mdate ;
    UNION ;
    SELECT ml_number,00000.00,0000.0,sv_date,SUM(sv_cost),;
      sv_invoice,sv_type+SPACE(5),00000.00 ;
      FROM idowe,exsvc ;
      WHERE sv_custid = cu_custid ;
      AND sv_date <= mdate ;
      GROUP BY 6 ;
      ORDER BY 1,6 ;
      INTO CURSOR temp
```

This query includes several points of interest. First, notice that the first SELECT contains several *placeholders*. Placeholders are representations of what the field would contain if such a field existed in the result from this one SELECT in the UNION. For example, neither of the tables in the first SELECT contain a "type" or "amount" field. However, other SELECTs in the UNION do. To allow for this, we create a character placeholder (such as SPACE(7)) and a numeric placeholder (such as 00000.00).

Also, if you look at the last SELECT, you can see that even when a matching field (such as sv_type) does exist, you still need to match the length of the field as defined in the first SELECT. In this case, the type field was defined as being seven characters wide. Because the service type field is only two characters wide, you need to pad the result with five spaces (as in sv_type+SPACE(5)).

While we are on the topic of placeholders, let's discuss some of the issues involved with numeric values and memos.

Numeric Placeholders

Numeric placeholders must match the width and precision of the largest underlying value. For instance, if two different numeric values will be placed in this field in the result, and one is five characters wide with two decimal places (as in 99.99) and the other is seven characters wide, with two decimal places (as in 9999.99), the placeholder has to be seven characters wide with two decimal places (as in 0000.00). If the placeholder is smaller than the value placed within it, the value will be truncated to match.

If the first SELECT uses a FoxPro function that produces a numeric result (such as SUM(field1)), the resulting table is automatically constructed with a 10 position field. Because there is no underlying field with a structure that can be used to determine the numeric width and precision, FoxPro uses the default for a numeric value when creating a table. This happens to be a width of 10 and no decimal places. To shorten this figure, you have to create in the first SELECT a placeholder that is smaller than this default and still large enough to hold the largest possible value (for example, 00000.00).

Memo Fields

Memo fields also require special handling, because they are special constructs that do not necessarily exist in other database languages. As such, memo fields do not have a data "type," such as character, numeric, date, or even logical. In fact, the memo "type" is merely a pointer stored in the header of the table to locate the information in the associated memo file (.FPT).

Therefore, there is no simple construct for emulating a memo field. However, Jerry Ela offers this clever work-around:

1. Create a SQL CREATE CURSOR file that contains a single field with a memo data type:

   ```
   CREATE CURSOR memohold (Memofld M)
   ```

2. Include this cursor in the first SELECT in the UNION, as follows:

   ```
   SELECT field1,field2,memofld ;
   FROM table1,memohold ;
   WHERE field3 = mycondition ;
   UNION ;
   SELECT field1,field2,fldmemo ;
   FROM table2 ;
   INTO CURSOR tempsql
   ```

This query allows the memo field contents from the second SELECT to be included in the result, even though the first SELECT table does not actually have a matching memo field. The cursor's memo field acts as a placeholder.

 Caution: Notice that we have not specified a join condition between the MEMOHOLD cursor and the TABLE1 table. Therefore, SQL SELECT tries to create a Cartesian product whereby it joins all the records in TABLE1 with all the records in the cursor, MEMOHOLD. Fortunately, there are no records in the cursor, so there is no problem. However, make sure that you never populate the placeholding cursor; otherwise your query is affected by the Cartesian product.

Following are a few more restrictions on the use of UNIONs:

- The ORDER BY and INTO/TO clauses affect the entire result rather than any individual SELECT in the UNION, and can therefore appear only in the final SELECT statement.

- GROUP BY and HAVING clauses are applied to the intermediate table that is used to filter the rows *before* they are moved into the result. Therefore, these clauses may appear in any or all of the SELECTs within the UNION.

 Tip: A final note on UNIONs. Because the UNION is a clause and not a subquery technique, all the SELECTs are considered to be a single SQL statement. An improperly constructed SELECT can therefore be very difficult to debug. A suggestion is to run each of the SELECTs individually, even if the result is meaningless, before placing them together in the UNION.

continues

continued

If you have a UNION with many SELECTs, add each SELECT one at a time and test the entire UNION rather than adding all the SELECTs at one time. This gives you a chance to find errors in UNIONing the various SELECTs without having to attempt to determine, *after* you have them all joined together, which SELECTs don't match.

Outer-Joins

SQL makes the following assumption about the nature of related tables: Every parent will have a child. In fact, when joining tables together, SQL goes from the child side to the parent. If the parent has no children, SQL simply ignores the parent.

For example, suppose we want a list of all clients and, if they have any projects, the projects names as well. This seems like a fairly simple query:

```
SELECT cl_company,pj_name ;
FROM tsclient,tsproj ;
WHERE pj_clid = cl_clid ;
AND cl_company <> "" ;
AND NOT DELETED() ;
INTO CURSOR temp
```

However, if the client does not have a project, SQL simply ignores the parent record, and clients without projects therefore do not appear in the result.

Most commercial SQL products get around this problem by including the capability to include a mathematical *null*. A null is an indicator that denotes a lack of a match in a related table. SQL products that allow for nulls also provide functions that let you test for the existence of the null on one or both sides of the join.

The FoxPro implementation of SQL does not provide for a null concept. To work around this problem, we need to construct a UNION consisting of two SELECTs. The first SELECT gets all parents with children:

```
SELECT cl_company,pj_name ;
FROM tsclient,tsproj ;
WHERE pj_clid = cl_clid ;
AND cl_company <> " " ;
UNION ALL ;
```

The second SELECT gets all the parents without children:

```
SELECT cl_company,SPACE(30) ;
FROM tsclient ;
WHERE cl_company <> "" ;
AND cl_clid NOT IN(SELECT DISTINCT pj_clid ;
                FROM tsproj)
```

The UNION ALL puts the two result sets together, providing a composite list of all clients and their projects, if any.

Additional SQL Notes

A final note or two of general SQL interest:

First, SQL matches empty records when tables are joined, creating a mini-Cartesian product. You need to be aware of this and use the EMPTY() function or an expression like "field<>SPACE(len(field))" to guard against empty records in the result.

Second, SQL obeys the setting of DELETED. If DELETED is SET ON, SQL does not include any deleted records in the result. However, if DELETED is SET OFF (the default), SQL includes any deleted records that match the search criteria.

Third, and finally, you can use the "really equals" evaluator (= =) to control whether strings must match exactly or whether shorter strings (such as "Micro") match longer strings (such as "Micro Endeavors").

The = = operator dictates that the strings used in both sides of the evaluator match character for character. The = = operator is not Rushmore-optimizable, however, and substantially reduces performance. If you need to ensure that only exact matches are found, pad the shorter string with spaces, as follows:

```
mvar="MICRO"
mvar=PADR(mvar,LEN(tsclient.cl_company))
SELECT * FROM tsclient WHERE cl_company=mvar
```

 Note: In FoxPro versions 2.5a and later, the == operator will be Rushmore-optimizable.

A Final Word

The SQL SELECT command has changed forever the way in which FoxPro programmers write reports, present query results, and calculate statistics. What once required many commands to SET RELATION, SCAN FOR, SEEK, and SKIP through records now can be accomplished with a single command. Add a thorough mastery of the SQL SELECT command to your arsenal, and watch your development time decrease, at the same time the performance of your applications increases!

The Report Writer

When I originally plotted the course for this book, I did not intend to include a specific chapter on the Report Writer. "After all," I thought, "several books are available that explain how to place objects in the different bands of a report. In addition, the developers who will read this book will be more than capable of figuring out how to use the Report Writer without assistance."

A brief survey of friends, students, and colleagues, however, indicated a different approach. Many suggested that a brief treatise on the concepts and applications of the Report Writer was in order. Others suggested the inclusion of a "tips and traps" chapter.

So, I asked **Melissa Dunn** to distill into a small chapter for the book some of the most important concepts, tips, and traps she found while creating the Micro Endeavors FoxPro 2.5 training materials. I also asked **Bruce Troutman** to include a brief discussion of his favorite mail merge report.

The result is the following chapter that explains as concisely as possible the underlying principles, and exposes the advanced capabilities, of the FoxPro Report Writer. By the way, those of you who would like a more detailed look at the Report Writer will want to read Lisa Slater's and Steve Arnott's excellent books, *Using FoxPro 2.5*, Special Edition, and *Using FoxPro for Windows*, Special Edition, also from Que.

Starting the Report Writer

We can access the Report Writer in one of three ways:

`CREATE REPORT <reportname>`

or

`MODIFY REPORT <reportname>`

or

`MODIFY REPORT ?`

The `CREATE REPORT <reportname>` always calls an empty report form. If `SAFETY` is `SET OFF`, the `CREATE REPORT <reportname>` command automatically overwrites an existing report of the same name. For this reason, I prefer to use the `MODIFY REPORT <reportname>` command. If a report already exists by the specified name (for example, TSCSTLST.FRX), FoxPro opens the Report Writer with the contents of that report table. If there is no matching report, FoxPro opens an empty report form.

Understanding Objects

We use the FoxPro Report Writer by placing *objects* in *bands* (bands are described shortly). The six types of objects described in Table 11.1 are available in the Report Writer, and each is represented on the tool bar on the left side of the Report Writer screen.

Table 11.1. Text objects available in the Report Writer.

Icon	Purpose
A	Text
ab	Fields, calculations, user-defined functions, and in-line code
+	Straight lines
□	Squares and rectangles

Icon	Purpose
	Rounded Rectangles
	Pictures

Creating Objects

To place fields, lines, boxes, and pictures in a report, you need only click the tool bar icon of your choice and then click and drag an appropriately sized box onto the report form. FoxPro fills the box with an object of the type you selected. You create text objects by clicking the text tool bar icon, clicking an appropriate spot on the report, and typing the required text.

Moving and Resizing Objects

You can resize any object except text. To resize an object you must first select the object by clicking it. Then position the cursor on the appropriate *handle* (a small, darkened square appearing along the dotted outline) and drag. The shape and size of the object will follow the direction of the handle.

Moving an object is as simple as select and drag.

Tip: The Windows Report Form consists of two grids: a ruler grid, which you can see, and an invisible grid onto which the objects "snap." When you move or resize an object, the invisible grid dictates the degree of change in the position or size. Because this grid is invisible, you may find that you cannot use the mouse to move or size an object exactly the way you want.

To achieve greater control (*micro-adjustment*), use the arrow keys to move the object by finer gradients, or press the Shift key and the appropriate arrow key to micro-adjust the size of an object.

Using the Selection Marquee

The *selection marquee* enables you to move several objects simultaneously. You create a marquee by first clicking an empty region of the report and then dragging the resultant marquee until it touches or surrounds all the objects to be selected.

When you release the mouse button, the objects will be temporarily grouped together. You can now drag these objects to a new location or use the Object menu to assign attributes to all selected objects. To release the objects from the temporary group, click an unoccupied portion of the report, or click an object that is not part of the temporary group.

 Tip: If the selection marquee touches any part of an object, the object is included in the group. The marquee does not have to completely surround the object.

Grouping Objects

Although the objects within a marquee appear to be grouped, they aren't. Attempting an activity such as centering all objects on the line results in a "pile up," as all the objects will center independently.

Before you can successfully perform an activity such as centering multiple objects, you must convert the marquee into a true group. You can achieve this by choosing the Group option of the Object menu. After you convert the marquee, you can choose the Object menu's Center option. All selected objects will now auto-center and keep their position relative to the other members of the group. When the centering is complete, you choose the Object menu's Ungroup option to restore the objects' independence.

Working with Text

FoxPro for Windows allows multiline text objects. In other words, pressing Enter continues the text object on the next line. To exit from a text object, select the pointer tool bar icon, or click another object or an empty space in the report.

Use the Object menu's Text Alignment option to control the appearance of multiline text objects.

Using the Object menu's Text Alignment option, you can justify text *flush left* (all lines starting at the same left-hand column), *flush right* (all lines starting at the same right-hand column), or you can *center* the text (each line in the text object centering automatically based on the size of the longest line of text). The spacing beween lines of multiline text objects can be changed from the default single space to $1^1/_2$ or double-spacing.

If you find that you need to change the contents of a text object, do not delete the object. Instead, choose the text icon from the tool bar. Position the I-bar at the appropriate position in the text object, click, and begin typing or erasing. When the change is complete, choose the pointer icon.

Understanding Bands

As I mentioned earlier, objects are placed in bands. As each band occurs in the report, the objects contained in the band are evaluated and printed. The Report Writer always reads the report form from left to right and from top to bottom. Therefore, the order in which the bands and objects appear is important.

The following sections describe the bands, in order from top to bottom.

The Title Band

The Title band prints once at beginning of the report. By default, the Title band prints at the top of the first page. Optionally, the New Page check box forces the band to print on a separate page that appears before the rest of the report.

The Page Header Band

The Page Header band is one of three default "startup" bands. (The other two are the Detail and Page Footer bands, described in later sections.) Objects placed within the Page Header band print once at the top of each page in the report.

The Column Header Band

Column Header bands are available only when the column spinner in the Page Layout dialog indicates more than the default single column. There are two types of columnar reports:

- *Snaked.* The extreme left column prints from the top to the bottom of the page, the next left column prints top to bottom, and so on. This columnar report type is the default.

- *Label.* The top row of information prints across all columns before proceeding to the next row.

The Group Header Band

Group Header bands appear for each data group that you designate by using the Report menu's Data Grouping option. You can identify up to 20 data groups. Objects located within the Group Header band are printed whenever the value of the group changes.

To take proper advantage of group breaks, however, you must ensure that the data presented to the Report Writer is in the same order as the group break expressions *before* the report begins. You can accomplish this by establishing a master index, by sorting or copying the database into the proper sequence, or by using a SQL SELECT command with an ORDER BY clause.

The Detail Band

Objects in the Detail band are printed once per record in the master table for the report.

The Group Footer Band

Because footer bands are evenly matched to header bands, there is one Group Footer band for each Group Header band. Objects located in the Group Footer band print when the next record in the master table contains a different group value.

The Column Footer Band

There is one Column Footer band for every Column Header band. Column Footer bands are available only when the column spinner in the Page Layout dialog indicates more than the default single column.

The Page Footer Band

Objects in the Page Footer band are printed at the bottom of each page in the report.

The Summary Band

Located with the Title band on the Report menu, Summary band objects print once at the end of the report. Although the Summary band defaults to printing on the bottom of the last report page, you can optionally print the Summary band on a separate page.

Sizing the Bands

Each of these bands is identified by a *band marker,* which goes across the entire report form. The area *above* the band marker belongs to the stated band.

If the amount of allocated space is incorrect, you can resize the band region by clicking and dragging the push button to the left of the band marker. When you release the mouse button, the band is resized accordingly. All bands located below the resized band are shifted as well.

Alternatively, you can double-click the push button and open the Band dialog. This dialog enables you to use a spinner to reallocate the band size.

Using the Quick Report Option

When no objects have been placed on the report form, the Quick Screen option of the Report pad can be used. The Quick Report option places all fields from the selected table on the form. The order of the fields on the form is the same as the order of the fields in the table structure.

If the combined width of the fields in the selected table exceeds the specified width of the report, the Report Writer shortens the field lengths to force all the fields on the form. To prevent this from happening, choose the Picture check box, which causes the Report Writer to place the objects vertically rather than horizontally (the default). After the objects are on the form, you can adjust their size and position according to your needs.

Creating a Simple Report

Let's start with a simple report that lists clients by state. In addition to the clients' names and addresses, we need to know the total number of clients and how many clients we have in each state.

Given the nature of the report, we know that the data must be in state order. Here is a simple solution:

```
SELECT tsclient
SET ORDER TO cl_state
MODIFY REPORT tsclnts
```

A common request for such a client listing report is to list two clients per line. We can satisfy this request by using the column spinner in Page Layout dialog to create quickly a two-column report form.

With the report form set for two columns, we use the **Quick Report** option to place all fields from the TSCLIENT database on the form. Because the combined sizes of the fields exceed the width of the established columns, we choose the vertical placement check box on the Quick Report dialog.

Changing the Format

After the objects are on the form, we can use the Object menu options to assign color, font, style, and justification attributes. We can also center objects by selecting the Center option of the Object menu.

Previewing the Report

We can preview the report, page by page, at any time by selecting the Page Preview option of the Report menu. Page Preview reveals that our report works but does not contain the state and grand totals required. Our next step, then, is to create calculated field objects.

Specifying Calculations

The Report Writer has capabilities that exceed the mere printing of static objects. One of these is the capability to calculate totals on the fly.

Creating totals requires us to take the following steps:

1. Create a field object in the appropriate band.

2. Include in this field object an expression to be calculated. (*Note:* This expression is evaluated once for every record in the master database. In other words, this expression is evaluated once for every Detail band that appears in the report.)

3. Choose the Calculate... check box of the Field dialog.

4. Select the type of total needed (for example, Sum, Count, or Average).

5. Identify the point at which the total should be reset to zero and the calculations begun again. The End Of Report and End Of Page options are always available. If the report has more than one column, there is an End Of Column reset option. Each assigned data group also has a reset option. (*Note:* The reset option defaults to the band in which the object resides.)

For our purposes, we are going to count the number of times that the client ID occurs. Therefore, our field expression is `cl_clid`, and our calculation type is `COUNT`. For fun, we will try placing this object in various bands in the report to see the effect band position has on calculated fields:

1. Let's start with the Detail band. When we bring up the Report Expression dialog and choose Calculate..., we establish the reset point as the End Of Report. This means that for each new record, the count for our created field is increased by one. Page Preview shows that placing the calculation in the Detail band produces a running total.

2. After making a copy of the report expression, we move the copy into the state Group Footer. In the Calculation dialog of the copy, we need to change the reset point to the end of the current group (for example, `cl_state`). Page Preview now shows that we have created a group subtotal by state.

3. Now we move a copy of the calculated field into the Column Footer, change the reset point, and choose Page Preview. We now have a column subtotal.

4. We place the report expression into the Page Footer, change the reset point to Page Footer, and then run Page Preview. The Report Writer now can give us running page totals.

5. Finally, by placing the calculated field into the Summary band with the correct reset point, we can calculate a grand total.

We now know that the Report Writer can generate running totals, group, column, and page subtotals, and a summary total.

Handling Groups

To specify group options, we use the Group Info dialog box shown in Figure 11.1. We can access the Group Info dialog in two ways: we can either go through the Report menu's Data Grouping option or double-click the push button associated with the Group Header band marker.

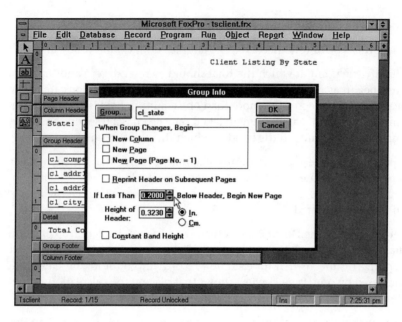

Figure 11.1. The Group Info dialog.

This dialog includes three options regarding paging and new Group Headers. The first option, New Column, starts the new group in a new column on the current page. The second option, New Page, starts the new group on a new page but continues with the next sequential page number. The third option, New Page (Page No. = 1), starts the new group on a new page and resets the page number to 1.

This last option gives your report a tailored, mini-report effect. In other words, each group is treated as if it were a separate report.

Changing Group Order

Because you can have as many as 20 nested groups, it is possible to add the groups in the wrong order. This means that Group Header and Group Footer bands may be out of order on the report form.

If you discover that you need to change the sequencing order of the groups to correct this placement, you do not have to delete the group. The Data Grouping dialog has mover bars located next to each group. All you have to do is click and drag the groups into the proper order. When you have completed this process, the Report Writer reorders the bands for you, complete with their contents.

Preventing Widows

A *widow* is a group heading that appears at the bottom of a page *without* any detail information.

To avoid widows, the document must start the group on the next page if there is not sufficient room to print any of the detail lines. Fortunately, the Report Writer's Group Info dialog includes a spinner control that enables the developer to designate how close to the bottom of a page a Group Header can print. FoxPro evaluates the If Less Than ... Below Header, Begin New Page value *before* printing the next Group Header. If there are fewer than the specified number of inches, or partial inches, left on the page, the current page is ejected and the Group Header is printed on the top of the next page.

Windows allows for the use of proportional fonts, so remember that you must take into account the pitch and size of the font(s) being used. For example, smaller fonts can mean more lines per page, leaving too much space at the bottom if you make the number bigger.

Preventing Orphans

Orphans exist when detail information is printed at the top of a page without a Group Header. Because it's difficult to determine to which group such a set of detail lines belongs, the data is considered "orphaned."

To avoid orphans, the Group Header must print at the top of the page even though the group started on a previous page. Like widows, orphans can be handled in the Group Info dialog. In fact, you need only check the Reprint Header box to direct FoxPro to reprint the Group Header whenever a new page is encountered.

Notice the spinner titled Height of Header. You can use this spinner to adjust the amount of room (inches or centimeters) used by the Group Header band. This option appears when you access the Group Info dialog by pressing the push button next to the Group Header band marker. This option is not available, however, when you access the Group Info dialog by using the Report menu. A similar dialog option also appears when you access the Group Info dialog by using the Group Footer band.

Suppressing Repeated Information

Typically, when we include a group, we also have information about that group which we want to print. For instance, the state field (`cl_state`) is printed with each client. However, if we have grouped the report by state, we usually only want the state field to print once per state group.

We can accomplish this in several ways:

- We can move the group information into the Group Header band. Now the state is printed only when the group changes (that is, whenever there is a new state).

- We can use the Print When dialog (described in the next section).

  By default, the Report Writer prints repeated values on each detail line, in the first band of a new page or column, and when the indicated group value changes. When you choose the No radio button, the check boxes in the Also Print region of the dialog are enabled.

- We can gain further control over when an expression is printed by using the Only When Expression is True... check box and putting the conditional expression into the traditional Expression Builder.

Using Print When for Conditional Formatting

We access the Print When dialog by activating the Print When check box in the Report Expression dialog. Figure 11.2 shows an example of this very important dialog.

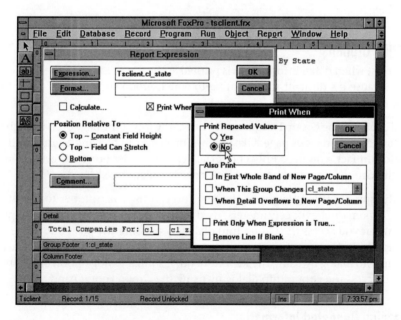

Figure 11.2. The Print When dialog.

Suppose that you are printing invoices and you want to use bold italics to draw attention to any outstanding invoice balance of over $10,000. First, you should create a balance field with normal attributes and direct FoxPro to print only this field WHEN balance<10000. Then, you should create a copy of the balance field and position it directly over the first balance field. Set the duplicate field's font style to Bold Italic and direct FoxPro to print it only WHEN balance>=10000.

The Remove Line If Blank check box suppresses the printing of field expressions that have no value. For example, if the second address line is blank, choosing this option moves any subsequent lines up one.

Note that if you want a line to be removed, all items in the line must be blank, and all items in the line must have the Remove Line if Blank option checked. In addition, you have to be careful how you line up your objects. If even one pixel from an object intrudes onto a line, FoxPro will not "close up" the line.

Finishing the Report

Enough digressions. To finish our client list we must create a field that we can COUNT in the Group Footer band (the number of clients per state) and in a Summary band (the total number of clients).

Finally, we could "dress up" the report by placing the state name in the Group Header so that it appears only once rather than with each client. We can also remove the second address line rather than having the Report Writer leave an empty line in the report.

Creating a Complex Report

Having completed a simple report, let's move on to one which is slightly more complex. For example, we want report that provides a detailed list of all hours, by employee and project, for each client.

Furthermore, we want three sets of figures. At the project level, we want the number of employees assigned and the total and average number of hours. For clients, we want the total number of projects, total and average hours. At the summary level, we want the total number of clients, and the total and average number of hours.

Getting the data for this report merely requires the use of a SQL SELECT:

```
SELECT cl_company,cl_clid,pj_projid,pj_desc,pj_name,;
  (ti_week+ti_day)-7 AS tidate,;
  ti_hours,ti_empid,em_first,;
  em_middle,em_last ;
  FROM tsclient,tsproj,tstime,tsempl ;
  WHERE pj_clid = cl_clid ;
  AND ti_projid = pj_projid ;
  AND em_empid = ti_empid ;
  ORDER BY cl_clid, pj_projid, ti_empid, tidate DESC ;
  INTO CURSOR temp
```

Notice that this query includes a "calculated" field, `((ti_week+ti_day)-7)`, which creates a field containing the date the hours were worked. We subsequently order the result table in descending date order. When the query is completed, the records will be in order by the client, project, employee, and descending date of work.

However, both the total counts (employees, clients, and projects) and the averages (hours for employees, clients, and projects) present a problem.

The Report Writer has only a single Detail band that prints each time a new time sheet record is encountered. Although we can suppress the multiple printing of the employee, project, and client information by using either the Group band or the Suppress field dialog option, internally FoxPro still encounters these fields on each Detail band.

Therefore, if we try to calculate a count on the employee ID, for example, we still end up with the number of hours, *not* the number of employees. As for the average number of hours, if we use the CALCULATE average, the Report Writer gives us the average number of hours based on the total days worked.

We need some way to count the middle "many" (employees, projects, and clients) in our multitable report. After we can count the number required, we can divide the sum of all hours by this count and have the average.

To get the counts we must use an embedded UDF, and we can calculate the averages by using report variables.

Specifying Report Variables

Located under the Report menu, *report variables* are standard FoxPro memory variables that are created and used in the report as it is printed. The created report variables appear in the Memory Variables list in the Expression Builder and can be used as fields or as parts of field expressions.

Figure 11.3 shows the Report Variables dialog. Notice that mover bars are associated with each of the variables. The reason for this association is fairly simple: FoxPro updates or evaluates report variables according to their placement within the Variables list. If the placement of the related variables is incorrect, the value of the variable can be wrong.

For example, suppose we have a variable, `avgbal`, that is the result of two other variables (`sumbal`, which is the sum of all line item extended prices, and `kcount`, which is the number of invoices). We created the `avgbal` variable before we created `sumbal`. Unfortunately, the value stored in `avgbal` will always be short one line item extended price, because the average is computed *before* the line item sum is updated.

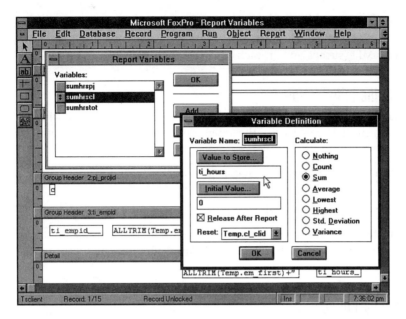

Figure 11.3. The Report Variables and Variable Definition dialogs.

Therefore, we should carefully think through the relationships (if any) among the variables before declaring them in the Variables list. However, if we find that the values are incorrect because of the variables' placement in the Variables list, we simply can use the mover bars to correct the update order.

Our report needs three "count" variables: employees on projects (cntpj), projects for clients (cntcl), and clients (cnttot). We also need three "sum" variables for the total number of hours for each group (sumhrspj, sumhrscl, and sumhrstot).

After we choose to add a report variable, we need to define it. We accomplish this by using the Variable Definition dialog, which also appears in Figure 11.3.

We can use the Variable Definition dialog to give the variable a reference ID (Variable Name), an update value (Value to Store...), and an initial value (Initial Value...). We also use this dialog to specify what type of calculation, if any, we want the Report Writer to perform (Calculate) and at what point in the report we want the value to be reset to the initial value and the calculation to begin again (Reset).

Specifying the Value To Store

The Value to Store... tells FoxPro what to evaluate each pass through the Detail band. We can enter the Value to Store... either by typing in the text box or by choosing the push button to access the Expression Builder.

225

In our report, for example, we have three report variables: the sum of hours for each project (`sumhrspj`), the sum of hours for each client (`sumhrscl`), and the total number of hours for MEI (`sumhrstot`). In each case, the Value to Store... is `ti_hours`.

Indicating the Initial Value

The Initial Value... is the value before any calculations are performed. As with the Value to Store..., the Initial Value... can either be entered directly into the text box or through the Expression Builder.

All the variables in our report use zero as the initial value.

Selecting a Variable Calculation

The Calculate box enables us to specify a calculation to be performed on the variable. Because each of our report variables is actually just a subtotal, we choose the Sum radio button.

Releasing Variables

By default, report variables are released from memory as soon as the report form has completed. If you unselect Release After Report, you can use report variables after printing the report.

Setting the Reset Points

The last of the areas in the Variable Definition dialog is a popup containing a list of possible reset points. These reset points behave in exactly the same manner as the reset points in the Field Calculate dialog.

You can always set the variable's value back to its initial state at the End Of Page and End Of Report. Optionally, you can reset the value whenever a Group changes (if any groups exist) or, if there are columns, when a column ends.

Each of our report's variables has a different reset point. The sum of hours for the project (`sumhrspj`) resets whenever the project ID changes. The sum of hours for the client (`sumhrscl`) resets whenever the client ID changes. Finally, the total number of hours for the report resets at the End Of Report.

The purpose of this exercise, however, is not to create subtotals (we can use the Calculate option of the Field dialog to do that), but averages. Where then are the averages?

The averages are computed in the appropriate Group Footers. For instance, suppose we place the following field in the project Group Footer:

```
sumhrspj/cntpj
```

When the Report Writer encounters this field, it executes the calculation and writes the average to the form. We will place similar calculated fields in all the appropriate Group Footers and the Summary band.

Embedding UDFs

Notice that I haven't said anything about the counter variables, cntpj, cntcl, and cnttot. We are going to use a UDF not only to determine when the value of the counters should be incremented, but also when they should be set back to zero. The initialization of the variables (cntpj = 0) occurs in the report control program (TSRPTIME.PRG). Figure 11.4 shows how to embed a UDF in a report.

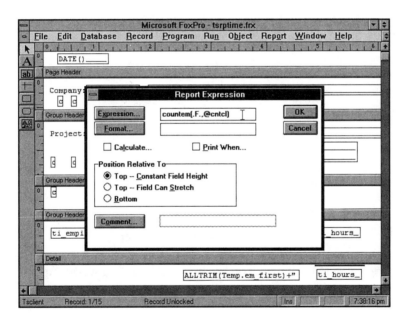

Figure 11.4. Embedding a UDF in a report.

Even though we have set the report variables, the report still won't work properly, because the Report Writer doesn't know how and when to update the value of the counters.

To update the counters, we are going to use a simple user-defined function called countem:

```
* countem.prg
* p_reset=.t. to reset, or false not to reset
* p_var = variable, passed by reference
```

continues

```
PARAMETERS p_reset,p_var
IF p_reset
  p_var=0
ELSE
  p_var=p_var+1
ENDIF
RETURN " "
```

The countem function is designed to receive two parameters: the indicator for handling the value of the counter, and the counter.

If we pass countem() a .T. (as in countem(.T.,@cntcl)), the value of the counter increases by one. If countem() receives an .F., the value is reset to zero.

Finally, the UDF return value is what the Report Writer will print. In the case of countem(), the return value is a null space, so the Report Writer doesn't print anything.

Placing the UDF onto the report form is easy. The general rule is that any report object that is not text, a line (box or rounded rectangle), or a picture must be a field. Therefore, we use the field icon and call the function in the Expression text area:

```
COUNTEM(.T.,@cntcl)
```

Placing the Calls

Now that we know how to update the value of the counters, we have to decide when the calls should be made. Putting the calls in the proper place on the report form requires a bit of knowledge about how the Report Writer operates.

The Report Writer executes, or prints, the objects on the report form, starting at the upper-left and going to the lower-right, line by line. Within a line, the Report Writer goes from left to right. For the UDF call, this means that we must be sure to place the counter and reset in the proper spot in the proper band.

Most often, you will want to place calls to UDFs like countem in the Group Header. We use the header rather than the footer to avoid accidentally setting the value up by one or back to zero too soon.

For example, if we set cntcl back to zero in the client Group Footer, we have to be very careful that the reset doesn't occur *before* the average calculation field. If we reset the value at the wrong point, we get a "division by zero" error because cntcl was zero when the average (sumhrscl/cntcl) was calculated.

For this reason, we use the Group Headers instead. In our report, we will need to have several of the headers do double duty.

For example, the client Group Header will have to reset the value of the client counter (countem(.F.,@cntcl)) for use in the client Group Footer. On the other hand, the total report counter will have to increment with each new client (countem(.T.,@cnttot)).

The project Group Header will reset the project counter and increment the client counter.

Finally, the employee Group Header, which we haven't used at all so far, will host the call to increment the project counter.

Creating Form Letters and Labels

Our next report example creates form letters and matching mailing labels. Because we want to be able to use a variety of letters in our form letter program, we create the database TSLTR.DBF. Here is the structure for TSLTR.DBF:

```
Structure for table:     f:\george\bruce\tsltr.dbf
Number of data records: 1
Date of last update:     02/27/93
Memo file block size:   64
Field  Field Name  Type       Width    Dec    Index
    1  LT_ID       Character     10
    2  LT_CONTENT  Memo          10
** Total **                      21
```

Here is the content of a sample lt_content memo field:

```
Micro Endeavors would like to congratulate you, <<FNAME>>
for your continued good service to our customers.
Since <<EMPMONTH>>, <<EMPYEAR>> we have been lucky
to have you on our team.

Please accept our best wishes for your continued
success in <<CITY>>.

Sincerely,



<<BOSS>>
```

At runtime, this report replaces the names surrounded by <<>> with strings from the employee database and memory variables. Here is the code for the controlling report program:

```
* tsltr.prg
* Mail merge program
CLOSE DATA
USE tsltr IN SELE(1)
SELECT * FROM tsempl ;
  ORDER BY em_zip,em_last ;
  INTO CURSOR temp
boss="FRED FOX"
REPORT FORM tsltr PREVIEW
use in temp


FUNCTION merge
* Store the content of the tsltr.lt_content memo field
* to the m.contents memvar. While we're at it,
* use STRTRAN() to replace the string <<FNAME>>
* with the content of the em_first field.
m.contents=STRTRAN(tsltr.lt_content,"<<FNAME>>",;
  ALLTRIM(em_first))
* Replace the string <<EMPMONTH>> with the content
* of the CMONTH() value of the em_empdate field.
m.contents=STRTRAN(m.contents,"<<EMPMONTH>>",;
  CMONTH(em_empdate))
m.contents=STRTRAN(m.contents,"<<EMPYEAR>>",;
  STR(YEAR(em_empdate),4))
m.contents=STRTRAN(m.contents,"<<CITY>>",ALLTRIM(em_city))
m.contents=STRTRAN(m.contents,"<<BOSS>>",m.boss)
RETURN m.contents
```

The report, shown in Figure 11.5, is very simple. Notice that the Data Grouping in the TSLTR report is on RECNO(). When we direct FoxPro to begin each group on a New Page, the result will be one form letter per employee (see Figure 11.6).

After the letters are printed, we need to generate supporting mailing labels. In FoxPro 2.5 for Windows, you create mailing labels in the Report Writer. When you issue the MODIFY LABEL command, FoxPro displays a pick list of available preformatted reports. After you select one of these, FoxPro sends you to the Report Writer.

For this exercise, we will simply copy the address information from the TSLTR.FRX report layout onto another report form. In page layout, we will choose three columns and then resize the fields as necessary. Figure 11.7 shows the result.

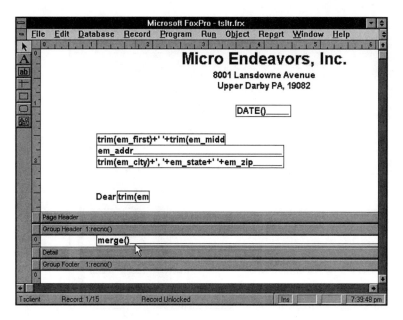

Figure 11.5. The form letter report layout.

Figure 11.6. The form letter page preview.

231

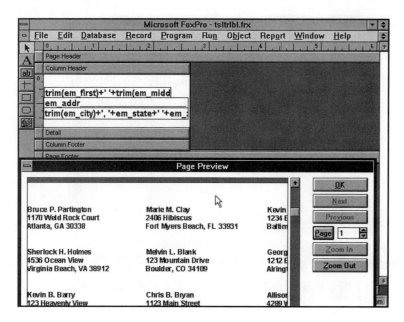

Figure 11.7. Mailing label page preview.

Windows Considerations

You can create all the reports discussed so far, except the columnar report, in either DOS or Windows. Whether created with DOS or Windows, the reports have the same functionality. The next report contains elements that you cannot transport into DOS (see Chapter 21, "Cross-Platform Issues," for more information on how the Transporter handles reports).

Picture Objects

The picture icon on the tool bar creates a report form picture object. This picture can come from either a bitmap (.BMP) file or a general field. What is displayed on the screen form is the size of the picture frame. Figure 11.8 shows a finished brochure as seen in Page Preview.

Where on the report form should you place pictures? The answer depends on what each picture represents. As a rule, if the picture comes from a general field that changes as the record changes, you should put the picture object into the Detail band. If the picture comes from a file, such as a company logo, you should place it in the Page Header band.

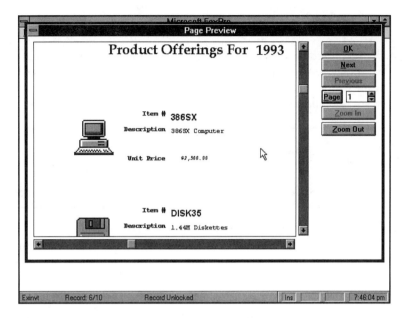

Figure 11.8. Pictures in reports.

General fields can contain a variety of images, which means that all the images in the same report might not be the same size as the picture frame into which the general field is placed. Because of this, the Report Writer provides three sizing options for picture objects: Clip Picture, Scale Picture-Retain Shape, and Scale Picture-Fill the Frame.

With Clip Picture, the image retains its original size. The image begins in the upper-left corner and is painted until the frame is filled. The remainder of the image is clipped. To solve this problem, you can use the original design tool (Paintbrush, for example) to copy the desired part of the image into another file and then insert the new file into the general field or directly onto the form.

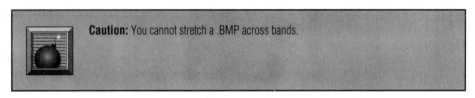

Caution: You cannot stretch a .BMP across bands.

With Scale, you can either Retain Shape, which protects your picture from vertical or horizontal distortion, or Fill the Frame, which can cause visual distortion. The severity of the distortion depends on the degree of scaling: The larger and wider you scale the image from its original proportions, the worse the distortion.

Fonts

The Report Writer provides two types of font controls. One is the Font push button in the Page Layout dialog. You can use this button to access the Windows Select Font dialog. The font you select in this dialog acts as the global default font for all new objects placed in the report form.

 Note: Existing objects are not changed by changing the global report font default.

The second font control mechanism is object-specific. You can select any object and then use the Font option from the Object menu to assign object specific fonts and styles. You can change the font for a group of objects by using the selection marquee to group the objects. The Font option you select from the Option menu then applies to all selected objects.

Another problem with fonts and reports is that the way characters appear on-screen may not be the way they appear when printed. You must rely heavily upon the Page Preview in order to get a better idea of what the finished report will look like.

To correct the appearance of the printed version, you sometimes have to place some objects "over" others. For example, Figure 11.8 shows the finished brochure as seen in Page Preview. Figure 11.9 shows what the report form looks like.

Notice that the current year field in the Page Header appears to overlap the heading text. This problem is not uncommon when you use proportional fonts. To adjust the heading and the field until they are properly spaced on the printed report, we have to rely on the Page Preview mechanism.

Printing the Report

We have now designed several different types of reports, some of which contain Windows-specific elements. The only remaining question is how to print what we have designed.

You run reports by using the REPORT FORM command, which has the following options:

- TO PRINT directs output to the current print device.

- PROMPT is available only for the Windows version of the product. When placed directly after the PRINTER keyword, PROMPT accesses the Windows Printer Setup Dialog. Within this dialog, the user can adjust the printer settings. Thereafter, the Windows Print Manager handles the printer drivers and setups.

- TO FILE directs output to the specified file name. If you use the ADDITIVE keyword, the original contents of the specified file are added to rather than replaced by the new information.

- OFF prevents output from being echoed to the screen while being printed.

- SUMMARY generates reports that suppress the printing of the Detail band. In other words, only header, footers, Title, and Summary bands are printed.

- HEADING adds an additional line to the page header.

- PREVIEW enables the user to access the Page Preview function from the Report Writer.

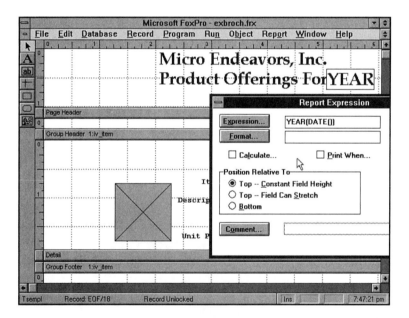

Figure 11.9. Be careful with fonts in the Report Writer.

Although the Windows product offers a Page Preview that you can move forward and backward through the contents of the resulting report, the DOS product has no such feature.

The Page Preview in the DOS product enables you to view the report only in a downward direction. If you go past the point of interest on the report, you have to generate the entire report before the Preview option takes control.

To avoid this problem in DOS, you can send reports to a file, and then review the file on-line by using the MODIFY FILE <name> NOMODIFY command.

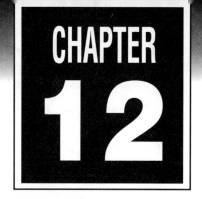

The BROWSE Command

FoxPro's BROWSE command is so important to the language that it plays a central role in Chapter 5 ("Employees and Projects"), Chapter 6 ("Time Sheets"), Chapter 7 ("Updating Time Sheets"), Chapter 8 ("Time Sheet Reporting"), and Chapter 20 ("A Data Dictionary"). Therefore, you might wonder why I chose to include a separate chapter focusing on the BROWSE command.

I asked **Dr. Mike Brachman** to write this chapter to ensure that this book covers all the BROWSE command's most important options. Some of the topics may be covered elsewhere in the book, and some of the ideas provide alternatives to solutions offered elsewhere in the book.

However, this chapter introduces plenty of new ideas, and even the old ones get a fresh treatment from Mike and from **Rich Wolf**, who also contributed to this chapter.

Introducing the *BROWSE* Command

The BROWSE command is the single most complex command in all of FoxPro. The command includes over 35 clauses, and the help screen for BROWSE is the longest help screen available. BROWSE is so powerful that you can write many small applications by using it alone. By the end of this chapter, you should have a feel for the power of BROWSE and consider using it in your programs.

We use the BROWSE command for data presentation, pick lists, and data entry. You can put a Browse window where you want, with the fields you want, and have it allow or disallow changes as required. Everything in BROWSE is programmable.

As the following example of a single BROWSE demonstrates, the command can get very complex:

```
BROWSE FIELDS ;
      checkem:1:H=" ", ;
      cbinvs.in_name:23:H="Investor", ;
      ci_name:20:H="Contact Name":W=.F., ;
      ci_phone:17:H="Phone":R, ;
      x=UPPER(cbinvs.in_slsp):H="Salesperson" ;
      WINDOW invwind ;
      TITLE "Investors And Contacts Who Have Received Reports" ;
      NOAPPEND NODELETE NOMODIFY ;
      WHEN chkoffx4() ;
      VALID:F chkonx4() ;
      FREEZE checkem ;
      NOWAIT
```

We typically use multiple lines to define the BROWSE command. Because each field is individually programmable, we usually put each on its own line. The easiest way to develop a BROWSE command is by using the Command window. By using the command-line continuation character (;) in the Command window, you can develop your BROWSE command interactively and then paste it into your program when you are finished.

You can turn the BROWSE command on its side and present the fields vertically. This is the EDIT face, which you can invoke directly by substituting the keyword EDIT for the word BROWSE. All the other clauses are the same. Although the rest of this chapter focuses on the BROWSE command, keep in mind that all the information also applies to the EDIT command, because it is actually the same command as the BROWSE.

Putting the *BROWSE* in a Window

If you simply issued a BROWSE command, it might or might not look the way you intended. BROWSE normally creates a window in the upper-left corner of the desktop, displays all fields using the field names as column titles, and uses the alias name of the current work area as the Browse window's title.

Note: If you invoke a BROWSE command without a WINDOW clause and have defined and activated a window, the resulting Browse window takes on the appearance of that window.

Within a program, you probably should not let FoxPro decide these things. You should decide where the Browse appears, the heading at the top of each of the columns, and even the title of the Browse. Programming the appearance of a Browse is an entire language in itself.

The first thing to do is to gain control of where the Browse window appears and how it looks. You should DEFINE a window by describing the size, placement, and title you want. If you are using FoxPro for DOS, you also should specify which color scheme you want (typically SCHEME 10) and whether you want a shadow. Do not activate the window, however.

When FoxPro sees a WINDOW clause in a BROWSE command, it automatically creates a new copy of the named window. If you activate the window first, you get two copies of the window and must deactivate the extra copy. It is far simpler to let BROWSE activate its own copy and then remove the copy when it is done. In either case, you must RELEASE the DEFINEd window to return the memory used by the DEFINEd window back to the memory pool.

As the preceding example shows, the BROWSE FIELDS clause is followed by a field list. Each field can be programmed individually. Options applied to fields are listed after the field name and separated by a colon or a forward slash. Don't use the forward slash, because it can become ambiguous later when you create calculated fields.

If you use the Micro Endeavors conventions for field names (see Chapter 9, "Micro Endeavors Naming Conventions"), the first thing you should do is supply a heading for each column. 'Date of birth' is certainly easier to decipher than ex_dob. To change the heading of a column, use the option :H= followed by the title.

If the title is shorter than the column width, FoxPro for Windows centers the title for you. If the title is longer than the column width, the column width expands to contain the entire title. You can override FoxPro's choice of width by using the :## option; that is, a colon followed by a number. This option tells FoxPro to make the column the width indicated by the number following the colon, regardless of the length of title or field. If you choose a length that is smaller than the title, the title is cut off, as are the contents of any field that is wider than you specify in the option.

If you let FoxPro automatically size your fields, your choice of font makes a difference. FoxPro automatically sizes the column to whichever is wider—the title or the field. With a fixed-width font such as Courier or FoxFont, this isn't a problem. With a proportional font, such as Arial or MS Serif, the contents of the first record determine the width of the field. If your title is short and the first record contains many blanks or thin characters, FoxPro may choose a width that is too narrow for subsequent records. If this happens, you should either switch to a fixed-width font or use the `:##` option to size the column yourself.

BROWSE Field Formatting

After you select a heading and a width, you probably will want to apply some formatting to some of the fields. The `:P=` option enables you to create a formatting string similar to that used in a SAY or GET field. You can apply almost any PICTURE function. The following are the most common PICTURE functions:

@!	Uppercase only
@R	Non-template characters (area code, Social Security number, ZIP+4, and so on)
@$	Currency
@L	Lead zero fill
@Z	Zero blanking
@B,I,J	Left- or right-justify, or center

Normally, character strings, dates, and logicals are left-justified and numbers are right-justified.

The standard, character-level PICTURE codes apply here as well. Most often, we use number formatting and the Y code to convert a logical T/F to Y/N. The `'@R'` function also requires a character string and is quite useful for Social Security numbers, telephone numbers, ZIP codes, and so on.

BROWSE Validation

You must decide whether you want to allow data entry within the Browse window. To support your decision, FoxPro provides the following BROWSE command options:

- The `:R` field clause renders a field read-only.
- The BROWSE NOMODIFY clause prevents changes to any field in any record in the Browse window.
- The FREEZE clause locks the user into a single column of the Browse.

Note: Unlike FoxPro for DOS, the default behavior for FoxPro for Windows BROWSE command is to select a field on entry, so that even a single keystroke replaces the field's contents. To achieve similar behavior using FoxPro for DOS, you must include the `:P="@K"` picture clause field argument.

Each field has its own WHEN and VALID as well. The :W= option determines whether the cursor is even allowed into the field. The option :W=.F. causes the cursor to jump over a particular field. The expression supplied to the :W and :F arguments can be a UDF.

The :V= option is a field-level VALID. If the expression supplied returns logical False, you cannot leave the field unless you press Esc. If you press Esc, the field reverts to its previous value and you can leave regardless of what the :V= expression returns.

To validate data, the '@M' selector works perfectly well as part of a :P= option. The '@M' selector enables the user to select from a preset number of choices by pressing the space bar to cycle through the choices. The use of "@M" selector in READs has fallen out of vogue since FoxPro 2.0 introduced radio buttons and popups for mutually exclusive choices, but the selector is still quite useful in a Browse. Users can't make mistakes in data entry if they can choose only from valid options.

The :V= expression is evaluated only if the field is altered. If you must force the validation routine to be executed regardless of whether a change is made, then add the :F option after the :V= expression. If the user enters data that causes the validation expression to return a logical False, the message Invalid Input is displayed in the upper-right corner of the screen if the status bar is not activated, or in the status bar if it is activated. If you want your own error message to appear, use the :E= option to supply an alternative character string.

A slightly less flexible form of validation uses the :B= option to restrict input to a certain range. As with the :V= option, the range is not evaluated unless a change is made. You can force a range check by applying the :F option after the range.

Here is an example of a BROWSE command that includes all these clauses:

```
BROWSE FIELDS ;
    ix_field1:H="Title of field 1":12, ;
    ix_field2:W=fwhen():V=fvalid():F;
    :E="Wrong Thinking Is Punished", ;
    ix_field3:B=12000,24000:F:P="@$ 999,999", ;
    ix_field4:5:P="@M Yes,No,Maybe", ;
    ix_field5:W=.F.:H=[Don't Enter]
```

Calculated *BROWSE* Fields

The BROWSE command also supports calculated fields. You create a calculated field by supplying a dummy variable name, followed by an equals sign, followed by any valid FoxPro expression. This expression can include a mathematical relation between fields or constants, a FoxPro function, a UDF, or any combination of these. It can be an IIF() function whose content is determined by other fields or outside factors.

You can also use calculated fields to show a field a second time. Normally, if you instruct a BROWSE to show a field with one heading and then the same field with another heading, the field is displayed only one time with the second heading. If your data is too wide to fit on one screen and the user must scroll to the right to see the rest of the information, you can put critical identifying fields on the far left simply by creating a calculated field whose expression is the field to be redisplayed. For example, in a contact management system, you might have a BROWSE like the following:

```
BROWSE FIELDS ;
    co_comp:12:H="Company", ;
    co_name:30:H="Contact Name", ;
    co_phone:H="Telephone":P="@R (###) 999-9999 9999", ;
    co_areasrv:H="Area Served", ;
    co_union:H="Union Shop":P="Y", ;
    co_vol:H="Volume of Business":P="@$ 999,999,999", ;
    x1=co_comp:12:H="Company" ;
    WHEN bwhen() ;
    VALID bvalid()              && see below
```

You can use the BROWSE WHEN clause to determine whether you have the right to modify a record. If the expression returns a logical False, the record becomes read-only. As with other WHEN and VALID clauses, you don't have to use this expression to evaluate something about this record. You can use it to refresh other parts of the screen, or toggle a highlight marker indicating which is the current record.

The BROWSE VALID clause determines whether you can leave a record at all, either by using the cursor keys, the mouse, or the Control menu. As with the :V= option, this expression is evaluated only if a field is changed. You can force evaluation even when the field is not changed by including the :F switch. Be aware that if users press the Esc key, they leave the Browse window, even if the VALID expression returns a logical False. If you want to prevent this, you can trap the Esc key with an ON KEY LABEL command, as follows:

```
ON KEY LABEL ESC *
BROWSE VALID vbrow():F
ON KEY LABEL ESC
```

Browse Window Aesthetics

As mentioned previously, many factors determine the physical appearance of the Browse window. If you define a window and then invoke it as part of the BROWSE command by using the WINDOW clause, the Browse window assumes the shape of that window. After you are done with the BROWSE, don't forget to release the defining window to return the memory to the pool. Here is a simple example:

```
DEFINE WINDOW jorge FROM 10,10 SIZE 20,40
BROWSE FIELDS ;
     ix_field1:H="Title of field 1", ;
     ix_field2:H="Alternate Title" ;
     WINDOW jorge ;
     NOAPPEND NOMODIFY NODELETE ;
     TITLE "Demo Browse Window"
RELEASE WINDOW jorge
```

Caution: BROWSE NOMODIFY has a "hole" in it. If you create a new record in a Browse session, the user will be able to edit that record until exiting the record. To prevent this behavior from happening, use BROWSE WHEN .F. rather than BROWSE NOMODIFY.

If you issue the IN WINDOW clause, the Browse window appears in that window with the scroll bars cut off. If you want your Browse to appear in another window but still have the scroll bars, you must define another window and use both the WINDOW and IN WINDOW clauses. Figure 12.1 shows the results of the following sample program:

```
CLEAR ALL
CLEAR
USE paycheck IN 0 ALIAS pay1
USE paycheck AGAIN IN 0 ALIAS pay2
USE paycheck AGAIN IN 0 ALIAS pay3

SELECT pay1
DEFINE WINDOW t1 FROM  0,0 ;
      SIZE 10,39 DOUBLE
BROWSE WINDOW t1 NOWAIT

SELECT pay2
DEFINE WINDOW t2 FROM 13,39 ;
      SIZE 10,39 DOUBLE
ACTIVATE WINDOW t2
BROWSE IN WINDOW t2 NOWAIT
```

continues

```
SELECT pay3
DEFINE WINDOW t3 FROM 27,0 ;
      SIZE 12,39 DOUBLE
ACTIVATE WINDOW t3
DEFINE WINDOW t4 FROM 1,1 SIZE 8,35 IN WINDOW t3
BROWSE IN WINDOW t3 WINDOW t4 NOWAIT
```

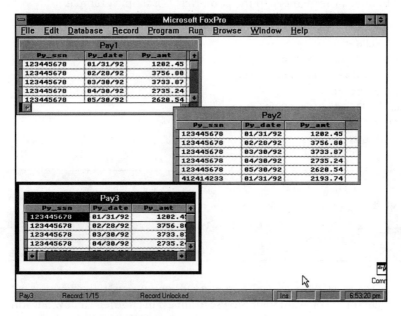

Figure 12.1. The *BROWSE WINDOW*, *BROWSE IN WINDOW*, and *BROWSE WINDOW IN WINDOW* commands.

Miscellaneous Browse Window Options

The user can manipulate a Browse window in several ways—split it into two pieces, unlink the partitions, have either half appear in Edit mode, suppress the field grid lines, and so on. You can do all these things programmatically by using clauses such as `PARTITION nnn`, `LPARTITION`, `NOLINK`, `LEDIT`, `REDIT`, `NOLGRID`, and `NORGRID`.

You can assign a font to the entire Browse window, and also assign a style such as italics or underline. You can also apply the bold face style, but note that column headings are always bold face regardless of the style you choose. For the best appearance, you should probably use a TrueType font for larger point sizes.

In FoxPro for Windows, you can control only the background color, the color of the selected field, the color of selected text, and the outside border. Don't bother trying to color the border, though, because it doesn't do much to enhance the appearance of the Browse window. Windows controls the color of the thin highlight bars that indicate the selected record. To change the color of the bars, you must use the Control Panel/Colors applet.

 Note: When you close a Browse window, FoxPro takes a snapshot of its appearance and records this in the FOXUSER file. This process takes time. If you want maximum performance, you should SET RESOURCE OFF; you will be amazed at how much faster control returns following the closing of a Browse.

A Browse by Any Other Name

To manipulate a Browse window programmatically, you must know the name of the Browse window. As a simple rule of thumb, the Browse's name is the first word (up to 10 characters) of the Browse's title. How do you assign the title to a Browse window? The simplest way is to use the TITLE clause of the BROWSE command and assign it yourself. If there is no TITLE clause, FoxPro uses the title of the window used to define the Browse window. If it can't find that, FoxPro uses the alias of the database.

As just mentioned, the name of the Browse window differs from its title: The name is the first word of the title. In FoxPro, a word is any combination of letters and numbers. Nonalphanumeric characters serve as delimiters. Table 12.1 lists some examples.

Table 12.1. FoxPro Browse window naming conventions.

Browse Title	Browse Window Name	Reason
Choose New Customers	CHOOSE	The space is a delimiter.
Noninverting Transforms	NONINVERTI	The first 10 characters are used.
Upside-down Antlers	UPSIDE	The hyphen is a delimiter.
T141 Snapshot	T141	Alphanumeric characters are valid.

You must know the name of the Browse window later if you want to REFRESH, ACTIVATE, or DEACTIVATE the Browse window programmatically. Let's review each of these processes one at a time.

Browse windows show the contents of many records at a time. If you change the content of one or more of those records programmatically, you have to use the following command to force the Browse to show an updated view:

```
SHOW WINDOW <window name> REFRESH
```

In this case, you must supply the name of the Browse window as described by the preceding rules.

If you have a Browse window on the screen and it is not active, you might want to programmatically place the user in that Browse window. (An example of this is presented later.) In this case, you must issue the following command:

```
ACTIVATE WINDOW <<browse window>>
```

Again, you must know the name of the Browse window.

If you want to remove a Browse window programmatically, you can certainly do that by closing the database. However, a less drastic step is to issue the command

```
DEACTIVATE WINDOW <<browse window>>
```

using the Browse name. This command closes only the specified window. Remember, to DEACTIVATE the window named in the WINDOW clause does no good, because that window was never ACTIVATEd in the first place.

If you use the IN WINDOW clause and DEACTIVATE the parent window, its contents, including the Browse window, disappear. If you ACTIVATE the parent window again, the Browse reappears. If you release the parent window, the Browse window disappears for good.

Using Browse as a Pick List

One of the most popular uses of the Browse window is for pick lists. You can use other methods to display options, including menu-style popups, scrollable lists, and button-style popups. Each has its use, and each has its drawbacks. However, because this chapter focuses on the Browse, let's concentrate on creating Browse pick lists. Consider the following Browse:

```
BROWSE FIELDS ;
    co_coname:24:H="Company", ;
    co_addr1:H="Address", ;
    co_csz:H="City, ST ZIP", ;
```

```
co_phone:H="Telephone", ;
co_faxno:H="Fax" ;
FONT "FoxPrint",10 ;
PARTITION 28 LPARTITION REDIT ;
TITLE "Contractors" ;
WINDOW t1
```

Figure 12.2 shows the resultant Browse window.

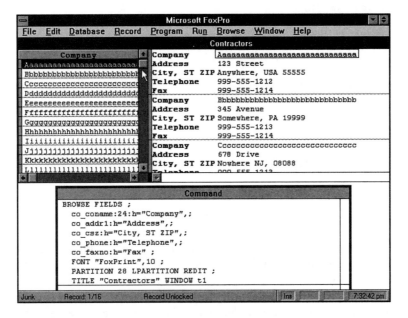

Figure 12.2. Using partitions can enhance the value of Browse as a lookup.

The Browse shown in Figure 12.2 is a great pick list, for several reasons. The Browse is split in half, with the left side an ordinary BROWSE and the right side in Edit mode. As you scroll down the left side, the right side automatically tracks and shows all the information associated with the name on the left side. You are no longer limited to the width of the screen for display of an individual's data but rather height of the screen.

To enable the user to select a single item, we typically arm a key with an ON KEY LABEL so that user presses only one key to make a selection. A library routine called L3HOTW arms both the Enter key and the right mouse button. This routine is self-clearing, so that if the program bombs out while the Enter key is reprogrammed, you can get control of it by pressing Enter again. Another method is to type ON KEY in the Command window and press Shift+Enter, which has the same effect as pressing Enter but is ignored by the ON KEY LABEL trap. The ON KEY command clears all ON KEY LABELs.

Here is the program:

```
PROCEDURE l3hotw
PARAMETERS l_what
IF TYPE("khotw")  = 'U'
  PUBLIC khotw,klk,krk
ENDIF
ON KEY LABEL ENTER
ON KEY LABEL RIGHTMOUSE
IF TYPE("l_what") = 'L'
   STORE .T. TO khotw
   KEYBOARD(CHR(23)) PLAIN
ELSE
   IF l_what = "IN"
      ON KEY LABEL ENTER DO l3hotw
      ON KEY LABEL ENTER DO l3hotw
      STORE .F. TO khotw
   ELSE
      STORE LASTKEY() TO klk
      STORE READKEY() TO krk
   ENDIF
ENDIF
RETURN
```

The usage is simple. You call L3HOTW to arm the Enter key and the right mouse button. You then issue your BROWSE command. The user exits by pressing Enter, Esc, or the right mouse button, or by clicking the window closed. You then call L3HOTW again to disarm the keys, just in case they are still armed. You examine the variable khotw—if it is a logical True, the user has made a choice; if it is a logical False, the user has decided not to make a choice. If you press the Enter key, this routine actually calls itself, using the following trick: If the routine is called because of the ON KEY LABEL trap, no parameter is passed, so the variable l_what is type Logical; the routine records this fact and then stuffs a Ctrl+W in the keyboard buffer to exit the Browse. Here is an example of the routine's use:

```
DO l3hotw WITH "IN" && arm the <Enter> key and RM button
BROWSE FIELDS ;
     choice1:H="Heading 1", ;
     choice2:H="Heading 2", ;
     choice3:H="Heading 3" ;
     NOAPPEND NODELETE NOMODIFY ;
     TITLE "Choose 1" ;
     WINDOW c1
DO l3hotw WITH "OUT" && disarm the keys, just in case
```

```
IF khotw && khotw = .T. means selection made
    * select action here
ELSE
    * no item was selected
ENDIF
```

Note that this Browse is specified as NOAPPEND NODELETE NOMODIFY because it is a pick list rather than a data entry screen. We don't want the user to modify anything. When we return from the Browse, we examine the state of the variable khotw to see whether a selection was made. We also have two other variables that tell us what LASTKEY() and READKEY() returned, if that is of interest.

Doing Incremental Searches in a Browse Window

This style of lookup is fine for a small-to-medium list. If the list is very large, however, the user may have trouble scrolling the record of interest. We want to do the following:

1. Present the user with the Browse list.

2. Enable the user to type characters.

3. Trap each keystroke as the user types each character.

4. Append each character to a "search string" as each keystroke is trapped.

5. SEEK in the current database the search string as each character is appended to that search string.

For example, suppose that the user wants to look up a client by company name in the time sheet application. To enable the user to accomplish this, we need only the following few lines of code:

```
SELECT tsclient
SET ORDER TO cl_company
DO l3srch WITH "cl_company:h=[Company]:20,cl_clid:h=[Id]"
```

Figure 12.3 shows the results of this short program. The source code disk includes the code for L3SRCH.PRG.

L3SRCH accomplishes its goals by using an API routine called L3SRCH.FLL. The source code disk includes l3SRCH.FLL, and Chapter 17, "The C Connection," discusses the techniques involved in L3SRCH.FLL's operation.

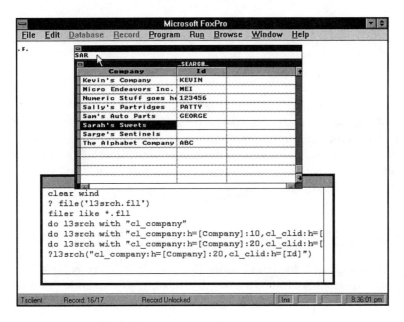

Figure 12.3. Using L3SRCH to search a Browse window incrementally.

Selecting Multiple Records in a Browse Window

Chapter 8, "Reporting on the Time Sheet Application," discussed one good method for selecting multiple records from a database. In that case, we used a DEFINE POPUP, an IIF(), and a memory variable with one character per record in the database. We can easily adapt this technique to a Browse window.

Here is the code:

```
* multpick.prg
* Use a memory variable with one character per record
CLOSE DATA
USE tsclient
m.pickvar=SPACE(RECCOUNT())
ON KEY LABEL f5 DO toggle
BROWSE FIELDS ;
  CALC=IIF(LEN(m.pickvar)>=RECNO(),SUBSTR(m.pickvar,RECNO(),1),"");
  :W=.F.,cl_company,cl_clid

ON KEY LABEL f5

PROCEDURE toggle
IF LEN(m.pickvar)<RECNO()
  m.pickvar=PADR(m.pickvar,RECNO())
```

```
ENDIF
m.pickvar=STUFF(m.pickvar,RECNO(),1,;
   IIF(SUBSTR(m.pickvar,RECNO(),1)="*"," ","*"))
```

This technique is the fastest available solution for those occasions when you want to select multiple records from a database. However, as was noted in Chapter 8, this solution is limited to databases that have less than 65,000 records.

By using Chapter 8's L3BITMP2.PRG, we can increase this limit to 520,000 records, but even this may not be sufficient when working with very large databases. Fortunately, a solution is available that handles databases of any size.

When we are selecting a relatively small number of records from a very large database, we need code such as the following:

```
* multpic2.prg
* Use an indexed cursor
CLOSE DATA
CREATE CURSOR multpic2 (RECNO N(13),STATUS C(1))
INDEX ON RECNO TAG RECNO
SELECT 0
USE tsclient ORDE cl_company
SET RELATION TO (RECNO()) INTO multpic2
ON KEY LABEL f5 DO toggle
BROWSE FIELDS ;
   calc=multpic2.status:H="Sel":W=.F.,cl_company,cl_clid

ON KEY LABEL f5
USE IN multpic2

PROCEDURE toggle
IF RECNO("tsclient")<>multpic2.recno
   INSERT INTO multpic2 (RECNO,STATUS) VALUES ;
      (RECNO("tsclient"),"*")
ELSE
   REPLACE multpic2.status WITH IIF(multpic2.status="*"," ","*")
ENDIF
```

When we select more than one out of every eight records from a large database, code such as the following may be more efficient:

```
* Multpic3.prg
* Use a cursor with one record per record in the
* original database.
CLOSE DATA
CREATE CURSOR multpic3 (STATUS C(1))
```

continues

251

```
SELECT 0
USE tsclient ORDE cl_company
SET RELATION TO RECNO() INTO multpic3
ON KEY LABEL f5 DO toggle
BROWSE FIELDS ;
  CALC=multpic3.status:H="Sel":W=.F.,cl_company,cl_clid

ON KEY LABEL f5
USE IN multpic3

PROCEDURE toggle
IF RECNO("tsclient")>RECCOUNT("multpic3")
  FOR l_xx=RECCOUNT("Multpic3") TO RECNO("tsclient")
    INSERT INTO multpic3 (STATUS) VALUES (" ")
  ENDFOR
  GOTO (RECNO("tsclient")) IN multpic3
ENDIF
REPLACE multpic3.status WITH IIF(multpic3.status="*"," ","*")
RETURN
```

Notice that MULTPIC3.PRG takes advantage of a peculiar FoxPro "feature" that descends directly from FoxPro's Xbase language heritage. When you use a numeric expression to establish a relationship INTO a database that has no master index order established, FoxPro uses the record number of the target database as an index. In MULTPIC3, every time the record pointer is moved in the TSCLIENT database, FoxPro essentially issues the following command:

```
GOTO (RECNO("tsclient")) IN multpic3
```

Data Entry

Browses are not restricted to pick lists. They are excellent for data review and in some cases data entry. If you are creating a single-user application, you don't have to worry about locking problems, so you can enable the user to alter record contents directly. If you are working in a multiuser system, things get more complicated. This section discusses the issues involved.

If you do enable the user to do data entry in a Browse, you must retain some control over the quality of information entered. Field-level VALIDs are okay and the BROWSE VALID clause allows for some record level error checking. However, as previously mentioned, you must trap the Esc key if you want total control over when the user can exit a Browse. This might be dangerous if users get into the data entry section by mistake, or on purpose, and cannot provide valid information. You must provide some method for users to exit gracefully under those conditions.

If you are using some sort of ID field that the system assigns, you cannot expect the user to enter that data in a new record. You must provide a control mechanism—a push button, menu bar, or ON KEY LABEL—to trigger the creation of a new record.

When a user requests a new record, you provide the record and mark it with the unique identifier before you give access to the user. To prevent the user from modifying the ID field, either define the ID field with the :R flag or simply omit the ID field from the Browse. If users decide to abort the addition of a new record, they must delete the record.

In general, it is preferable to add records to Browse windows by creating an .SPR for the addition of records. Then, you arm a hot key to call that .SPR when the user elects to add a record to the Browse.

Once "in" the .SPR, you can validate all the information for the new record *before* the record is added to the database. The following sample program demonstrates this approach:

```
SELECT company
ON KEY LABEL F4 DO addrec
BROWSE FIELDS ;
        co_coname:20, ;
        co_addr1, ;
        co_city, ;
        co_state, ;
        co_zip, ;
        co_telephone ;
        co_faxno ;
  NOAPPEND NODELETE NOMODIFY ;
  TITLE  "Company Review    <F4> Add New"
ON KEY LABEL F4

PROCEDURE addrec
PUSH KEY CLEAR
STORE 0 TO action
DO addrec.SPR  && screen contains necessary VALIDs
IF action = 1  && can only happen if record is OK
  IF NOT l3uniq_a(m.co_compid,"company")
    DO l3msgw WITH "Sorry. Not a unique id!"
  ENDIF
ENDIF
POP KEY
RETURN
```

For more information about adding records to Browse windows, review Chapters 5 ("Employees and Projects"), 6 ("Time Sheets"), and 7 ("Updating Time Sheets").

Multiple Databases, One Browse Window

The BROWSE command enables the programmer to include fields from multiple databases. In the following example, we want to provide the user with a list of pay checks in order of pay date, along with the name of the employee associated with each check:

```
* pay1.prg
SELECT paycheck
SET ORDER TO py_idate
SET ORDER TO em_ssn IN employee
SET RELATION TO py_ssn INTO employee
BROWSE FIELDS ;
   employee.em_name:H="Name":22, ;
   employee.em_phone:14:H="Telephone":P="@R (###) 999-9999", ;
   py_date:H="Date", ;
   py_amt:H="Amount":P="@$" ;
   NOAPPEND NODELETE NOMODIFY ;
   TITLE "Paychecks" ;
   FONT "Arial",10 STYLE "B"
```

Figure 12.4 shows the result of the PAY1.PRG program.

With the advent of FoxPro 2.0, we can now do one-to-many relations. This has the advantage of showing parent records that have no children, a feat we cannot achieve with the traditional many-to-one relationship. Creating a Browse with the one-to-many set has the added advantage of giving a visual indicator of related records. The following is the same example as shown to demonstrate the many-to-one Browse, run from the parent side:

```
* pay2.prg
SELECT employee
SET ORDER TO em_name
SET ORDER TO py_ssn IN paycheck
SET RELATION TO em_ssn INTO paycheck
SET SKIP TO paycheck
BROWSE FIELDS ;
   employee.em_name:H="Name":22, ;
   employee.em_phone:14:H="Telephone":P="@R (###) 999-9999", ;
   py_date:H="Date", ;
   py_amt:H="Amount":P="@$" ;
   NOAPPEND NODELETE NOMODIFY ;
   TITLE "Paychecks" ;
   FONT "Arial",10 STYLE "B"
```

Figure 12.5 shows the result of the PAY2.PRG program.

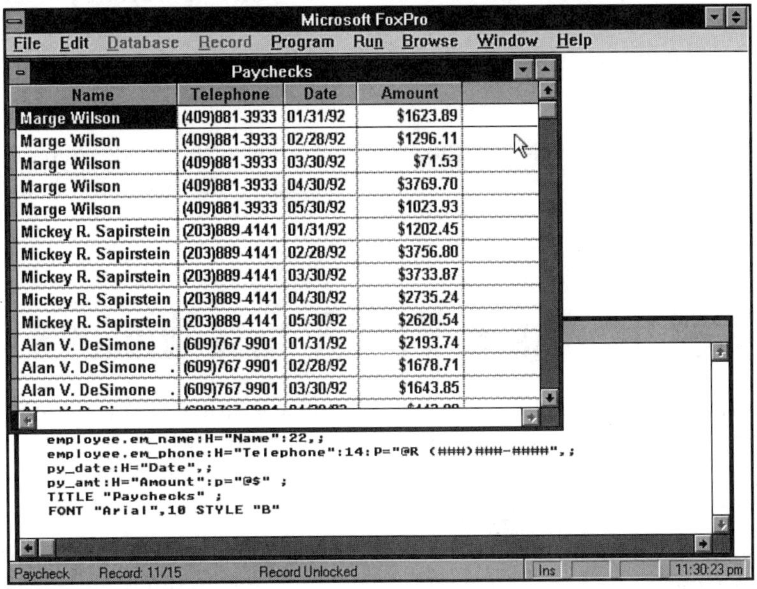

Figure 12.4. A many-to-one Browse window of two databases.

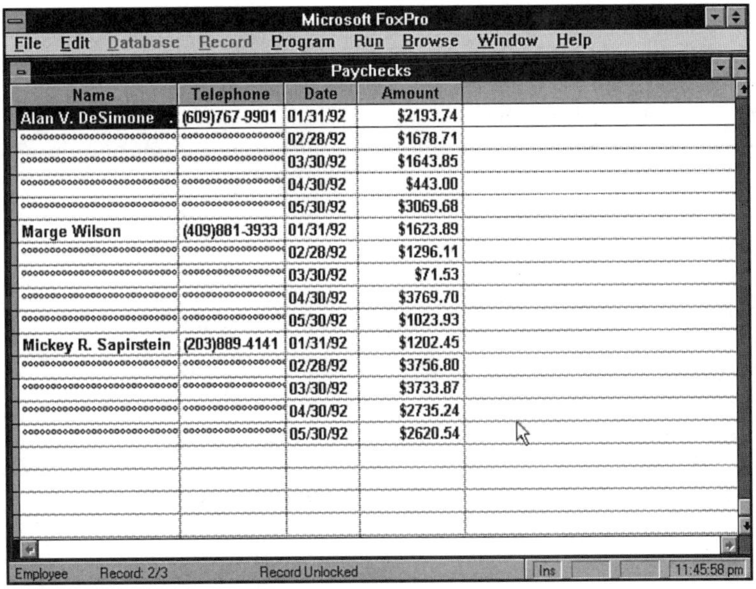

Figure 12.5. A one-to-many Browse of two databases.

Although this presentation is a handy way to look at data, a problem arises if you have so many pay checks that the employee name scrolls off the screen before you get to the next person. In this case, we can include a calculated field on the far right that is simply the employee's name. Here's the code:

```
x = em_name:H="Name":20
```

Because x is a calculated field, FoxPro does not produce the shading character in duplicate records, so the user can always scroll over to the right to see what data is being displayed.

Many Related Databases, Many Browse Windows

For our next trick, we present the user with three related Browse windows. In window number one, we have the client database. In window number two, we have the projects associated with the current client. In window number three, we present the time sheet records associated with the current client and project.

The display in Figure 12.6 is nice, but what makes it special is the code, or lack of code, required to create this sophisticated display. Here is the simple code for MULTBROW.PRG:

```
* multbrow.prg

CLOSE DATA
* Open databases, and establish relationship from:
*   tsclient into tsproj into tstime into tsempl
USE tsclient ORDER cl_company
USE tsproj ORDER pj_clid IN 0
USE tstime ORDER clproj IN 0
USE tsempl ORDER em_empid IN 0
SET RELATION TO cl_clid INTO tsproj
SELECT tsproj
SET RELATION TO pj_clid+pj_projid INTO tstime
SELECT tstime
SET RELATION TO ti_empid INTO tsempl
**   Set up three windows
DEFINE WINDOW one AT 1,0 SIZE 10,SCOLS()/2 FLOAT ;
  FONT "Arial",10
DEFINE WINDOW two AT 1,SCOLS()/2+2 SIZE 10,SCOLS()/2-4 ;
  FLOAT FONT "Arial",10
DEFINE WINDOW three AT 12,0 SIZE 10,SCOLS() FLOAT ;
  FONT "Arial",10
```

```
** Do the browses
SELECT tsclient
BROWSE FIELDS cl_company,cl_clid NOWAIT WINDOW one
SELECT tsproj
BROWSE FIELDS pj_projid,pj_clid,pj_name NOWAIT WINDOW two ;
  KEY tsclient.cl_clid
SELECT tstime
BROWSE FIELDS DATE=ti_week-7+ti_day,ti_projid,ti_clid,;
  tsempl.em_last NOWAIT WINDOW three ;
  KEY tsproj.pj_clid+tsproj.pj_projid
ON KEY LABEL f8 DO finish
mvar=.F.
READ VALID mvar

PROCEDURE finish
RELEASE WINDOW tstime,tsproj,tsclient
mvar=.T.
CLEAR READ
```

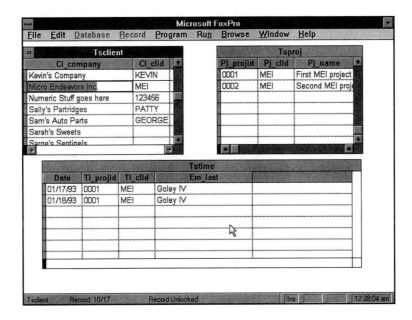

Figure 12.6. Three related Browse windows.

An Integrated Browse

In Chapter 6, "Time Sheets," I spent a great deal of time explaining how to integrate a Browse window with a READ CYCLE session. One thing I did not discuss is a method for enabling the user to enter a Browse window with a keystroke rather than a mouse click.

The following command does the job nicely:

```
ON KEY LABEL Shift+F12 ACTIVATE WINDOW tasks
```

To enable the user to exit the Browse window and move to the time sheet week window, we might include the following command:

```
ON KEY LABEL Shift+F11 ACTIVATE WINDOW tstimewk
```

However, what if we want the user to enter the Browse window automatically when he or she tabs past the last GET on the screen? At first glance, the solution seems simple: Place a WHEN clause on an invisible button that follows the last GET on the screen. That WHEN clause should reference a UDF that includes code such as the following:

```
PROCEDURE winvisible
ACTIVATE WINDOW tasks
RETURN .F.
```

Unfortunately, this doesn't work. Instead, we must resort to the following kludge:

```
PROCEDURE winvisible
_CUROBJ=0
KEYBOARD "{Shift+F12}"
RETURN .F.
```

Identifying the Current Record in a Browse Window

If you do use an integrated Browse, you need some method of indicating to the user which record is currently selected. Of course, this is no problem when you are in the Browse, because highlight bars indicate the current record. But when you are outside the Browse, the current record in the Browse is not indicated.

To add an indicator, you must do the following:

1. Include a calculated field in the Browse.

2. Update a variable containing the record number of the current Browse record each time you enter a new record in the Browse.

3. Reset the marker variable to zero when you move to a new record in the same Browse window.

Here is the code to add a record indicator:

```
* browmark.prg
CLOSE DATA
** Set up a Browse window for the client database
DEFINE WINDOW mymark AT 1,0 SIZE 10,75 FLOAT FONT "Arial",10
USE tsclient
client=RECNO() && Mark variable
BROWSE FIELDS ;
   t1=IIF(RECNO("tsclient")=m.client,">"," "):H="":1:w=.F.,;
   cl_company NOWAIT WHEN bmw() VALID :F bmv(@client,"tsclient") ;
   WINDOW mymark
DEFINE WINDOW myread AT 15,0 SIZE 10,75 FLOAT FONT "Arial",10
ACTIVATE WINDOW myread
SCATTER MEMVAR MEMO
@ 2,5 GET m.cl_company
@ 4,5 GET m.cl_city
@ 6,5 GET m.cl_state
READ CYCLE

PROCEDURE bmw
* Refresh the read window
SCATTER MEMVAR MEMO
SHOW GETS WINDOW myread
* Refresh the marker variable
client=RECNO("tsclient")
RETURN .F.

PROCEDURE bmv
PARAMETERS p_var,p_window
IF UPPER(WONTOP())==UPPER(p_window)
   * If he moved to a new record in the same Browse window,
   * set the marker variable to 0, so that the marker column
   * for the current record in the Browse will be blanked.
   p_var=0
ENDIF
RETURN .T.
```

Multiuser Considerations

When editing Browse records in a multiuser environment, we have the following choices for record locking:

- Enable the user to edit the Browse directly and perform no explicit record locking. Instead, rely on FoxPro's implicit record locking to attempt to lock any record that the user attempts to change in the Browse.

- Allow no editing of Browse windows. Enable a hot key that calls an .SPR file to edit an individual Browse record. Place explicit record-locking logic in the control program for the .SPR.

- When browsing the children of a parent record, lock the parent record before enabling the user to access the Browse window. If all programmers follow this convention, after you have the lock on the parent record, you can assume that FoxPro can lock all the parent record's children.

- When browsing the children of a parent record, lock the parent and all the children when the user elects to edit this group of records.

- Issue a BROWSE WHEN RLOCK() command to lock explicitly each record the user enters. Use VALID :F l3unlock() or a similar UDF to unlock each record as the user exits.

- When browsing the children of a parent record, copy the children to a cursor when the user elects to edit. Perform all changes to the records in the cursor and lock only the original records to save changes made in the cursor.

Final Words

The BROWSE command is the most complex, most powerful, and most flexible command in all of FoxPro. You can make it do almost anything if you work hard enough at it. It's safe to say that no application passes through the doors of Micro Endeavors that doesn't have at least one Browse in it. Some applications contain only Browses and their support code.

Mastering the BROWSE command requires study of field-level programming as well as record-level programming. The help screens in FoxPro are useful, and the techniques discussed in this chapter also provide a guide to some common situations. The best thing to do is to stop reading this and start experimenting. Good luck!

CHAPTER

13

Multiuser Discussions

There is no one "right" way to handle record locking, error trapping, and data contention in FoxPro. Indeed, there is no one right way to handle those issues in any language.

No matter what language you use to develop applications, the application dictates whether you use an active or passive locking scheme. The application determines whether you must track changes by user. The application determines whether a batch or real-time approach to multirecord updates is optimal.

In this chapter, I identify the most important alternatives. Along the way, I give you the source code you need to implement each technique.

Specifically, the following topics are discussed:

- Opening databases in a multiuser environment
- Choosing between active and passive locking schemes
- Adding a record to a shared database
- Enforcing unique, user-assigned IDs
- Enforcing unique, system-generated, sequentially assigned IDs
- Updating multiple records in multiple tables
- Trapping errors

Opening Databases in a Multiuser Environment

The USE command opens databases. However, it is insufficient simply to USE a database in a multiuser environment, because one or more of the following unfortunate events can occur:

- The file is in use in another work area.

- Another user has EXCLUSIVE use of the file.

- Another user has SHAREd use of the file, but you need EXCLUSIVE use of the file.

- The file does not exist.

- The .CDX file is missing or corrupt.

- The .FPT file is missing.

- The database is corrupted.

Obviously, the prudent programmer must consider the possibility that, for one of these reasons, a file that is required for a session, report, or process might not be available. I'll show you a UDF that can facilitate this cautious behavior shortly.

First, though, the programmer should open all databases required for an activity before beginning any portion of the activity. In addition, after a database is opened in preparation for an activity, you should leave that database open for the duration of the activity.

The following is the scenario you are trying to avoid by leaving the database open for the duration of the activity. Suppose you want to post a new invoice. This activity requires that you add an invoice header, look up a customer record, add some number of line item records, and update some number of inventory records.

Here is pseudocode demonstrating the *wrong* way to accomplish this posting:

```
USE invoice
INSERT INTO invoice FROM memvar
USE IN invoice
USE customer
SEEK custid
REPLACE ytdsales WITH ytdsales+total
USE IN customer
USE lineitem
APPEND FROM ARRAY lineitems
USE IN lineitem
USE inventor
FOR l_xx=1 to ALEN(lineitems,1)
```

```
    SEEK lineitems(l_xx,2)
    REPLACE onhand WITH onhand-lineitems(l_xx,3)
ENDFOR
USE IN inventor
```

The approach presented in this block of pseudocode suffers from the possibility that a file needed to complete the transaction might not be available at the time of the transaction. For example, if someone obtains exclusive use of the INVENTOR.DBF database during the posting of line items, this application cannot finish the transaction.

Further, the application might not be able to undo the changes already made to the invoice, customer, and line item databases, because another user may have obtained exclusive use of those files during the time that this application spent attempting to USE the INVENTOR.DBF database.

Instead, the programmer should open the invoice, customer, line item, and inventor databases *before* beginning the transaction. If any of those databases is unavailable, the transaction should not be started.

What we need is a UDF that enables us to write code like the following:

```
IF all_files_can_be_opened
  DO transaction
ELSE
  DO message
ENDIF
```

One of the drawbacks of such a UDF is that using the UDF is often more difficult than directly using the database. Here are two examples:

```
* Block 1
IF NOT USED("tsclient")
  USE tsclient IN SELECT(1) AGAIN
ENDIF
SET ORDER TO cl_clid IN tsclient

* Block 2
DO myopen WITH "tsclient","cl_clid",.T.,SELECT(1)
```

In the first example, FoxPro allows almost total flexibility in the positioning of the many clauses available on the USE command. On the other hand, MYOPEN.PRG requires that the arguments be passed in a specific order, and that, to open a database, the programmer learn (and remember) a new "language."

As a result, one of the first requirements for the l3open UDF is that it enable the programmer to use FoxPro syntax to open databases. Here are all the requirements for L3OPEN.PRG:

- Support FoxPro syntax for opening files, including all USE command clauses.

- Handle all errors that can occur in opening files.

- Determine whether a file is already in use.

- Support multiple alias names for the same database file.

- Be able to switch a database from EXCLUSIVE to SHAREd mode, and vice versa.

- Be able to change master order for an already open database.

- Close any databases it opened if it fails to open any one of the requested databases.

- Return a string that identifies the database that caused the error, and the content of the error message.

In our TSTIME data entry screen program, we open five databases. This consumes some 20 lines of code in the tstimeopen procedure. The following block of code attempts the same thing by using l3open:

```
l_badopen=l3open(;
  "tsempo order em_empid",;
  "tsclient order cl_clid",;
  "tsproj order clproj",;
  "tstime order empdte",;
  "tsweek order empdte"))
IF NOT EMPTY(l_badopen)
  DO l3msg WITH "The following error occurred when I "+;
    "tried to open databases:¦"+l_badopen
  RETURN
ENDIF failed to open the databases
```

If you don't feel like telling the user exactly why you can't open the databases, you can rewrite this code segment as follows:

```
IF NOT EMPTY(l3open(;
  "tsempo order em_empid",;
  "tsclient order cl_clid",;
  "tsproj order clproj",;
  "tstime order empdte",;
  "tsweek order empdte")
```

```
      DO 13msg WITH "An error occurred when I tried to "+;
        "open databases!"
      RETURN
   ENDIF failed to open the databases
```

Here is the source code for the L3OPEN.PRG program:

```
* 13open.prg
* Opens databases if possible.
* Pass each parameter as a complete USE statement, without
* the USE command. For example:
*     IF 13open("tsclient order cl_clid")
*     l_badnews=13open("tsclient","tsproj orde pj_id")
PARAMETERS p_dbf01,p_dbf02,p_dbf03,p_dbf04,p_dbf05,p_dbf06,;
  p_dbf07,p_dbf08,p_dbf09,p_dbf10,p_dbf11,p_dbf12,p_dbf13,;
  p_dbf14,p_dbf15,p_dbf16,p_dbf17,p_dbf18,p_dbf19,p_dbf20,;
  p_dbf21,p_dbf22,p_dbf23,p_dbf24;

PRIVATE ALL LIKE l_*
** Preserve old error trap
l_olderr=ON("error")
** Establish error trap for 13open
ON ERROR kerror=MESSAGE()
l_qty=PARAMETERS() && How many database USE commands were passed
l_retval="" && Value to return to user
l_oldsele=SELECT() && Preserve initial work area
** Create an array to hold work areas of newly opened databases,
** in case we need to close them.
DIMENSION l_sofar(l_qty)
FOR l_xx=1 TO l_qty && Process all requests
  ** Use the loop counter to store the content of the
  ** next parameter in the m.l_dbf string
  l_dbf="p_dbf"+TRAN(l_xx,"@L ##")
  l_dbf=ALLTRIM(EVAL(l_dbf))+" "
  ** Look for an ALIAS clause in this string
  DO CASE
    CASE " ALIA "$UPPER(l_dbf)
      l_spot=ATC(" ALIA ",l_dbf)+6
      l_len=AT(" ",SUBSTR(l_dbf,l_spot+1))
      l_alias=SUBSTR(l_dbf,l_spot,l_len)
    CASE " ALIAS "$UPPER(l_dbf)
      l_spot=ATC(" ALIAS ",l_dbf)+7
      l_len=AT(" ",SUBSTR(l_dbf,l_spot+1))
      l_alias=SUBSTR(l_dbf,l_spot,l_len)
```

continues

265

```
      OTHERWISE
         l_alias=LEFT(l_dbf,AT(" ",l_dbf)-1)
   ENDCASE find the alias clause
   ** Look for an ORDER clause in this string
   DO CASE
      CASE " ORDE "$UPPER(l_dbf)
         l_spot=ATC(" ORDE ",l_dbf)+6
         l_len=AT(" ",SUBSTR(l_dbf,l_spot+1))
         l_order=SUBSTR(l_dbf,l_spot,l_len)
      CASE " ORDER "$UPPER(l_dbf)
         l_spot=ATC(" ORDER ",l_dbf)+7
         l_len=AT(" ",SUBSTR(l_dbf,l_spot+1))
         l_order=SUBSTR(l_dbf,l_spot,l_len)
      OTHERWISE
         l_order=""
   ENDCASE find the ORDER clause
   ** If there isn't an AGAIN clause in the string,
   ** put an AGAIN clause on the end of the string
   l_dbf=l_dbf+IIF(" AGAI "$UPPER(l_dbf) .OR. ;
      " AGAIN "$UPPER(l_dbf),""," AGAIN")

   ** Check to see whether this alias is already in use.
   ** L3openex() checks to see whether the database needs to
   ** be reopened to establish the proper shared or
   ** exclusive use state. If the file needs to be reopened,
   ** L3openex() will close the file, and return .T.

   kerror="" && set error flag
   IF NOT USED(m.l_alias) OR l3openex()
      ** File needs to be opened
      IF SELECT(1)=0
         ** Oops. No more work areas
         l_retval="No work area available for "+l_dbf
         EXIT
      ELSE && at least one work area is free
         IF " IN "$UPPER(l_dbf)
            ** Programmer told me IN which work area to open
            ** this database.
            USE &l_dbf.
            l_sofar(l_xx)=.f. && In case we can't find it
            FOR l_yy=1 TO 225
               IF UPPER(ALIAS(l_yy))==UPPER(m.l_alias)
                  l_sofar(l_xx)=l_yy && remember work area
```

266

```
                EXIT
              ENDIF is this the right one
            ENDFOR look for this alias
          ELSE && no IN clause in the USE command
            ** Assume that he wants to open the database in
            ** an unopened work area.
            l_sofar(l_xx)=SELECT(1) && remember work area
            USE &l_dbf. IN SELECT(1)
          ENDIF has an IN argument
        ENDIF no WORK areas available
      ELSE && database is already in use
        ** It's already in use, so just check for set order
        IF NOT EMPTY(m.l_order) AND ;
           NOT UPPER(m.l_order)==ORDER(m.l_alias)
           SET ORDER TO (m.l_order) IN (m.l_alias)
        ENDIF sent me an ORDER, AND it doesn't match the current order
      ENDIF NOT already IN USE
      IF NOT EMPTY(kerror)
        ** Kerror has been assigned an error message because the
        ** ON ERROR kerror=MESSAGE() command we established at the
        ** beginning of l3open has been triggered by an error
        ** when we tried to "USE" the database.
        l_retval="Error ["+kerror+;
           "] attempting to USE "+l_dbf
        EXIT
      ENDIF an error occurred
ENDFOR try TO OPEN ALL DATABASES
IF NOT EMPTY(m.l_retval)
   ** Because we failed to open one of these databases,
   ** close all of the databases we did open
   FOR l_yy=1 TO MIN(225,l_xx)
      IF TYPE("l_sofar(l_yy)")="N" AND USED(l_sofar(l_yy))
         USE IN (l_sofar(l_yy))
      ENDIF work area is in use
   ENDFOR close all databases we did open
ENDIF an error occurred
SELECT (m.l_oldsele)
ON ERROR &l_olderr
RETURN m.l_retval

PROCEDURE l3openex
* Returns .T. if the file needs to be reopened to
* establish shared/exclusive use status.
```

continues

```
IF NOT USED(m.l_alias)
  RETURN .T.
ELSE
  SELECT (m.l_alias)
  DO CASE
    CASE " EXCL"$UPPER(m.l_dbf) AND UPPER(SYS(2011))#"EXCLUSIVE"
      * now shared, want exclusive
      USE                           && close it first
      RETURN .T.
    CASE ATC(" EXCL",m.l_dbf)=0 AND UPPER(SYS(2011))="EXCLUSIVE";
         AND (SET('EXCL')="OFF" OR " SHAR"$UPPER(m.l_dbf))
      * now exclusive, want shared
      USE                           && close it first
      RETURN .T.
    OTHERWISE
      RETURN .F.
  ENDCASE
ENDIF NOT IN USE
```

Note that performance should not be much of an issue for L3OPEN.PRG, because we should not be opening and closing our files very often!

The Principle of Data Currency

The only user of a shared database who is certain that he or she is looking at the current copy of a record is that user who has the record locked.

The following demo makes for one of the liveliest sessions in our FoxPro training classes. It also proves the aforementioned rule of data currency.

1. Jane and John use INVENTOR.DBF at the same time.

2. INVENTOR.DBF has only one record and only one field. This field is the onhand field.

3. Jane and John both issue the command ? onhand.

4. Jane and John both see that there are currently 24 somethings on hand.

5. Jane locks the record.

6. John issues the command ? onhand and sees that there are still 24 somethings on hand.

7. Jane sells six somethings and replaces onhand with onhand-6.

8. Jane and John both issue the command ? onhand.

9. Jane sees 18, but John sees 24!

10. Jane, out of the goodness of her heart, issues the UNLOCK command to release her lock on the record.

11. Jane and John both issue the command ? onhand.

12. Jane sees 18, but John still sees 24!

13. John moves his record pointer by issuing a GO TOP command.

14. John then issues the command ? onhand, and finally sees 18—just as Jane locks the record and replaces onhand with onhand-8!

Before students can recover, I ask them to use INVENTOR.DBF. Then I give each student a number, and ask them to issue the following command:

```
REPLACE onhand WITH number
```

Finally, we ask them to issue the command ? onhand.

Each of the 24 students sees *the number he or she entered*—that is, 24 people, looking at the same record in the same database at the same time, see 24 *different values for that same record.*

Try these tests yourself, because nobody believes me when I tell them they must lock a record to ensure that it is current. That's why I do the exercises in class. The explanation for this phenomenon is simple: Each of the 24 workstations on the network maintains a copy of that workstation's current INVENTOR.DBF record.

FoxPro does not get a new copy of the current record every time the program queries that record. This is fortunate, because if FoxPro did get a new copy of a record every time a command queried the current record, no network would be fast enough to handle the traffic. Further, if FoxPro got a new copy of the current record every time a command referenced the current record, we would be faced with the following problem:

```
SELECT inventor
SEEK mvar
m.name=inventor.name  && record as of 09:00.01 AM
m.price=inventor.price && record as of 09:00.02 AM
** At this moment, another user changes the inventor.price field
m.myprice=inventor.price*discount && New value for price!!
```

Even if FoxPro were to look for the current record with every reference to the current record, you still would not be assured that the copy of the record the user is viewing is the current copy of the record. After all, between the time FoxPro got the new copy of the record and the time you presented that record to the user, another user might have changed the record.

In effect, so long as time is a dimension in our reality (which I fearlessly predict will be the case for some time to come), the only user of a shared database who is certain that he or she is looking at the current copy of a record is that user who has the record locked.

I make a point of this data currency issue because understanding this basic principle of multiuser access is crucial when choosing between passive and active locking schemes. Well, now that I've made my point, I guess we can talk about passive and active locking schemes.

Active versus Passive Locking

Whenever you want to change the content of a record in a shared database, you must lock that record. This section answers *when* and *how long* to lock those records.

In the *active locking scheme,* the records to be changed are locked at the beginning of an editing session, and they remain locked until the editing session is complete. Data entry screens that use an active locking scheme usually feature an Edit button such as the one found in the TSTIME program.

Until the user presses the Edit button, the GETs on-screen are disabled and the underlying records are not locked. When the user presses the Edit button, the underlying records are locked and the user is enabled to edit the GETs on-screen.

In the *passive locking scheme,* the records to be changed are not locked until the user, or the programmer, elects to save the user's changes. In this scheme, there is often no Edit button. Instead, the user is placed in Edit mode immediately on entry into the data entry screen. The programmer usually provides a Save button, or may decide simply to save changes whenever the user selects an option that moves to another record in the underlying database(s). Therefore, in the passive locking scheme, the records in question are locked only for the time it takes to save the changes.

Each of these approaches has its benefits and its drawbacks. Table 13.1 lists a few of each.

Table 13.1. Benefits and drawbacks of active and passive locking.

Active Locking Benefits	Passive Locking Benefits
Guarantees the user that the data presented is current.	Reduces contention for records, because records are locked only for the duration of the replace, gather, delete, or other action.

Active Locking Benefits	Passive Locking Benefits
Guarantees the user that any changes made can be saved, because his or her workstation locks the affected records.	Enables the programmer to create "modeless" screens, which do not require the user to select Edit before changing the displayed data.
Enables the user to directly edit general fields.	
Makes coding simpler for the programmer, which means less debugging and more reliable code.	

Active Locking Drawbacks	Passive Locking Drawbacks
If the user goes "out to lunch," the record remains locked, preventing other users from accessing the record.	The user may be editing an "old" copy of the record. If so, the changes are be saved.
In active systems, it may be virtually impossible to FLOCK( ) a file while editing is taking place.	While user A is editing the record, user B may change the record, causing user A's edits to be invalid. User A's changes will be lost
In an event-driven application, the user may move to another session and leave the record in the current session locked indefinitely.	The programmer must check for data currency before saving changes, which means more initial coding and more debugging.
	Editing general fields is virtually impossible.

 Note: To address the most critical issues resulting from these drawbacks, programmers who use active locking must take steps to avoid the "out-to-lunch" syndrome (which can occur when a user begins an edit, thereby locking a record, and then leaves the system unattended), while programmers who use the passive locking scheme must take steps to ensure data currency.

Before moving to other topics, let's review some examples of both active and passive locking techniques presented in earlier chapters.

Passive Locking Techniques

In Chapter 4, "More Clients," the TSCLIENT data entry provides a good example of a passive locking scheme. The user of the TSCLIENT.PRG program is immediately placed in edit mode. There is no separate Edit button. Whenever the user presses a push button or selects a menu option, changes are saved.

Before saving the user's changes, however, we lock the TSCLIENT record and check whether any changes were made since the user moved to the current record. To verify that the user has indeed been editing the most current copy of the record all along, we must do the following:

1. `SCATTER TO l_old` at the same time that I `SCATTER MEMVAR`.

2. Lock the record before saving the changes.

3. `SCATTER TO l_new` after the record lock to get the most current version of the record.

4. Compare the `l_old` array with the `l_new` array. If the two arrays are not equal, the user has not been working with the most current version of the record, and the changes must be aborted.

If the database in question includes fields that are not being edited in this data entry screen but that may be updated by another process during an edit, I must amend my approach. Suppose, for example, that the TSCLIENT database is enhanced to include a `cl_ytdsale` field that holds a running total of year-to-date sales for each client. The `cl_ytdsale` field is not edited on the TSCLIENT data entry screen.

Because I sincerely hope that there is vigorous activity taking place in the order entry and invoicing portions of our system, I can expect that changes will often take place to the `cl_ytdsale` field while users are editing the other fields in the TSCLIENT database. If so, when I compare `l_old` to `l_new`, I will frequently discover that one of the fields in the TSCLIENT database has changed since the user began working with the current TSCLIENT record. Therefore, I will frequently discard changes the user makes to TSCLIENT records.

Because the user cannot directly change `cl_ytdsale`, I may want to adjust my SCATTER and GATHER commands as follows:

```
SCATTER MEMVAR MEMO FIELDS cl_clid,cl_company, etc.
SCATTER TO l_old MEMO FIELDS cl_clid,cl_company, etc.

IF RLOCK()
  SCATTER TO l_new MEMO FIELDS cl_clid,cl_company,etc.
  IF the l_new and l_old arrays match
    GATHER MEMVAR MEMO cl_clid,cl_company, etc.
```

Another solution to the running total problem is to place the running total in a separate database along with the client ID. This solution not only relieves our l_new versus l_old comparison problems, it also improves posting performance by reducing the size of the database to which ytdsales are posted.

Many programmers are unwilling to live with the possibility that the user may start with an old copy of a record. Others are unwilling to live with the possibility that user A may not be able to save his changes because user B has changed the record while user A was editing. In many cases, programmers choose to address either problem by using a *flag field* in the database.

Before the introduction of the SCATTER TO command, we frequently used flag fields at Micro Endeavors. Now, however, we rarely use the technique. I discuss it here only because it is still very popular among long-time Xbase programmers.

Here is some pseudocode that demonstrates the important aspects of the flag field technique:

```
PROCEDURE vcontrol
DO CASE
  CASE m.control="EDIT"
    IF RLOCK()
      IF NOT EMPTY(tsclient.flag)
        UNLOCK
        DO l3msg WITH tsclient.flag+" is using the record now."+;
          " Please try again later."
      ELSE
        REPLACE tsclient.flag WITH kuserid
        SCATTER MEMVAR MEMO
        UNLOCK
      ENDIF
    ENDIF
  CASE m.control="SAVE"
    IF RLOCK()
      IF m.flag<>tsclient.flag
        UNLOCK
        DO l3msg WITH "Someone overrode your lock! No changes"+;
          " saved!"
      ELSE
        m.flag=""
        GATHER MEMVAR MEMO
      ENDIF
    ENDIF
ENDCASE
```

This approach is popular for the following reasons:

- It lets the user know who has a record locked.

- It greatly reduces the possibility that the user's changes won't be saved.

- It locks the record only long enough to check for a flag at the beginning of the edit session, and then again when the user elects to save changes.

- Until the inclusion of the SCATTER TO command in the FoxPro language, there was no easy way to determine whether a record had changed because the beginning of an edit. Programmers who subscribe to the "If it isn't broken, don't fix it" school of development continue to use the flag field technique because they've "always done it this way."

The following are the problems with the flag field approach:

- Every database must include an extra field.

- The technique works only if every programmer checks the flag field before making changes.

- The application must ensure unique user IDs.

- Extra network traffic occurs because two record locks result in two reads of the database.

- The application must include a "clear flags" utility to clear the flags placed by workstations that have disconnected from the LAN, locked up, rebooted, or otherwise failed to maintain their own flags.

Active Locking Techniques

The active locking scheme is demonstrated in Chapters 6 ("Time Sheets") and 7 ("Updating Time Sheets") during discussions of the TSTIME multifile data entry screen. However, because so much goes on in those chapters, you might have over-looked the basic active locking approach.

For a simple, single-file data entry screen, the following vcontrol() segment handles most of the work of the active record locking scheme:

```
PROCEDURE vcontrol
DO CASE
  CASE m.control="EDIT"
    IF NOT RLOCK()
      DO l3msg WITH "Sorry. Someone else is using this record"+;
        " right now. Please try again later."
    ELSE
```

```
      ** Get "current" copy of the record
      SCATTER MEMVAR MEMO
      SHOW GETS
    ENDIF
  CASE m.control="SAVE"
    GATHER MEMVAR MEMO
    UNLOCK
ENDCASE
```

Notice that we don't need to compare arrays to ensure that the record is not changed during the time the user is editing the record. We know that the record has remained unchanged during the user's edit because this user has the record locked.

In addition, we don't have to worry about failing to obtain a record lock when the user elects to save changes. After all, we already have the record locked. Finally, because the record is locked, we are assured that the user is working with the current copy of the record.

Despite of the obvious coding advantages afforded by the active locking scheme, many programmers always use the passive locking scheme. They do this to avoid the "out-to-lunch" problem, which can occur when a user begins an edit (thereby locking a record) and then leaves the system unattended.

Active Locking Solutions to the Out-to-Lunch Problem

In some applications, the out-to-lunch problem can be a significant challenge. Fortunately, there is a solution to this problem: The READ TIMEOUT clause directs FoxPro to attempt to exit a READ CYCLE command if no activity takes place for a designated number of seconds.

To test this feature, create and run the following code segment:

```
ACTIVATE SCREEN
CLEAR
@ 2,5 GET mvar DEFAULT 0
t1=SECO()
READ CYCLE TIMEOUT 5
t2=SECO()
WAIT WINDOW "Timed out after "+LTRIM(STR(t2-t1,10,4))+;
  " seconds of inactivity"
```

The TIMEOUT occurs only if the user does not press a key or click the mouse. You can use the Screen Builder to apply the READ TIMEOUT clause in one of two ways.

First, you can include the following line in the setup snippet of the Screen Layout dialog:

```
#READCLAUSES TIMEOUT 120
```

Second, you can include the TIMEOUT clause as part of one of the READ clause expressions, as shown in Figure 13.1.

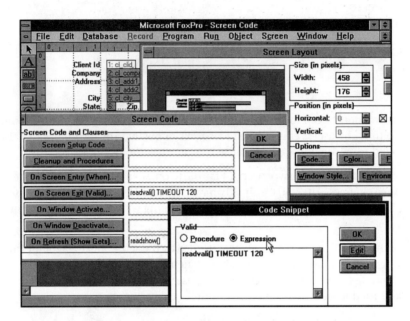

Figure 13.1. Including a *READ TIMEOUT* in the *READ VALID* expression.

When you generate this screen, GENSCRN.PRG generates the following READ CYCLE command:

```
READ CYCLE;
    VALID readvali() TIMEOUT 120;
    SHOW readshow()
```

Because you might want your program to take a specific action when a TIMEOUT occurs, you should create the following readvali UDF:

```
PROCEDURE readvali
IF READKEY(1)=6  && Timed out
  IF l_editing && variable set when the edit starts
    GATHER MEMVAR MEMO
    UNLOCK
  ENDIF
ENDIF
RETURN .T.
```

Fortunately, the READ TIMEOUT clause is in effect even if the user is currently resting in a BROWSE NOWAIT window. Unfortunately, the READ TIMEOUT clause is not in effect if the user clicks a menu pad without selecting an option. In other words, the user can sit in a menu popup forever, regardless of the READ TIMEOUT command.

Active Locking Solutions to the Running Total Problem

If your application requires a running total, the active locking scheme seems to pose another problem. For example, if your customer record contains a cu_ytdsale field, and user A has a customer record locked to change the address, user B cannot update that customer record's cu_ytdsale field to reflect a new sale to the customer.

The first solution to the problem is not to create running total fields. After all, FoxPro can summarize records very quickly, so you might not need a running total field.

If you determine that a running total field is necessary, consider creating a separate database to contain only the running total field(s) and the unique ID associated with a master file record. Not only does this solution make using the active locking scheme safer, it significantly increases throughput during posting by reducing the size of the file that must be searched to update the ytdsales field.

Did the User Change Anything?

In the time sheet application, we use the TSCHANGE.PRG program to determine whether the user changed any values on the screen during the current edit session. Chapter 4, "More Clients," includes the listing for the TSCHANGE program.

Why not just use the FoxPro UPDATE() function? Unfortunately, any change to any GET on the screen, including push buttons, causes the UPDATE() function to return True. Further, once the UPDATE() function returns .T., it returns .T. until the current READ CYCLE is exited.

The TSCHANGE solution is easy to understand and easy to use. However, the next solution to the UPDATE() function problem provides some additional functionality, although it requires significant extra effort on the part of the programmer.

In several applications, we have:

1. Created an l_original array.

2. Created a l_changed variable of character type.

3. Included the l3chv() UDF in the VALID clause expression of every GET that we want to monitor for change.

4. Included the l3chw() UDF in the WHEN clause expression of every GET that we want to monitor for change.

Every GET in a READ CYCLE has an object number. The current object number is returned by the _CUROBJ system variable. We will use this _CUROBJ value as an index to a single character in the l_changed variable, and as an index to a single element in the l_original array.

To the l3chv() and l3chw() UDFs we pass the content of the GET with which they are associated. Here are a few sample @...GET commands generated by a screen in which we have placed the appropriate references to the l3chv() and l3chw() UDFs:

```
@ 1.231,10.000 GET m.nmcmname ;
   SIZE 1.000,36.000 ;
   DEFAULT " " ;
   FONT "MS Sans Serif", 8 ;
   PICTURE "@!" ;
   WHEN l3chw(m.nmcmname) ;
   VALID vnmcmname() and l3chv(m.nmcmname) ;
   MESSAGE "Enter the company name"
@ 0.077,45.000 GET m.nm_last ;
   SIZE 1.000,20.000 ;
   DEFAULT " " ;
   FONT "MS Sans Serif", 8 ;
   WHEN l3chw(m.nm_last) ;
   VALID l3chv(m.nm_last) ;
   MESSAGE "Last name"
@ 0.077,67.333 GET m.nm_suffix ;
   SIZE 1.000,12.000 ;
   DEFAULT " " ;
   FONT "MS Sans Serif", 8 ;
   WHEN l3chw(m.nm_suffix) ;
   VALID l3chv(m.nm_suffix) ;
   MESSAGE "Suffix. E.g. Jr., III, Esq., etc."
```

The l3chw UDF checks whether the original value for the GET in question resides in the l_original() array. If it does not exist, the l_original array is resized as necessary, and the content passed to l3chw() is placed in the appropriate element of the l_original array. Here is the code for l3chw():

```
* l3chw.prg
* Maintains the "change" arrays for a screen.
* l_changed string has one character per object on the screen.
*    if position is blank, this is the first time the
*    GET has been entered.
*    If the position has an 'N', this GET has not been changed.
*    If the position has a 'C', this GET has been changed.
*    l_original() array = original content of all objects
*
```

```
PARAMETERS p_val,p_obj
PRIVATE m.l_thisobj
m.l_thisobj=IIF(TYPE('p_obj')="N",p_obj,_CUROBJ)
IF m.l_thisobj>0
  ** See whether the string and array are big enough
  IF LEN(m.l_changed)<m.l_thisobj
    ** Make them big enough
    DIMENSION l_original(m.l_thisobj)
    m.l_changed=PADR(m.l_changed,m.l_thisobj)
  ENDIF array not big enough
  ** See whether this is the first entry to this GET
  IF SUBSTR(m.l_changed,m.l_thisobj,1)=" "
    ** First time into this GET
    l_original(m.l_thisobj)=m.p_val
    m.l_changed=STUFF(m.l_changed,m.l_thisobj,1,"N")
  ENDIF this is the first entry to this GET
ENDIF in a get field
l_lastobj=_CUROBJ
RETURN .T.
```

So, when the user enters a GET for the first time, the 13chw() UDF registers the initial value of the GET in the l_original array, and places the letter *N* in the appropriate character of the l_changed variable. Now, we are ready for the user to exit the field and trigger the following 13chv() UDF:

```
* 13chv.prg
* Maintains the "change" arrays for a screen.
* l_changed string has one character per object on the screen.
*    if position is blank, this is the first time the
*    GET has been entered.
*    If the position has an 'N', this GET has not been changed.
*    If the position has a 'C', this GET has been changed.
* m.l_original() array = original content of all objects
*
* p_val = value to be compared
* p_obj = object number to use, defaults to _curobj
PARAMETERS p_val,p_obj
PRIVATE m.l_thisobj,m.l_oldenable
m.l_thisobj=IIF(TYPE('m.p_obj')#"N",_CUROBJ,p_obj)
m.l_oldenable="C"$m.l_changed
IF m.l_thisobj>0
  m.l_changed=STUFF(m.l_changed,m.l_thisobj,1,;
    IIF(l_original(m.l_thisobj)==m.p_val,"N","C"))
ENDIF
```

continues

279

```
** Turn the SAVE and CANCEL buttons on
** or off depending on the existence of
** a changed GET.
IF NOT l_oldenable AND "C"$m.l_changed
   ** Before this GET, there were no changes pending.
   ** The user changed this GET, so we will enable
   ** the SAVE and CANCEL buttons for this screen.
   IF OBJNUM(m.pbsave)>0
     SHOW GET m.pbsave enabled
   ENDIF
   IF OBJNUM(m.pbcanc)>0
     SHOW GET m.pbcanc enabled
   ENDIF
ENDIF changed
IF l_oldenable AND NOT "C"$m.l_changed
   ** This GET was the only pending change on the
   ** screen, and the user changed it back to its
   ** original value. So, we will disable the
   ** SAVE and CANCEL buttons for this screen.
   IF OBJNUM(m.pbsave)>0
     SHOW GET m.pbsave disabled
   ENDIF
   IF OBJNUM(m.pbcanc)>0
     SHOW GET m.pbcanc disabled
   ENDIF
ENDIF he undid his change
l_lastobj=_CUROBJ
IF NOT EMPTY(kaction)
   ** This must have been triggered by a menu action
   CLEAR READ
ENDIF
RETURN .T.
```

The l3chv() UDF compares the passed value to the value that the l3chw() UDF stores in the l_original array. If the values don't match, the appropriate character in the l_changed variable is set to "C". If the values do match, the appropriate character in the l_changed variable is set to "N".

The l3chv() UDF takes the extra step of enabling or disabling the m.pbsave and m.pbcanc push buttons, if those push buttons exist. In other words, a data entry screen that takes full advantage of l3chv() includes a Save push button and a Cancel push button.

As the user enters the screen, these push buttons are disabled. However, as soon as the user changes the content of a GET, and therefore triggers the l3chv() UDF, the l3chv() UDF enables the Save and Cancel push buttons. Interestingly, if the user undoes the changes, l3chv is smart enough to disable the Save and Cancel buttons as needed.

All that remains is to provide the programmer with an easy way to determine whether any fields have been changed. You can accomplish this by testing for the existence of a "C" in the l_changed variable. If a "C" exists, at least one change is pending on this screen. The following is an example that uses this information:

```
IF "C"$l_changed AND l_butt#"CANC" AND l_butt#"SAVE"
   ** Something changed, so call pbsave to save changes
   DO pbsave
   ** Reset the change trackers
   l_changed=""
   l_original=.f.
ENDIF something changed
```

Obviously, the l3chw() and l3chv() approach to monitoring changes is very powerful. Equally obvious, however, is the amount of overhead associated with ensuring that all of the GETs on a screen are appropriately assigned l3chw() and l3chv() references. Because I hate clicking into every field dialog on a screen and typing in the appropriate l3chw() and l3chv() references, I wrote the following routine to automate the process:

```
* l3allwv.prg
* Sets all WHEN and VALID clauses to use l3chw and l3chv
* respectively
* P_options=
*      scx=[mecomp] name of scx to read and update
*      for=[upper(name)="M.CM_"] condition for which
*      updates should be made
** Example: The following command will "tag" all of the m.cm_*
**      GETs in the mecomp.scx file with the appropriate
**      l3chw() and l3chv() references.
**      DO l3allwv WITH "scx=[mecomp]for=[upper(name)='M.CM_']"
PARAMETERS p_options
PRIVATE ALL LIKE l_*
p_options=IIF(TYPE('p_options')#"C","",p_options)
m.l_parse=ATC("SCX=[",m.p_options)
m.l_scx=IIF(m.l_parse=0,GETFILE("SCX","Screen to when/valid");
  ,SUBSTR(m.p_options,m.l_parse+ 5,AT("]",;
  SUBSTR(m.p_options,m.l_parse+ 5))-1))
IF EMPTY(m.l_scx)
  RETURN
ENDIF
```

continues

```
m.l_parse=ATC("FOR=[",m.p_options)
m.l_for=IIF(m.l_parse=0,"",SUBSTR(m.p_options,;
  m.l_parse+ 5,AT("]",SUBSTR(m.p_options,m.l_parse+ 5))-1))
m.l_scx=UPPER(m.l_scx)
m.l_scx=IIF(RIGHT(m.l_scx,4)#".SCX",m.l_scx+".SCX",m.l_scx)
IF USED('l3allwv')
  USE IN l3allwv
ENDIF
USE (l_scx) IN SELECT(1) ALIAS l3allwv AGAIN
SELECT l3allwv
IF EMPTY(m.l_for)
  GETEXPR "Condition for screen" TO m.l_for ;
    TYPE "L" DEFAULT "not empty(name)"
ENDIF empty for clause
REPLACE ALL WHEN WITH IIF(EMPTY(WHEN),"",TRIM(WHEN)+" and ")+;
  "l3chw("+TRIM(name)+")",;
  whentype WITH 0 FOR &l_for. AND NOT "L3CHW("$UPPER(WHEN)
REPLACE ALL validtype WITH 0,;
  VALID WITH "l3chv("+TRIM(name)+")"+;
  IIF(EMPTY(VALID),""," and "+TRIM(VALID)) ;
  FOR &l_for. AND NOT "L3CHV("$UPPER(VALID)
USE IN l3allwv
RETURN
```

Adding a Record to a Shared Database

When we attempt to add a record to a shared database in FoxPro, one of the following results are possible:

- The record is added successfully.

- The record is not added because another user has the file locked.

- The record is not added because other users are adding records at the same time.

- The record is not added because another user has the target database in EXCLUSIVE use. (*Note:* The INSERT INTO command tries to open the target database if the target database is not already in use. Therefore, the user may attempt to INSERT INTO a database that is in EXCLUSIVE use by another user.)

- The record is not added because of another error condition. (For example, insufficient disk space.)

Chapter 4, "More Clients," introduced the concept of adding records to shared databases. In that chapter, we used the FLOCK() function to help ensure that the client ID the user proposed was in fact a new ID. In effect, if the program can obtain an FLOCK() on a database, a subsequent attempt to INSERT or APPEND a record will succeed.

However, although an FLOCK() is in place on a database, no other users can obtain an RLOCK() or FLOCK() on that database. Further, no other users can add a record to that database. More importantly, if any user has an RLOCK() in the database, an attempt to obtain an FLOCK() will fail.

For these reasons, most FoxPro programmers eschew the use of the FLOCK() function. Instead, most write a UDF like l3insert(). The l3insert() UDF attempts to add a record with an INSERT INTO command and returns .T. if that attempt succeeds, or .F. if that attempt fails. Here are three examples using l3insert():

```
** Try to INSERT INTO .... FROM MEMVAR in the
** current work area
IF l3insert()

** Try to INSERT INTO ... FROM MEMVAR in the
** tsclient work area
IF l3insert("alia=[tsclient]")

** Try to INSERT INTO tsclient (cl_clid) VALUE (m.cl_clid)
IF l3insert("comm=[tsclient (cl_clid) VALUES (m.cl_clid)]")

** Try forever to INSERT INTO tsclient FROM MEMVAR
IF l3insert("alia=[tsclient]retr=[-1]")
```

Here is the source code for the l3insert() UDF:

```
* l3insert.prg
* adds one or more record(s) via insert into
* insopts  = character string with the following options:
*    alia=[alias] Alias into which l3insert will insert. ALIAS()
*        if not passed
*    comm=[] = The remainder of the insert into command. If not
*            passed, (ALIAS()) FROM MEMVAR is assumed.
*    retr=[0] Number of times to retry. Defaults to 0 for
*            try until user escapes. -1 means try forever.
*            Number > 0 is times to try before failing.
*    time=[.2] Time between attempts. Defaults to 0.2 seconds.
*    noer=[] Indicates that your error trap routine will update
*            kerror for me. So...I won't reset the error trap.
*    msg=[Attempting to add your customer...] Message to be
```

continues

283

```
*           displayed during retries. Defaults to "Attempting to add"
*           I will add the "Please wait" or "Press Escape" to exit
*           as needed.
PARAMETERS p_insopts
PRIVATE l_msg,l_noer,l_time,l_retr,l_sofar,l_thiskey,l_olderr
** Parse out the parameters from the p_insopts parameter
m.l_sofar=0
m.l_success=.F.
m.l_insopts=IIF(TYPE('m.p_insopts')#"C","",m.p_insopts)
m.l_parse=ATC("COMM=[",m.l_insopts)
m.l_comm=IIF(m.l_parse=0,"",SUBSTR(m.l_insopts,m.l_parse+
6,AT("]",SUBSTR(m.l_insopts,m.l_parse+ 6))-1))
m.l_parse=ATC("RETR=[",m.l_insopts)
m.l_retr=IIF(m.l_parse=0,0,VAL(SUBSTR(m.l_insopts,m.l_parse+ 6)))
m.l_parse=ATC("TIME=[",m.l_insopts)
m.l_time=IIF(m.l_parse=0,0,VAL(SUBSTR(m.l_insopts,m.l_parse+ 6)))
m.l_parse=ATC("MSG=[",m.l_insopts)
m.l_msg=IIF(m.l_parse=0,"Attempting to add...",;
  SUBSTR(m.l_insopts,m.l_parse+ 5,AT("]",;
  SUBSTR(m.l_insopts,m.l_parse+ 5))-1))
m.l_parse=ATC("ALIA=[",m.l_insopts)
m.l_alia=IIF(m.l_parse=0,ALIAS(),SUBSTR(m.l_insopts,m.l_parse+;
  6,AT("]",SUBSTR(m.l_insopts,m.l_parse+ 6))-1))
m.l_noer="NOER=[]"$UPPER(l_insopts)
IF NOT l_noer
  l_olderr=ON('error')
  ** Set up a local error trap
  ON ERROR kerror=ERROR()
ENDIF
* Start trying to add the record(s)
DO WHILE .T.
  * Reset error flag
  kerror=0
  IF NOT EMPTY(m.l_comm)
    ** He passed me the rest of the INSERT INTO command,
    ** so I'll just use it.
    INSERT INTO &l_comm.
  ELSE
    ** Because she didn't pass me the rest of the INSERT INTO
    ** command, I'll assume that she wants to
    ** INSERT INTO FROM MEMVAR
    INSERT INTO (m.l_alia) FROM MEMVAR
  ENDIF
```

```
   ** Now, see how we made out.
   DO CASE
     CASE kerror=0                            && success!!!!!!!!!
       m.l_success=.T.
       EXIT
     CASE m.l_retr=-1                         && try forever
       ** I failed, and he wants me to try forever.
       WAIT WINDOW m.l_msg+"Attempting to add..."+;
       "Please wait." NOWAIT
       =INKEY(m.l_time,"MH") && Pause between lock attempts
     CASE m.l_retr=0   && try till success, or they say to stop
       ** I failed, and she wants me to try until the user
       ** presses escape, or until I succeed.
       WAIT WINDOW m.l_msg+"Press [Esc] to abort." NOWAIT
       **  Pause between lock attempts
       m.l_thiskey=INKEY(m.l_time,"MH")
       IF m.l_thiskey=27                     && escape key pressed
         m.l_success=.F.
         EXIT
       ENDIF
     CASE m.l_sofar<=m.l_retr                 && try some number of times
       ** I failed, and he wants me to try some number of times
       m.l_sofar=m.l_sofar+1
       =INKEY(m.l_time,"MH") && Pause between lock attempts
     OTHERWISE
       ** failure....
       m.l_success=.F.
       EXIT
   ENDCASE
   WAIT CLEAR && get rid of lingering WAIT WINDOW messages
ENDDO try some number of times to add the records
IF NOT m.l_noer
   ** Put the error trap back the way I found it.
   ON ERROR &l_olderr
ENDIF
RETURN m.l_success
```

If you are curious about the manner in which we pass multiple values to the
l3insert() UDF in the same parameter, you will find Chapter 19, "Library Routines,"
particularly beneficial. In the meantime, note that the only way to determine the
possible success or failure of an INSERT INTO command is to attempt the command and
then check for errors.

Adding Unique IDs

Often, we want to add a record only if the record's ID is unique. In Chapter 4, "More Clients," we created a TSCLIENT.PRG program that uses an FLOCK() to ensure that two users do not simultaneously attempt to add the same client ID, resulting in non-unique client IDs in the TSCLIENT.DBF database.

In a single-user environment, we can protect against duplicate IDs as follows:

```
SELECT tsclient
IF NOT SEEK(m.cl_clid)
  INSERT INTO tsclient FROM MEMVAR
ELSE
  DO l3msg WITH "ID is a duplicate!"
ENDIF
```

In a multiuser environment, this solution is unreliable because two users can simultaneously SEEK the same proposed ID in the TSCLIENT database, discover that the ID is not yet in the database, and then add the duplicate proposed ID.

The FLOCK() solution demonstrated in Chapter 4 prevents this problem by ensuring that only one user can perform the SEEK at a time. As we discussed earlier in this chapter, however, the FLOCK() solution has several undesirable side effects. So, I propose the use of the l3uniq_a() UDF, as follows, to ensure unique IDs:

```
IF l3uniq_a(m.cl_clid)
  DO l3msg WITH "Client added successfully!"
ELSE
  DO l3msg WITH "Client id is a DUPLICATE!"
ENDIF
```

Here is the code for the l3uniq_a() UDF:

```
* l3uniq_a.prg
* uses new APPEND FROM technique to add unique records
* p_key = key value to seek in the database
* p_options is a string containing one or more of the following
* alia=[cust] Alias in which to place newly unique record.
*             defaults to current alias().
* retr=[10] Number of times to retry the add
* time=[.33] Time to wait between attempts to add record.
*  msg=[Adding Customer] Message to be displayed while retrying
*      APPEND FROM
* orde=[cu_custid] Order for seek in the target file.
* arra=[arrayname] array name containing content of new record.
```

```
*                    If not included, assume the use of memvar.
* nogo=[] Don't GOTO the newly added record
PARAMETERS p_key,p_options
PRIVATE ALL LIKE l_*
IF PARAMETERS()<1
  DO 13msg WITH "No key passed to 13uniq_a.prg.¦No record added."
  RETURN .F.
ENDIF
IF TYPE('p_options')#"C"
  p_options=""
ENDIF no optional parameters passed
* parse optional arguments
m.l_parse=ATC("ALIA=[",m.p_options)
m.l_alia=IIF(m.l_parse=0,ALIAS(),;
  SUBSTR(m.p_options,m.l_parse+ 6,AT("]",;
  SUBSTR(m.p_options,m.l_parse+ 6))-1))
m.l_parse=ATC("RETR=[",m.p_options)
m.l_retr=IIF(m.l_parse=0,10,VAL(SUBSTR(m.p_options,m.l_parse+ 6)))
m.l_parse=ATC("TIME=[",m.p_options)
m.l_time=IIF(m.l_parse=0,.33,VAL(SUBSTR(m.p_options,m.l_parse+ 6)))
m.l_parse=ATC("MSG=[",m.p_options)
m.l_msg=IIF(m.l_parse=0,"Attempting to add record to "+;
  ALIAS(),SUBSTR(m.p_options,m.l_parse+ 5,;
  AT("]",SUBSTR(m.p_options,m.l_parse+ 5))-1))
m.l_parse=ATC("ORDE=[",m.p_options)
m.l_orde=IIF(m.l_parse=0,ORDER(l_alia),;
  SUBSTR(m.p_options,m.l_parse+ 6,AT("]",;
  SUBSTR(m.p_options,m.l_parse+ 6))-1))
m.l_parse=ATC("ARRA=[",m.p_options)
m.l_arra=IIF(m.l_parse=0,"",SUBSTR(m.p_options,m.l_parse+;
  6,AT("]",SUBSTR(m.p_options,m.l_parse+ 6))-1))
m.l_nogo="NOGO=[]"$UPPER(m.p_options)
* make sure the target database is open
l_oldsele=SELECT()
IF NOT USED(m.l_alia)
  USE (m.l_alia) AGAIN IN SELECT(1)
ENDIF
* select the target database
SELECT (m.l_alia)

IF EMPTY(m.l_arra)
  * If they didn't pass us an array to add,
  * create an array with the content of the
```

continues

```
      * memvars that should have been created
      * with a SCATTER MEMVAR
      DIMENSION l_memvar(FCOUNT())
      FOR l_xx=1 TO FCOUNT()
         l_memvar(l_xx)=IIF(TYPE(FIELD(l_xx))="G",.F.,;
            EVAL("m."+FIELD(l_xx)))
      ENDFOR
   ENDIF no array passed
   * If the l3uniq_a alias is in use, close it
   IF USED('l3uniq_a')
      USE IN l3uniq_a
   ENDIF
   * Open the target database again under the l3uniq_a alias
   USE (DBF(m.l_alia)) AGAIN IN SELECT(1) ALIAS l3uniq_a ;
      ORDER (m.l_orde)
   * Set flags and counters
   l_sofar=0
   l_retval=.T.
   DO WHILE l_retr<=0 OR l_sofar<=l_retr
      * set error trap flag
      * We assume that l3error or similar error trap will
      * issue kerror=error() if the append from fails
      kerror=0
      IF NOT EMPTY(m.l_arra)
         APPEND FROM ARRAY (m.l_arra) FOR NOT SEEK(p_key,'l3uniq_a')
      ELSE
         APPEND FROM ARRAY l_memvar FOR NOT SEEK(p_key,'l3uniq_a')
      ENDIF no array passed
      * check to see if we succeeded
      DO CASE
         CASE _TALLY>=1 AND kerror=0
            * we succeeded in adding a record!
            IF NOT l_nogo
               GOTO (RECNO('l3uniq_a')) IN (m.l_alia)
            ENDIF
            l_retval=.T.
            EXIT
         CASE _TALLY<=0 AND kerror=0
            * this is a duplicate
            l_retval=.F.
            EXIT
         CASE l_retr<0
            * try forever
            WAIT WINDOW l_msg NOWAIT
```

```
      CASE l_retr=0
        * try until success or keystroke
        IF CHRSAW()
          l_retval=.F.
          EXIT
        ELSE
          WAIT WINDOW l_msg+" Press a key to abort" NOWAIT
        ENDIF
      CASE l_retr>=0
        * try some number of times
        l_sofar=l_sofar+1
        WAIT WINDOW l_msg NOWAIT
        l_retval=.F.
    ENDCASE
    * wait the designated length of time before trying again
    l_seco=SECONDS()
    DO WHILE SECONDS()+l_time<=l_seco+l_time AND SECONDS()>=l_seco
    ENDDO time between tries
  ENDDO
  * cleanup
  WAIT CLEAR
  SELECT (l_oldsele)
  USE IN l3uniq_a
  RETURN l_retval
```

When FoxPro attempts to add a record or records to a shared database, it first locks the header of that database. The l3uniq_a() UDF takes advantage of this behavior as follows:

1. Opening the target database AGAIN in another work area.

2. Copying the memvars associated with the fields in the target database into an array called l_memvar().

3. Using the command

   ```
   APPEND FROM ARRAY l_memvar FOR NOT SEEK(p_key,"l3uniq_a")
   ```

   to add the content of the l_memvar() array to the target database only if a SEEK() of the key value in the duplicate work area for the target database returns False.

This technique works because the APPEND FROM command locks the file header of the target database *before* it evaluates the FOR clause, and it keeps the file header locked *while* it evaluates the FOR clause. Therefore, no two users can SEEK(p_key,"l3uniq_a") at the same time.

This is a simple, foolproof solution to the unique ID problem. I would therefore love to take full credit for the idea. However, this one came from my friends on the Microsoft FoxPro development team. Thanks, folks!

Sequentially Assigned IDs

Frequently applications require the assignment of sequential IDs to records in a database. For example, invoice numbers are usually system-generated, and almost always sequential. Other examples include check numbers, purchase orders, and project IDs.

The following method works acceptably in single-user environments:

```
SELECT paycheck
GOTO BOTTOM
m.pc_num=pc_num+1
INSERT INTO paycheck FROM MEMVAR
```

In a multiuser environment, this approach fails because two users can simultaneously arrive at the last record in the file and thereby create two pay check records with the same pc_num.

For most applications, the best solution to the sequentially assigned ID number problem involves the use of a separate "system" file, which contains a record, which contains a field, which contains the value of the next available check number. Here is a sample data structure for a system database:

```
Structure for table:    c:\book\dbf\tssyst.dbf
Number of data records: 0
Date of last update:    01/21/93
Field  Field Name  Type       Width   Dec   Index
    1  SY_NUMBER   Numeric      10
    2  SY_TAG      Character    10            Asc
** Total **                     21
```

The sy_tag field contains the name of the databases for which sequentially assigned IDs are required. The sy_number field contains the next available number for each of these databases.

The TSSYST.DBF database includes one record per database that receives sequentially assigned numbers. For example, suppose we use a process or data entry screen to fill with values the memory variables associated with the TSPAYCH.DBF database. All that remains is to add to the TSPAYCH.DBF a record with the next available pay check number. Here is one method of creating that new TSPAYCH.DBF record:

```
l_retval=.F.
SELECT tssyst
SEEK "TSPAYCH"
IF RLOCK()
  m.pc_num=sy_number
  IF l3insert("alia=[tspaych]")
    REPLACE sy_number WITH sy_number+1
    l_retval=.T.
  ENDIF successfully added the tspaych record
  UNLOCK
ENDIF able to lock this system record
RETURN l_retval
```

Notice that the TSSYST record remains locked while we attempt to add the TSPAYCH record. By incrementing the sy_number field only if a TSPAYCH record is successfully added, we ensure that the numbering scheme has no "holes."

Because most applications include sequentially assigned IDs in one or more tables, you might expect to find a library routine that facilitates the process of applying sequentially assigned IDs. The name of the library routine is l3nextid(), and you can see the source code and usage in Chapter 19, "Library Routines."

Some developers prefer not to create and maintain a system table. So, here is an alternative method for generating sequentially assigned IDs:

```
SELECT tspaych
SET ORDER TO pc_num
GO BOTTOM
m.pc_num=tspaych.pc_num+1
DO WHILE NOT l3uniq_a(m.pc_num)
  m.pc_num=m.pc_num+1
ENDDO
```

Multitable, Multirecord Updates

Until now, our discussions have focused on adding, editing, and deleting one record at a time. However, most applications require the simultaneous addition, deletion, or update of multiple records in multiple tables.

Here is a general approach for updating multiple records in one or more tables:

1. Store all user additions, changes, and deletions in temporary files, memory variables, or arrays.

2. When the user elects to save changes, attempt to lock all permanent records the changes will affect. If you cannot lock a permanent record, unlock all records and start over.

3. Attempt to add any new records. If the attempt fails, unlock all records and start over.

4. If all permanent records are locked and all new records have been added, update all permanent records and unlock all records.

Here's a little memory jogger that can be useful: *T*emp, *L*ock, *A*dd, *R*eplace/delete, u*N*lock (*TLARN*).

Why Bother with Temporary Files?

Why not just treat every change, addition, and deletion as an individual transaction? After all, we didn't use any temporary files in the time sheet application.

Whenever possible, I try to treat each change of a record as an individual transaction, because doing so greatly reduces programming effort. This approach is successful in time sheet application because each entry into the TSTIME database is atomic. In other words, if I were adding 25 time sheet entries to the system but posted only 12 because the power went out, because my workstation became disconnected from the network, or because someone locked the file in which I wanted to work, the 12 records I added would still be viable. Referential integrity would still be maintained. No running totals would be out of balance.

Developers are not always so lucky, however. For example, adding, editing, or deleting an invoice often requires that records be changed in the customer, invoice, line item, and inventory databases. Further, if one part of the invoice is not posted, the entire invoice is invalid.

Finally, if the user decides to cancel the invoice before it is complete, undoing changes made to permanent files is difficult.

Because the invoice example is so common, and because it presents a significant number of challenges, we'll walk through some of the steps required to post new or changed invoices in an application.

Adding a Multirecord, Multitable Transaction

The user will be changing values found in the invoice and line item files. We use some of this information to change values found in the customer and inventory databases. We store pending changes/additions to the invoice file in memory variables and store pending changes/additions to the line item file in a cursor.

To prepare for our invoice and line item activities, we include code such as the following at the beginning of our invoicing program:

```
* ppinvoic.prg
SELECT ppinvoic
SCATTER MEMVAR MEMO
SELECT ppline
** Put structure of ppline.dbf into linestru array
=AFIELDS(linestru)
** Make room for two extra fields
DIMENSION linestru(ALEN(linestru,1)+2,ALEN(linestru,2))
** Make a field for the record number of the
** ppline.dbf record associated with this temp record
linestru(ALEN(linestru,1)-1,1)="recno"
linestru(ALEN(linestru,1)-1,2)="N"
linestru(ALEN(linestru,1)-1,3)=13
linestru(ALEN(linestru,1)-1,4)=0
** Make a field to hold (A)dd, (E)dit, or (D)elete
** to signify action taken on this temp record
linestru(ALEN(linestru,1),1)="action"
linestru(ALEN(linestru,1),2)="C"
linestru(ALEN(linestru,1),3)=1
linestru(ALEN(linestru,1),4)=0
** Use linestru array to create temp cursor into
** which we will place all pending changes, additions,
** and deletions to the ppline database
CREATE CURSOR templine FROM ARRAY linestru
```

When the user elects to add a new invoice, we can execute the following simple procedure to prepare for the new information:

```
PROCEDURE startadd
SELECT ppinvoic
SCATTER MEMVAR MEMO BLANK
SELECT templine
ZAP
RETURN
```

After the user fills the invoice and line item information as necessary, we must accomplish the following to add this new invoice information to the permanent files:

1. Validate and lock the customer record associated with the invoice.

2. Ensure that at least one line item is entered.

3. Lock all the inventory items that the new line items will update.

4. Obtain an invoice number for the invoice.

5. Add an invoice record to the PPINVOIC database.

6. Apply an invoice number to all line items.

7. Add temporary line items to the PPLINE database.

8. Update all associated inventory items.

9. Update customer.

10. Unlock all records.

In the following program, we assume that a data entry screen program has taken care of populating the TEMPITEM cursor and the m.iv_* variables. Further, the data entry program must place the letter N for (N)ew in the tempitem.action field of every TEMPITEM record that should be added to the line item database.

The addinvoice procedure is provided for your review. This program includes no data, although you can find the code in the EXINVOI.PRG program, which is included on your source disk. Here is the code:

```
PROCEDURE addinvoice
IF EMPTY(m.iv_custid) .OR. !SEEK(m.iv_custid,'ppcust')
  DO l3msg WITH "Invalid Customer id!"
  _CUROBJ=OBJNUM(m.iv_custid)
ELSE                            && VALID custid
  IF NOT RLOCK("ppcust")
    DO l3msg WITH "I can't lock the customer record now."+;
      " Invoice not added."
  ELSE
    SELECT templine
    COUNT TO l_qtyitems FOR templine.action="N" AND NOT DELETED()
    IF l_qtyitems=0
      UNLOCK ALL
      DO l3msg WITH "You must have at least one line item"+;
        " to add an invoice!"
    ELSE
      ** Lock all the inventory items associated with this
      **    new order
      l_alllock=.T.
      SELECT templine
      SCAN FOR templine.action="N" AND NOT DELETED()
        IF (NOT SEEK(li_item,"ppinvt")) OR (NOT (RLOCK("ppinvt"))
          l_alllock=.F.
          EXIT
        ENDIF couldn't find inventory item, or couldn't lock item
```

```
ENDSCAN
IF NOT l_alllock
  ** not able to lock all inventory items
  UNLOCK ALL
  DO l3msg WITH "I couldn't lock one or more of your "+;
    "inventory items, so I couldn't save your new invoice."
ELSE
  ** Since we were able to lock everything, let's
  **    try to get a new invoice number
  l_newivno=0
  l_newivno=l3nextid("sysd=[ppsyst]syst=[sy_tag]"+;
    "sysn=[sy_number]id=[INVOICE]retr=[20]")
  IF l_newivno=0
    ** Couldn't GET a new invoice number
    UNLOCK ALL
    DO l3msg WITH ;
      "Sorry. The system could not generate an "+;
      "invoice number at this time. ¦No records added."+;
      "¦Please try again later."
  ELSE
    ** got the new invoice number
    ** put header record in ppinvoic file
    m.iv_ivno=STR(l_newivno,6)
    m.iv_status="UNPOSTED"
    IF NOT ;
      (l3insert("alia=[ppinvoic]msg=[Invoice Header]") ;
      AND RLOCK("ppinvoic"))
      UNLOCK ALL
      DO l3msg WITH "Sorry. The system could not add your"+;
        " invoice header at this time ¦No records added."+;
        "¦Please try again later."
    ELSE
      SELECT templine
      ** update temporary records with new invoice number
      REPLACE li_ivno WITH STR(l_newivno,6) FOR ;
        templine.action="N" AND NOT DELETED()
      COPY TO ARRAY l_templine FOR ;
        templine.action="N" AND NOT DELETED()
      ** Try to put new temporary records in line items
      ** database.
      IF NOT l3insert("comm=[ppitem FROM ARRAY l_templine]"+;
          "msg=[Line items]")
        ** Update invoice record
        REPLACE ppinvoic.iv_status WITH "CANCELLED"
```

continues

295

```
                              UNLOCK ALL
                              DO l3msg WITH ;
                                  "Sorry. The system could not add your"+;
                                  " line items at this time ¦No records added."+;
                                  "¦Please try again later."
                           ELSE
                              ** Successfully added the new line items, so
                              **   update the associated inventory records
                              SELECT templine
                              l_newsale=0
                              SCAN FOR templine.action="N" AND NOT DELETED()
                                 ** Note: We can be sure that the inventory record
                                 ** exists, and is locked, because we previously
                                 ** found and locked all inventory items for this
                                 ** invoice!
                                 =SEEK(templine.li_item,"ppinvt")
                                 REPLACE ppinvt.iv_qty WITH ;
                                   ppinvt.iv_qty-templine.li_qty
                                 l_newsale=l_newsale+li_qty*li_price
                              ENDSCAN
                              ** Update the invoice record
                              REPLACE ppinvoic.iv_status with "POSTED"
                              ** Update customer ytd sales
                              REPLACE ppcust.cu_ytdsale WITH ;
                                ppcust.cu_ytdsale+m.l_newsale
                              UNLOCK ALL
                              DO l3msg WITH "Successfully added invoice "+;
                                 ppinvoic.iv_ivno+;
                                 " for "+ppcust.cu_company
                           ENDIF able to add line item records
                        ENDIF able to add the invoice header record
                     ENDIF able TO crank up A VALID invoice NUMBER
                  ENDIF able to lock all of the associated inventory items
               ENDIF 1 OR more VALID items
            ENDIF able to lock the customer record
         ENDIF VALID customer id
```

Remember, the addinvoice procedure is presented here for discussion purposes only. It is not part of the time sheet application.

Because we are discussing addinvoice, however, we should probably take another look at this series of commands:

```
COPY TO ARRAY l_templine FOR ;
  templine.action="N" AND NOT DELETED()
```

```
** Try to put temporary records in line items database.
IF NOT l3insert("comm=[ppitem FROM ARRAY l_templine]"+;
  "msg=[Line items]")
  ** Update invoice record
  REPLACE ppinvoic.iv_status WITH "CANCELLED"
  UNLOCK ALL
```

In this case, we have called on the l3insert() UDF to add multiple records to the line items database by using a single INSERT INTO command. Notice that FoxPro does not lock the file when adding multiple records. Also, FoxPro simply ignores the extra fields in the l_templine array.

Note: If the user elects not to save a newly created invoice, we simply ZAP the templine cursor and reset the m.iv_* memory variables. We don't have anything to undo because we don't write anything to the permanent files until the user elects to save the new invoice.

Editing a Multirecord, Multitable Transaction

When it is time to edit an existing invoice, we must do the following:

1. Lock the invoice header.

2. Lock and copy each of the line items associated with the invoice to the TEMPLINE cursor.

3. Enable the user to add, edit, and delete invoice header and line item data.

4. Save the changes to the permanent file.

Here is the code that we execute when the user elects to edit the current invoice record:

```
PROCEDURE startedit
m.l_reval=.F.
IF NOT RLOCK("ppinvoi")
  DO l3msg WITH "I can't lock this invoice."
ELSE
  SELECT ppinvoi
  SCATTER MEMVAR MEMO
  SELECT templine
  ZAP
  SELECT ppline
```

continues

```
    SEEK ppinvoi.iv_ivno
    SCAN WHILE ppline.li_ivno=ppinvoi.iv_ivno AND RLOCK()
      SCATTER MEMVAR MEMO
      m.recno=RECNO() && Remember where this line item came from
      m.action=" " && No action until user edits or deletes this
      ** Put this record in the temp file
      INSERT INTO templine FROM MEMVAR
    ENDSCAN
    IF ppline.li_ivno=ppinvoi.iv_ivno
      ** IF sitting on a line item for the current invoice,
      ** must not have locked all of the line items for
      ** the current invoice.
      UNLOCK ALL
      DO l3msg WITH "I can't lock the line items for "+;
        "this invoice."
    ELSE && Locked and copied all of the line items
      m.l_retval=.T.
    ENDIF didn't lock them all
  ENDIF couldn't lock the invoice header
  RETURN m.l_retval
```

Now that we have the placed a duplicate of this invoice into memory variables and a cursor, we enable the user to edit the contents of the memory variables and cursor. When the user finishes editing, we must accomplish the following to save the changes:

1. Save changes to the invoice header.

2. Handle changes made to existing line items.

3. Handle newly added line items.

4. Handle line items that the user has flagged for deletion in the TEMPLINE database.

Of course, we must update the inventory and customer records as necessary. Here is the code:

```
PROCEDURE editsave
IF NOT RLOCK("ppcust")
  DO l3msg WITH "I can't lock the customer record now."+;
    " Invoice not changed."
ELSE
  l_alllock=.T.
  SELECT templine
  ** Find and lock the inventory record associated with
  ** any templine record that is (N)ew, (D)eleted, or (E)dited
  SCAN FOR templine.action$"NDE" AND NOT DELETED()
```

```
    IF (NOT SEEK(li_item,"ppinvt")) OR (NOT (RLOCK("ppinvt"))
      l_alllock=.F.
      EXIT
    ENDIF couldn't find inventory item, or couldn't lock item
  ENDSCAN
  IF NOT l_alllock
    ** not able to lock all inventory items
    UNLOCK ALL
    DO l3msg WITH "I couldn't lock one or more of your "+;
      "inventory items, so I couldn't save your changes."
  ELSE
    ** Determine previous invoice total
    SELECT SUM(li_qty*li_price) FROM ppline WHERE ;
      li_ivno=m.iv_ivno INTO ARRAY l_totprice
    l_oldtot=IIF(_TALLY=0,0,l_totprice)
    SELECT templine
    ** update temporary records with new invoice number
    REPLACE li_ivno WITH STR(l_newivno,6) FOR ;
      templine.action="N" AND NOT DELETED()
    COPY TO ARRAY l_templine FOR ;
      templine.action="N" AND NOT DELETED()
    ** Try to put temporary records in line items database.
    IF NOT l3insert("comm=[ppitem FROM ARRAY l_templine]"+;
        "msg=[Line items]")
      UNLOCK ALL
      DO l3msg WITH "Sorry. The system could not add your"+;
        " new line items at this time ¦No records changed."+;
        "¦Please try again later."
    ELSE
      ** Successfully added the line items, so
      **    update the associated inventory records
      SELECT templine
      l_newtot=0
      SCAN FOR templine.action$"NED" AND NOT DELETED()
        ** Note: We can be sure that the inventory record
        ** exists, and is locked, because we previously
        ** found and locked all inventory items for this
        ** invoice!
        =SEEK(templine.li_item,"ppinvt")
        IF templine.action<>"N"
          ** Find the original record
          GOTO (templine.recno) IN ppline
        ENDIF not a new one
```

continues

299

```
      DO CASE
        CASE templine.action="D"
          ** Deleted this line item, so increase inventory
          REPLACE ppinvt.iv_qty WITH ppinvt.iv_qty+ppline.li_qty
          ** Delete the original record
          SELECT ppline
          DELETE
        CASE templine.action="N"
          ** Newly added line item, so decrease inventory
          REPLACE ppinvt.iv_qty WITH ;
            ppinvt.iv_qty-templine.li_qty
          l_newtot=l_newtot+templine.li_qty*templine.li_price
        CASE templine.action="E"
          ** Note: The edit routine does not allow the user to
          ** change the li_item field in a line item. If the
          ** user wishes to change the item for a line item,
          ** the user has to delete and re-add.
          ** Changed the line item, may have changed the qty
          REPLACE ppinvt.iv_qty WITH ppinvt.iv_qty - ;
            ppline.li_qty+templine.li_qty
          ** Change the original
          SCATTER MEMVAR MEMO
          SELECT ppline
          GATHER MEMVAR MEMO
          l_newtot=l_newtot+templine.li_qty*templine.li_price
      ENDCASE
    ENDSCAN
    ** Update the invoice record
    SELECT ppinvoic
    GATHER MEMVAR MEMO
    ** Update customer ytd sales
    REPLACE ppcust.cu_ytdsale WITH ;
      ppcust.cu_ytdsale-l_oldtot+l_newtot
    UNLOCK ALL
    DO l3msg WITH "Successfully changed invoice "+;
      ppinvoic.iv_ivno+;
      " for "+ppcust.cu_company
  ENDIF able to add line item records
 ENDIF able to lock all of the associated inventory items
ENDIF able to lock the customer record
```

Deleting a Multirecord, Multitable Transaction

As you might suspect, deleting multiple records in multiple tables is nearly identical to editing multiple records in multiple tables. Here is the source code:

```
PROCEDURE delinvoice
IF NOT RLOCK("ppcust")
   DO l3msg WITH "I can't lock the customer record now."+;
     " Invoice not deleted."
ELSE
  IF NOT RLOCK("ppinvoic")
     DO l3msg WITH "I can't lock the invoice header."+;
        "Invoice not deleted"
     UNLOCK ALL
  ELSE
     l_alllock=.T.
     SELECT ppline
     SEEK ppinvoic.iv_ivno
     ** Find and lock all line items for this invoice.
     ** In addition, find and lock the inventory record associated
     ** with any ppline record that is part of this invoice
     SCAN WHILE ppline.li_ivno=ppinvoic.iv_ivno AND RLOCK() AND ;
         SEEK(ppline.li_ivno,"ppinvt") AND RLOCK("ppinvt")
     ENDSCAN
     IF ppline.li_ivno=ppinvoic.iv_ivno
       ** not able to lock all inventory items or line items
       UNLOCK ALL
       DO l3msg WITH "I couldn't lock one or more of your "+;
          "line items so I couldn't delete this invoice."
     ELSE
        l_oldtot=0
        SELECT ppline
        SEEK ppinvoic.iv_ivno
        SCAN WHILE ppline.li_ivno=ppinvoic.iv_ivno
          ** Note: We can be sure that the inventory record
          ** exists, and is locked, because we previously
          ** found and locked all inventory items for this
          ** invoice!
          =SEEK(templine.li_item,"ppinvt")
          l_oldtot=l_oldtot+ppline.li_qty*ppline.li_price
          ** Deleted this line item, so increase inventory
          REPLACE ppinvt.iv_qty WITH ppinvt.iv_qty+ppline.li_qty
```

continues

```
      ** Delete the original record
      SELECT ppline
      DELETE
    ENDSCAN
    ** Update the invoice record
    SELECT ppinvoic
    DELETE
    DO l3skip WITH 1
    ** Update customer ytd sales
    REPLACE ppcust.cu_ytdsale WITH ;
      ppcust.cu_ytdsale-l_oldtot
    UNLOCK ALL
    DO l3msg WITH "Successfully deleted invoice "+;
      ppinvoic.iv_ivno+;
      " for "+ppcust.cu_company
  ENDIF able to lock all of the associated inventory items
 ENDIF able to lock invoice record
ENDIF able to lock the customer record
```

Error Trapping

In a multiuser environment, we must protect against two classes of errors:

- *Resource contention errors.* These include the inability to INSERT INTO a database while someone has the database FLOCKed, and the inability to edit a record in a Browse window while another user has that record locked.

- *Programming errors.* These include syntax errors, missing variables, misspelled fields, and missing files.

At Micro Endeavors, we handle the two classes of errors as follows:

- When a resource contention error occurs, we want the error trap to assign a value to kerror quickly and return control to the application. The application is responsible for testing the value of kerror following any activity that can result in a resource contention error.

- When a programming error occurs, we want the error trap to give the user the option of ignoring the error, quitting from FoxPro, or saving information about the error. If we are in the development phase of the application, we also want the error trap to present us with options to suspend or cancel the offending program.

FoxPro provides the ON ERROR command to trap these errors. As this chapter has shown, the following command traps an error and, instead of interrupting the program, simply assigns the number of the error to the kerror variable before proceeding to the next command:

```
ON ERROR kerror=ERROR()
```

Although the preceding command satisfies our requirements for handling resource contention errors, to satisfy our requirements for handling programming errors we need a command such as the following:

```
ON ERROR DO l3error WITH ERROR(),SYS(16),LINENO(),;
   MESSAGE(1),MESSAGE(),SET('CONSOLE'),SET('DEVICE'),;
   SET('PRINT'),SET('TALK')
```

Because we can have only one error trap in place at a time, we could design L3ERROR.PRG to assign ERROR() to kerror whenever an error occurs. In this case, when a resource error occurred, l3error would simply return control to the current program after assigning a value to kerror.

Although this solution is acceptable, we can speed processing a bit by using the IIF() and INLIST() functions as follows:

```
ON ERROR kerror = ;
   IIF(INLIST(ERROR(),108,109,110,111,;
   130,1101,1502,1503,1705,1718),ERROR(),;
   l3error(ERROR(),SYS(16),LINENO(),;
   MESSAGE(1),MESSAGE(),;
   SET("CONSOLE"),SET("DEVICE"),;
   SET("PRINT"),SET("TALK")))
```

When this error trap is in place, and a 108, 109, 110, 111, 130, 1101, 1502, 1503, 1705, or 1718 error occurs, the value of ERROR() is assigned to kerror and control returns immediately to the current program. If the error is not one of these resource contention errors, FoxPro evaluates the l3error() UDF.

Trapping Resource Contention Errors

Table 13.2 lists the resource contention errors and their definitions.

Table 13.2. Resource contention errors.

Error Number	Error Message
108	File is in use by another
109	Record is in use by another
110	Exclusive open of file is required
111	Cannot write to a read-only file
130	Record is not locked
1101	Cannot open file
1502	Record is in use: Cannot write
1503	File cannot be locked
1705	File access denied
1718	File is read-only

If you use UDFs such as l3open and l3insert, and if you RLOCK() any records you want to change before attempting to change them, you should almost never encounter one of the resource contention errors. However, if you install an error trap such as the one described in the preceding section, you can adjust l3open and l3insert so that they do not have to set and reset the error trap.

After all, l3open and l3insert simply depend on their internal error trap to assign a value to kerror. If our global error trap accomplishes this task, we can improve l3open() and l3insert() performance by removing their extraneous ON ERROR commands.

You might wonder why we pass so many parameters to the l3error procedure. After all, why not just let the l3error routine determine those values for itself?

The reason we must pass parameters such as the error number and the name of the procedure is that the value returned by the functions in question change after we enter L3ERROR.PRG. In other words, we want to know what the values of ERROR(), SYS(16), and so on are at the time of the error, not at the time we evaluate those functions in the l3error routine.

For your convenience, Table 13.3 lists functions with values that are most often passed to an error trap routine.

Table 13.3. Return values frequently passed to error trap routines.

Function	Return Value
ERROR()	The error number
SYS(16)	The procedure name and the name of the file in which the procedure resides
LINENO()	The line number of the command that triggered the error trap
LINENO(1)	The line number of the command that triggered the error trap, relative to the first line of the procedure in which the error occurred
MESSAGE()	The text of the error message
MESSAGE(1)	The text string containing the command that triggered the error trap

Trapping Programming Errors

Every program in the world contains bugs. Further, users can introduce bugs by erasing files, changing system configurations, and rebooting without exiting properly.

The l3error routine that I am about to show helps both the user and the developer handle bugs. First, however, you must understand the difference between the RETRY and RETURN commands: RETRY re-executes the command that triggered the error, and RETURN returns control to the line of code *following* the command that triggered the error.

Here's the code for L3ERROR.PRG:

```
* l3error.prg
* error trapping
* example:
*ON ERROR DO l3error WITH ERROR(),SYS(16),LINENO(),MESSAGE(1),;
*  MESSAGE(),SET("CONSOLE"),SET("DEVICE"),SET("PRINT"),SET("TALK")

PARAMETERS errnum,errprog,errline,errcomm,errmsg,errcons,errdevi,;
  errprnt,errtalk
PRIVATE ALL LIKE l_*
IF TYPE("kerror")="U"
  PUBLIC kerror
ENDIF
```

continues

```
m.kerror=m.errnum
* Check to see whether we are in development or production mode
IF TYPE("ktesting")<>"L"
  PUBLIC ktesting
  * Look for a DOS environment setting of SET FOXTEST=ON
  ktesting=UPPER(GETENV("FOXTEST"))=="ON"
ENDIF
* Set the environment so that we can talk to the user
SET DEVICE TO SCREEN
SET TALK OFF
SET CONSOLE ON
SET PRINT OFF
m.l_action="RETURN"
* Determine the program calling tree
prgrms=""
xx=1
DO WHILE ""#SYS(16,xx)
  prgrms=prgrms+SYS(16,xx)+"¦"
  xx=xx+1
ENDDO
* Determine which options to give the user.
erropts="\<Retry;\<Save;\<Ignore;\<Quit"+;
  IIF(ktesting,";S\<uspend;\<Kill","")
* Use l3msg to present the user with a message, and options
m.l_ans = UPPER(l3msg("Error is : "+LTRIM(STR(m.errnum))+;
  "¦Desc     : "+errmsg+;
  "¦Code     : "+errcomm+;
  "¦Line#    : "+LTRIM(STR(errline))+;
  "¦Program  : "+errprog+;
  "¦Program  : "+prgrms,erropts,"bell=[2]just=[l]"+;
  "titl=[ An error has occurred! ]"))
* Process the user's selection
DO CASE
  CASE m.l_ans="SAVE"
    * User wants to save information about this error in the
    * l3error database.
    m.l_oldsele=SELECT()
    IF !USED('l3error')
      IF NOT FILE('l3error.dbf')
        * IF l3error doesn't exist, create it
        CREATE TABLE l3error ;
          (er_desc C(80),;
          er_date D,;
          er_time C(8),;
```

```
              er_type C(1),;
              er_station C(10),;
              er_memvars m,;
              er_windows m,;
              er_envi m,;
              er_statmem m,;
              er_info m)
      ELSE
        * If it does exist, open it
        SELECT 0
        USE l3error
      ENDIF
    ENDIF not already open
    IF !USED('l3error')              && failed to open it
      DO l3msg WITH "Can't open the error history file!"+;
        "¦Error not saved."
    ELSE
      * Call l3errsav to save information about the error
      SELECT l3error
      DO l3errsav WITH (errmsg),"E",(m.l_oldsele)
      USE                           && close error database
      SELECT (m.l_oldsele)
    ENDIF
    m.l_action="RETURN"
CASE m.l_ans="RETRY"
    m.l_action = "RETRY"
CASE m.l_ans="KILL"
    ** The developer wants to directly access the program that
    ** caused the error. By removing our error trap, and
    ** retrying the command that caused the error, we allow
    ** FoxPro to place the user in the program that caused
    ** the error.
    ON ERROR  && remove error trap
    m.l_action="RETRY" && cause the error to occur again
CASE m.l_ans="IGNORE"
    m.l_action="RETURN"
CASE m.l_ans="QUIT"
    IF l3msg("Are you sure you want to quit?","\!\<No;\?\<Yes")=;
        "Yes"
      QUIT
    ELSE
      m.l_action="RETRY"
    ENDIF
```

continues

307

```
    CASE m.l_ans="SUSPEND"
       PUSH KEY CLEAR && kill OKL mapping, for now
       ** Put miscellaneous information into the l3errinf.txt file
       DO l3errinf WITH "l3errinf"
       ** Load font information into an array for display as part
       ** of the LIST MEMO command
       =AFONT(errfont)
       ** Append LIST MEMO and LIST STATUS info to the l3errinf.txt
       ** file
       LIST MEMO TO l3errinf.txt ADDITIVE NOCONSOLE
       LIST STAT TO l3errinf.txt ADDITIVE NOCONSOLE
       ** Open the l3errinf.txt file for review by the programmer
       MODI FILE l3errinf.txt NOWAIT
       ZOOM WINDOW l3errinf MIN
       ** Find a program file to open
       l_thisfile=SUBSTR(errprog,RAT(" "," "+errprog))
       ** Open the program, query, screen, report, or menu file
       ** that contains the error
       DO l3eropen WITH l_thisfile,errline
       ACTIVATE WINDOW COMMAND
       ** Put the trace window on the desktop, so the developer
       ** can step, cancel, etc.
       ACTIVATE WINDOW trace
       PUSH MENU _msysmenu
       ** Put system menu back for developer
       SET SYSM TO DEFAULT
       ** Suspend processing
       SUSPEND
       POP MENU _msysmenu
       POP KEY
       m.l_action="RETRY"
    ENDCASE
    ** Put settings back the way we found them
    IF errcons#"ON"
      SET CONS OFF
    ENDIF
    IF errdevi#"SCREEN"
      SET DEVI TO &errdevi.
    ENDIF
    IF errtalk#"OFF"
      SET TALK ON
    ENDIF
    IF errprnt#"OFF"
      SET PRINT ON
```

```
ENDIF
IF m.l_action = "RETRY"
  m.kerror=0
  RETRY
ELSE
  m.kerror=m.errnum
  RETURN m.kerror
ENDIF


*: EOF: l3error.PRG

PROCEDURE l3errsav
* l3errsav.prg
*# Saves errors to l3error.dbf
PARAMETERS p_desc,p_type,p_oldsele,p_overwrite
PRIVATE ALL LIKE l_*
l_oldfull=SET('fullpath')
SET FULLPATH ON
* Create and fill a record in the l3error database.
IF !m.p_overwrite
  APPEND BLANK
ENDIF
REPLACE er_desc WITH m.p_desc,er_type WITH m.p_type
REPLACE er_date WITH DATE(),er_time WITH TIME(),;
  er_station WITH ALLTRIM(SYS(0))
** Save memory variables to er_memvars memo field
=AFONT(errfont)
SAVE TO MEMO er_memvars
RELEASE errfont
IF NOT _windows
  ** Save windows only in the DOS environment. Takes too much
  ** space in the Windows environment.
  SAVE WINDOW ALL TO MEMO er_windows
ENDIF
** Save relationships, filters, etc., for easy re-creation
tempfile=SYS(3)
CREATE VIEW (tempfile)
APPEND MEMO er_envi FROM (tempfile+".vue")
ERASE (tempfile+".vue")
SET CONSOLE OFF
** Save memvar contents in an easy to read format
LIST MEMO TO FILE (tempfile+".txt")
APPEND MEMO er_statmem FROM (tempfile+".txt")
```

continues

```
** Save status in an easy to read format
LIST STATUS TO FILE (tempfile+".txt")
APPEND MEMO er_statmem FROM (tempfile+".txt")
** Gather additional information
DO l3errinf WITH tempfile
APPEND MEMO er_info FROM (tempfile+".txt")
SET CONSOLE ON
ERASE (tempfile+".txt")
SET FULLPATH &l_oldfull.
RETURN


PROCEDURE l3errinf
** Gather additional information
PARAMETERS p_tempfile,p_oldsele
PRIVATE errinf,l_xx,l_fh,l_yy
p_oldsele=IIF(TYPE('p_oldsele')="N",p_oldsele,SELECT())
SET CONSOLE OFF
RELEASE WINDOW l3errinf
SET ALTERNATE TO (p_tempfile+".txt")
SET ALTERNATE ON
** Pick up any database information not covered in LIST STATUS
FOR l_xx=1 TO IIF(_windows OR UPPER(VERS(1))=;
    "FOXPRO 2.5 (X)",225,25)
  IF ""#DBF(l_xx)
    ? "**** Area "+LTRIM(STR(l_xx))+" "+REPL("*",25)
    ? IIF(l_xx=p_oldsele,"CURRENT WORK AREA",'')
    ? "DBF=",DBF(l_xx)
    ?? " Alias=",ALIAS(l_xx)
    ?? " Recno=",LTRIM(STR(RECNO(l_xx)))
    ?? " Reccount=",LTRIM(STR(RECC(l_xx)))
    ?? " Memblck=",SYS(2012)
    ?
    =AFIELDS(errinf)
    FOR l_yy=1 TO ALEN(errinf,1)
      ? PADR(errinf(l_yy,1),11)
      ?? errinf(l_yy,2)+" "
      ?? STR(errinf(l_yy,3),4)
      ?? STR(errinf(l_yy,4),2)
    ENDFOR
    RELEASE errinf
  ENDIF this work area is in use
ENDFOR process all work areas
```

```
** Put in some miscellaneous stuff
?
? "Disk remaining      ",DISK()
? "Disk size           ",SYS(2020)
? "Disk cluster size   ",SYS(2022)
? "sys(12)             ",SYS(12)
? "Avail mem           ",SYS(1001)
? "Mem in use          ",SYS(1016)
? "EMS                 ",SYS(23)
? "EMS limit           ",SYS(24)
? "Current directory   ",SYS(5)+SYS(2003)
? "FoxPro start dir    ",SYS(2004)
? "Resource file       ",SYS(2005)
? "Temporary file drive ",SYS(2023)
? "Graphics card       ",SYS(2006)
? "Files in Config.sys ",SYS(2010)
? "Printer             ",SYS(6)
? "Printer status      ",SYS(13)
? "sys(0)              ",SYS(0)
? "Version             ",VERSION(1)
? "Error message 2     ",SYS(2018)
? "Config.fp           ",SYS(2019)
?
l_fh=FOPEN(SYS(2019))
IF l_fh>0
  ? "***** CONFIG.FP  *******"
  DO WHILE NOT FEOF(l_fh)
    ? FGETS(l_fh)
  ENDDO
  =FCLOSE(l_fh)
  ? "***** EOF config.fp *****"
ENDIF
? "Program calling tree"
l_xx=1
DO WHILE ""#SYS(16,l_xx)
  ? SYS(16,l_xx)
  l_xx=l_xx+1
ENDDO
SET ALTERNATE OFF
SET ALTERNATE TO
RETURN .T.
```

continues

```
PROCEDURE l3eropen
* Opens the program, menu, screen, or report associated with
* this error.

PARAMETERS p_file,p_line
PRIVATE l_name
l_name=LEFT(p_file,LEN(p_file)-4)
DO CASE
  CASE UPPER(RIGHT(p_file,4))==".FXP"
    IF FILE(l_name+".PRG")
      ** Use l3goline and the line number of the error
      ** to position the user on the offending line
      DO l3goline WITH l_name+".PRG",p_line
    ENDIF
  CASE UPPER(RIGHT(p_file,4))==".MPX"
    IF FILE(l_name+".MNX")
      MODI MENU (l_name) NOWAIT
    ENDIF
  CASE UPPER(RIGHT(p_file,4))==".SPX"
    IF FILE(l_name+".SCX")
      MODI SCREEN (l_name) NOWAIT
    ENDIF
  CASE UPPER(RIGHT(p_file,4))==".FRX"
    IF FILE(l_name+".FRX")
      MODI REPORT (l_name) NOWAIT
    ENDIF
  CASE UPPER(RIGHT(p_file,4))==".QPX"
    IF FILE(l_name+".QPR")
      MODI QUERY (l_name) NOWAIT
    ENDIF
  OTHERWISE
    IF FILE(p_file+".PRG")
      ** Use l3goline and the line number of the error
      ** to position the user on the offending line
      DO l3goline WITH p_file+".prg",p_line
    ENDIF
ENDCASE
RETURN .T.
```

Note that, based on the value of ktesting, l3error presents one set of options to users and another set of options to the programmer. This is as it should be, because users and programmers have different requirements for error handling.

The user, when encountering a bug, wants to save information for the developer but primarily wants to keep working. The l3error routine accomplishes this by providing options to Save or Ignore errors.

If the user elects to save errors, information is written to the L3ERROR.DBF file. If the user elects to ignore, L3ERROR simply issues a RETURN command.

The developer, when encountering an error, primarily wants to fix the bug. To do this, the developer needs ready access to the object that caused the error, and information about the environment in which the error occurred.

To handle the environmental information, we output miscellaneous information about disk space, memory available, environmental settings, and databases to a text file called L3ERRINF.TXT. Then we simply LIST MEMO and LIST STAT to the end of the L3ERRINF.TXT file. Next, to place the information on the desktop, we issue the following command:

```
MODI COMM l3errinf.txt NOWAIT
```

Finally, we minimize the window that contains the L3ERRINF.TXT information.

We aren't done yet, though. To be really useful, the L3ERROR trap should take the developer as close as possible to the source code that caused the error. Because the SYS(16) function passes both the name of the current procedure *and* the name of the file in which that procedure resides, we have a chance to place the bug-toting file on the desktop for use by the developer.

The l3eropen procedure uses the file extension associated with the error-producing program to determine whether to look for a program, a query, a menu, a screen, or a report. When the procedure completes its deliberations, it issues a MODIFY...NOWAIT command to place the object on the desktop.

However, if the file containing the bug is a .PRG file, we can do more than just place the .PRG file on the desktop: We also can open the .PRG file with the offending line selected. To do this, we use the value passed by the LINENO() function, some low-level file I/O work in L3GOLINE, and the RANGE clause of the MODIFY command. Here is the code for L3GOLINE.PRG:

```
* l3goline.prg
* Begins editing of a file at a specified line
PARAMETERS p_file,p_line
PRIVATE ALL LIKE l_*
l_fh=FOPEN(p_file)
l_retval=0
```

continues

```
IF l_fh>0
  l_xx=1
  l_start=0
  l_end=0
  DO WHILE l_xx<=p_line AND NOT FEOF(l_fh)
    l_start=FSEEK(l_fh,0,1)+1
    l_null=FGETS(l_fh,2048)
    IF l_xx=p_line
      l_end=FSEEK(l_fh,0,1)-1
      EXIT
    ENDIF
    l_xx=l_xx+1
  ENDDO go to the bottom
  =FCLOSE(l_fh)
  MODI COMM (p_file) RANGE l_start,l_end NOWAIT IN SCREEN
ENDIF able to open it
RETURN l_retval
```

The *SET REPROCESS* Command

We're almost done; but I couldn't finish this discussion of multiuser concepts without talking about SET REPROCESS and SET REFRESH.

SET REPROCESS determines FoxPro's behavior when an attempt is made to lock a shared resource. For example, SET REPROCESS determines what happens when an RLOCK() is initially unsuccessful. Table 13.4 lists the available settings.

Table 13.4. Settings available for *SET REPROCESS.*

SET REPROCESS TO	Behavior
AUTO	FoxPro presents in the status bar a message that says Attempting to lock... Press ESC to cancel. If the user presses Esc, RLOCK() returns .F.; otherwise FoxPro continues to try to lock the record.
0	Same as AUTO.
-1	FoxPro presents a message that says Waiting for lock... and then waits until the RLOCK() succeeds. The user has no opportunity to interrupt.

SET REPROCESS TO	Behavior
<<Number between 1 and 36000>>	FoxPro attempts the RLOCK() the designated number of times. If all attempts fail, the RLOCK() returns .F. No messages are presented.
<<Number between 1 and 36000 >> SECONDS	FoxPro attempts the RLOCK() for the designated number of seconds. If time expires before an RLOCK() is obtained, the RLOCK() returns .F. No messages are presented.

Tip: Students frequently ask what the best setting is for REPROCESS. I almost always use SET REPROCESS TO 1. In my applications, if an RLOCK() or FLOCK() fails, I want to know immediately so that my application can take appropriate action.

The *SET REFRESH* Command

The SET REFRESH command supports two arguments. The first argument determines how frequently FoxPro will update Browse windows that are based on shared databases. The second argument determines the maximum age of local data buffers. Table 13.5 lists some sample settings.

Table 13.5. Settings for *SET REFRESH*.

SET REFRESH TO	Browse Windows Are Refreshed	Local Data Buffers Are Refreshed
0	Never	If older than 5 seconds or when forced
0,10	Never	If older than 10 seconds or when forced
0,0	Never	Only when forced
5	Every 5 seconds	If older than 5 seconds or when forced

FoxPro buffers records at the local workstation, which is one of the reasons FoxPro provides such phenomenal performance on a network. When FoxPro looks for a record, it first looks in local memory. If it finds the record in local memory, FoxPro then checks the "age" of the buffer. Depending on the setting of SET REFRESH, FoxPro may or may not retrieve a new copy of records stored in local memory if the age of the buffer in which those records reside is too great.

 Note: Locking a record, inserting a record, locking a file, opening a file, accessing more records than can fit in memory, and many other activities can force a REFRESH of a local buffer.

Some developers are distressed by the thought that their data is not *absolutely* current. As we discussed at the beginning of this chapter, however, the only time a record is *absolutely* current is when that record is locked.

So, if we must ensure that the copy of a record is current, we must lock the record or file. On those occasions that we can live with the fact that a record may not be absolutely current, we can greatly increase network throughput by issuing the following command:

```
SET REFRESH TO 0,0
```

This command directs FoxPro to get new copies of records only when forced to do so. As a result, many operations will take place on records that are available in the local workstation's RAM, reducing the number of times FoxPro must access data on the network.

Event-Driven Programming

In the beginning (about 13 years ago by the PC calendar), developers created menu-driven interfaces for their applications. And users saw that it was good. Or at least it was a lot better than the mainframe interfaces to which they had grown accustomed.

Developers were happy too, because menu-driven programs fit nicely with the structured, third generation languages in use at the time. Even the top-down, step-wise development methodologies of the period lent themselves to the creation of menu-driven applications.

However, it wasn't long before an apple was placed in this menu-driven garden of Eden—a Macintosh Apple, to be precise—and developers were cast out of the relative safety of menu-driven interfaces and into the terrifying world of mice, windows, icons, and, worst of all, *event-driven programming!*

Okay, okay. So it's not the book of Genesis. For some people, however, event-driven (E-D) programming is a religious issue, so perhaps the analogy is not that far off.

Happily, there is nothing mystical, religious, or even god-like in the creation of event-driven applications. In fact, at the end of the first day of our Advanced Programming class, everyone in the room can write a fully event-driven application from scratch.

Although I can't guarantee that you will be able to write an event-driven application from scratch when you finish this chapter, I can guarantee that you will understand all the issues involved. I can also guarantee that you will have an approach for every challenge facing the FoxPro developer of event-driven applications.

What Is an Event-Driven Program?

If users of your application can branch to any session in your application without first closing their current session, and if they can return to the previous session when they close their current session, and if they can do all this without losing any work in any session, your application is fully event-driven. Usually, the user moves to another session by making a menu selection, by clicking another window, or by pressing a hot key.

Before going any further, you need to understand the terms *session, event, control loop,* and *control variable.* Understanding these terms is a prerequisite to developing truly event-driven applications.

Sessions

A *session* is simply a READ CYCLE or BROWSE command. A user is considered to be "in" a session while sitting "in" the READ CYCLE or BROWSE.

Events

An *event* occurs when the user performs an action that triggers a program associated with one of the following FoxPro constructs:

GET WHEN	READ DEACTIVATE
GET VALID	BROWSE WHEN
READ WHEN	BROWSE VALID
READ VALID	ON KEY LABEL
READ SHOW	ON SELECTION
READ ACTIVATE	

In other words, when a user exits a GET field that has a valid clause, he or she is said to have triggered the GET VALID event. When the user leaves a GET window in a READ CYCLE session that includes a READ DEACTIVATE clause, the user is said to have triggered the READ DEACTIVATE event.

Control Loop

The *control loop* for an event-driven application is a simple DO WHILE .T. loop located in the main program of the application. Inside this DO WHILE .T. loop is a DO CASE construct that tests the content of the kaction variable to see which session should be processed next. The TSMAIN.PRG program listed in Chapter 2, "Menus and Data-bases," contains a standard control loop.

Control Variable

In the time sheet application, kaction is the *control variable.* This variable contains the name of the next session to process. When an event occurs that should take the user to a new session, the program associated with that event must fill the kaction variable with the name of the desired session and then force an exit from the current session.

What Are the Challenges for the FoxPro Programmer?

In a perfect world, we could accomplish this jumping from session to session with commands such as the following:

```
ON SELECTION BAR 1 OF POPUP george DO inventory
ON KEY LABEL F5 DO sales
ON SELECTION WINDOW inventory DO inventory
```

Unfortunately, FoxPro doesn't include an ON SELECTION WINDOW command. Further, although the ON SELECTION BAR and ON KEY LABEL commands do exist, we can't use them, for the following reasons:

- You can nest FoxPro programs only 32 levels deep; that is, one program can call another program, which calls another program, and so on, down 32 levels.

- You can nest only five read levels; that is, while the user is sitting in a READ CYCLE, you can DO a program that contains another READ CYCLE. While the user is in this second READ CYCLE, you can DO a program that contains another READ CYCLE, and so on—but only four times.

- FoxPro is not *re-entrant.* That is, while sitting in inventory, you DO customer; then, while sitting in customer, you DO inventory. FoxPro does not return to the previous instance of INVENTORY.PRG, but instead starts a new instance of INVENTORY.PRG. As a result, if you attempt to DO programs directly while sitting in sessions, sooner or later the user will hit one of the nesting limits previously mentioned.

The rest of this chapter discusses work-arounds for these seemingly insurmountable obstacles to the development of event-driven programs in FoxPro. Separate sections cover the following topics:

- Selecting local events (push buttons, hot keys, and so on)

- Moving from session to session without exiting the current session

- Leaving multiple sessions on the desktop simultaneously and choosing among them by clicking windows

- Returning to the previous session when the current session is closed

- Remembering the location of windows when reopening a session

- Remembering the content of memory variables when returning to a session

- Closing leftover sessions

- Coping with Browse windows

Selecting Local Events

For your application to be event-driven, it first must enable users to click push buttons and have an action occur. In other words, while in the middle of changing a field on the data entry screen, the user must be able to move immediately to a push button and perform an action.

If you read the first eight chapters of this book, you already know that FoxPro handles this level of E-D for you. All you have to do is place a valid clause on the push button object in the Screen Builder.

Choosing a New Session While in the Current Session

Next, while the user is working in one session, your program must enable her to choose another session directly without first requiring the user to exit the current session. As noted earlier, FoxPro does not handle this aspect of E-D programming for you. Instead, you must follow these steps:

1. Create a `kaction` variable.

2. Establish `ON SELECTION` and `ON KEY LABEL` events.

3. Start an event loop.

4. Establish a session.

While the user sits in a session, you must give the user access to menus and `ON KEY LABEL`s that cause the program to move to another session. Fortunately, menus built with the menu builder are active during a session by default. Further, ON KEY LABELs are active during sessions.

When one of the ON SELECTION or ON KEY LABEL events is triggered, you must do the following:

1.   Assign a value to kaction.

2.   Exit the current session.

Because the entire time sheet application demonstrates the proper implementation of these concepts, I won't duplicate the code from TSMAIN.PRG, TSMENU.MPR, and TSDO.PRG. However, if you haven't already worked through the creation of the time sheet application, you might want to review Chapter 2, "Menus and Databases."

How Event-Driven Do You Need To Be?

The time sheet application is semi-event-driven. As the user resides in any session, the time sheet application enables the user to move directly to another session by making a menu selection. However, when the user moves to the new session, the current session is closed.

As a result, only the windows associated with the current session are on the desktop at any given time. Further, when users close the current session, they are not returned to the previously open session. Finally, when a user returns to a previously opened session, that session does not "remember" information about the last time the user worked in this session.

The level of E-D demonstrated in the time sheet application is satisfactory for 80 percent of development. Indeed, many users insist that their application *not* be more E-D, to prevent user confusion.

In many ways, the semi-event-driven approach demonstrated in the time sheet application is the best compromise between the effort required for fully E-D applications and the "user-hostile" interface of old-fashioned menu-driven applications.

However, as Windows becomes the dominant operating environment on PCs, users will become increasingly accustomed to fully E-D applications. Indeed, many of MEI's clients have already begun insisting on fully E-D applications. To accommodate those clients and to anticipate the needs of our future clients, we have developed an approach and a series of routines that allow us to develop fully event driven FoxPro applications.

Allowing Multiple Sessions on the Desktop

Our first task will be to allow multiple sessions to reside on the desktop simultaneously. For example, we may want to have the client data entry screen on the desktop alongside the employee data entry screen in the time sheet application.

To accomplish this, we have to follow these steps:

1. Disable the Close Windows option of the Screen Generator dialog.

2. Place the name of each window we create in an array called kw() along with the name of the session with which this window is associated.

3. Use the READ DEACTIVATE clause to establish the next kaction.

Later we will want to remember the location of each window, so we create the kw array with three columns per row, as follows:

```
DIMENSION kw(1,3)
```

To "register" a window, we simply place into the kw array the title of the window and the session with which that window is associated. To make this as easy as possible, I wrote L3WS.PRG, which we invoke like this:

```
DO l3ws WITH kw,"Customer Data Entry","Customer"
```

We call L3WS.PRG once for each window that exists in the application. The best place to issue the DO l3ws command is just before we issue the DO .SPR command in the screen control program. Here is the code for L3WS.PRG:

```
* l3ws.prg
* Attaches session names to window titles.
* thisarr = name of array holding titles and sessions
* thistitle = title of window
* thissession = session name
PARAMETERS thisarr,thistitle,thissession
PRIVATE ALL LIKE l_*
IF ALEN(thisarr,2)=0
  l_spot = ASCAN(thisarr,UPPER(thistitle)+CHR(255))
  IF l_spot=0  && title not already in the array
    IF !EMPTY(thisarr(1))
      DIMENSION thisarr(ALEN(thisarr)+1)
    ENDIF
    l_spot=ALEN(thisarr)
  ENDIF
  thisarr(l_spot)=UPPER(thistitle)+CHR(255)+thissession
ELSE && this is a two-dimensional array
  l_spot = ASCAN(thisarr,UPPER(thistitle)+CHR(255))
```

```
  IF l_spot=0  && title not already in the array
    IF !EMPTY(thisarr(1))
      DIMENSION thisarr(ALEN(thisarr,1)+1,ALEN(thisarr,2))
    ENDIF
    l_spot=ALEN(thisarr)
  ENDIF
  l_row=ASUBSCRIPT(thisarr,l_spot,1)
  thisarr(l_row,1)=UPPER(thistitle)+CHR(255)+thissession
ENDIF this is a single dimension array
RETURN thistitle  && for use in title clauses
*: EOF: L3WS.PRG
```

Now when the user clicks another window on the desktop, the program can search the kw array to see what session is associated with that window. After finding this session name in the kw array, we want to store the session name in the kaction variable. Fortunately, the READ DEACTIVATE event is triggered whenever the user exits a GET window. This makes the readdeac() UDF a perfect place to query the kw array for the name of the newly selected window.

Here is a sample readdeac() UDF:

```
PROCEDURE readdeac
kaction=l3winses(@kw,WTITLE(WONTOP()))
RETURN .T.
```

The l3winses UDF simply searches the kw array for the title of the window that the user has placed on top of the desktop. The l3winses UDF then returns that session name, which readdeac places in the kaction variable. When readdeac returns .T., the program exits the current READ session.

Here is the code for L3WINSES.PRG:

```
* l3winses.prg
* Returns the session name associated with a window title.
* thisarr = array to search
* thistitle = title to look up
PARAMETERS thisarr,thistitle
EXTERNAL ARRAY thisarr
PRIVATE ALL LIKE l_*
l_spot = ASCAN(thisarr,UPPER(thistitle)+CHR(255))
RETURN IIF(l_spot=0 OR l_spot=LEN(thisarr(l_spot)),"",;
  SUBSTR(thisarr(l_spot),AT(CHR(255),thisarr(l_spot))+1))
*: EOF: l3WINSES.PRG
```

We must attend to one more piece of business before we can achieve the goal of leaving multiple sessions on the desktop for easy access by users. Because we have disabled the

Close Windows option of the Screen Generator dialog, we must take responsibility for releasing any windows that we create in .SPR files.

Here is a simple vcontrol() procedure that solves this problem:

```
PROCEDURE vcontrol
PARAMETERS m.control
DO CASE
  CASE UPPER(m.control)="MENU"
    ACTIVATE WINDOW exev12cu
    CLEAR READ
  CASE UPPER(control)="CLOSE"
    CLEAR READ
    RELEASE WINDOW exev12cu
ENDCASE
RETURN .T.
```

Returning to a Previous Session

On entry to the application, the user selects customer entry as his first session of the day. Without closing the customer session, the user selects the inventory session as his second session of the day. After finishing her work with the inventory screen, the user elects to close the inventory session.

In this case, we should return the user to the customer session. If the user elects to close the customer session, we should return the user to the main control loop, where a READ VALID .T. command enables the user to select a menu option at leisure.

To accomplish this goal, we follow these steps:

1. Create an array named khistory() to maintain a history of sessions entered.

2. Register each session in khistory() on entry into that session.

3. Remove each session from khistory() when the user elects to close each session.

4. In the main event loop, we check khistory() for something to do when kaction is empty.

The khistory array contains the name of the session and the name of the program associated with that session. We create the khistory array as follows:

```
DIMENSION khistory(1,2)
```

Each time we enter a session, we place the name of that session and that session's program name into the first row of the khistory array. If other sessions are already in the khistory array, they are moved down one row to make room. If the current session already exists in the khistory array, the earlier reference to the current session is removed from the khistory array and a new reference is placed in the first row of khistory.

To make this process as easy as possible, I created the L3PSHARR.PRG procedure, which we can call like this:

```
DO l3psharr WITH khistory,"Customer","exev17cu"
```

Here is the code for L3PSHARR.PRG:

```
* l3psharr.prg
*# Pushes an element on to the top of an array.
* If the element is new, the array is resized.
* If the element already exists in the array,
*    the element is simply moved to the top of the array.
PARAMETERS thisarr,elem1,elem2,elem3,elem4,elem5,elem6
PRIVATE ALL LIKE l_*
l_spot=ASCAN(thisarr,elem1)
IF ALEN(thisarr,2)>0
  DIMENSION l_parm(6)
  l_parm(1)=elem1
  l_parm(2)=elem2
  l_parm(3)=elem3
  l_parm(4)=elem4
  l_parm(5)=elem5
  l_parm(6)=elem6
  IF l_spot>0
    l_row=ASUBSCRIPT(thisarr,l_spot,1)
    =ADEL(thisarr,l_row)
  ELSE
    DIMENSION thisarr(ALEN(thisarr,1)+1,ALEN(thisarr,2))
  ENDIF
  =AINS(thisarr,1)
  FOR l_xx=1 TO ALEN(thisarr,2)
    thisarr(1,l_xx)=l_parm(l_xx)
  ENDFOR
ELSE
  ** One-dimensional array
  IF l_spot>0
    =ADEL(thisarr,l_spot)
  ELSE
    DIMENSION thisarr(ALEN(thisarr)+1)
  ENDIF
```

continues

```
    =AINS(thisarr,1)
    thisarr(1)=elem1
ENDIF two dimensional
* Return .t. if element already existed.
RETURN l_spot>0
*: EOF: l3PSHARR.PRG
```

When the user closes a session, the session is removed from the khistory array with a command like this:

```
DO l3poparr WITH khistory,""
```

Here is the code for L3POPARR.PRG:

```
* l3poparr.prg
*# "Pops" a single element off the top of an array,
* then resizes the array.
* Thisarr = name of the array
* emptyval = value to be placed in the 1st element of the array
*              in the event that the pop empties the array.
PARAMETERS thisarr,emptyval
PRIVATE l_xx
=ADEL(thisarr,1)
IF ALEN(thisarr)>1
  IF ALEN(thisarr,2)>0
    DIMENSION thisarr(ALEN(thisarr,1)-1,ALEN(thisarr,2))
  ELSE
    DIMENSION thisarr(ALEN(thisarr,1)-1)
  ENDIF two dimensions
ELSE
  IF ALEN(thisarr,2)>0
    FOR l_xx=1 TO ALEN(thisarr,2)
      thisarr(1,l_xx)=emptyval
    ENDFOR
  ELSE
    thisarr(1)=emptyval
  ENDIF two dimensions
ENDIF more than one element in the array
* Returns the size of the newly resized array
RETURN ALEN(thisarr,1)

*: EOF: l3POPARR.PRG
```

All that remains is for the event loop to test the khistory array before placing the user in a READ VALID .T. session.

Here is the code:

```
DO WHILE .T.
  DO CASE
    CASE UPPER(kaction)="CUST"
      kaction=""
      DO exev13cu
    CASE UPPER(kaction)="INVE"
      kaction=""
      DO exev13iv
    CASE UPPER(kaction)="EXIT"
      EXIT
    OTHERWISE
      IF EMPTY(khistory(1))
        *** activate menu _msysmenu pad sessions
        READ VALID .T.
      ELSE
        kaction=khistory(1)
        DO l3poparr WITH khistory,""
      ENDIF
  ENDCASE
ENDDO
```

Remembering Window Locations

When the user reopens a session that he or she previously closed, we want to restore the windows associated with that session to their previous screen locations. We can accomplish this by never releasing any windows. Or, we can simply deactivate any windows associated with closed sessions—but unfortunately, this approach can consume more than 100K of RAM per window in FoxPro for Windows. So, instead, we will try the following approach:

1. Use the second and third columns of the kw() array to hold the wlrow() and wlcol() values for each window.

2. Use the l3winpos UDF to store window locations when the session closes.

3. Use the l3winpos() UDF as an "output" (@...SAY) object in each .SCX to move the window to its proper position before the window becomes visible.

Saving the location of a window when the session closes is as simple as this:

```
DO l3winpos WITH kw,"exev15cu"
```

Here is the code for L3WINPOS.PRG:

```
* l3winpos.prg
* Puts window coordinates in the second and third
* column of the array row associated with the
* named window.
* p_array = array to process
* p_winname = window name to search
* p_moveit = .t. to move the window to the appropriate
*            coordinates. .F. to store wlrow() and
*            wlcol() for this window in the array.
PARAMETERS p_array,p_winname,p_moveit
EXTERNAL ARRAY p_array
PRIVATE ALL LIKE l_*
l_spot = ASCAN(p_array,UPPER(WTITLE(m.p_winname))+CHR(255))
IF l_spot>0
  l_row=ASUBSCRIPT(p_array,l_spot,1)
  IF m.p_moveit
    ** Wants us to move it.
    IF TYPE("p_array(m.l_row,2)")="N" AND ;
        TYPE("p_array(m.l_row,3)")="N"
      MOVE WINDOW (m.p_winname) TO p_array(m.l_row,2),;
        p_array(m.l_row,3)
    ENDIF numeric values available for row/col coordinates
  ELSE
    ** Wants us to store values.
    p_array(m.l_row,2)=WLROW(m.p_winname)
    p_array(m.l_row,3)=WLCOL(m.p_winname)
  ENDIF wants us to post values to the array
ENDIF found it
RETURN ""
```

When the third parameter passed to l3winpos is .T., l3winpos moves the window to the position stored in the kw array. If the third parameter passed to l3winpos is .F., l3winpos stores the location of the window in the kw array.

All that remains is to create an output object in each screen that has the following expression:

```
l3winpos(@kw,woutput(),.t.)
```

Remembering Variables

Upon returning to a session, the user should find the screen's memory variables the same as when the user left the session. We accomplish this as follows:

1. Create a cursor that contains two fields: one character field for the session name, and one memo field to save the memory variables associated with the session.

2. Use l3fndses() to create a record in the cursor for each session as the session is entered.

3. Use SAVE TO MEMO to save the content of memory variables if the session is open.

4. Use RESTORE FROM MEMO to restore memory variables on re-entry into the session if there are memory variables to restore.

Here's how we create the cursor:

```
CREATE CURSOR exsyst ;
  (sy_session C(20),sy_memvar m(10))
```

Here's how we use l3fndses() to register each session in the exsyst cursor, and how you restore the memory variables you saved the last time the user was in this session:

```
IF l3fndses("Customer") AND NOT EMPTY(exsyst.sy_memvar)
  RESTORE FROM MEMO exsyst.sy_memvar ADDITIVE
ENDIF
```

Here is the code for L3FNDSES.PRG:

```
* l3fndses.prg
* Finds the exsyst record associated with a
* particular session.
* P_session = session name
PARAMETERS p_session
PRIVATE l_oldsele,l_result
IF USED('exsyst')
  l_oldsele=SELECT()
  SELECT exsyst
  IF NOT UPPER(sy_session)=;
      LEFT(UPPER(m.p_session),LEN(sy_session))
    ** I'm not sitting on it, so look for it.
    LOCATE FOR UPPER(sy_session)=;
      LEFT(UPPER(m.p_session),LEN(sy_session))
    IF NOT FOUND() && Not on file
      INSERT INTO exsyst (sy_session) VALUES ;
        (m.p_session)
    ENDIF couldn't find it
  ENDIF not sitting on it
  SELECT (l_oldsele)
ENDIF the exsyst file is in use
RETURN .t.
```

Here's how to save memory variables for a session when we leave the session without closing it:

```
=l3fndses("Customer")
IF WEXIST("exev16cu")
  * Save everything except public variables. This is one
  * of the primary reasons for the MEI K* public variable
  * naming convention.
  SAVE TO MEMO exsyst.sy_memvar ALL EXCEPT K*
ELSE
  REPLACE exsyst.sy_memvar WITH ""
ENDIF Window is still up, so session is still open
RETURN
```

Closing Leftover Sessions

If the user opens multiple sessions and then chooses to exit from the entire application, we are left with the problem of having lots of windows laying around the desktop. We can solve the problem with a single command like this:

```
CLEAR WINDOW
```

Unfortunately, if there were pending changes in any of those windows, this solution would be unsatisfactory. Instead, to enable the application to close all open sessions, we should follow these steps:

1. Use a second column in khistory() to store the name of the .PRG associated with a session.

2. Adjust each session .PRG to accept a parameter that may contain the word "CLOSE".

3. In the READWHEN UDF for each session, call vcontrol("CLOSE") to close the session if the parameter passed directed the session to "CLOSE".

4. When it is time to close all open sessions, loop through the khistory array, closing any open sessions.

Here is the code to register both the program and the session name in the khistory array:

```
DO l3psharr WITH khistory,"Customer","exev17cu"
```

Here is the parameter statement for each session:

```
PARAMETERS kmessage
```

Here is the READWHEN UDF for each session:

```
PROCEDURE readwhen
IF TYPE("kmessage")="C" AND UPPER(kmessage)="CLOSE"
  DO vcontrol WITH "CLOSE"
ENDIF
RETURN .T.
```

Here is the code to close all open sessions:

```
PROCEDURE exev17closall
=ACOPY(khistory,kcloser)
FOR l_xx=1 TO ALEN(kcloser,1)
  IF NOT EMPTY(kcloser(l_xx,1))
    =EVAL(kcloser(l_xx,2)+"([Close])")
  ENDIF
ENDFOR
```

Handling Troublesome Browse Windows

Browse windows pose special problems for the developer of event-driven applications. Unfortunately, FoxPro does not trigger the READ DEACTIVATE event when a user exits from a Browse window. Further, FoxPro does not trigger the READ ACTIVATE event when the user enters a Browse window.

As a result, some event-driven methodologies call for the exclusion of Browse windows from applications. Micro Endeavors believes that Browse windows can be productive members of the event-driven society if we implement the following measures:

- Include a BROWSE VALID :F clause to capture an exit from a Browse window.

- In the READ DEAC clause, prevent access to empty Browse windows.

- When attempting to exit from a READ CYCLE session with a CLEAR READ, always activate the READ window before returning to the READ CYCLE.

Here is a sample BROWSE command containing a BROWSE VALID clause:

```
BROWSE FIELDS vn_name,vn_contact,vn_id ;
  WINDOW exev17vnbr TITLE "VENDLIST" ;
  NOMENU NOMODIFY NOAPPEND NODELETE NOWAIT ;
  WHEN NOT showem() VALID :F UPPER(WONTOP())="VENDLIST" ;
  OR readdeac()
```

Here is the associated READ DEACTIVATE UDF:

```
PROCEDURE readdeac
kaction=l3winses(@kw,WTITLE(WONTOP()))
IF UPPER(kaction) <> "VENDOR"
  DO vcontrol WITH "MENU"
ELSE
  kaction=""
  IF UPPER(WONTOP())="VENDLIST"
    ** Wants to move into the Browse window.
    IF EOF('exvend') && no records in the browse
      ?? CHR(7)
      ACTIVATE WINDOW exev17vn
    ELSE
      DO vcontrol WITH "SAVE"
    ENDIF
  ELSE && just left the browse window
    IF NOT WEXIST("VENDLIST")
      DO exev17vnbr
    ENDIF
  ENDIF just left the exev17cu window
ENDIF clicked on a window from a different session
RETURN .F.
```

Finally, here is the control code for a session that includes a Browse window:

```
PROCEDURE vcontrol
PARAMETERS m.control
DO CASE
  CASE UPPER(m.control)="MENU"
    ACTIVATE WINDOW exev17vn
    CLEAR READ
  CASE UPPER(m.control)="SAVE"
    SELECT exvend
    GATHER MEMVAR MEMO
  CASE UPPER(m.control)="CLOSE"
    ACTIVATE WINDOW exev17vn
    CLEAR READ
    DO l3poparr WITH khistory,""
    DO l3winpos WITH kw,"exev17vn"
    DO l3winpos WITH kw,"VENDLIST"
    RELEASE WINDOW exev17vn,vendlist
ENDCASE
RETURN .T.
```

Benefits and Drawbacks of Event-Driven Programs

There are both benefits and drawbacks to creating event-driven programs. Here are some of each.

Benefit	Drawback
The user has easier access to many activities.	Requires more work from the programmer, who must manage "session logic." The programmer also must consider the effects of all actions on other open sessions.
The desktop, and the sequence of actions, are user-configurable.	Imposes a slight performance penalty when switching sessions.
Makes for "sexy" demos, which can lead to lucrative contracts.	Confusing for infrequent users. The annual report might not benefit from E-D.
Invaluable for interrupt-driven tasks such as sales, telephone support, and management.	Less hand-holding is available because user has so many options at any given time.
Makes "what-if" analysis easier.	Troublesome in naturally modal applications such as manufacturing and payroll, although you can make sessions modal and be E-D when possible.

If you must create event-driven applications in FoxPro, this chapter should hold all the answers you need. However, don't think that every application you write *must* be event-driven to be valuable. Sometimes, a simpler, if less flexible, menu-driven approach is appropriate.

Finally, don't forget that there are degrees of event-drivenness. Pick the one that's right for your application.

CHAPTER 15

Performance

Sometimes it seems that I spend half my professional life talking about the performance of database management systems. Whether I am creating benchmarks for a feature story in *Data Based Advisor* magazine or running comparison benchmarks for clients, performance tests never seem to be far from the top of my list of things to do.

As you might expect, much of the time associated with benchmarking is spent arguing with vendors or supporters of products that did not fare well on the latest benchmark tests. This is understandable, because the commercial success of a database product is partly based on the public's perception of the database product's performance.

I actually enjoy these calm, rational, discussions with vendors. (*Note:* I also enjoy kick boxing, professional wrestling, and heavy metal music in the same way.) However, what I really enjoy about database performance is helping clients make their FoxPro applications perform brilliantly. Because this is my book, and I can therefore talk about anything I like, I'm going to talk about issues that will help you make your FoxPro applications perform brilliantly.

Before I start, though, I encourage you to read the last section in this chapter. I think you'll find it enlightening.

The Importance of Speed

Frequently, vendors confront me and suggest that speed is unimportant, or at least much less important than some other feature of their product. Other times, developers who use products other than FoxPro insist that their product is "fast enough" for their purposes, so any difference in performance between their product and FoxPro is irrelevant. As a result, clients often suggest that speed is not an important factor in selecting a database management product.

In general, these are informed, intelligent, decision makers. In addition, they are all very wrong about performance. Outstanding performance, like that found in FoxPro, provides the following benefits:

- Core business questions are answered faster.

- Larger projects can be accomplished on PCs.

- Less tweaking time is required of the developer.

- Performance issues have less impact on database design.

- Users have time to ask more questions.

- The business can afford to acquire and store more data.

- Hardware costs are reduced.

At least in the world of PC databases, speed doesn't kill, it gives life. Speed gives life to the creativity of developers who, freed of the burden of constantly tuning applications to provide acceptable performance, can turn their attention to providing information systems solutions for business problems.

Speed gives life to information systems group budgets by enabling even large projects to reside on PC-based LAN platforms.

Speed gives life to systems analysts, who don't have to spend hours debating the relative performance of one database design over another. Instead, with FoxPro, they have time to try both designs and see which is faster. Or, they can simply create the best design to support the development of the application, and depend on FoxPro to make the application fly.

Speed gives life to the imagination of users, who get answers to their common questions so quickly they have time to ask the uncommon questions, the kinds of questions that give their companies competitive advantages.

Speed gives life to management by enabling information systems to acquire and store more data, and by enabling managers to turn that data into information quickly. The more useful information managers have, the more likely they are to make good decisions. The more good decisions they make, the more likely the business is to grow.

Finally, speed gives life to core business activities by enabling users to process orders faster, or respond to requests for information more quickly, or find key suppliers faster. The mail-order firm that processes and ships orders 10 percent faster than its competition has a significant competitive advantage, as does the manufacturer who can instantly identify the best suppliers for a needed part.

FoxPro's Place in the World of Speed

FoxPro 2.5 currently is the fastest database management product available for the PC platform. Indeed, when it comes to querying databases, FoxPro 2.5 is faster than most database management products running on much more expensive mainframe and minicomputer platforms.

At Micro Endeavors, we develop large applications for large companies. As a result, performance is *always* an issue for our clients. We use FoxPro for these large applications' development efforts because FoxPro is the fastest product available. Further, Microsoft, and Fox Software before it, has made speed the number one issue in marketing FoxPro. Therefore, it is firmly committed to ensuring that FoxPro remains the fastest database management system available for PCs.

Introducing Rushmore

Rushmore is the name Microsoft uses to identify a series of algorithms and procedures used by FoxPro to optimize queries. In general, when you issue a command in FoxPro that attempts to retrieve records from one or more databases based on a condition, FoxPro applies Rushmore algorithms to expedite the retrieval of those records.

For example, suppose that you have a database of items ordered that contains 680,000 records consuming more than 50M of disk space. Further, suppose you want to know how many bullwhips were ordered last week. The code to obtain this information is trivial:

```
SELECT COUNT(it_item),SUM(it_qty) ;
  FROM oritem WHERE it_item="BULLWHIP" AND ;
  it_date>={03/07/93} AND it_date<={03/13/93}
```

As it turns out, there were 30 orders with a total quantity of 94 bullwhips last week. Interestingly, it took FoxPro only *1.38 seconds* to determine this.

No, that's not a misprint. No, I'm not drinking. No, I did not run this query on a Cray. I ran the query on a 486/33 with 8M of RAM, and a relatively slow (18ms access, 365K transfer) hard disk. Yes, FoxPro is unbelievably fast.

Let's put this in perspective. It took FoxPro 1.38 seconds to find and summarize 30 records in a database containing 680,000 records. This is no fluke: I have run queries on 2,500,000-record, 100M+ databases that completed in less than one second.

On queries like this, FoxPro is faster than any database product with which I have ever worked, including several minicomputer and mainframe databases.

In fact, when querying the same database for similar data, FoxPro can appear to take no time at all in delivering an answer. For example, after completing the previous query, I wondered how many bullwhips ordered last week were part of a multiple bull-whip order. Here is the query:

```
SELECT COUNT(it_item),SUM(it_qty) ;
  FROM oritem WHERE it_item="BULLWHIP" AND ;
  it_date>={03/07/93} AND it_date<={03/13/93} ;
  AND it_qty>2
```

This query ran in 0.02 seconds. The results were virtually instantaneous.

One of the best things about the Rushmore technology is its invisibility. The developer does not have to do much at all to take full advantage of this phenomenal speed. There are a few guidelines, however, which the next section discusses.

What Are Rushmore's Requirements?

When a command is issued to retrieve records from a database conditionally, FoxPro checks which index keys are available for that database. If possible, FoxPro uses the indexes associated with the database to determine which records in the database match the query criteria, *before accessing the database.*

In other words, you need indexes to use Rushmore. Further, for Rushmore to take effect, you must compare a static value to an existing index key expression. (A *static value* is a constant, expression, or memory variable that does not change value during the query.)

To demonstrate proper and improper utilization of Rushmore, I use the following database:

```
Structure for table:    c:\devcon\fast.dbf
Number of data records: 106960
Date of last update:    02/05/93
Field  Field Name  Type        Width   Dec   Index
    1  NAME        Character     10           Asc
    2  AGE         Numeric       10           Asc
    3  DOB         Date           8           Asc
** Total **                      29
```

As you can see, FAST.DBF contains only 106,960 records, and consumes only about 3.1M of disk space. I chose this relatively small database because I intend to demonstrate both correct and incorrect attempts to utilize Rushmore. Improperly utilizing Rushmore on a two million record database is punishable by a several minute, or even several hour, wait.

The first query takes proper advantage of Rushmore to retrieve quickly all records in which the age is 10:

```
mvar=10
SELECT * FROM fast WHERE age=mvar
```

FoxPro retrieved 33 records in 0.22 seconds. This query obeys all the rules of Rushmore:

- It compares a static value to an existing index key expression.

- It uses an =, <, >, <=, >=, <>, #, or != operator.

This seems simple enough, and it is. However, misusing Rushmore is also fairly easy. The following query looks correct, but isn't:

```
LIST FOR name="B0"
```

This command required 16 seconds to retrieve and display 35 records. Obviously, something is wrong.

The LIST command benefits from Rushmore optimizations, so that's not the problem. The = operator is a valid operator, so that isn't it. The constant "B0" is certainly static, so that isn't the problem.

Finally, the command includes an index tag named name, so that isn't it. Or is it? Here are the index tags and expressions for FAST.DBF:

```
Select area:  1, Table in Use: C:\DEVCON\FAST.DBF    Alias: FAST
   Structural CDX file:    C:\DEVCON\FAST.CDX
               Index tag:   NAME               Key: NAME+STR(AGE,10)
               Index tag:   AGE                Key: AGE
               Index tag:   DOB                Key: DOB
               Index tag:   ANYTHING           Key: DELETED()
         Lock(s): Exclusive USE
```

We have an index tag named name, but we don't have any index key expressions based on name. We do, however, have an index based on name+str(age,10). So, we retry the list this way:

```
LIST FOR name+str(age,10)="B0"
```

This command required 2.3 seconds to retrieve and display the same 35 records as the first LIST. The rule is simple: the left side of a Rushmore optimizable expression must match the index key expression of one of the tags in the queried database.

Now we can look at another demonstration. The following query took 23.78 seconds to return 220 records:

```
select * from fast where age+0>10 and age+0<20
```

Why did it take so long? Because no index tags are built on the expression age+0. The following query took 4.17 seconds to return the same 220 records:

```
select * from fast where age+0>10 and age<20
```

We know that the age+0>10 portion of the query is not optimizable. However, we also know that the age<20 portion of the query is optimizable. Fortunately, FoxPro knows this too.

In short, when a query includes optimizable and nonoptimizable expressions, FoxPro first performs the optimizable portions and then applies the nonoptimizable conditions to the result. Therefore, for FoxPro to return an answer quickly, not every expression in a query must have a corresponding index key expression.

Which Commands Can Participate in Rushmore Optimizations?

As we have seen, the SQL SELECT command takes full advantage of Rushmore. SQL SELECT is not alone, however. When combined with an optimizable FOR clause, each of the following commands can take advantage of Rushmore:

AVERAGE	INDEX
BROWSE	LABEL
CALCULATE	LIST
CHANGE	LOCATE
COPY TO	RECALL
COPY TO ARRAY	REPLACE
COUNT	REPORT
DELETE	SCAN
DISPLAY	SORT
EDIT	SUM
EXPORT	TOTAL

Reducing Indexes

Why should we care about partially optimizable queries? After all, if we simply index every field in every database, all our queries will be fully optimizable, right?

Right. However, we might want to add a record to the databases occasionally, and every index we create is an index FoxPro must maintain.

In multiuser applications, the single most important factor in the performance of FoxPro during file updates is the number of index tags associated with the database. In other words, the more indexes FoxPro must maintain, the longer it takes to add or change a record.

On a Novell Netware 3.11 LAN, utilizing 16-bit Ethernet cards, with 486/50 workstations with 8M of RAM and local hard drives, FoxPro can add 40 records per second per workstation to a database with three indexes. Amazingly, FoxPro performance does not degrade when we add as many as eight workstations. Even with 36 workstations, FoxPro maintains more than 25 appends per second per workstation. However, with no indexes, FoxPro can add 200 records per second per workstation with no degradation up to 36 workstations. (I stopped checking after 36 workstations.)

In other tests, with 36 workstations simultaneously querying and updating the same database, FoxPro produces nearly 3,400 seeks, and nearly 750 replaces of nonindexed fields per second.

One of MEI's manufacturing clients runs a system that must support 30 simultaneous data entry stations, each of which produces 20 transactions every 12 seconds. At the same time, as many as 30 users can query these same tables. These rather remarkable numbers are of interest for two reasons. First, FoxPro is fast enough for use in very demanding, real-time systems. Second, even when maintaining many indexes, FoxPro is probably fast enough to handle your data entry needs.

For this reason, you should design your system with all the indexes that you might reasonably expect to use in a query. If you discover that data entry speed is unsatisfactory, you can always go back and remove an index or two to improve throughput.

Special *SELECTs*

If you issue a SQL SELECT command that is fully Rushmore-optimizable, that references only a single database, that uses only fields from that table, that uses no field name aliases, that uses no column functions, that includes no GROUP BY or ORDER BY clauses, and that directs its output to a cursor, FoxPro can create a very special cursor very quickly.

Instead of copying the result of the query to a separate table, FoxPro identifies all the records that belong in the result, reopens the source database in another work area, and establishes a filter on that new work area. The result is nearly instantaneous response to single table queries of this type.

The Dilemma of *DELETED()* Records

When you SET DELETED ON in FoxPro, all data retrieval commands are supposed to ignore deleted records. Rushmore optimization consists mostly of checking indexes before testing records in the database. When you issue a COUNT or SELECT COUNT() command, Rushmore enables us to return the count without ever accessing the database.

However, the DELETED() flag is stored in the database. So, if SET DELETED is ON, COUNT and SELECT COUNT() commands are forced to test the database records before returning a value. As a result, COUNT and SELECT COUNT() run much more slowly with SET DELETED ON.

To resolve this problem, include an index like the following in each database that the SET DELETED ON slows down:

```
INDEX ON DELETED() TAG anyname
```

When you include an index based on the DELETED() expression, FoxPro can once again determine all the records that match your query, without accessing the database. In this case, after obtaining a list of records that match your count condition, FoxPro can check the anyname tag to determine which records should be counted.

Using *SET ORDER TO*

On learning that Rushmore utilizes indexes to perform its magic, developers often try to "help" Rushmore by setting the master order of a database before executing a command. Here is an example:

```
CLOSE ALL
USE fast ORDER name
t1=SECO()
LIST FOR name+STR(age,10)="B0"
t2=SECO()
WAIT WINDOW STR(t2-t1,10,4)  && 23.63 seconds

CLOSE ALL
USE fast
t1=SECO()
LIST FOR name+STR(age,10)="B0"
t2=SECO()
WAIT WINDOW STR(t2-t1,10,4) && 2.2 seconds
```

As you can see, such "helping" can hurt a lot. The problem is that FoxPro uses Rushmore to determine which records have names that start with "B0". This is accomplished in less than two seconds. However, after figuring out which records belong, FoxPro must go back and read the entire index to determine what order to present the records.

 Note: SQL SELECT ignores any established orders, and therefore suffers no performance penalty when a database has an established order.

Solutions to the *SET ORDER* Problem

In theory, or in a book, it's easy to say "don't set an order before doing a BROWSE FOR or a COPY FOR." In the real world, however, clients want to see their records in a particular order. Fortunately, there are several solutions available.

Before settling on one of the available solutions, you must first determine whether your user will need to process all records in the result set, or whether your user will only need to see one screen of records. To demonstrate the importance of this question, I wrote the SETORDE.PRG program that follows.

SETORDE.PRG tests the efficacy of five different approaches to presenting a filtered list of records to the user in order. SETORDE.PRG doesn't stop there though. It tests the efficacy of all five methods both for presenting a single screen of data, and for processing the entire result set.

Each test begins with a bold faced comment. The scores for each test are summarized at the end of the listing.

```
* setorde.prg
* Test speed of various filtered, ordered,
* browse solutions.
CLEAR
SET EXCL OFF
CLOSE DATA
USE fast
t1=SECO()

** Browse FOR no order
BROWSE FOR age=10 NOWAIT
t2=SECO()
CLOSE DATA
```

continues

```
USE fast ORDER name
t3=SECO()
```

```
** Browse FOR after SET ORDER
BROWSE FOR age=10 NOWAIT
t4=SECO()
CLOSE DATA
USE fast
t5=SECO()
```

```
** Scan FOR no ORDER
SCAN FOR age=10
   mvar=name
ENDSCAN
t6=SECO()
CLOSE DATA
USE fast ORDER name
t7=SECO()
```

```
** SCAN FOR after SET ORDER
SCAN FOR age=10
   mvar=name
ENDSCAN
t8=SECO()
CLOSE DATA
t9=SECO()
```

```
** BROWSE tricky
SELECT RECNO() AS tricky FROM fast WHERE age=10 ;
   ORDER BY name INTO CURSOR george
SET RELATION TO tricky INTO fast
BROWSE FIELDS fast.age,fast.dob,fast.name NOWAIT
t10=SECO()
CLOSE DATA
t11=SECO()
```

```
** Scan tricky
SELECT RECNO() AS tricky FROM fast WHERE age=10 ;
   ORDER BY name INTO CURSOR george
SET RELATION TO tricky INTO fast
SCAN
   mvar=fast.name
ENDSCAN
```

```
t12=SECO()
CLOSE DATA
t13=SECO()


** BROWSE after SELECT ORDER
SELECT * FROM fast WHERE age=10 INTO CURSOR george ;
  ORDER BY name
BROWSE NOWAIT
t14=SECO()
CLOSE DATA
t15=SECO()


** SCAN after SELECT ORDER
SELECT * FROM fast WHERE age=10 INTO CURSOR george ;
  ORDER BY name
SCAN
  mvar=name
ENDSCAN
t16=SECO()
CLOSE DATA
t17=SECO()


** BROWSE after INDEX FOR
USE fast
INDEX ON name FOR age=10 TO george COMPACT
BROWSE NOWAIT
t18=SECO()
CLOSE DATA
t19=SECO()


** SCAN after INDEX FOR
USE fast
INDEX ON name FOR age=10 TO george
SCAN
  mvar=name
ENDSCAN
t20=SECO()


? "BROWSE FOR no order       ",t2-t1   && 1.321
? "BROWSE after SELECT ORDER ",t14-t13 && 1.343
? "BROWSE tricky             ",t10-t9  && 1.497
? "BROWSE after INDEX FOR    ",t18-t17 && 2.948
? "BROWSE FOR after SET ORDER",t4-t3   && 4.581
```

continues

345

```
? "SCAN FOR no order       ",t6-t5   && 0.993
? "SCAN after SELECT ORDER  ",t16-t15 && 1.315
? "SCAN tricky             ",t12-t11 && 1.388
? "SCAN after INDEX FOR     ",t20-t19 && 2.786
? "SCAN FOR after SET ORDER ",t8-t7   && 9.488
```

The first five tests present to the user one Browse window's worth of records. All records have age=10 and are presented in name order. The BROWSE FOR no order test is presented as a baseline, because its records are not presented in name order. Notice that, in this case, it is faster to first SELECT...ORDER BY and then BROWSE than it is to simply BROWSE with an order set.

Unfortunately, the SELECT ORDER BY technique yields a read-only result set. Fortunately, the BROWSE tricky and INDEX ON FOR solutions enable the user to directly edit the FAST.DBF records that match the search criteria.

Notice the efficacy of SELECT ORDER BY when the entire result set must be processed. Whether you are running a report, copying the results to another table, or performing a global calculation, if you must process all the records in the result set, the SQL SELECT command should be your first choice.

At first glance, the SELECT ORDER BY approach also seems to be the best solution when the user wants to see only one screen full of records. However, this particular query returns only 33 records from a 106,000 record table. To see what happens if the majority of the records in a large table met a criterion, run the SETORDE.PRG after changing the filter condition from age=10 to age<>10. Here are the timings:

```
? "BROWSE FOR no order       ",t2-t1   && 0.364
? "BROWSE after SELECT ORDER ",t14-t13 && 88.288
? "BROWSE tricky             ",t10-t9  && 111.838
? "BROWSE after INDEX FOR     ",t18-t17 && 54.525
? "BROWSE FOR after SET ORDER",t4-t3   && 1.344

? "SCAN FOR no order         ",t6-t5   && 22.937
? "SCAN after SELECT ORDER   ",t16-t15 && 105.257
? "SCAN tricky               ",t12-t11 && 1456.929
? "SCAN after INDEX FOR       ",t20-t19 && 1396.914
? "SCAN FOR after SET ORDER   ",t8-t7   && 1358.100
```

Once again, SELECT ORDER BY is the clear choice when the entire result set is to be processed. However, the BROWSE FOR with a SET ORDER is the hands-down winner when it comes to presenting the user with a single screen full of records.

In fact, this BROWSE FOR with a SET ORDER is even faster than the first query's BROWSE FOR with a SET ORDER. The reason is simple: In the second query, the first 30 records or so that FoxPro finds in the name index fill the Browse window. In the first query, FoxPro must search the entire name index to find the 30 records that match the search criteria.

 Tip: If the criteria for your query are always the same, one more solution is available to you. FoxPro enables you to include a conditional index tag in a .CDX file. For example, if your boss constantly wants to see a list of all open invoices in order by date, the following index tag can help present a Browse window full of records instantly:

```
INDEX ON iv_date TAG open FOR iv_balance>iv_amtpaid
```

After creating this tag, you can instantly present your boss with a list of open invoices in date order, like this:

```
SET ORDER TO open
BROWSE
```

Obviously, the filtered index tag technique works only if the query criteria are static. This technique can also slow data entry slightly, by adding another index that FoxPro must maintain while adding or changing a record.

The *SORT*, *INDEX*, or *SET ORDER* Commands

As the previous section demonstrates, it is often faster to SORT or SELECT...ORDER BY a file rather than to list a file by using a preexisting index tag. This is counterintuitive. After all, the SORT or SELECT...ORDER BY must physically reorder the records before processing the result. Using an existing tag, on the other hand, involves no physical reordering of the data before processing begins.

Scanning an indexed table takes longer than scanning an unindexed table. This is easy to understand. After all, when FoxPro processes a database in indexed order, it must move back and forth in the database searching for the next record in the index.

The following table helps demonstrate the problem.

Key Value	Record Number
A	100,231
B	7
C	96,325
D	43
E	106,002

When FoxPro attempts to process this database in index order, it first moves to record 100, 231. Then, it moves to record 7. Then, it moves to record 96,325. Then, it moves to record 43. Finally, it moves to record 106,002. If you project this kind of jumping around to all 106,000 records in this table, you can understand why it takes longer to process the database in indexed order than in record number order.

So we now understand that FoxPro can process an unindexed table in *x* seconds less than the time it takes to process an indexed table. What is unexpected is FoxPro's capability to sort the database into the desired order in much less than *x* seconds.

The Decision Tree for *SORT* versus *INDEX*

Although SORTing is usually faster than using an existing index, there are times when you should use an existing index. In fact, there are even times when you are better off building an index than sorting the database.

Before you make this decision, you should learn two general rules, which apply to most of your queries:

- If the table contains less than a few thousand records, or if the query returns less than 50 records, the method you choose doesn't matter. FoxPro handles small tables so quickly that the differences in approach are of little consequence.

- Always use the SQL SELECT approach first. It is the easiest, and usually the best way to retrieve the records you need. You should investigate other solutions only if the SQL SELECT approach provides unsatisfactory results.

When the best possible performance is an absolute must, you might have to decide whether to index or SELECT...ORDER BY. The following decision tree should help you decide:

```
IF (memo_exists and is populated) OR insufficient_disk_for_sort
  IF tag_exists
    SET ORDER
  ELSE
    INDEX ON
  ENDIF
ELSE
  IF records_in_order_of_index_already
    SET ORDER
  ELSE
    IF very_big_records
      IF TAG
        SET ORDER
```

```
    ELSE
      INDEX ON
    ENDIF
  ELSE
    SORT/SELECT..ORDER BY
  ENDIF very_big records
 ENDIF records match INDEX
ENDIF MEMO involved
```

Notice the test that checks whether the records in the database are already in order of the index. Remember the table of indexed records? What if that table looked like the following table instead?

Key Value	Record Number
A	1
B	2
C	3
D	4
E	5

When FoxPro attempts to process this database in index order, it doesn't have to do much jumping around at all. Therefore, processing this table in indexed order doesn't take much longer than processing it in unindexed order. You can use either of these approaches to get your database in sync with its most commonly used index:

```
** "Copy to" approach
USE fast
SET ORDER TO name
COPY TO temp
USE
ERASE fast.dbf
ERASE fast.cdx
USE temp
RENAME temp.dbf TO fast.dbf
USE fast
** Rebuild all indexes


** "SELECT ORDER BY" approach
SELECT * FROM fast INTO TABLE temp ORDER BY name
USE IN fast
USE IN temp
```

continues

```
ERASE fast.cdx
ERASE fast.dbf
RENAME temp.dbf TO fast.dbf
USE fast
** Rebuild all indexes
```

Obviously, a database can only match one index at a time, so this approach helps only procedures that must process the FAST.DBF database in name order.

Foreign Key *ORDER BY* Solutions

Often we want to present the content of a file, ordered on the content of another file. For example, we might want to list open invoices in company name order.

We can solve this problem by relating invoices into customers and indexing the invoice database on the related customer name. Or, we can solve the problem by relating customers into invoices, SET SKIP TO invoices, and SET ORDER TO customer name. Or, we can use a SQL SELECT with an ORDER BY clause.

Here is a program that exercises all three options and then tests the speed of each technique for BROWSE and for SCAN:

```
SET SAFE OFF
SET TALK ON
SET TALK WINDOW ON
CLOSE DATA
t1=SECO()
** Index ON browse
USE bkinvc
USE bkcust IN SELE(1) ORDER cu_custid
SET RELATION TO iv_custid INTO bkcust
INDEX ON bkcust.cu_company+iv_ivno TO temp
GO TOP
BROWSE FIELDS bkcust.cu_company,iv_ivno NOWAIT
t2=SECO()
CLOSE DATA
t3=SECO()
** Set skip BROWSE
USE bkcust ORDER cu_company
USE bkinvc IN SELE(1) ORDER bkinvcid
SET RELATION TO cu_custid INTO bkinvc
SET SKIP TO bkinvc
GOTO TOP
```

```
BROWSE FIELDS cu_company,bkinvc.iv_ivno NOWAIT
t4=SECO()
CLOSE DATA
t5=SECO()
** Index on SCAN
USE bkinvc
USE bkcust IN SELE(1) ORDER cu_custid
SET RELATION TO iv_custid INTO bkcust
INDEX ON bkcust.cu_company+iv_ivno TO temp
SCAN
   mvar=bkcust.cu_company
ENDSCAN
t6=SECO()
CLOSE DATA
t7=SECO()
** SET SKIP SCAN
USE bkcust ORDER cu_company
USE bkinvc IN SELE(1) ORDER bkinvcid
SET RELATION TO cu_custid INTO bkinvc
SET SKIP TO bkinvc
SCAN
   mvar=bkcust.cu_company
ENDSCAN
t8=SECO()
CLOSE DATA
t9=SECO()
** SQL SELECT BROWSE
SELECT cu_company,iv_ivno FROM bkcust,bkinvc ;
   WHERE cu_custid=iv_custid ORDER BY cu_company ;
   INTO CURSOR temp
BROWSE NOWAIT
t10=SECO()
CLOSE DATA
t11=SECO()
** SQL SELECT SCAN
SELECT cu_company,iv_ivno FROM bkcust,bkinvc ;
   WHERE cu_custid=iv_custid ORDER BY cu_company ;
   INTO CURSOR temp
SCAN
   mvar=cu_company
ENDSCAN
t12=SECO()
```

In case you can't guess the results, here are the times:

```
Index on...browse        22.382
Set skip...browse         0.562
Select...browse          12.608
Index on...scan          66.850
Set skip...scan          52.895
select...scan            13.165
```

Notice that the SET SKIP solution is the best for presenting one Browse window's worth of records. However, SQL SELECT once again takes top honors when it comes to processing the entire database.

Conditionally Displaying Records: *BROWSE KEY* versus *BROWSE FOR*

We can use both BROWSE KEY and BROWSE FOR to display records conditionally in a Browse window. BROWSE KEY usually is faster than BROWSE FOR when the records must be in the same order as the conditional expression.

We can run the following program to test this assertion:

```
*brforkey.prg
DEFINE WINDOW george FROM 1,0 TO 20,75
CLOSE DATA
USE mename
t1=SECO()
BROWSE FOR nm_compid="T" NOWAIT WINDOW george
t2=SECO()
CLOSE DATA
USE mename ORDER nm_compid
t3=SECO()
BROWSE KEY "T" NOWAIT WINDOW george
t4=SECO()
CLOSE DATA
USE mename ORDER nm_compid
t5=SECO()
BROWSE FOR nm_compid="T" NOWAIT WINDOW george
t6=SECO()
```

Here are the times recorded for a 20,000 record database on a LAN:

FOR	0.445
KEY	0.493
FOR with order set	0.755
FOR	0.117
KEY	0.259
FOR with order set	0.749

Use BROWSE KEY when you can. BROWSE FOR is more flexible, but generally slower.

Sometimes EXCLUSIVE use is slower than SHAREd use. On Novell networks, using a file EXCLUSIVEly can actually degrade performance. Notice that two sets of times are reported for the BRFORKEY.PRG. The first set of times was recorded on the LAN with EXCLUSIVE SET ON. The second set of times was recorded with EXCLUSIVE SET OFF. This seems to occur only on Novell networks, and only when an optimizable query returns a small subset of records.

SEEK WHILE versus *FOR*

Which of the following code segments is faster?

```
* Segment 1
SET ORDER TO keyfield
SEEK mvar
SCAN WHILE keyfield=mvar
  DO something
ENDSCAN

* Segment 2
SET ORDER TO 0
SCAN FOR keyfield=mvar
  DO something
ENDSCAN
```

The answer is, *it depends*. The closer the physical order of the records is to the indexed order of the records, and the fewer the number of records that match the criteria, the more likely the SEEK/SCAN WHILE approach is to win.

The *APPEND FROM* Command

The APPEND FROM command is the fastest way to add a group of records to a database. The APPEND FROM command does not require an FLOCK() and can be used to APPEND FROM a currently open database, from a database that is not open, from an array, or from a DOS file in one of several formats.

 Note: You often can add large batches of records to an existing database more quickly if you first delete all index tags in the database. Then, after the records have been appended, the index tags are rebuilt. FoxPro, like all database management systems, can build B+ tree indexes faster than it can maintain them.

INSERT INTO versus *APPEND BLANK*

INSERT INTO is faster than APPEND BLANK/REPLACE or APPEND BLANK/GATHER. The reason is pretty simple: When you APPEND BLANK and then update the fields in your new record by using GATHER or REPLACE, you make two changes to every index tag in the database.

The first change occurs when you create the blank record with APPEND BLANK. Then, when you update the blank record, FoxPro changes the blank entries in the .CDX tags to reflect your changes.

The difference in performance can be two and one-half times or more, depending on the number of index tags in the database. This difference occurs only when you add records to shared files.

The Fastest Popup Solutions

Often an application must present the user with a popup of valid values. In heavy data entry environments, how quickly the program presents the popup to the user, and how quickly the user can scroll the options, can significantly affect the perceived value of the product.

To put it another way, popup speed can matter a lot if you have an irate customer on the phone and you need to find his or her order in a popup. The next program includes four different methods for creating popups to be displayed when the user triggers a valid clause:

```
* poptestw.prg
* Tests four different popup solutions.
PUBLIC t1,t2,t3,t4,t5,t6,t7,t8,t9,t10
STORE 0 TO t1,t2,t3,t4,t5,t6,t7,t8,t9,t10
USE mecomp ORDER cm_compid
DEFINE WINDOW big FROM 1,0 TO 23,79
ACTIVATE WINDOW big
SELECT cm_compid+" "+cm_name FROM mecomp ORDER BY ;
  cm_compid INTO ARRAY goodcomp
m.compid=SPACE(10)
@ 2,0 GET m.compid VALID poptest1(@t1,@t2,@m.compid)
@ 3,0 GET m.dummy DEFA 1
KEYBOARD "{tab}"
READ CYCLE
@ 2,0 GET m.compid VALID poptest2(@t3,@t4,@m.compid)
@ 3,0 GET m.dummy DEFA 1
KEYBOARD "{tab}"
READ CYCLE
@ 2,0 GET m.compid VALID poptest3(@t5,@t6,@m.compid)
@ 3,0 GET m.dummy DEFA 1
KEYBOARD "{tab}"
READ CYCLE
@ 2,0 GET m.compid VALID poptest4(@t7,@t8,@m.compid)
@ 3,0 GET m.dummy DEFA 1
KEYBOARD "{tab}"
READ CYCLE
SET ALTERNATE TO poptest.txt ADDITIVE
SET ALTERNATE ON
? VERS(1),DATE(),TIME()
? "Browse 1x           ",t2-t1
? "Define popup 1x     ",t4-t3
? "Scrollable list array",t6-t5
? "@ menu to 1x        ",t8-t7
SET ALTERNATE TO

PROCEDURE poptest1
PARAMETERS start,END,thisvar
m.start=SECO()
DEFINE WINDOW george FROM 2,15 TO 10,75
PUSH KEY
ON KEY LABEL enter KEYB "{ctrl+w}" PLAIN
KEYBOARD "{pgdn}{pgdn}{enter}"
BROWSE WINDOW george FIELDS cm_compid,cm_name WHEN .F.
```

continues

```
POP KEY
RELEASE WINDOW george
m.thisvar=cm_compid
m.end=SECO()
KEYB "{ctrl+w}"
RETURN .T.


PROCEDURE poptest2
PARAMETERS start,END,thisvar
m.start=SECO()
DEFINE POPUP george FROM 2,15 TO 10,75 PROMPT FIELD ;
  cm_compid+" "+cm_name
ON SELECTION POPUP george DEACTIVATE POPUP george
KEYBOARD "{pgdn}{pgdn}{enter}"
ACTIVATE POPUP george
m.thisvar=cm_compid
m.end=SECO()
KEYB "{ctrl+w}"
RETURN .T.


PROCEDURE poptest3
PARAMETERS start,END,thisvar
m.start=SECO()
KEYBOARD "{pgdn}{pgdn}{enter}"
@ 2,15 GET poptest3 DEFA 1 FROM goodcomp SIZE 9,60
READ
m.thisvar=LEFT(goodcomp(poptest3),10)
m.end=SECO()
KEYB "{ctrl+w}"
RETURN .T.

PROCEDURE poptest4
PARAMETERS start,END,thisvar
m.start=SECO()
KEYBOARD "{pgdn}{pgdn}{enter}"
@ 2,15 MENU goodcomp,10,ALEN(goodcomp)
poptest4=1
READ MENU TO poptest4
m.thisvar=LEFT(goodcomp(poptest4),10)
m.end=SECO()
KEYB "{ctrl+w}"
RETURN .T.
```

Here are the times for each solution:

```
Browse                    1.390
Define popup              0.260
Scrollable list array     0.760
@ menu to                 0.233
```

Each method has its merits, but the DEFINE POPUP solution provides the best mix of speed and compliance with the rest of the FoxPro interface. Here are the times turned in by FoxPro 2.5 for DOS:

```
Browse 1x                 0.981
Define popup 1x           0.192
Scrollable list array     0.145
@ menu to 1x              0.014
```

Obviously, FoxPro for DOS displays and scrolls popups faster than FoxPro for Windows. Further, the @ MENU TO command is the fastest popup solution available on either platform, but the difference is truly noticeable on the DOS platform.

Using Macros Selectively

Macros are faster than they once were, particularly when using the extended mode version of FoxPro for DOS and when using FoxPro for Windows. This does not mean that we should attempt to use more macros. It simply means that we no longer must avoid macros at all costs.

Referencing Objects: Macros versus Name Indirection

As the next program demonstrates, when we use a macro to reference the name of an object indirectly, we can use simple name indirection; that is, instead of issuing the command USE &mvar., we can issue the command USE (mvar). There is a slight performance benefit to name indirection.

```
* macro.prg
* Speed of macro vs. name indirection
SET TALK OFF
SET SAFE OFF

CREATE TABLE george (name C(10))
USE IN george
mvar="george"
```

continues

```
george=7
t1=SECO()
FOR xx=1 TO 100
   DEFINE WINDOW &mvar. FROM 1,0 TO 10,50
   mvar2=&mvar.
   USE &mvar.
ENDFOR
t2=SECO() && 5.3 seconds elapsed time
t3=SECO()
FOR xx=1 TO 100
   DEFINE WINDOW (mvar) FROM 1,0 TO 10,50
   mvar2=(mvar)
   USE (mvar)
ENDFOR
t4=SECO() && 4.4 seconds elapsed time
WAIT WINDOW STR(t2-t1,10,4)+STR(t4-t3,10,4)
```

Evaluating Expressions: Macros versus *EVAL()*

When the purpose of using a macro is to evaluate an expression stored as a string in a memory variable, we can increase performance by using the EVAL() function rather than a macro expansion. In the following example, the EVAL() function is faster than a macro expansion:

```
* Macro2.prg
* Tests the speed of macros vs. EVAL()
mvar="mvar1=7"
mvar1=8
t1=SECO()
FOR xx=1 TO 100
   IF &mvar.
      george=7
   ENDIF
ENDFOR
t2=SECO() && 0.1899 Seconds elapsed time
t3=SECO()
FOR xx=1 TO 100
   IF EVAL(mvar)
      george=7
   ENDIF
ENDFOR
t4=SECO() && 0.122 Seconds elapsed time
WAIT WINDOW STR(t2-t1,10,4)+STR(t4-t3,10,4)
```

However, sometimes macros are faster than EVAL(), as in MACRO3.PRG:

```
* Macro3.prg
* Macro vs. EVAL on multirecord commands
SET TALK OFF
CLOSE DATA
USE fast
mvar="age=10"
t1=SECO()
BROWSE FOR &mvar. NOWAIT  && 1.192 seconds
t2=SECO()
USE
USE fast
t3=SECO()
BROWSE FOR EVAL(mvar) NOWAIT && 111.897 seconds
t4=SECO()
t5=SECO()
answer=&mvar. && 0.002 seconds
t6=SECO()
t7=SECO()
answer=EVAL(mvar) && 0.002 seconds
t8=SECO()
USE
? t2-t1,"browse &"
? t4-t3,"browse eval()"
? t6-t5,"=&mvar"
? t8-t7,"=eval(mvar)"
```

Simply put, the expanded macro in this case is Rushmore-optimizable. The macro is expanded only once, and then FoxPro applies Rushmore to the problem, yielding a fast return. The EVAL(), however, must be evaluated for every record in the database, which takes *100 times longer* in this case.

As a general rule, we use macros for multirecord commands and use EVAL() for single evaluations.

Substring Searches

Substring searches are not Rushmore-optimizable. Therefore, trying to find, for example, a company name that includes the word "Inc." anywhere in the title can take a very long time.

One solution is to maintain two tables for company information. One table includes the company ID, the company name, and all address and contact information. In the other table, we include only the company name.

When we want to perform a substring search against the name field, we select the name-only database and perform the substring search. When we find the record(s) of interest, use the record number of the name-only database to find the associated record in the master company database. Because the name-only file is smaller than a company file containing additional company information, the search is faster. Here is a sample program:

```
USE mecomp
USE mecompnm IN 0
SELECT mecompnm
LOCATE FOR "INC."$UPPER(nm_name)
IF FOUND()
   SELECT mecomp
   GOTO RECNO("mecompnm")
ENDIF
```

Even this solution is insufficient if the searches must be completed in seconds rather than minutes. One of MEI's clients came up with the following solution.

The client built one index tag for every character in the name field and then performed a series of SEEKs to find the record of interest. (In the actual case, the name field was 40 characters long, but to reduce the program length, pretend that the name field is only 10 characters long.) First, we need the following indexes:

```
INDEX ON UPPER(cm_name) TAG name01
INDEX ON UPPER(SUBSTR(cm_name,2)) TAG name02
INDEX ON UPPER(SUBSTR(cm_name,3)) TAG name03
INDEX ON UPPER(SUBSTR(cm_name,4)) TAG name04
INDEX ON UPPER(SUBSTR(cm_name,5)) TAG name05
INDEX ON UPPER(SUBSTR(cm_name,6)) TAG name06
INDEX ON UPPER(SUBSTR(cm_name,7)) TAG name07
INDEX ON UPPER(SUBSTR(cm_name,8)) TAG name08
INDEX ON UPPER(SUBSTR(cm_name,9)) TAG name09
INDEX ON UPPER(SUBSTR(cm_name,10)) TAG name10
```

If 30 more characters were in the cm_name field, we would add 30 more index tags. Now, when we want to find a cm_name field that contains the characters "INC.", we call a UDF such as the following:

```
* fastfind.prg
PARAMETERS p_s
l_found=.t.
```

```
IF EMPTY(LOOKUP(cm_name,UPPER(p_s),cm_name,"name01"))
  IF EMPTY(LOOKUP(cm_name,UPPER(p_s),cm_name,"name02"))
    IF EMPTY(LOOKUP(cm_name,UPPER(p_s),cm_name,"name03"))
      IF EMPTY(LOOKUP(cm_name,UPPER(p_s),cm_name,"name04"))
        IF EMPTY(LOOKUP(cm_name,UPPER(p_s),cm_name,"name05"))
          IF EMPTY(LOOKUP(cm_name,UPPER(p_s),cm_name,"name06"))
            IF EMPTY(LOOKUP(cm_name,UPPER(p_s),cm_name,"name07"))
              IF EMPTY(LOOKUP(cm_name,UPPER(p_s),cm_name,;
                "name08"))
                IF EMPTY(LOOKUP(cm_name,UPPER(p_s),cm_name,;
                  "name09"))
                  IF EMPTY(LOOKUP(cm_name,UPPER(p_s),cm_name,;
                    "name10"))
                    l_found=.F.
                  ENDIF name10
                ENDIF name09
              ENDIF name08
            ENDIF name07
          ENDIF name06
        ENDIF name05
      ENDIF name04
    ENDIF name03
  ENDIF name02
ENDIF name01
return l_found
```

Databases that include large memo fields pose another performance challenge. FoxPro searches memo fields for strings very quickly. Sometimes, however, users need instant response. One approach calls for the indexing of keywords in memo fields to provide virtually instantaneous access to all memo fields that contain one or more user-specified keywords.

In this approach, every unique word in a memo field is stored, along with the record's unique ID, in a separate file. That file is indexed both by record ID and by word. Here are some sample database structures:

```
Structure for table:     d:\devcon\wordtest.dbf
Number of data records: 52
Date of last update:     03/13/93
Memo file block size:    64
Field  Field Name  Type        Width    Dec    Index
    1  WT_ID       Character     12             Asc
    2  WT_CONTENT  Memo          10
** Total **                      23
```

continues

```
Structure for table:      d:\devcon\fastword.dbf
Number of data records: 1203
Date of last update:     03/13/93
Field  Field Name  Type         Width    Dec    Index
    1  FW_ID       Character      10             Asc
    2  FW_WORD     Character      20             Asc
** Total **                       31
```

Here are the indexes:

```
Select area:  1, Table in Use: D:\DEVCON\WORDTEST.DBF
  Alias: WORDTEST
  Structural CDX file:    D:\DEVCON\WORDTEST.CDX
     Master Index tag:   WT_ID              Key: WT_ID
           Memo file:    D:\DEVCON\WORDTEST.FPT
     Lock(s): Exclusive USE


Currently Selected Table:
Select area:  2, Table in Use: D:\DEVCON\FASTWORD.DBF
  Alias: FASTWORD
  Structural CDX file:    D:\DEVCON\FASTWORD.CDX
          Index tag:    FW_ID          Key: UPPER(FW_ID)
          Index tag:    FW_WORD        Key: UPPER(FW_WORD)
          Index tag:    IDWORD         Key: UPPER(FW_ID+FW_WORD)
          Lock(s): <none>
```

When a new WORDTEST.DBF record is added, or when the content of a wt_content memo field is changed, we call the following program to parse the words in the memo field and to create the appropriate entries in the FASTWORD.DBF:

```
* fastword.prg
* Registers all of the unique words in a string in the
* fastword database.
PARAMETERS p_s,p_id
l_uniq=CHR(255)
l_strlen=LEN(p_s)
l_totwords=0
l_uniqwrds=0
l_xx=1
l_oldsele=select()
SELECT fastword
SET ORDER TO idword
DO WHILE l_xx<l_strlen
```

```
   ** Skip over any nonword characters.
   DO WHILE NOT UPPER(SUBSTR(p_s,l_xx,1))$;
       "ABCDEFGHIJKLMNOPQRSTUVWXYZ01234567890" AND l_xx<l_strlen
     l_xx=l_xx+1
   ENDDO
   ** Accumulate characters for the current word.
   l_word=""
   DO WHILE UPPER(SUBSTR(p_s,l_xx,1))$;
       "ABCDEFGHIJKLMNOPQRSTUVWXYZ01234567890" AND l_xx<l_strlen
     l_word=l_word+UPPER(SUBSTR(p_s,l_xx,1))
     l_xx=l_xx+1
   ENDDO
   l_totwords=l_totwords+1
   IF NOT CHR(255)+l_word+CHR(255)$l_uniq
     l_uniqwrds=l_uniqwrds+1
     l_uniq=l_uniq+l_word+CHR(255)
     IF NOT SEEK(p_id+PADR(l_word,20),"fastword")
       INSERT INTO fastword (fw_id,fw_word) VALUES (p_id,l_word)
     ENDIF not on file
   ENDIF
 ENDDO
SELECT fastword
SET ORDER TO 0
SCAN FOR fw_id=p_id
  IF NOT CHR(255)+ALLTRIM(l_word)+CHR(255)$l_uniq
    DELETE
  ENDIF old word does not exist in string
ENDSCAN
select (l_oldsele)
RETURN str(l_uniqwrds)+str(l_totwords)+str(l_strlen)
```

When the user wants to see a list of all records whose wt_content field includes the word GEORGE, we can obtain that list instantly, as follows:

```
SELECT fastword
SET RELATION TO fw_id INTO wordtest
BROWSE FOR fw_word="GEORGE" ;
  FIELDS wordtest.wt_id,wordtest.wt_content
```

This substring search solution is not perfect. Obviously, you should rewrite FASTWORD.PRG as a C routine for better performance. Further, only whole words or the beginning of whole words can be searched in this way. Finally, there is no support for phrases.

Don't Reuse *DELETED()* Records

Many Xbase programmers address the problem of deleted records by reusing deleted records. The approach is to blank each record as it is deleted. Then, when it is time to add a record, the program first searches for a blank record to reuse before INSERTing a new record.

Indeed, many programmers go so far as to append many blank records to active database "at the beginning of the day," so that there are plenty of blank records to find.

This technique is often used in applications where it is not possible to PACK the database. This situation occurs when there is insufficient disk space to perform a PACK and when the application is required to be "live" 24 hours a day, seven days a week.

Other times, programmers employ this technique so that they can locate and lock an empty record before beginning a transaction, thereby ensuring that attempts to add a new record are successful.

Most often, programmers employ this technique in the mistaken belief that it is faster to reuse deleted records than to create new records. This belief probably stems from our ecologically sensitive times, in which it just seems that recycling deleted records is more responsible than consuming more disk space with an INSERT INTO.

At Micro Endeavors, programmers don't reuse blank deleted records, for the following reasons:

- It is faster to INSERT a new record than it is to SEEK and GATHER into an existing blank record.
- Reusing blank records creates twice as much index activity as INSERTing a new record, which increases network contention and reduces performance.
- Reusing blank deleted records requires additional code.
- Reusing blank records forces records out of index key order.
- Reusing blank deleted records helps to unbalance index tags.

Nine Speed Tips for Fun and Profit

The following is a list of some favorite performance tips:

- The location of procedures has no impact on performance.
- Defragment local hard drives frequently.
- Keep the number of files in any given subdirectory under 256.

- When SELECT...GROUP BY and SELECT DISTINCT yield the same result, SELECT...GROUP BY returns the result faster.

- If you have SHARE loaded, and you have SET EXCLUSIVE OFF, .DBFs on local hard drives are opened in SHAREd mode. Open these databases with USE...EXCLUSIVE for better performance.

- Once you open a database, leave it open. Opening and closing databases are two of the slowest things you can do in FoxPro.

- PUSH MENU consumes a minimum of 15K of RAM per issuance. Try releasing or restoring menu elements by hand instead.

- Instead of always using a UDF to lock a record, try IF RLOCK() .OR. MYLOCK(). If the RLOCK succeeds, your program won't incur the overhead of calling your UDF.

- It is faster to @...SAY an expression than it is to @...GET an object.

The Great Client-Server Myth

Within the past year, a major PC trade publication ran a story benchmarking most of the major client-server database products available on PCs. On the first page of the article was an impressive graphic illustrating one of the most popularly held misconceptions in the database industry.

One half of the graphic showed a picture of a PC connected to a LAN running a file-server database product. The other half of the graphic showed a picture of a PC connected to a LAN running a client-server database product.

According to the graphic, when the PC running the file-server DBMS queried the database on the LAN, the entire database was transmitted over the network to the PC, where the PC tested all records in the database. When large databases are involved, this huge volume of network traffic should render file-server-based PC DBMS unusable, according to the graphic.

The client-server half of the graphic showed how the PC running the client-server DBMS sent a request to the server, where the server processed the database and returned only those records that matched the criteria. Obviously, this approach creates much less network traffic and should, according to the graphic, produce breathtakingly better performance than a file-server solution.

The idea that a client-server DBMS is inherently faster than a file-server DBMS, and that only a client-server DBMS can possibly handle large databases with high transaction volumes, makes so much sense that everyone believes it. In fact, while teaching a class of more than 20 database specialists, I once asked the question, "How many of you have sold database products to clients by explaining that client-server products must, by virtue of their design, outperform file-server products?" Everyone in the room raised a hand.

I then ran the following FoxPro query on the equivalent of the world's slowest LAN:

```
SET EXCL OFF
SELECT li_ivno,li_invntry FROM bkitms WHERE ;
  li_ivno="199100000001" OR ;
  li_ivno="199100100000"
```

This query returns the first two, and last five records from a 449,996 record, 40M+ database, in *less than 1.5 seconds.*

I'll repeat that for speed readers: FoxPro, a file-server DBMS, queried a 40M+ database, over a LAN, in less than 1.5 seconds. If you are good with math, you know that such a LAN has to be able to transfer data at more than 40M per second, that the PC has to be able to read 40M per second, and FoxPro has to be able to filter more than 40M of data per second, if, as we all know, file-server products drag the entire database across the network every time they perform a query.

A company's MIS group, which held the common misconceptions of the "limitations" of file-server products in handling large databases, came to MEI's offices one day. I let them test the accuracy of their perceptions of file-server databases by having all five of them simultaneously query the same 680,000-record, 70M+ database. Their first queries required some two seconds to complete. Subsequent queries, some of which were fairly complex, finished in less than one second.

Obviously, if five users can simultaneously query the same 70M+ database on an EtherNet LAN, FoxPro does not drag the entire database across the network with every query. If you take advantage of Rushmore, and of indexes in general, your applications should rarely saturate a network.

If you let many users simultaneously query your client-server-based database, however, your application may frequently saturate your server. The truth is that there are fast client-server products and there are slow client-server products; there are fast file-server products and there are slow file-server products. So it's not the philosophy behind the DBMS that determines the DBMS' performance, but the implementation of that philosophy that determines the performance of the DBMS.

Regardless of philosophy, regardless of the size of the database, regardless of the volume of transactions, FoxPro is the fastest database product available for PCs, with no exception.

Final Thoughts

I love making applications run fast. I love getting answers for people in seconds when it used to take days. I love listening to users ask questions they never even thought of when they were spending their time waiting for their applications to run.

If you love doing these things too, use FoxPro, and the simple tips in this chapter, and you'll be a very happy developer.

CHAPTER 16

Beautifying Windows

The time sheet application that we developed in the first eight chapters of this book is a remarkably plain looking application. Colors, fonts, and styles are used sparingly. Graphics are avoided altogether. Sound is not even discussed.

I like fonts. I like colors. I like styles. I really like graphics. I even like sound effects, in small doses. However, I like functioning applications more. So, I postponed the discussion of cosmetic issues until I had covered all the functionality issues.

In addition, I wanted the time sheet program to be as cross-platform-compatible as possible. Because the DOS version of FoxPro cannot support fonts, styles, or graphics, I kept the use of these Windows-specific features to a minimum.

Writing a Windows application that doesn't take advantage of fonts, styles, graphics, and sounds cheats your user by withholding valuable interface tools, and cheats you by dramatically reducing the fun associated with writing Windows applications. So, I included two chapters to ensure that you had full command of all the tools available to FoxPro for Windows developers.

In Chapter 18, "Sharing the Windows Environment with OLE and DDE," you can read all about DDE and OLE. In this chapter, **Mike Brachman** discusses issues related to the use of fonts, graphics, color, and styles. He also provides some tips to help you more easily create and align objects in FoxPro for Windows.

The Problem of Cross-Platform Applications

The ideal cross-platform application would operate the same across platforms and look as good as possible. The problem is that to create this ideal application, you are forced to use the lowest common denominator. For screens, you must use fixed-width fonts, plain backgrounds, and screen controls built out of characters. You must assume an 80 x 25 or 80 x 50 screen. For reports, you must use a fixed-width font with limited print styles.

FoxPro 2.5 can create applications that are customized to the platform. By that I mean attention to the cosmetics. The core program still runs the same. The program would automatically detect the platform and call the proper code. Your DOS screens would be tailored for DOS and your Windows screens would look like Windows screens. Your reports would be fixed-width font for DOS but use TrueType fonts for Windows. The next few sections tell you how to get the most out of Windows and give your applications not only the look and feel of Windows, but some pizzazz as well.

Screens 1: Background

When designing screens in FoxPro for Windows, I strongly suggest that you use the Screen Builder. FoxPro for Windows uses fractional row and column numbers for object placement, and letting FoxPro calculate these position numbers is much easier than doing it by hand.

When you first use the Screen Builder, you can save alignment time by using a fixed-width font such as FoxFont or Courier. After you have everything placed and aligned, you can change fonts. Here are a few more tips for aligning items on screens:

- To preserve your vertical alignment, try to use the same point size as your layout font.

- For smaller fonts, use a sans-serif font such as Arial.

- Reserve serif fonts such as Times New Roman for larger point sizes.

- If you have an input field in which every position is important, use a fixed-width font such as Terminal or even leave it in FoxFont to prevent "wiggle" on data entry. (*Note:* Using a proportional font may even hide your last character or two if you use the same screen to review your data.)

After you become experienced at using the Screen Builder to design screen layouts, you can get brave and start designing directly in the display font. You can set the default font of the screen by using the Screen pad, Layout... bar, and Font... option, as shown in Figure 16.1.

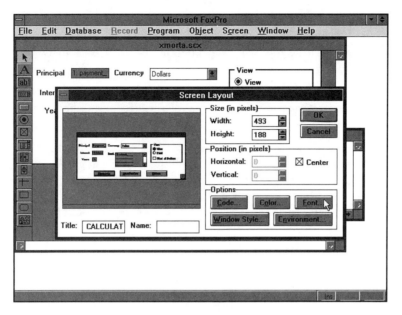

Figure 16.1. Selecting a default font for the Screen Builder.

There are a number of techniques you can use to align objects. The most important is to enable the Show Position option on the Screen menu. The status bar now will show all the relevant statistics whenever you select an object, as shown in Figure 16.2.

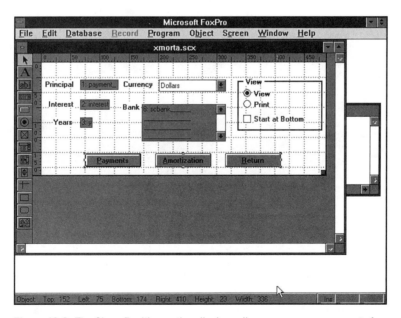

Figure 16.2. The Show Position option displays all necessary measurements for a selected object.

When you start a screen, you should use the Snap to Grid option of the Screen menu and make the grid visible. This will make it easier to make gross alignments for objects. When it is time to fine tune your sizing and alignments, you'll want to use the cursor keys.

You can use the cursor keys to make single-pixel adjustments of a selected object. By using the Shift+ cursor keys, you change the size of an object by a single pixel. By using the Ctrl+ cursor keys, you disable the grid while you move that object.

Try to maintain a consistent font for similar objects. You can use boxes or color sparingly to set special objects apart from others. If you are using different fonts or point sizes, a good rule of thumb is to align the bottom of letters, not descenders. The eye will interpret two fonts as misaligned if the bottoms of letters are not aligned regardless of descenders. This is especially true if you are using a serif font or mixing a serif font with a sans-serif font.

Colors and Wallpaper

Windows opens up many opportunities for color. Some colors, such as those used for the title band and border, are not controlled by the program. The Windows control panel settings set these colors. However, object colors and background are under your control. By using the menus, you can set the color of individual objects as well as their fonts and whether they are transparent or opaque. To control the background color of a window, first select the Layout... option of the Screen menu. Then, select the Color... push button, as I have done in Figure 16.3.

 Tip: You can create pastel shades from the standard 16 colors offered by Windows. First create a small .BMP file with dimensions of 10 pixels by 10 pixels. Then fill in every other pixel with color, staggering every other row. This creates a lighter version of the fill color. Make your text objects transparent rather than white so that they are visible against your background. Contrast is the key. If you are using a dark background, use light letters or dark letters in opaque mode. If you are using a light background, use dark letters.

Wallpaper

You can also use an icon file to create a background. If you use an icon as wallpaper, I suggest that you use opaque mode for your text objects so they can be seen against an unhomogeneous background. This also applies to wallpaper made from pictures.

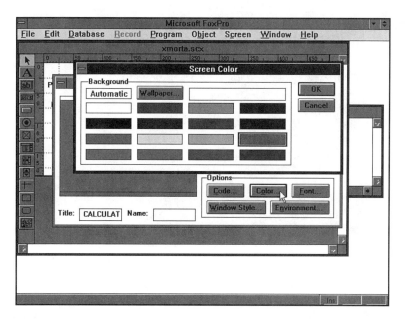

Figure 16.3. Use the Screen Color dialog from Screen Layout to select the background color or wallpaper.

Wallpaper uses .BMP or .PCX files to fill the background with repeating images. If the original .BMP is bigger than the window, it will be a clipped image. If smaller, the .BMP tiles multiple images together. If you are using a homogeneous pattern, you have to adjust the size of the image so that the "seams" are invisible. If you are using a picture or whimsical background, you probably don't care about the seams.

Figure 16.4 shows a .BMP file showing some fish with the text objects on the left transparent and the ones on the right opaque. You can see that the text on the left is nearly invisible whereas the text on the right stands out.

Screens 2: Bitmap Files for Controls

FoxPro for Windows allows you to use .BMP or .ICO files for check boxes, radio buttons, and push buttons. There are many advantages to using .BMP files for controls. For example, it makes the function easier to decipher. For example, you can show a magnifying glass to represent Zoom, or a file folder closing to represent Close.

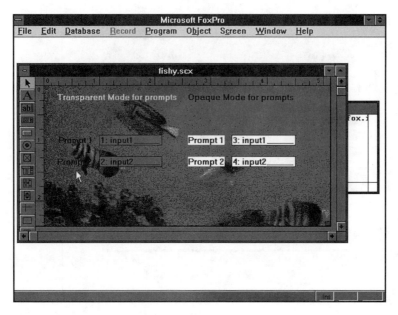

Figure 16.4. The selection of object mode depends on the background; opaque is required if there isn't enough contrast.

Picture controls allow you to create international applications with less work. You can use internationally recognized icons for selected operations or you can distribute your application with .BMP files tailored for the local setting. In this way, you avoid the hassle of translating the text of your controls for each language version of your application.

Methods for Using Icons

Figure 16.5 shows push buttons, radio buttons, and check boxes presented in three formats. The first group is the standard, text-only control.

The second group is icon-assisted. This might be the type you use if you substitute different .BMP files for different localities. The icon remains the same, except the text is adapted for each locality.

Note: Icons not only facilitate the development of applications for different languages, they also make it easier to remember what each control does. This is especially true when the application is not used daily.

The third group shows a pure icon form of each type of control. In this case, you do not need a different version for each locale, because no language element is included.

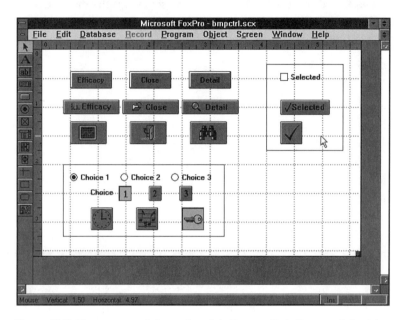

Figure 16.5. Three representations of push buttons, radio buttons, and check boxes.

Using .BMP files for controls has a downside as well. For push buttons and radio buttons, you must return the selected value as a number. You cannot prefill the variable behind the control with a string and receive the selected character string as you can with text-only controls. Also, you cannot assign a default push button with the metacommand \ !, nor an Escape push button with \?. You can't even assign a hot key to these controls because you have to make those assignments with individual ON KEY LABEL commands.

Changing the Icons

If you choose to use .BMP files to represent your radio buttons or push buttons, you can have up to three bitmaps assigned to each button. The first bitmap is the normal, unselected representation, the second is the selected representation, and the third is assigned to disabled controls. Unfortunately, there is no way to assign these push buttons by using the Screen Builder.

If you want to use this feature, you can use one of three methods. First, you can let FoxPro change the color when a push button or radio button is selected or disabled. The selected and unselected states look about the same, but the disabled state looks somewhat different.

Second, you can use the READ WHEN or READ ACTIVATE clause to issue the following command:

```
SHOW GET pb,1 PROMPT "s1.bmp,s1.bmp,s1d.bmp"
```

This repaints the GET field with the new attributes. Note that the variable is referred to as pb,1. This is important. You must assign a new attribute to each subobject within each GET object. If you omit the ,1, you receive an error message.

The third way to alter the appearance of .BMP files in controls is to use the Screen Builder's comment field of the object. First, include your additional .BMP file names in the comment field of the object in question. Then, adjust the anybitmapctrl procedure in GENSCRN.PRG to concatenate the comment field to the end of the picture clause for your control.

 Tip: One word of advice: If you are modifying GENSCRN.PRG, save a copy of it somewhere *before* you start modifying it. You may need it some day!

Reports 1: Using Fonts

Windows provides a marvelous array of fonts and printing technology. If you use True-Type, you don't have to worry whether your printer is PostScript- or LaserJet-compatible: In either case, the output is the same. The Report Writer in FoxPro for Windows is quite reminiscent of the Screen Builder. The rules and techniques for alignment are the same.

As you begin designing screen layouts, you may want to use a fixed-width font such as FoxFont until you get the hang of alignment. You can change fonts after the fields are properly aligned. Remember to align the bottom of letters, not the descenders, if you are mixing fonts or point sizes on the same line. Use horizontal or vertical lines to aid in alignment, and make sure you use the Show Position option so that you can use the cursor keys to fine-tune alignment.

Choosing Fonts

The basic version of Windows provides numerous fonts, and you can add hundreds more. How do you choose which fonts to use to create an effective report? This section provides a few rules of thumb that can help you decide which fonts to use.

At standard VGA resolution, you can see sans-serif fonts such as Arial more easily on-screen than a serif font. However, this is not true for printed output. Most people find a serif font such as Times New Roman easier on the eyes for lengthy output. Therefore, our first rule of thumb is to use a serif font for the body of the text. Within the Report Writer, this would correspond to the Detail band. (See Chapter 11, "The Report Writer," for a description of bands.)

Many people find that using a sans-serif font such as Arial works better for column headings, because such fonts make the headings quite distinguishable from the body text in the Detail band. If you really want the headings to stand out, you can underline them or put them in reverse (that is, if the body text shows dark letters against a light background, the headings present light letters against a dark background).

If your report includes program listings, try using a fixed-width font such as Courier New or FoxPrint. Both are TrueType fonts and thus infinitely scalable.

If you need yet another font, say for a header or footer, try Century Schoolbook. This serif font has a wider aspect ratio and a heavier basic stroke weight than Times New Roman.

Just using these four fonts will make a very attractive report. Figure 16.6 uses all these rules of thumb.

Although you can apply other font characteristics, you should do so sparingly to prevent your report from looking too "busy." You can use bold face for emphasis, small capital letters for tables, and so on. Also, you can stop using underlining to indicate italics and start using actual italics.

Inserting Objects with OLE

By combining the advantages of OLE and the Report Writer, you can really let your creativity blossom. For example, you can insert OLE objects such as .BMP files, MS Graph objects, and MS Draw objects into a general field and then have the Report Writer place them in the proper place on your report. You also can include pictures of products in an inventory report, or pictures of people in a personnel report, and use indicators to mark unique sections or flag special items (see Chapter 18, "Sharing the Windows Environment with OLE and DDE").

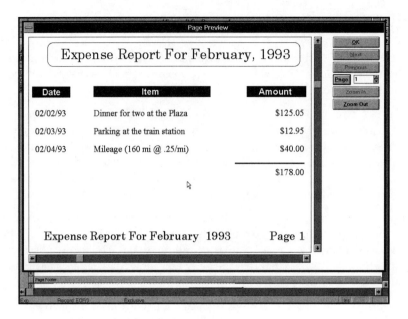

Figure 16.6. Sample use of fonts in a report.

Reports 2: Previewing and Printing

In the old days, if you wanted users to have a bidirectional scroll, you printed your report to a file and then issued a MODIFY COMMAND textfile.txt NOMODIFY. Unfortunately, you cannot easily do this with FoxPro for Windows.

There is no real loss here, though. The PREVIEW clause applied to the REPORT FORM command produces a different style of preview from that offered by the DOS product. The PREVIEW feature in FoxPro for Windows is bidirectional to start, so you don't have to create one.

Saving and Printing to a File

If you need to recall a previous report, you have more work ahead of you. Your best bet is to use a SELECT statement to produce a cursor and then produce the original report off of that cursor. If you need to reprint the report or recall and preview the report, you should save the cursor to a table and then produce the report off of the table.

The problem is that the output of the Report Writer is basically a bitmap and there is no real way to save it to a file. If you use a PostScript printer, you can send the output of the Report Writer to an encapsulated PostScript file, but there is no way to preview that file. However, you can reprint the report by simply copying the file to your PostScript printer.

If you really need to print to a file, you have several options. First, you can create a FoxPro 2.5 for DOS report format and invoke it directly from FoxPro for Windows. If you do that, you can send the output to a file and it will be stored strictly as ASCII characters. Of course, you lose all the power and flexibility of TrueType that way. If you do a PREVIEW of a FoxPro 2.5 for DOS report in FoxPro for Windows, you see a DOS-style, unidirectional preview rather than the Windows version.

Another alternative is to select Generic / Text Only to FILE: as your printer. Windows then will send the output to a file that you specify. Make sure that you do not use any font styles such as Bold, because FoxPro for Windows substitutes multiple copies of the same print object in an attempt to produce a darker look on a simple print device.

A more complex method is to edit your WIN.INI file directly and add a new print device, which is a file of your choice with a device driver of TTY. If you select this device as your printer, FoxPro for Windows does not prompt for a file name before printing to a file.

Although none of these techniques is perfect, perhaps one or a combination of methods can produce the effect you want.

Switching Printers

You can switch printers in several ways. You can apply the PROMPT clause on your REPORT FORM command and FoxPro for Windows will ask you to select a printer for that report. If you are doing many reports, this method may not be very efficient.

Another method is to issue the following command:

```
RUN /N CONTROL PRINTERS
```

This command runs the Printer Selection applet from the control panel. You can select a new default printer and, because this applet writes to WIN.INI, the choice remains in effect until you change it again. This allows all applications to read what the current default printer should be.

At Micro Endeavors, we use a small library routine that uses an .FLL file to call COMMDLG.DLL, which brings up the common dialog for selecting printers. After selecting a printer in this dialog, you write the choice directly to WIN.INI so that all applications can see the change. This method is slightly dangerous because it modifies WIN.INI. However, Word, Excel and other applications use this method. It is the "Windows way!"

Adding Pizzazz

Windows 3.1 offers a rich set of choices that you can use to enhance screens and reports. Adding sound to your program is an easy way to make it livelier or even fun. You can easily include sound effects by embedding .WAV files in a general field and then playing them at certain points in your program. You also can SET BELL TO wavefile.wav, 0 — then whenever the bell would have sounded, you hear a sound of your choice instead.

If you don't have a sound board installed, you can still get sounds from your computer by acquiring a copy of the Microsoft Sound Driver for the PC Speaker, which is in the public domain and available on CompuServe. Just follow the instructions in the README file. You can get surprisingly good sound from the built-in PC speaker. It is certainly adequate for the type of sound effects you might add to your program.

You can add other OLE objects beyond .BMP or .WAV files. You also can add graphs, draw objects, and many other types covered in Chapter 18, "Sharing the Windows Environment with OLE and DDE."

Windows is such a rich (and fun) environment that you really should try to add a little pizzazz to your applications. FoxPro for Windows makes it easy to give your applications that Windows look and feel that make people want to use your program to its fullest. Have fun!

CHAPTER
17

The C Connection

Dr. Michael Brachman is the industry's leading authority on FoxPro's API. A frequent public speaker on the topic, and an author of several articles and papers on the topic, Mike has been writing C programs on a variety of platforms for more than a decade.

Around the office, no one is ever able to finish the following question, "Mike, can we use FoxPro to..." Before the questioner comes close to explaining the requirements, Mike enthusiastically answers "Yes!" When pressed for an explanation of his unfaltering confidence in FoxPro's suitability to any task, Mike explains that FoxPro's API allows us to use C and Assembler to accomplish any programming task.

So far, Mike's bold declarations have been as accurate as they are frequent, and his reminders of those successes are as frequent as they are welcome. I asked Mike to share some of his secrets with those of us who will use C to enhance FoxPro's native function and command set. I think you'll like what he conjured up.

How and Why To Use C in FoxPro

Although FoxPro is a complete applications development system, there are some applications (for example, a data-logger that reads from an A/D converter) that FoxPro cannot execute unaided. Other applications are in .DLL format, which we can access only if there is a link to FoxPro.

Fortunately, since the advent of FoxPro 2.0, there is an Application Programming Interface (API) that lets us add new functions and capabilities to FoxPro. These capabilities include the ability to read or write to an A/D converter, a digital I/O port, a serial communications port, and so on. By using the API, we can add graphics, encryption, and network functions. We can also access an unlimited number of Windows applications and .DLLs by using the API.

You use the SET LIBRARY TO command to attach external libraries, called *.FLL files,* that are created for the API. Typically, .FLL files are written in C or assembly language. Microsoft's Library Construction Kit (LCK) includes all the programs necessary for creating .FLL files and also includes a library of functions that allows access to .DBF files, windows, mouse events—all the constructs of the FoxPro environment.

After purchasing the LCK and installing it according to the directions, you need to have access to a standard C compiler such as the Watcom C 9.0 or Microsoft C/C++ 7.0 versions. You then have all the tools necessary to create, compile, and link C programs in .FLL format. The following section shows how to use the API to create and attach a simple function to FoxPro. I then describe how to identify and rewrite certain sections of FoxPro programs for increased performance. The next section shows you how to rewrite existing C functions to be compatible with FoxPro. In the last section, I cover how to use the API to access the Windows API and other .DLL files.

The Elements of a C Program

Xbase is a *weakly typed* language. That is, in Xbase, you can create variables as one type, such as a date, and later convert it to another type, such as a character string. C, however, is a *strongly typed* language. When you use C, you must predeclare variables as a certain type and they can never change.

Headers

You must predefine all C functions by describing their input parameters and return values. Rather than requiring you to retype these predefinitions or cut-and-paste them into new programs, C has a compiler directive, #include, that you can use to include special files, called *headers,* which contain these predefinitions.

Header files typically have an extension of *.H.* The compiler vendor supplies some header files, and the developer creates others. The LCK also comes with a special header, PRO_EXT.H, which includes all the structure and function definitions unique to FoxPro.

Global Variables

As with FoxPro, all variables created when you call a function are released when you exit that function. C provides for global variables and structures, similar to PUBLIC variables. Global variables are created whenever you declare them outside of a function and remain intact as long the function is loaded.

Code

C is a very simple, yet powerful, language. It has very few operators. All statements in C must be terminated with a semicolon. Parentheses are used to indicate all C functions. Code belonging to a function is enclosed in a symmetrical pair of curly braces ({}), as are control structures. You delineate comments by using the /* and */ symbols.

Return Values

All C functions are defined by the values they are expected to return. Typically, functions are declared as type int, float, or char. Another function type, void, does not return any value. All API functions called directly from FoxPro must be type void. This does not mean you cannot get a return value, it just means you cannot use the normal return mechanism. The LCK provides special functions to return numbers, character strings, logical values, and so on. These functions give FoxPro more control over the use of memory and formatting.

The FoxInfo Structure

FoxInfo is the link between FoxPro and the routines written in C. The FoxInfo structure contains the following:

- The name of the function as it is called by FoxPro
- The name of the C function
- The number of parameters and their type

You need one entry in the FoxInfo table for every function you want to call from FoxPro.

A Simple Function

The simplest way to get up to speed in the creation of an API library routine is to use an actual example. The following is the complete listing of a C function, called ARGUTYPE.C, which is similar to the TYPE() function but returns the data type as a complete string rather than a single character.

```
/*        A R G U T Y P E . C

   demonstration 'C' library - adds the following:
   argutype    -  returns type of argument passed */



#include <stdlib.h>
#include <pro_ext.h>

/* Create the type code lookup table. */
char *types[ ] = {
   "Character","Date","Integer","Float",
   "General","Logical","Memo","Numeric",
   "Picture","Reference","Unknown"
};

/*
  FUNCTION ARGUTYPE

  Called from FoxPro as:
    argutype(varname)  varname can be a constant,
    variable, or expression
  Returns:
    argument type as a character string */

void far argutype(ParamBlk FAR *parm)
{
  int ix;                           /* this is line 1! */
  int tp = parm->p[0].val.ev_type;     /* tp holds type code */
  for (ix = 0; ix < 10 && tp != types[ix][0]; ix++); /* look it up */
  _RetChar(types[ix]);              /*  link up to FoxPro */

FoxInfo myFoxInfo[ ] = {
    {"ARGUTYPE", argutype, 1, "?"},
};
```

```
FoxTable _FoxTable = {
    (FoxTable FAR *)0, sizeof(myFoxInfo) / sizeof(FoxInfo),
        myFoxInfo
};
```

This chapter previously described the #include directives and explained the need to declare this function as type void. The function is only four lines long, and can be less. C lends itself to very compact routines that are not the easiest things to follow. Some programmers refer to C as a *write-only* language, but it needn't be that bad. Consider the preceding listing. The first line declares variable ix, which is just a counter. The second line defines the variable tp. To understand how the variable is initialized, you must understand how the API receives its parameters.

All parameters must be passed to the API using a special structure called the ParamBlk structure. Structures in C are groups of elements treated as a whole. They are somewhat like arrays in FoxPro in that each element can be of a different type.

With FoxPro, you can pass parameters to the API by using *call-by-value* or *call-by-reference*. To capture the parameter, each type requires a unique structure. Call-by-value is handled by a Value structure, and call-by-reference is handled by a Locator structure.

When two structures physically overlap, they create a *union*. The ParamBlk structure is the union of a Value structure and a Locator structure. The programmer must decide which face of the union applies. The first byte of the structure holds the type of call and tells which face to use.

Dissecting the assignment of the segment provides a good opportunity for decoding C nomenclature:

```
tp = parm->p[0].val.ev_type;
parm->      pointer to ParamBlk structure
p[0].          first parameter in structure
val.        use Value face of Parameter structure
ev_type     this element contains the data type
```

This particular routine uses call-by-value. The ParamBlk structure is a subscripted structure enabling multiple parameters to be passed. Subscripts in C are indicated by square brackets ([ ]). Arrays in C always begin with element 0.

This routine then takes the single letter of the parameter type and compares that type to the first letter of the expanded definitions. If a match is found, the expanded data type is returned. If no match is found, the routine returns the string "Unknown". The function _RetChar() returns the contents of the array. _RetChar() expects a pointer to a null-terminated string as its only argument.

At the end of the listing for ARGUTYPE.C is the FoxInfo structure. This structure defines each new function to be added to FoxPro. The first item supplied is the name that FoxPro uses to access the new function. The name must be enclosed in quotation marks and must be in all uppercase letters. The second item is the name of the C function. This function name need not be the same as the FoxPro name. However, it must match the name of the C function exactly, because C is case-sensitive. The third argument is the number of parameters to be passed, and the fourth argument, enclosed in quotation marks, describes their types. The third and fourth arguments let FoxPro check the number and type of arguments being passed before the API is ever invoked. The program is stored in a file with an extension of .C and is ready to be compiled.

As was previously mentioned, the `ParamBlk` structure is actually the union of a Value structure and a Locator structure. The first element of each structure overlaps and is used to indicate whether the parameter is being passed by value or by reference. The Value structure of the `ParamBlk` structure is defined as follows:

```
typedef struct {
    char        ev_type;
    char        ev_padding;
    short           ev_width;
    unsigned short  ev_length;
    long        ev_long;
    double          ev_real;
    MHANDLE         ev_handle;
} Value;
```

The first element, `ev_type`, must be one of the following: C, N, I, D, G, L, or M. If it is an R, the parameter was passed by reference and you should use the Locator face. Assuming that `ev_type` is one of these values, the definition of the rest of the elements of the Value structure depends on the type of parameter being passed. Table 17.1 describes what each field is used for as a function of the parameter type.

Table 17.1. Fields in the *typedef* structure.

Element Type	Character	Numeric	Integer	Date	Logical	Memo/Gen
ev_type	'C'	'N'	'I'	'D'	'L'	'M'
ev_width		Display width	Display width			FCHAN
ev_length	String length	Decimal places			Logical	

Element Type	Character	Numeric	Integer	Date	Logical	Memo/Gen
ev_long			Long integer			Length of memo field
ev_real		Double precision		Date		Offset of memo field
ev_handle	MHANDLE to string					

You use the Locator structure to pass parameters by reference, and also to pass arrays, memo fields, and general fields. Here is the definition of the Locator structure:

```
typedef struct {
    char  l_type;
    short l_where;
    short l_NTI;
    short l_offset;
    short l_subs;
    short l_sub1;
    short l_sub2 ;
} Locator;
```

The first element, l_type, must be an 'R' for the following definitions in Table 17.2 to be valid.

Table 17.2. Locator fields and their uses.

Locator Field	Field Use
l_type	'R'
l_where	–1 for memory variable or work area number
l_NTI	Name table index
l_offset	Field number (if database) 0-based
l_subs	0 for a memory variable, or the number of subscripts (if array)
l_sub1	First subscript (if array)
l_sub2	Second subscript (if two-dimensional array)

Compiling

To compile the ARGUTYPE.C program (using the Watcom C 9.0 compiler as an example), you issue the following DOS command:

```
wcc /ol /of /s /d2 /ml /fpc argutype
```

This invokes the Watcom compiler WCC.EXE. The command-line options are as follows:

```
/ol  loop optimization
/of  generate traceable stack frames
/s   removes stack overflow checks
/d2  embed symbolic debugging information
/ml  use the large model
/fpc use only the floating point library, not the coprocessor
```

If successful, the compiler produces the file ARGUTYPE.OBJ. Note that, although this example uses the Watcom C 9.0 compiler, you can also use other compilers, such as the Microsoft C/C++ 7.0. Other compilers will be supported later.

Linking

You must combine the file ARGUTYPE.OBJ with a front-end as well as any library functions invoked before you can load it into FoxPro. We typically use a .LNK file to tell the linker what we want to include in our .FLL file. The file ARGUTYPE.LNK contains the following:

```
debug all
sys windows dll
lib clibl
lib windows
lib proapiwl
name ARGUTYPE.exe
option symfile = ARGUTYPE.map
option heapsize=5k
option map
option oneautodata
file libentry.obj
file ARGUTYPE.obj
```

This instructs the linker, WLINK.EXE, to combine the file LIBENTRY.OBJ, which the compiler supplies along with ARGUTYPE.OBJ. Any general C functions or Windows-specific functions that the routine requires come from the library files WINDOWS.LIB and CLIBL.LIB, which are also supplied with the compiler. Finally, any FoxPro-specific functions come from the file PROAPIWL.LIB, which is supplied with the LCK. If successful, this command produces the file ARGUTYPE.EXE.

At this point, you must take several actions to guarantee that this file is recognized as a Windows 3.1 file and loadable by FoxPro. The following are the required commands:

```
rc -31 ARGUTYPE.exe
copy /b ARGUTYPE.exe+ARGUTYPE.map
del ARGUTYPE.fll
rename ARGUTYPE.exe ARGUTYPE.fll
```

The first line invokes the resource compiler, which brands ARGUTYPE.EXE as a Windows 3.1 executable. The second line combines the file and a symbol table into a single file. The third line deletes any existing copies of the file. The last line renames the executable as type .FLL, which is the default for FoxPro for Windows library files. Typically, you place this whole sequence in a batch file or use the Watcom MAKE facility.

Adding a New Function to FoxPro

After you create an .FLL file, attaching it inside FoxPro is as simple as issuing the following command: ·

```
SET LIBRARY TO argutype
```

If you were to LIST STATUS or DISPLAY STATUS, you would see something like the following:

```
API library                    Instance Handle
c:\foxprow\winapi\argutype.fll    0031B994

Function                       Address
ARGUTYPE                       08D7:0130
```

To test the function, you could just ?argutype(DATE()), which should print the string "Date" to the screen. Try each of the known data types. In each case, the function should return a string expanding the function type to a readable word. Because FoxPro does not normally let you declare numbers as integer, you may be surprised to see that Integer is one of the valid data types. Integer math is more efficient in C, so if FoxPro detects that you are trying to pass an integer to the API, it converts the integer for you. If you return an integer to FoxPro by using the _RetInt() function, FoxPro automatically converts the integer back to floating point.

You can attach multiple libraries by using the following command:

```
SET LIBRARY TO library1, library2,
```

and adding as many libraries as necessary. You can attach additional libraries by using the following command:

```
SET LIBRARY TO library3 ADDITIVE
```

You must use the `ADDITIVE` keyword; otherwise, FoxPro first unloads any other libraries. By using the command `SET LIBRARY TO` with no other arguments, you can unload all libraries. Finally, you can release a particular library by using the `RELEASE LIBRARY` command.

Other Types of Arguments and Returns

If you examine the listing for ARGUTYPE.C, you see that the last argument in the FoxInfo structure is a question mark. This indicates to the API that any data type is valid as an argument. However, you can restrict the types of arguments by using any of the following designations: C (character), D (date), F (float), I (integer), L (logical), and N (numeric). An R indicates call-by-reference, which is used when the value is contained in a database field or array or if the explicit call by reference operator (@) is used.

You can return values by using `_RetXXXX()` functions. These include `_RetInt()` and `_RetChar()`, which were mentioned previously, `_RetLogical()`, `_RetDateStr()` for dates as strings, `_RetFloat()`, and finally `_RetVal()`. The `_RetVal()` function is a general-purpose routine that can return any type, including a new type—that of a pointer to the contents of a memo/general field.

Many third-party vendors of libraries have already written routines to extend FoxPro for DOS, and we expect similar products to be announced for FoxPro for Windows. Table 17.3 has a partial list of library routines currently available for the DOS version.

Table 17.3. Some library routines available in FoxPro for DOS.

Category	Product Names
Graphics	Espia, dGE, SilverPaint, FoxGraph, and SunShow
Serial communications	CommTools and SilverFox SPCS
NetWare libraries	NetLib, FPNet, GPLib, and NetWare (which comes with FoxPro)
Client-servers	Biton/ORACLE and RaSQL

Note: Other libraries are available for data encryption and decryption, compression and decompression, and so on.

Improving Performance Using the API

The API can be also be used to improve the performance of routines that can be written in FoxPro. In this section I present two examples, but first I must explain a little about the mechanics of FoxPro.

There are two types of high-level languages: compiled and interpreted.

- Languages such as FORTRAN and C are *compiled;* that is, they are translated ultimately into machine language, which is the most elemental and compact language. Compiled languages feature fast throughput and the smallest executables, but require recompiling every time you make a modification. This slows down the development process, but produces applications that have the highest performance.

- *Interpreted* languages, such as BASIC and APL, do not require recompiling. They are stored exactly as you type them (in a tokenized form) and each statement is reinterpreted every time it is encountered. Interpreted languages are slower than compiled languages, but program development is easier because you do not need to wait for recompilation to test your changes. Interpreted programs can be smaller than the equivalent program written in a compiled language, but you must include the size of the interpreter to gauge accurately how much memory you need to execute them.

FoxPro is a hybrid of a compiled and interpreted language. The code you type in a .PRG must be compiled into an .FXP, which makes FoxPro a compiled language. The .FXP contains a very compact set of instructions called *p-code.* FoxPro reads in and interprets each line of p-code every time it encounters it. This makes FoxPro an interpreted language also.

Between lines of code, FoxPro checks for other events, such as mouse clicks and keystrokes. The master control loop that controls program execution and external events is called the *event loop,* and the part of the program that reads and executes code is called the *inner loop interpreter.* By using the API, you can insert your own processes into FoxPro's event loop. These processes usually look for events like keystrokes, mouse clicks, serial port I/O, or other conditions, and then perform an action based on the event.

You can instruct FoxPro to run your process at every iteration of the inner loop interpreter, or you can instruct FoxPro to run your process only during *idle time*—that is, while FoxPro awaits keyboard input. The next section provides a real-life example that may make this concept easier to understand.

Adding a Process to the Event Loop

FoxPro's BROWSE is a very powerful tool. It is easily the single most complicated piece of programming in the entire language. You can use BROWSE for data entry as well as

391

lookup tables. If the table is very large, you need to give the end-user a method—besides simply pressing PgDn—for navigating to the desired record. The simplest method is to use 26 ON KEY LABELS to arm 26 hot keys so that pressing any alphabetic key causes a SEEK to the first record beginning with that letter. This method works, but is somewhat imprecise.

A better method is the so-called *incremental search*. In such a search, as the user types more and more keys, the resulting SEEK gets closer and closer to the desired record.

At Micro Endeavors, we have gone through several generations of incremental searches during a BROWSE. Our first attempt used a series of single character GETs. The VALID clause of each GET field performed the SEEK. The cursor keys were trapped so, if close to the desired record, the user could still use these keys to navigate to the record. We made the BROWSE part of the READ so that the user could still use the mouse. When you finally got to the record of choice, you merely had to press Enter or click the right mouse button, which used an ON KEY LABEL to terminate the BROWSE. This technique worked, but was fairly slow.

Our next version of the routine used INKEY() to trap keystrokes and was much faster. The only problem was that we lost the use of the right mouse button because INKEY() does not trap for it. Instead, we simply wrote an API routine, called RMDOWN(), that was patterned after the MDOWN() function. The function RMDOWN() checks the mouse status and returns a logical .T. if the right mouse button is down. Thus, our second generation incremental search was quite a bit faster but looked and acted like the original version, thanks to the API.

The current version of our routine is the ultimate incremental search. The routine, called L3INCR.FLL, is available from Micro Endeavors. (It also appears on the disk.) It uses the API to add a new process to the event handler during the BROWSE. The user sees only a BROWSE—but what a BROWSE it is! Keystrokes between A through Z and 0 through 9 are trapped, a SEEK string is built, and a SEEK is performed after every keystroke. We used an API function, RMDOWN(), to trap the right mouse button. This routine is blazingly fast but otherwise acts just like a normal BROWSE. In this particular case, the API improved performance tremendously.

A simpler form of the L3INCR.FLL routine, called SKEY.FLL, illustrates the minimal amount of code required to attach a keystroke detector to a BROWSE:

```
/*      S K E Y . C

   demonstration 'C' library - adds the following:
      skeyinit - arms keyboard for SEEK
      skeykill - disables keyboard trap
*/


#include <dos.h>
#include <pro_ext.h>
```

```
/* Global variables */
int       skeyid;
Value     val;
MHANDLE   mh;
char      *cp;
Point     pt;
WHANDLE   wh;

/* Function predefinitions */
void dbback();
void dbseek(char);
FAR SKHandler(WHandle, EventRec FAR *);

/* Initialization routine */
void FAR skeyinit(ParamBlk FAR *parm)
{
  wh = _WOnTop();              /* Get handle of window on top   */
  mh = _AllocHand(100);        /* Reserve some memory           */
  _HLock(mh);                  /* Lock memory so it stays still */
  val.ev_type = 'C';           /* Define search string...       */
  val.ev_length = 0;           /* ... as length 0 and ...       */
  val.ev_handle = mh;          /* ... points to memory handle   */
  cp = _HandToPtr(mh);         /* Figure out real pointer too!  */

  /*Now we attach our new event handler found below       */
  skeyid = _ActivateHandler(SKHandler);
}

/* Removal routine, cleans up after itself */
void FAR skeykill(ParamBlk FAR *parm)
{
  _HUnLock(mh);                /* Unlock and ...                */
  _FreeHand(mh);               /* ... free memory               */

  /* Remove our event handler from consideration           */
  _DeActivateHandler(skeyid);
}

/* This is the actual event handler ...                     */
/* ... it only looks at keyboard events for now             */
FAR SKHandler(WHandle SWin, EventRec FAR *ev)
{
  /* A return value of YES tells FoxPro that we trapped... */
```

continues

```
      /* ... event and to proceed with next event.  NO ...     */
      /* ... tells FoxPro that it should handle the current ...*/
      /* ... event.                                            */
      int retval = NO;

      if (ev->what == keyDownEvent) {
        /* Check to see if it is a legal character, uppercase.  */
        if ( (ev->message >= ' ' && ev->message < 'a') ||
             (ev->message >  'z' && ev->message <= 0x7E) ) {
          dbseek(ev->message);
          retval = YES;
        }
        else { /* Check for lowercase too! */
          if (ev->message >= 'a' && ev->message <= 'z') {
            dbseek(ev->message & 0xDF);  /* Make uppercase, */
            retval = YES;
          }
          else {  /* and check for backspace as well */
            if (ev->message == '\b') {
              dbback();
              retval = YES;
            }
          }
        }
      }
      return retval;
    }


/* This routine builds up a seek string by concatenating ...   */
/* ... the character sent as an argument then doing a SEEK ... */
/* ... then printing the character to the window on top.       */
void dbseek(char chr)
{
  val.ev_length += 1;
  cp[val.ev_length-1] = chr;  /* Add char to string */
  _DBSeek(&val);
  pt.h = val.ev_length;
  pt.v = 0;
  _WPosCursor(wh,pt);              /* Position cursor in window */
  _WPutChr(wh,chr);               /* Print character in window */
}


/* This routine erases 1 character if necessary and shortens...*/
/* ... the seek string and does a SEEK again.                  */
```

```
void dbback()
{
  if (val.ev_length > 0) {
    pt.h = val.ev_length;
    pt.v = 0;
    _WPosCursor(wh,pt);
    _WPutChr(wh,' ');  /* Erase last character typed */
    val.ev_length -= 1;
    _DBSeek(&val);      /* Seek against shorter string */
  }
  else  /* No characters left to trim, ring the bell  */
    _PutChr(7);
}


FoxInfo myFoxInfo[ ] = {
    {"SKEYINIT", skeyinit, 0, ""},
    {"SKEYKILL", skeykill, 0, ""},
};



FoxTable _FoxTable = {
  (FoxTable FAR *)0,sizeof(myFoxInfo)/sizeof(FoxInfo),myFoxInfo
};
```

To use this program, you need to define and activate a window to echo your keystrokes. You then call skeyinit() to arm the detector. Then you bring up a normal BROWSE. Don't forget to use skeykill() to disarm the trap when you are finished. The following program fragment illustrates this:

```
@23,1 SAY PADC("Press <Enter> To Select",80) COLOR GB+/B
SET LIBRARY TO skey  && attach API routine
USE laser ORDER utitle  && note tag is UPPER(title)
DEFINE WINDOW test FROM 4,15 TO  6,60 ;
  SHADOW SYSTEM TITLE "TITLE SEARCH" ;
  COLOR SCHEME(8)
ACTIVATE WINDOW test

= skeyinit()  && initialize keyboard trap
DEFINE WINDOW brow FROM 6,15 TO 20,60 SHADOW SYSTEM ;
  COLOR SCHEME(10)
ON KEY LABEL ENTER KEYBOARD CHR(23)
ON KEY LABEL RIGHTMOUSE KEYBOARD CHR(23)
```

continues

```
BROWSE FIELDS title:42 WINDOW brow  && display list

ON KEY
STORE LASTKEY() TO lk

= skeykill()  && disable keyboard trap
RELEASE WINDOW test
CLEAR

IF lk = 27
  RETURN "Escape Pressed"
ELSE
  RETURN title
ENDIF
```

Handling Computationally Intensive Loops

As previously mentioned, FoxPro uses an inner loop interpreter to read and execute code. Because of this, all executable statements entail some overhead, regardless of the instruction. This includes looping constructs such as SCAN/ENDSCAN and FOR/ENDFOR. This overhead becomes substantial during computationally intensive loops. On the other hand, the overhead for looping constructs in C is usually negligible. Thus, a routine in FoxPro that repeatedly executes the same code is a good candidate for rewriting in C. In most cases, an API routine executes faster, and sometimes much faster, than the equivalent code in FoxPro.

To demonstrate this, the following program was written and benchmarked in FoxPro, then rewritten in C and attached using the API. The program, called INTEREST.PRG, calculates the total accumulated value of $1000.00 invested in an account that pays 10 percent interest, compounded daily, for 100 years. Here is the FoxPro code:

```
result = 1000               && Starting balance
effint = (10/100) / 365     && Eff. daily rate
FOR year = 1 TO 100
  FOR day = 1 TO 365
    result = result + effint * result  && Add interest
  ENDFOR
ENDFOR
```

This program was run and benchmarked on a 33 MHz 486 DX machine with plenty of RAM. The program took 2.13 seconds to execute in FoxPro. Next, the inner loop was rewritten in C and called 100 times. This took .309 seconds to execute, an increase in throughput of a factor of 6.89. Then the outer loop was incorporated in the C program so that the entire API routine was only called once. This took .283 seconds, an increase in throughput of 7.53. This means a savings of almost 52 minutes on calculations that normally take an hour!

You can also misuse the API. Each call to the API entails its own overhead, because FoxPro is a 32-bit, extended mode product and the API routines are executed in 16-bit or standard mode. Each call to the API must flip the processor from protected mode to standard mode then back again. To illustrate this, we took just the innermost statement that actually calculates the daily interest, wrote it in C, and called it 36,500 times. This took 9.199 seconds, which is slower than the FoxPro code by a factor of 4.3. Table 17.4 summarizes the execution times and ratios for the different types of calls.

Table 17.4. Calls to the API.

Type of Call	Times Called	Execution Time (uS)	Ratio
FoxPro	n/a	2.130	1.00
Daily Interest	36,500	9.199	0.23
Interest for one year	100	.309	6.89
Interest for one Century	1	.283	7.53

The bottom line here is that you should include as much of the loop as possible in the API routine, and call it as infrequently as possible. Also keep in mind that in some cases using the API is inappropriate. Some quick benchmarking should tell you when you should or should not use the API to improve throughput.

Accessing the Math Coprocessor

If you tried the interest example on your machine, especially on a 386, you would probably get even better ratios. The machine used to produce these results has a 486 DX processor that has a built-in numeric coprocessor. FoxPro accesses the numeric coprocessor (as does Windows), which gives the FoxPro code a boost. When you use the /fpc switch in the wcc command line, the API-assisted routines do not use the coprocessor but rather 80387 emulator software. If you use the /fp87 or /fp387 switch, you route math calls directly to the math coprocessor.

We recompiled the API routine that calculates interest over one century with the /fpi387 switch and then tested it. The results were unbelievable! The execution time was .036 seconds, or a ratio of 59.17. Although there is some variability due to Windows multitasking, we always get ratios well above 50.

Tip: If your machine has a numeric coprocessor and you want to achieve similar results, you must observe two caveats. First, although you can mix routines that were compiled using the /fpc (emulator only) switch and the /fpi87 or /fpi387 (coprocessor only) switches, you cannot use the /fpi switch. The /fpi switch lets the code decide at runtime which library to use and is incompatible with the API. If you need to write routines that work on either type of machine, compile two versions of your routines: one with the /fpc switch and the other with either the /fpi87 or /fpi387 switch. Use _bios_equiplist() to check whether there is a coprocessor and then use that information to decide which version to call.

The second caveat concerns results from the coprocessor. If you use the coprocessor, do not use the _RetFloat() function to return results. The _RetFloat() function does not interpret the output of the coprocessor correctly. Use _RetVal() instead. The RetVal() function makes the necessary translations for you and returns the correct results.

In summary, you can use the API to turbo charge functions—such as event-driven programs and computationally intensive loops—that you normally write in FoxPro. Next, we will consider modifying existing programs that were already written for DOS or Windows.

Adapting Existing DOS Programs

Adapting an existing DOS or Windows program to work in FoxPro can be simple or exceedingly hard. We will take a simple example to illustrate some of the issues involved. This example assumes that we already have a program that works well from DOS or Windows, and that we no longer want to issue a RUN command to access this function. We now want to access the program directly from FoxPro.

Why make changes at all? First, you cannot use standard memory allocation functions such as malloc() to grab a block of memory. Second, FoxPro controls its own I/O. It is considered "ill-mannered" to write directly to the console or to use standard low-level file I/O such as fopen() or fwrite() to manipulate files. Third, FoxPro's debugging facilities are more limited, should a program not perform as expected.

None of these issues should be cause for concern, though. Certain functions are not permitted in API routines. In every case, whenever FoxPro takes away a function, a substitute is made available. In most cases, converting existing C programs to run in FoxPro is a simple matter of calling another function. In the worst case, this conversion is a matter of adding one or two extra lines of code.

We will explore an actual example of a function that was written for DOS and explore the steps necessary to make it work in FoxPro. Here is WFCOUNT.C along with WENGINE.C:

```
/*      W F C O U N T . C
   demonstration 'C' library - adds the following:
      wcount    -  returns number of words in a file
*/


#include <stdlib.h>
#include <dos.h>
#include <pro_ext.h>

/*

  FUNCTION WCOUNT

  Called from FoxPro as:
    wcount(filevar)  filevar can be a constant or char. variable
  Returns:
    integer number of words
    -1 means "File Not Found"
    -2 means "Insufficient Memory"
*/

void far
wcount(ParamBlk FAR *parm)
{
  /* SECTION 1 - DEFINE VARIABLES */
  FCHAN fh;              /* File Handle (int) */
  MHANDLE bmh;
  char far *buff,fname[40];
  int retval,filen;
  struct find_t finfo;

  /* SECTION 2 - SETUP NAME OF FILE */
  filen = parm->p[0].val.ev_length;
  _MemMove(fname,_HandToPtr(parm->p[0].val.ev_handle),filen);
```

continues

```
    fname[filen] = 0;   /* add null-terminator */

    /* SECTION 3 - GET SIZE OF FILE */
    _dos_findfirst(fname,_A_NORMAL,&finfo);

    /* SECTION 4 - SEE IF FILE EXISTS */
    fh = _FOpen(fname,FO_READONLY);
    if (fh < 1) {           /*  Illegal file name */
      retval = -1;          /*  Return of -1 means can't find it */
    }
    else {    /* File is legal */
      /* SECTION 5 - CREATE BUFFER FROM MEMORY POOL */
      bmh = _AllocHand(finfo.size);
      buff = (char far *)_HandToPtr(bmh);

      if (bmh < 1)
        retval = -2;    /* Return of -2 means not enough memory */
      else {
        /* SECTION 6 - LOAD BUFFER FROM DISK FILE */
        _FRead(fh,buff,finfo.size);

        /* SECTION 7 - CALL THE "ENGINE" */
        retval =  nowords(buff,finfo.size-1);

        /* SECTION 8 - CLEAN UP */
        _FreeHand(bmh);
        _FClose(fh);
      }
    }
    /* SECTION 9 - RETURN THE ANSWER */
    _RetInt(retval,10);
}

#include "wengine.c"


FoxInfo myFoxInfo[ ] = {
    {"WCOUNT", wcount, 1, "C"}
};

FoxTable _FoxTable = {
  (FoxTable FAR *)0,sizeof(myFoxInfo)/sizeof(FoxInfo),myFoxInfo
};
```

```
/* THE "ENGINE" W E N G I N E . C  ,
   It has two states: inword and !inword
   What it does with the next character depends on this state
   If you are inword and the next character is a delimiter,
      wc is incremented, and inword is toggled.
   If you are !inword and the next character is not a delimiter,
      inword is toggled.
*/
extern int
nowords(char far *bf,long sz)
{
  int inword,ix,wc;
  wc = 0;
  inword = !delim(bf[0]);  /* Initialize the "state" variable */

  for (ix=0; ix < sz; ix++) {
    if (inword) {
      if ( delim(bf[ix]) ) {
        wc = wc + 1;        /* Increment word counter */
        inword = 0;         /* Toggle state of inword */
      }
    }
    else {                  /* Not in word */
      if ( !delim(bf[ix]) )
        inword = 1;         /* Toggle state of inword */
    }
  }  /* endfor */

  /* All done except for... */
  if (inword != 0 && sz != 0)
    wc = wc + 1;            /* Still inword so it counts */

  return wc;
}

/* Uniform logic for word delimiter */
extern int
delim(char ch)
{
  return ( (ch == ' ') ||
           (ch == '.') ||
           (ch == ',') ||
           (ch == ';') ||
           (ch == '-') ||
```

continues

```
        (ch == '?') ||
        (ch == ':') ||
        (ch ==  13) ||
        (ch ==  10) ||
        (ch == '!') );
}
```

This example, a word counter originally written for DOS, is loosely organized into two parts. The first part is a front-end that reads the file into memory, calls a word-counting "engine," then reports the results back to the console. The engine is written to work in both FoxPro and DOS. This is not an accident, but the preferred technique for developing programs to work within the API. Obviously, you can't always use this technique, especially when databases or event-loop processes are involved. However, many of the debugging aids available from the DOS environment are unavailable in FoxPro, so you want to take advantage of them when you can. Now you can analyze the program.

Section 1: Defining Variables

Like most C programs written for DOS, the word counter starts with a procedure called main:

```
int
main(int argc,char *argv[ ])
{
   FILE *fp;                /* File Pointer (structure) */
```

The variable argc holds the number of arguments and argv is a list of pointers to the arguments. Typically, argv[0] is a pointer to the name of the program and argv[1] is a pointer to the first argument—in this case, to the file of interest.

Within the API, we call our functions directly, using the FoxInfo structure. Therefore, in the FoxPro version of this program, we must use the ParamBlk structure to pass the name of the file to be counted. The following code shows how you can use the ParamBlk structure to convert an argument into a standard, null-terminated string:

```
void far
wcount(ParamBlk FAR *parm)
{
   char fname[40];
   int filen;

   filen = parm->p[0].val.ev_length;
   _MemMove(fname,_HandToPtr(parm->p[0].val.ev_handle),filen);
   fname[filen] = 0;     /* Add null-terminator */
```

Note that the ParamBlk structure does *not* contain the string, but only a memory handle that is an index into a table of pointers. As a result, we need both the _HandToPtr() and the _MemMove() functions to convert the argument to a null-terminated string.

The function _HandToPtr() converts the handle into a real pointer. The function _MemMove() is used to copy the number of bytes indicated in the ev_length element into the vname variable. Strings in FoxPro are not guaranteed to be null-terminated, so we must explicitly null-terminate the fname string.

You should use _MemMove(), _StrCpy(), and similar functions in place of their DOS equivalents. These API library routines provide better control over memory boundaries and reduce the likelihood of transgressed (memory) handles. If your common routines use these functions, simply include the following #defines in your DOS front-end to reduce the number of changes required later:

```
#define    _MemMove    memmove
#define    _MemCmp     memcmp
#define    _MemFill    memfill
#define    _StrCpy     strcpy
#define    _StrCmp     strcmp
#define    _StrLen     strlen
```

Section 2: Low-Level File I/O

To open a file in a DOS program, you define a file pointer and then use fopen() to gain access to it. For example:

```
FILE *fp;                /* File Pointer (structure) */

fp = fopen(argv[1], "r" );
```

In an API routine, we use file channels (FCHAN), which are equivalent to file handles, and then use a function called _FOpen(). This looks like the following:

```
FCHAN fh;                /* File Handle (int) */

fh = _FOpen(fname,FO_READONLY)
```

For every low-level I/O routine such as fread() and fwrite(), there are API equivalents you should use. You can use a series of #defines to handle the function translation for the low-level I/O routines, also. Functions such as _FOpen() and _FWrite() are identical to the functions found in FoxPro. In fact, the file handle numbers used in FoxPro are compatible with those used in the API.

Section 3: Memory Management

As previously mentioned, you cannot use `malloc()` to grab a block of memory. Instead, you use the following to create a pointer to a block:

```
MHANDLE bmh;
char far *buff;


bmh = _AllocHand(finfo.size);
buff = (char far *)_HandToPtr(bmh);
```

If it can grant the number of bytes requested, the `_AllocHand()` function returns a memory handle, which is an integer pointer to a table. The `_HandToPtr()` function converts a memory handle into a pointer.

 Note: It is important to note that FoxPro can reorganize memory between calls to API routines. Therefore, you should derive the pointer each time you enter the API, or use the `_HLock()` function to lock a block of memory. When you finish with a block of memory, you should free it by using the `_FreeHand()` function (along with `_HUnLock()` if necessary) to prevent excessive drain on resources.

Section 4: Invoking the Engine

If things have gone well, you can now invoke the engine by using code that remains unchanged whether you use DOS or FoxPro. Admittedly, this works only under ideal circumstances. This particular word counter assumes that the files examined can always be held in memory. If that didn't work, you have to examine the input stream by using low-level file I/O. In this case, the `#define` technique might still preserve the code.

The point is, you want to do as much of your testing as possible in DOS, where better debugging tools are available. Symbolic debugging under FoxPro is somewhat tedious. You must use the function `_BreakPoint()` to hook into the processor's INT 3 trap and then manually align the segment and offset of your symbol table from within the debugger. Don't be surprised if you find yourself resorting to the old `printf()` (or, in this case, `_PutStr()`) method of debugging.

Section 5: Return Values

Many DOS programs use functions such as printf() to send their results to the console. In FoxPro, you should summarize your results in numbers, strings, or codes and return them to FoxPro by using one of the _RetXXXX() functions. FoxPro maintains the screen exclusively and has no knowledge of values printed there. If you need to return multiple values, one technique you might try is to send an array by using call-by-reference and to enter your return values by using _Store().

If you must return results to the screen, you should use functions such as _PutChr() and _PutStr() to print to the currently active window or screen. The API also contains all the functions necessary to create, select, maintain, and close windows. You have complete control over their size and shape and can poll the API about window characteristics. This technique should provide an adequate substitute for almost any console I/O you want to do in DOS.

FoxPro Unleashed

With FoxPro's API, there is no limit to what FoxPro can do. With relatively simple add-ons, you can create applications for instrumentation, data logging, process control, robotics, music, bar code reading and generating, spell checking, a thesaurus, text search, and more. If your API routine needs a function already implemented in FoxPro, you can get to it by calling FoxPro; you simply use the function _Execute() to execute a FoxPro command, or _Evaluate() to evaluate any valid FoxPro expression, including UDFs!

The following simple example creates a window, uses the API to activate it, and then uses INKEY() to read in a key:

```
Value Val;
_Execute("DEFINE WINDOW t1 FROM 0,0 TO 10,10 DOUBLE SHADOW ");
_Execute("ACTIVATE WINDOW t1");
_Evaluate(&Val, "INKEY(1)");
```

There are special codes you can use for call on load and call on unload for initialization and cleanup procedures. It is conceivable (though inefficient) that you could write an API routine that is called on load and never returns to FoxPro, using the _Execute() and _Evaluate() functions to treat FoxPro as a giant library instead. Once you master the use of the API, the whole world becomes available to you!

Accessing the Windows API

You can use the FoxPro API to access the Windows API, which has over 700 functions for font manipulation, graphics, and so on. Windows employs a technique for recycling library routines called *Dynamic Link Libraries* (*.DLL* files). You need to load these .DLL files only once. You can choose whether each instance of a particular library requires private memory or whether its memory can be shared.

FoxPro for Windows uses .FLL files, which are simply a special form of .DLL files. By using the .DLL mechanism, the .FLL files can load or attach to other libraries. There are many advantages to reaching the Windows API. You immediately gain access to common dialog boxes such as MessageBox and ChangePrinter. You also gain access to Windows graphic functions, multimedia, printer services, and font technology.

There are two ways to reach the Windows API. The first is to use an .FLL called FOXTOOLS.FLL, which is supplied with FoxPro for Windows. The second is to write your own equivalent of FOXTOOLS.FLL in C.

You can find the FOXTOOLS.FLL in the \GOODIES subdirectory, which is created when you install FoxPro. With this library, you use the function RegFN() to register a Windows API function. You then use CallFn() to call that function. Although this routine cannot reach all functions, it works for a surprisingly large number. The only restriction is that the functions you call must have parameters of type integer, long, float, double, char, or character string. The function must return a value that is also one of these types. You can pass parameters by using call-by-value or call-by-reference. For example, you can register the MessageBox function as follows:

```
SET LIBRARY TO foxtools
mbf = RegFn("MessageBox","ICCI","I")
```

The parameter list is interpreted as follows: function MessageBox; four arguments, type integer, character string, character string, and integer; returning type integer. You can then call this function by using the following command:

```
ans = CallFn(mbf,0,"Delete All Files?","Attention",36)
```

The 36 is a bit-encoded parameter that tells MessageBox to give only the choices Yes and No and to display the question mark icon.

The FOXTOOLS.FLL is also good for changing the cursor, finding default directories, manipulating the WIN.INI file for changing printers, and more.

Nonstandard Calls

If you are willing to write the necessary code, you can reach any function in any .DLL. You should attempt this only for functions that do not fit the requirements for FOXTOOLS.FLL.

You have to write the necessary C code to load in the .DLL. You then invoke the C Windows library function LoadLibrary(), which checks whether a .DLL is already loaded and, if not, loads the .DLL from disk. Then you use the Windows library function GetProcAddress() to find your function's address. At this point, you can invoke your function directly and supply it with whatever parameters it requires and receive whatever type of value it returns.

For example, you can invoke the ChangeFont dialog as follows:

```
LOGFONT lf;
CHOOSEFONT cf;

void NewFont(ParamBlk FAR *parm)
{
  HANDLE hLibrary;
  FARPROC fnCM;
  char szCommName[40];
  /* Set all structure fields to zero. */
  memset(&cf, 0, sizeof(CHOOSEFONT));
  cf.lStructSize = sizeof(CHOOSEFONT);
  cf.hwndOwner = 0;
  cf.lpLogFont = &lf;
  cf.Flags = CF_SCREENFONTS | CF_EFFECTS;
  cf.rgbColors = RGB(0,255,255);  /* light blue */
  cf.nFontType = SCREEN_FONTTYPE;
  _StrCpy(szCommName,"COMMDLG.DLL");
  hLibrary = LoadLibrary(szCommName);
  if (hLibrary >= 32) {
    fnCM = GetProcAddress(hLibrary,"CHOOSEFONT");
    (fnCM)(&cf);
  }
  return;
}
```

You can also reach your own .DLL files by using a similar mechanism. You can use your own .DLL for inter-instance communication or data translation. For a very simple example, you can send data from a FoxPro program to a Windows scrolling graph program. First, you create an .FLL with a memory buffer that you fill from FoxPro by using API calls. The graphing program invokes the same .FLL by using the LoadLibrary() function and then reads the buffer into its own memory. Here is the source code:

```
/*    D A T A P R O C . C
      Adds the following function to FoxPro:
      Function: dataproc()
*/
```

continues

```
#include <windows.h>
#include "pro_ext.h"

int idat[500][4];    /* the transfer buffer */

void far dloader(ParamBlk FAR *parm) /* Loads buffer from FoxPro */
{
  int i = parm->p[0].val.ev_long;
  int j = parm->p[1].val.ev_long;
  idat[i][j] = parm->p[2].val.ev_long;
}

int FAR _ _export PASCAL uldr(int i, int  j)  /* Unloads buffer */
{ return idat[i][j]; }

FoxInfo myFoxInfo[] = {
    {"DLOADER", dloader, 3, "I,I,I"},
};

FoxTable _FoxTable = {
 (FoxTable FAR *)0,sizeof(myFoxInfo)/sizeof(FoxInfo),myFoxInfo
};
```

The code to load in this library from a Windows function is similar to the preceding:

```
dll = LoadLibrary("DATAPROC.FLL");
if (dll >= 32) {
   DataProc = GetProcAddress(dll,"uldr");  /* The transfer func*/
   if (DataProc == NULL)
     MessageBox(NULL,"You got a NULL","DataProc Address",MB_OK);
   else {
    for (i=0; i<500; i++)
      for (j=0; j<4; j++)
        idat[i][j] = (DataProc)(i,j);
   }
   FreeLibrary(dll);
}
```

Final Thoughts

FoxPro provides an exceptional applications-development environment and superior database management tools. Under all circumstances, you should write your application in FoxPro and consider using the API only if you need a function that FoxPro cannot provide, such as access to new hardware, or if a particular section of code (most likely a looping construct) must run faster. Working in C is like walking a tightrope without a net: No one can help you if you fall. However, with a little bit of care, you can achieve spectacular results. Good luck!

CHAPTER 18

Sharing the Windows Environment with OLE and DDE

Each application is better at some tasks than others. For example, Excel is good at many parallel calculations, FoxPro is superior at manipulating databases, and MSGraph is best at handling graphs. One of the nice things about the Windows environment is that you can have multiple tasks running and have each task doing the things it does best. There are numerous ways of passing data back and forth and you learn about each one of them in this chapter.

Dr. Michael Brachman is among the best programmers and developers I have ever met. Because I had the good fortune of employing Mike, I persuaded him to share his insights with you in this chapter and in Chapter 17, "The C Connection." By the time you finish these chapters, you'll agree that Mike is every bit as good an author as he is a developer. Enjoy.

Exchanging Data in DOS

In the DOS world, if you had two tasks that were specialized to perform a certain function, you were limited in the number of ways you could hand data back and forth. Suppose that you had a program that performed an obscure calculation, written in some arcane language, and you had a FoxPro program with many records requiring that calculation.

If all you have, for example, is a DOS executable for your calculator, you have only one way to call the calculator: You must create a file from FoxPro in the format expected by the calculator, issue the RUN command to shell out to DOS, and execute the calculator. The calculator leaves its answer in another file, then returns control to FoxPro.

At this point, FoxPro must read in the file and place the answer in the appropriate record. You must do this once for each record requiring a calculation. Because there is a two to three second overhead in shelling out to DOS, even a small number of records takes a relatively long period of time to be processed.

A more efficient method is to create a batch file containing all the numbers to be calculated, shell out to DOS once, have the calculator process the numbers, then place the answers in a single file. FoxPro is responsible for wading through the output and distributing the answers to the appropriate places. This technique actually works. It is quite fast and can be used in many applications.

The most sophisticated method is to acquire the source code for the calculator and rewrite the code as a FoxPro API routine. This method eliminates the need to shell out to DOS and is as efficient a method as is possible.

If the calculator were a part of a spreadsheet like Excel, it is unlikely that Microsoft would give you the source code and even if it did, it would be impossible to rewrite the code as an API library routine. You would have to resort to the first or second method and use Excel macros to perform the calculations.

The bottom line is that although you can create an environment in which two tasks transmit data back and forth, this environment still runs only one task at a time.

Exchanging Data in Windows

Examples such as the one in the preceding section aren't too difficult to implement. Life gets much harder when the objects you want to pass back and forth are not simple numbers or strings but pictures, sounds, or graphs. There are, however, many ways to exchange data and objects among applications in Windows, including the following:

- The Windows Clipboard
- File-mediated transfer

- DLL-shared memory

- Task server

- Dynamic Data Exchange (DDE)

- Object Linking and Embedding (OLE)

Each of these methods is described separately in the following sections.

Single-Tasking Methods

Single-tasking methods of sharing data require a requesting program to begin and end a request for information before moving to other tasks. Multitasking methods of sharing data allow requesting programs to make a request, perform other activities, and respond to a message from the providing program when the requested information has been provided.

The Windows Clipboard

The first method is the simplest method for exchanging data in Windows—through the Windows Clipboard. The Clipboard is "intelligent"; it understands the nature of an object. You use the standard keyboard shortcuts—Ctrl+C to copy an object, Ctrl+X to cut an object, and Ctrl+V to paste one. The Clipboard even has its own application, called the Clipboard Viewer, which enables you to examine its contents and save these to an intermediate file. The Clipboard is especially useful for transferring text among Windows applications. Unfortunately, it can be difficult to manage programmatically.

File-Mediated Data Transfer

Can you call a calculator program from FoxPro for Windows in a manner similar to that for DOS? The answer, of course, is "yes!" This process is called *file-mediated data transfer*. Like FoxPro for DOS, FoxPro for Windows has a RUN command that enables you to shell out to DOS or execute another Windows application. If you use the /N option as part of the RUN command, you are instructing FoxPro to launch a Windows executable. Thus, you can still put your data in a file and launch the calculator program. It performs as it does in DOS, leaving the answer in a file. When program control returns to FoxPro, you read the file in and distribute the answers.

DLL Shared Memory

The third method is even more sophisticated—using a .DLL for the exchange. When you create a .DLL (or a FoxPro library file [.FLL]), you can specify whether the data segment is to be shared or nonshared. The .DLL loader looks at the memory flag each time it is requested to create a new instance. If the data segment is flagged as shared, each program that uses that .DLL has access to a common memory block. This memory block can be used for data exchange. The interface between the two applications is custom-designed to allow the most efficient transfer of data. The other task can be another instance of FoxPro or any other program that can understand and read in the common .DLL.

The following code shows an example of a small .DLL (actually an .FLL) that is used to transfer an array between a FoxPro program and a Windows application:

```c
#include <windows.h>
#include "pro_ext.h"
int idat[500][4];            /* The shared memory transfer buffer */
/* FoxPro API call to load up the buffer */
/* All functions must be void! */
void far dloader(ParamBlk FAR *parm)
{
  int i = parm->p[0].val.ev_long;            /* Grab the row */
  int j = parm->p[1].val.ev_long;            /* Grab the column */
  /* Stuff the value into the cell */
  idat[i][j] = parm->p[2].val.ev_long;
}

/* DLL call to unload from the buffer */
int FAR __export PASCAL uloader(int i, int  j)
{ return idat[i][j]; }          /* Just return cell requested */

FoxInfo myFoxInfo[] = {
    {"DLOADER", dloader, 3, "I,I,I"} };
FoxTable _FoxTable = {
(FoxTable FAR *)0,sizeof(myFoxInfo)/sizeof(FoxInfo),myFoxInfo};
```

As far as FoxPro is concerned, this is a standard .FLL file with a function called dloader(). You pass it a row, column, and value, and dloader() places it in an array called idat. The Windows application, a scrolling graph, attaches this .FLL as a standard .DLL. The application calls the function uloader() with a row and column, and uloader() returns the value stored in the array. Note that if you use this method, you need not worry about where the memory is mapped. The .DLL mechanism is used to the fullest advantage. You can easily adapt this program to work on a block of data.

Multitasking Methods

Although you can use all three of the preceding methods to transfer data, they are all custom-written. In addition, no matter which method you choose, you are still resorting to a single-task approach. To execute calculations, you stop executing FoxPro code, and you must wait until the calculations are finished before you continue. It is far more efficient to have our calculations going on while we continued doing other work—in other words, if the application applied a *multitasking* approach. We can take advantage of the fact that Windows is inherently multitasking to maximize our efficiency—but first a word about multitasking itself.

Running Windows on a single microcomputer requires a method called *cooperative multitasking*. This means that each application agrees to relinquish control at regular intervals so that other tasks can proceed as well. Windows NT, on the other hand, uses a technique called *preemptive multitasking,* which means that it is hardware-assisted and that tasks need not relinquish control. Windows NT takes care of saving and restoring memory and registers as it swaps one task for another. This is all done transparently, with each application behaving as if it were the only one in the queue. Windows NT is scalable and permits the use of multiple processors, which means that you can have a separate microprocessor running each task within the same computer. Windows for Workgroups, which enables multiple computers to share resources, can be considered multitasking in a way similar to that described for a print server or query server.

The Task Server

One multitasking technique requires the use of a network. You can easily program FoxPro to look at a shared database for commands and set up another machine to issue those commands. With very few lines of code, you can create a print server, a query server, or a report server. This *multiprocessor* approach to multitasking works great if you have the extra machines. But what do you do if you only have one computer? The following sections describe your options: DDE and OLE.

Linking with DDE

To use the three previously described methods for data transfer between applications, you must be able to program both ends of the process. This isn't always possible. It would be nice if a set of standards described the software interface for interprocess communication. That way, even if you did not have access to the inner workings of a program such as Excel or Word, you could still communicate with them by using Windows. Fortunately, Microsoft has created these standards in the form of *Dynamic Data Exchange (DDE)*. With relatively few commands, you can establish a channel for communication. The content of the exchange is up to you. DDE handles the protocol.

The paradigm for DDE is that of a conversation. You initiate a conversation with another application by referring to it by its service or application name. After you establish contact with the other task, you then pick a subject for conversation called a *topic.* After you begin a conversation, you cannot change a conversation to another topic or to another service (or application); you must end that conversation before you can switch to another topic or service (or application).

Applications engaging in DDE are either clients or servers. *Servers* provide the DDE service. *Clients* request DDE services.

415

DDE links between programs are either cold, warm, or hot. The distinction lies in how the client handles the delay from the request for data to when the data is actually available. You use DDEAdvise() (described in the following section) to inform the DDE server what type of link you want to establish.

If the client must specifically request data from the server, we call the connection between client and server a *cold link*. The official DDE name for this is a *manual link*. An example of a cold link is one between a document and a spreadsheet in which the data is required only as you are printing the document.

If the server in a conversation notifies the client that the requested data has been changed, we call the connection a *warm link*. The official DDE name for this type of link is a *notify link*. With a warm link, the client must still request the data from the server. An example of a warm link is a FoxPro READ in which you await user input and need only notify users that they should close the READ session to collect the new data.

If a client program is automatically executed whenever data changes in the server, we call the connection a *hot link*. The official DDE name for this is an *automatic link*. The client informs the server of the name of the routine, called a *callback routine*. The server then calls that routine directly whenever data has changed. Data is transferred automatically. Routines in FoxPro that receive hot link information have a special parameter sequence, which is discussed below.

All conversations take place over a *channel*. When you initiate a DDE conversation, you are assigned a *channel number*. A channel number of zero indicates that the conversation has failed. When a link is established, the server determines the topics available. All applications that support DDE have a topic called the *system topic*. The system topic typically provides a list of generic services available from that server.

The DDE Commands

FoxPro for Windows supports 12 functions that form a very thin layer over the native DDE functions found within the Windows API. Table 18.1 lists FoxPro's DDE functions in alphabetical order.

Table 18.1. The FoxPro DDE functions.

Function	Purpose
DDEAbortTrans()	Aborts a transaction that has not yet completed.
DDEAdvise()	Establishes a cold or warm link with another application.
DDEEnabled()	Enables or disables a channel, or enquires about its status.
DDEExecute()	Commands the DDE server to execute a command.

Command	Purpose
DDEInitiate()	Establishes a DDE channel with a DDE server.
DDELastError()	Returns a code explaining why a request failed. Errors include the following:
	`Service/Topic/Channel busy`
	`No such service/topic/bad channel`
	`Timeout for acknowledge/request/execute/poke/advise`
	`No DDEInitiate()`
	`Bad parameter`
	`Low memory/memory error`
	`Server died`
DDEPoke()	Sends data to server.
DDERequest()	Requests data from the server.
DDESetOption()	Sets or returns certain parameters, principally the timeout interval.
DDESetService()	Assigns a name to service provided (for example, RentData).
DDESetTopic()	Defines topic of conversation.
DDETerminate()	Closes the channel.

The following sections contain three DDE examples that show the DDE functions used in context. The first uses FoxPro as a client, receiving data from a spreadsheet. The second and third examples use FoxPro as a server. In the second example, FoxPro inserts data into a Word document. The exchange occurs within FoxPro, which technically makes it the client; however, the orientation is from Word, so FoxPro mimics a server. In the last example, FoxPro is used as a general database server, accepting queries and commands and running them in the background.

FoxPro as a DDE Client

Suppose you are the proprietor of a small restaurant and your landlady cuts you a break on your rent. She makes you only pay a small amount of fixed rent per month. The rest is proportional to the amount of your sales. So far, so good. The problem is that your landlady charges you a different rate for different types of sales. Cigarette sales command a higher proportion than food sales. Newspapers and other sundry items are measured at a lower rate. Using a spreadsheet to calculate the rent can simplify the job of calculating rent. DDE makes it easy to set up a spreadsheet in Excel, feed it sales from FoxPro, have it calculate rent owed, then return the answer to FoxPro.

Here is a facsimile of the spreadsheet, called CVRENT.XLS.

A	B	C	D	
1	Category	Gross Sales	Rental	Rent Due
2				
3	Cigarettes	$5,000	8%	$400
4	Food	$10,000	5%	$500
5	Sundry	$1,000	3%	$30
6			Pct. Rent	$930
7			Minimum Rent	$250
8			Total Due	$1,180

Column B is supplied from FoxPro, and cell D8 is returned to FoxPro as the total rent due.

To initiate the conversation with Excel, you must first make sure that it is running. Although you can use various methods, the simplest is to launch another instance of Excel, directing it to the worksheet previously described, called CVRENT.XLS. The following is the command line to do this:

```
RUN /N7 EXCEL.EXE CVRENT
```

As covered previously, the RUN command with the /N parameter indicates that the application to be run is a true Windows application. The N7 indicates that the application is to be minimized and inactivated so that the input focus can be returned to your FoxPro application.

The next command establishes the link between your FoxPro program and Excel:

```
iChannel = DDEInitiate("Excel","CVRENT.XLS")
```

If the function DDEInitiate() returns a positive number, a link is established and the DDE conversation can proceed. At this point, your program can tally sales for the various categories and send them to the spreadsheet with the following three commands:

```
= DDEPoke(iChannel,"R3C2",STR(cigsales,10))
= DDEPoke(iChannel,"R4C2",STR(foosales,10))
= DDEPoke(iChannel,"R5C2",STR(sunsales,10))
```

The command DDEPoke sends data to the DDE server. The string R3C2 tells Excel that the data is destined for row 3, column 2, and the third string is the actual data. At this point, the spreadsheet reflects your total sales in each of the three categories and performs the calculations necessary to arrive at the total rent due. You can command Excel to provide that total rent due by using the following command:

```
iReqTransNum = DDERequest(iChannel,"R8C4","CF_TEXT","iDone")
```

This command instructs Excel to return the result of the calculation, found in row 8, column 4, when it is finished. Similar to a hot link, the command calls this routine when Excel is ready rather than when FoxPro calls it. The string CF_TEXT indicates that the answer is to be standard text. The string iDone is the name of a UDF called the callback function. The following is the complete listing of the program iDone:

```
PROCEDURE iDone
PARAMETERS iChanNum, sAction, sItem, sData, sFormat, iStatus
DO cvrent.spr  && show the values return
nonote = .F.   && flag used to indicate done
rentdue = ""
FOR i=1 TO LEN(sData)  && loop strips commas and $$
  chrq = SUBSTR(sData,i,1)
  IF ISDIGIT(chrq)
    rentdue = rentdue + chrq
  ENDIF
ENDFOR
rentdue = VAL(rentdue)  && convert to a real number
```

The program iDone is called when the transaction is complete. Procedure iDone uses the following standard parameter string:

```
PARAMETERS iChanNum, sAction, sItem, sData, sFormat, iStatus
```

These parameters are returned for every transaction, so you must provide for them in your parameter line, even if you don't care what their values are. You can look at iChanNum if you are using the same callback function for multiple DDE channels. The argument sAction typically has values such as "INITIATE", "REQUEST", or "TERMI-NATE". You can use this argument to decide what to do with the data that returns. The client determines the argument sItem. In this example, the argument is the row and column of the answer, R8C4. The argument sData contains the actual data, as a string. You must convert the data to a number by using the VAL() function. sFormat tells you the format; in this example, the format is CF_TEXT. Finally, the iStatus argument returns a positive value indicating that the transfer was a success.

When you are finished with the spreadsheet, you can terminate the link with the following command:

```
= DDETerminate(iChannel)
```

You can close Excel altogether by invoking the following commands:

```
iChannel = DDEInitiate("Excel", "System")
= DDEExecute(iChannel, '[ERROR(FALSE)]')
= DDEExecute(iChannel, '[QUIT()]')
= DDETerminate(iChannel)
```

This uses the System topic, which is a standard topic that clears all errors and then instructs Excel to exit and return to Windows. Remember, all this is done while your FoxPro program continues to execute.

Although this example of using DDE with Excel is trivial, the techniques are the same even for the most complex spreadsheet. As long as you know the cells to POKE and the cell to read the answer, the level of complexity of the spreadsheet doesn't matter. After you get your first test program running, creating additional programs is just a matter of substituting different calls; however, the techniques stay the same.

These techniques are particularly useful if you want to graph results. By using Excel, you can easily construct any kind of chart imaginable and then fill it with data from FoxPro. The minimal code necessary to update cells in a graph is identical to that of a spreadsheet. The following is an example:

```
iChannel = DDEInitiate("Excel","CVGRAPH1.XLS")
= DDEPoke(iChannel,"R2C1",STR(val2bpoked[1],8))   && column 1
= DDEPoke(iChannel,"R2C2",STR(val2bpoked[2],8))   && column 2
* etc.
= DDETerminate(iChannel)
```

This sounds easy because it requires that you construct the graph in advance within Excel. If you must construct an original graph directly from FoxPro, you either must use the GraphWizard, which is part of the RQBE window, or learn Excel's macro language.

Interestingly enough, you can link in a graph to FoxPro by using OLE (described later in this chapter) and update it by using DDE from FoxPro. This makes a DDE-linked graph an active part of your application.

FoxPro as a DDE Server (Mostly)

Most people who have used a computer have used a mail merge program at some time. FoxPro can export a mailing list in .SDF format, which can be read in by Word's merge feature. This method of data transfer is an example of the traditional single-tasking orientation previously described. A more sophisticated method is to have Word request the data from FoxPro whenever it needs the data. In this case, FoxPro acts as a DDE server. To accomplish this, you must learn how to write scripts in WordBasic, which is a variant of Visual Basic. If you are already an accomplished FoxPro programmer, this may seem like a step backward.

 Note: Using FoxPro as a DDE server is quite different from using other servers because you can use the entire range of FoxPro's commands and functions, without needing to list each command as a topic.

There is another way to get Word to provide a template and have FoxPro supply the necessary information on demand. This method uses a feature of Word called a *bookmark*. Bookmarks are arbitrary spots in a document that are given a name. You can use DDE to insert anything you want at a bookmark if you know its name.

Like the Excel example, the following example starts by launching a new instance of Word that attaches the document to be merged. You launch this instance by invoking the following command:

```
RUN /N4 WINWORD
```

You must start a DDE conversation with Word by using the following command:

```
iChannel = DDEInitiate("WinWord","System")
```

As in the previous example, a positive number indicates that a conversation has begun. The next step is to open the template document, called CVRENT.DOC, by invoking the following command:

```
= DDEExecute(iChannel,'[FileOpen "CVRENT.DOC"]')
```

CVRENT.DOC is a prototype sales letter to be sent to the landlady along with the rent check each month. Four bookmarks are assigned: cigsales, foosales, sunsales, and rentdue. After calculating the total sales for the month and calling Excel to calculate the rent, we are ready to write the document. The commands are

```
= DDEExecute(iChannel,'[EditGoTo .Destination="cigsales"]')
= DDEExecute(iChannel,'[Insert "'+TRANSFORM(cigsales, ;
  "@$ 9,999.99"+'"]')
= DDEExecute(iChannel,'[EditGoTo .Destination="foosales"]')
= DDEExecute(iChannel,'[Insert "'+TRANSFORM(foosales, ;
  "@$ 9,999.99"+'"]')
= DDEExecute(iChannel,'[EditGoTo .Destination="sunsales"]')
= DDEExecute(iChannel,'[Insert "'+TRANSFORM(sunsales,;
  "@$ 9,999.99"+'"]')
```

continues

```
= DDEExecute(iChannel,'[EditGoTo .Destination="rentdue"]')
= DDEExecute(iChannel,'[Insert "'+TRANSFORM(rentdue, ;
  "@$ 9,999.99"+'"]')
```

At this point, the document is complete. We can instruct Word to print the document by using the following commands:

```
= DDEExecute(iChannel,'[FilePrintDefault]')
= DDETerminate(iChannel)
```

The whole sequence is repeated for the next and subsequent letters.

This technique is nearly identical to the Excel example. A location within the target file is identified and data is directly inserted into that spot. The key difference is that Excel is minimized and used just as an engine. Word is left open and visible so that the document is constructed before our eyes. If we want to cancel or change anything, we can do so by simply clicking the document.

If you want to do this from the Word side, you must learn WordBasic, which is a dialect of Visual Basic. WordBasic supports the following DDE commands:

```
DDEExecute

DDEInitiate()

DDEPoke

DDERequest$()

DDETerminate

DDETerminateAll
```

To write a program in WordBasic, you must create a macro by using the Macro... bar of the Tools menu (see Figure 18.1). You select the macro to edit and then click the Edit push button.

The following is a short WordBasic macro that sends any valid FoxPro command (in this case, TIME()) to FoxPro for Windows and then inserts the answer into the document:

```
Sub MAIN
ChanNum = DDEInitiate("FoxCommand", "WordFunc")
FPCmnd$ = "TIME()"
DDEPoke(ChanNum, "Command", FPCmnd$)
a$ = DDERequest$(ChanNum, "Answer")
DDETerminate(ChanNum)
Insert a$
End Sub
```

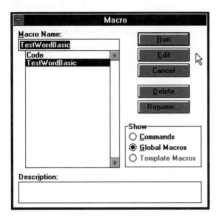

Figure 18.1. The dialog box for selecting a WordBasic macro to edit.

The following is the minimal FoxPro code required to support this macro:

```
** PROCEDURE wordtest
PUBLIC kans
kans = ""
_SERVER_ = "FoxCommand"
= DDEEnabled(.T.)
= DDESetService(_SERVER_, "define")
= DDESetService(_SERVER_, "request", .T.)
= DDESetService(_SERVER_, "poke", .T.)
= DDESetService(_SERVER_, "formats", "CF_TEXT, CF_CSV")
= DDESetTopic(_SERVER_, "WordExec", "WordExec")
SET PROCEDURE TO wordtest   && so it can find this later
RETURN


PROCEDURE WordExec
PARAMETERS iChanNum, sAction, sItem, sData, sFormat, iStatus
sAction = UPPER(sAction)
DO CASE
  CASE sAction = "POKE"
    rts = ""
    kans = &sData   && make sure this is a valid command!
  CASE sAction = "REQUEST"
    rts = kans
  OTHERWISE  && don't care
    rts = ""
    kans = ""
ENDCASE
= DDEPOKE(iChanNum, sItem, rts)
RETURN
```

423

Note that absolutely no error checking is in this code. If there is any error at all, FoxPro hangs up at the line in which the macro is evaluated, and your word processing seems to freeze. You must cycle through the active Windows tasks until you get to FoxPro and then correct the problem. To make this error-correction procedure even semi-automated, you must include enough code to handle ordinary types of errors so that FoxPro doesn't hang up during macro evaluation. As you will see in the following section, most of the FoxData server code is devoted to error handling.

Actually, the code presented is simply a skeleton of a program. Supplying the time is hardly a worthwhile use of FoxPro's power. But contained in this example are all tools necessary to incorporate FoxPro commands in a Word document. To make the whole thing fly, you must launch an instance of FoxPro and execute this program. At this point, you can minimize FoxPro and treat it as an engine that returns most anything. If you want FoxPro to act as a source for mail merge, you must supply the code necessary to open the database and find the records of interest.

FoxData: A General Purpose DDE Server

FOXDATA.APP allows FoxPro to act as a general-purpose server that can service not only Word documents and Excel spreadsheets, but in fact any Windows application that can act as a DDE client.

Microsoft supplies FOXDATA.APP and associated source code in its demonstration materials. An excellent illustration of a general-purpose database server, the example is also useful for demonstrating the limitations of DDE. Although this section does not cover all the code, you have the opportunity to do so when you install FoxPro for Windows.

The FOXDATA.APP is fairly simple. Most of the code is for handling errors. FoxPro is rather insistent on displaying messages on-screen when an error occurs, often even if you have an error trap set. This can disrupt the execution of your main application and should be avoided.

To invoke the server, just do FOXDATA.APP. A status screen appears, which you can then minimize if you want. At this point, FoxPro is behaving as a DDE server, and is ready to accept requests from DDE clients.

For the purposes of our discussions, we will use another instance of FoxPro as a client to the instance of FoxPro that is running FOXDATA.APP. Obviously, we could use Word, or Excel, or any other package capable of acting as a DDE client as a client to the instance of FoxPro that is running FOXDATA.APP.

Let's assume that you need FOXDATA to open a .DBF. You can do this in several ways, but the simplest way is to initiate a conversation by using the topic of TABLE. The syntax is as follows:

```
iChannel = DDEInitiate("FoxData","C:\FOXPROW;TABLE t161.DBF")
```

The string in front of the semicolon is the full path prefix, followed by the word TABLE, followed by the table or .DBF name. If a channel is opened successfully, you can now begin asking questions about the database. The following are some examples:

```
?TRIM(DDERequest(iChannel,"fieldnames")) && list field names
?TRIM(DDERequest(iChannel,"fieldcount")) && number of fields in DBF
?TRIM(DDERequest(iChannel,"firstrow"))   && return first record
?TRIM(DDERequest(iChannel,"lastrow"))    && return last record
?TRIM(DDERequest(iChannel,"prevrow"))    && return previous record
?TRIM(DDERequest(iChannel,"nextrow"))    && return next record
?TRIM(DDERequest(iChannel,"all"))        && return entire database
* above will include field names as well as data
?TRIM(DDERequest(iChannel,"data"))       && return all records
* this form does not return field names
?TRIM(DDERequest(iChannel,"1"))          && return record 1
?TRIM(DDERequest(iChannel,"1-5"))        && return records 1 to 5
```

You can run a SQL command directly. The following is the syntax for an example:

```
iChannel = DDEInitiate("FoxData","C:\FOXPROW;SQL SELECT re_cat,"+ ;
      "SUM(re_sales) AS sum FROM cvrent GROUP BY re_cat" + ;
      "INTO CURSOR sales")
```

After you run this command, CURSOR sales becomes the active table and you can then apply all the commands described for the TABLE topic.

You can also run a predefined query (.QPR file) by using similar syntax, as in the following example:

```
iChannel = DDEInitiate("FoxData","C:\FOXPROW;QUERY cvrent.qpr")
```

As with the other two topics, the output table of the query becomes the active table and you can ask questions about this table by using the previously described commands.

You can converse with FoxData about several other topics. For example, the DATABASE topic lets you ask for a list of file types. You can ask for a list of all databases, screen files, reports, queries, and other file types found in the path supplied, as in the following example:

```
iChannel = DDEInitiate("FoxData","C:\FOXPROW;DATABASE")
?TRIM(DDERequest(iChannel,"TableList"))
?TRIM(DDERequest(iChannel,"ScreenList"))
```

The Down Side of DDE

There are several drawbacks when using DDE, as listed:

- Not every application supports DDE, and those that do may require that you learn a new language such as Excel's macro language or WordBasic.

- Another drawback is speed. Because data is typically transferred as text, one line at a time, you don't get the same throughput as you do performing a query or any other database operation.

- Perhaps the most severe drawback is that you need a copy of each program that you want to link into your application. That means that you might have to convince a client that the company must purchase 150 licenses for Excel along with its 150 licenses to FoxPro if the client wants to use DDE to utilize Excel. This may not be a problem if these programs are already installed, but it is something to keep in mind.

To summarize, DDE is a well-defined, scalable (through NetDDE) software interface that you can use to transfer data between applications, taking advantage of each application's strengths. A sequence of commands is required to initiate the conversation, and some rules regarding protocol must be followed, but the content of the conversation is up to the developer.

General Fields: A Place for OLE

Before we discuss FoxPro's new general field type, you should understand what I mean by an *object*. In the preceding examples, we considered exchanging data between FoxPro and other applications one item at a time. We placed sales figures within individual cells of an Excel spreadsheet and looked at a specific cell for the total rent due. In a sense, data is data, and it doesn't matter which application is looking at it. The entire spreadsheet, however, is considered an object. This object includes not only the data but the formulas relating the cells to one another, as well as formatting information, preferences, and so on.

With the advent of Windows 3.x, we now have *OLE*, which stands for *Object Linking and Embedding*. We associate an application with the object, such as Excel for .XLS files, Paintbrush for .BMP files, and the Sound Recorder for .WAV files. Whenever we want to view or edit the object, Windows activates an instance of the controlling application.

FoxPro for Windows has a new type of field called a *general field*. It is similar to a memo field in that the data is stored in the .FPT file and only a pointer is kept in the actual database. A bitmap of the object or an icon is stored along with all the information necessary to access the application responsible for the object. Thus, a .BMP is stored in its entirety along with the information required to call Paintbrush. In the case of a .WAV file, an icon similar to that used for the Sound Recorder is stored in the general field, along with the .WAV file and the information necessary to call the Sound Recorder.

Before we look at the general field, let's establish some terminology. The application that provides OLE services is the *server,* and, as with DDE, the application subscribing to those services is the *client.*

After you place an object in a general field, you must choose whether or not the object should be linked or embedded. *Linking* retains a reference to the original object, which is not actually stored in the general field. Whenever the original object changes, the changes eventually appear in the copy in the general field. This makes updating multiple documents or applications simple, because all versions of the object faithfully reflect the original. This also takes less space on your disk, because only one copy of the object is maintained.

If you choose to *embed* the object, you sever the link to the original object, and FoxPro stores all information about the object in the general field. Your copy does not reflect changes to the original object. You can delete the original object and allow access to the copy of the object only through your application. You may find it interesting to note that OLE uses DDE between applications to maintain links and status information.

Any object type that is to become an OLE object must be registered within Windows registration database, called REG.DAT. To see what object types you have registered, issue the following command:

```
RUN /N REGEDIT
```

Each OLE server can perform one or more actions. These actions are called *verbs*. For example, the Sound Recorder can PLAY or EDIT a .WAV file. To see a list of verbs available, issue the following command:

```
RUN /N REGEDIT /V
```

This registration database is also used by the Windows File Manager, usually found in the Main workgroup. If an object is properly registered, you can simply double-click the object from the File Manager to launch the object's controlling application.

Try creating a database with the name TMEM and adding a field, making it type GENERAL. Suppose that the field is called ts_gen, for example. If you want to insert an OLE object into this field, add a record and open a window to the general field, either by using BROWSE, by double-clicking the word gen, or by issuing the following command:

```
MODIFY GENERAL ts_gen
```

If you see a window titled TMEM.TS_GEN, you are ready to add an OLE object. The following subsections demonstrate the methods for embedding or linking four objects: a .BMP file, an Excel spreadsheet, a .WAV file, and a Word document. Each object has its own nuances and uses.

Adding a .BMP Picture File

To link in a .BMP file, you must perform the following series of actions:

1. Open a window to a general field, as previously described.

2. Launch an instance of Paintbrush.

3. Create your own picture or load one that is already stored on disk.

4. Select an area to copy by using the Pick or Scissors tool.

5. Copy the region to the Clipboard by using Ctrl+C or the Edit menu.

6. Return to FoxPro.

7. Select Paste Special... from the Edit menu.

8. Select Paste Link.

Let's review each of the steps, one by one.

You can open a window to a general field by double-clicking the word gen in a Browse window or issuing the command MODIFY GENERAL. The screen might look like Figure 18.2.

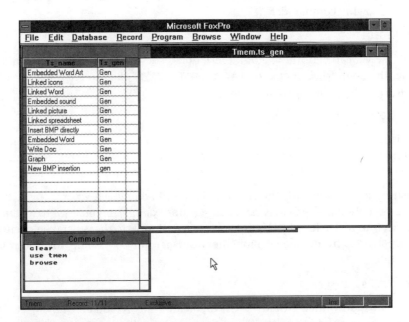

Figure 18.2. Preparing to insert a .BMP file into a general field.

Next you must run a copy of Paintbrush. Create your own picture or load one that is already stored on disk. Use the Pick or Scissors tool to select an area to copy. Use Ctrl+C or the Edit menu to copy the region to the Clipboard.

Now return to FoxPro and use the Edit menu to select Paste Special.... You now see a dialog box, shown in Figure 18.3, offering you the choice of Paste, Paste Link, or Cancel along with object types Paintbrush Picture Object, Bitmap, and Picture.

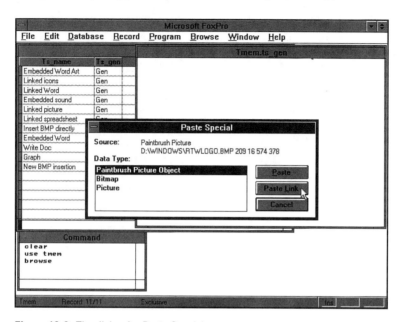

Figure 18.3. The dialog for Paste Special.

You should leave the data type as Paintbrush Picture Object to demonstrate the Paste Link option. Select Paste Link, and an image of your picture appears in the general field window. Tile your windows so that you can see the original along with the FoxPro general field window. Change the original picture. As soon as you finish each change, you see the FoxPro image change, as shown in Figure 18.4.

Note that you can see changes only when the OLE server is active. If you close your FoxPro application, change the picture, reopen FoxPro, and view the general field, you see the changes. If you close FoxPro, change the picture, close Paintbrush, reopen FoxPro, and view the picture, you do not see the changes but rather the image last seen when FoxPro and Paintbrush were in communication with each other. You can resynchronize the two images by double-clicking the general field. This automatically opens Paintbrush.

Double-clicking an OLE object does not always result in the same effect. The effect depends on the verbs that each OLE server supports. Typically, double-clicking means EDIT, but in the case of .WAV files, it means PLAY. You can tell what the effect of double-clicking is by reading the option listed below the Insert Object... bar of the Edit popup. If there is only one choice, such as Edit Paintbrush Picture Object, that is what will happen. If the OLE server has multiple verbs, the choice will indicate something like

Sound Object, with an arrow indicating a submenu. The first verb listed in that submenu is the action performed by double-clicking. Figures 18.5 and 18.6 show two examples.

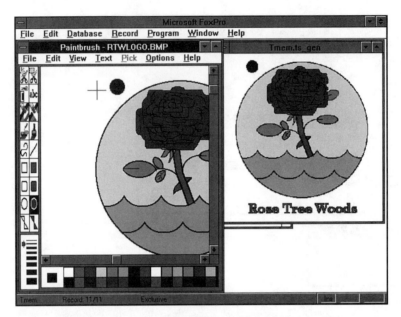

Figure 18.4. Changes in a linked .BMP file show instantly in the general field window.

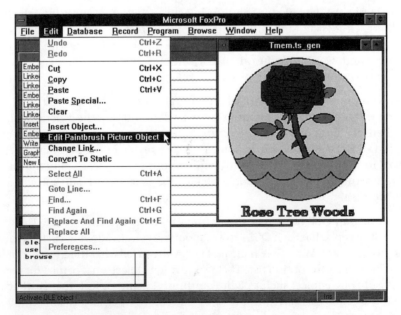

Figure 18.5. Deducing what action will occur when you double-click a .BMP file.

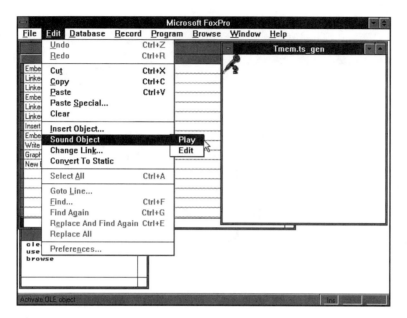

Figure 18.6. Deducing what action will occur when you double-click a .WAV file.

Using OLE, you can also embed Paintbrush pictures in a general field. You can cut or copy an image into the Clipboard and then simply paste the image into the general field. You can embed an image from a file by using the Insert Object... option from the Edit menu and selecting Paintbrush Picture Object from the list of object types.

Embedded objects are completely contained in the general field and never reflect changes to the original file. If you double-click an embedded .BMP file, you launch a new instance of Paintbrush, which looks like Figure 18.7.

At this point, you can modify the picture that was inserted into the general field. If you tile the windows so that you can see the general field window as well as the Paintbrush window, you see diagonal lines drawn through the general field. These denote an editing session active outside of FoxPro. Within Paintbrush, you are expected to modify the picture. If you try to open another .BMP file, you break the OLE link, and your activity then becomes a regular Paintbrush session. When you finish modifying the picture and are ready to return to FoxPro, the Exit item on the File menu of Paintbrush looks as shown in Figure 18.8.

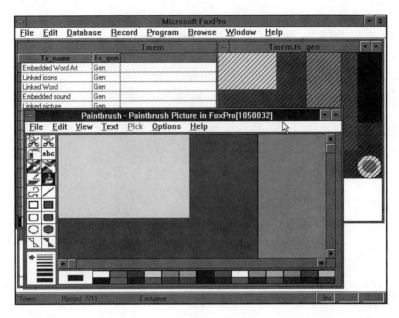

Figure 18.7. Editing an embedded .BMP object brings up a linked version of Paintbrush.

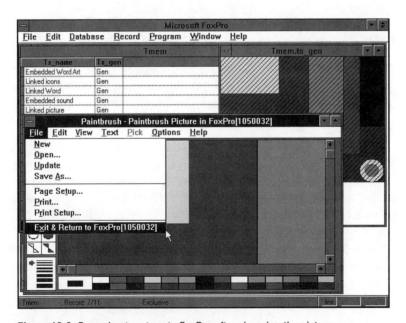

Figure 18.8. Preparing to return to FoxPro after changing the picture.

If you have modified the picture, when you exit you see the dialog box in Figure 18.9, asking whether you want to update the embedded object.

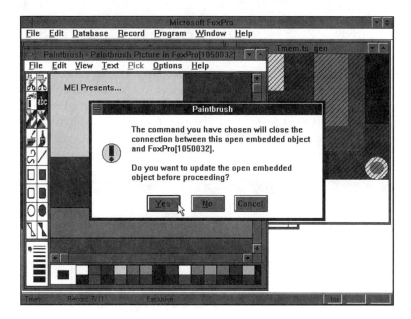

Figure 18.9. Windows asks whether you want to update the embedded object.

Typically, you answer Yes to update the general field image.

You might have noticed by now that, no matter what method you use to place an image in the general field, it probably doesn't look exactly like the original. FoxPro maintains the aspect ratio of the original image. If you increase the size of the general field window or maximize, you see a more accurate representation of your picture. Often, however, the representation is still not exact, probably because you created a picture with dimensions that were determined by Paintbrush. On a standard VGA system, such a picture would be a .BMP with the dimensions 640 by 480. On such a system, FoxPro for Windows cannot display the full object because it needs room for the border and its title band, menu bar, and so on. Try creating a smaller picture and you see that you can get a full representation of the .BMP file within the general field window.

After you link or embed a .BMP file in a general field, you can paint it to the screen by invoking the following command:

```
@0,0 SAY tmem.ts_gen
```

You do not need the keyword BITMAP. FoxPro figures out from the general field how to present the contents of the .BMP, and attempts to paint the image on the area provided. If the picture is 640 by 480, part of it is cut off. If the picture is smaller than

433

the screen, it is placed in the upper-left corner of the screen. You can center a small image by applying the CENTER clause to the SAY command. If the picture is larger than the screen and you want to see the full picture, you can add the clause ISOMETRIC, which maintains the aspect ratio of the picture but makes it small enough to fit on the screen. Alternatively, you can add the STRETCH clause, which causes the picture to fill the space available.

If you want to limit the area of the picture, use the SIZE clause to define its extent. If the image is smaller than the region specified, it appears in the upper-left corner. You can tell FoxPro to center the image by using the CENTER clause. If the image is larger than the region specified and you do not instruct FoxPro on how to fill the region, the picture is clipped. You can also apply the ISOMETRIC and STRETCH clauses to the @...SAY command. Figure 18.10 shows the appearance that results from some of these clauses.

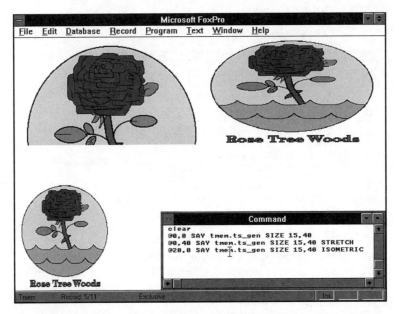

Figure 18.10. The effects of the various fill options associated with the *SIZE* clause.

In the upper-left corner, the image is restricted to a region 15 by 40. As you can see, the image is clipped. For the upper-right corner, we used the same SIZE clause but added the keyword STRETCH. The entire picture is shown, but it is stretched to fill the region. For the lower-left corner, the keyword ISOMETRIC is used to fill the same region. In this case, the aspect ratio of the regular picture is maintained, so some white space is created.

You also can use .BMP images within general fields to enhance reports and screens. For example, to create a letterhead, you can place at the top of letters a company logo alongside names and addresses from a database.

Adding Excel (.XLS) Spreadsheets and Graphs

You can link or embed spreadsheets as easily as pictures. To embed a spreadsheet, select from within Excel the cells to be included in the general field. Then copy the selected cells to the Clipboard. After you switch back to FoxPro, activate the general field window and select Paste Special..., as you did when adding the .BMP file. Then select Paste Link—that is all there is to it. As long as Excel is active, changes in the spreadsheet are reflected in the image presented in the general field. If you use a TrueType font in your spreadsheet, FoxPro scales the text as best it can. If you use a bitmapped font, such as MS Sans Serif, FoxPro scales the image as it does a .BMP file. The text of the spreadsheet image might become unreadable if the general field window is too small.

If you want to embed a spreadsheet, you use the same procedures as you do for a .BMP file. You can copy cells to the Clipboard and use a regular paste or you can use the Insert Object... bar on the Edit menu. If you have an embedded spreadsheet, you can still edit it by using the menu item or double-clicking the general field image. As with the .BMP files, if you are editing an embedded spreadsheet and examine the general field window while Excel is open, you see diagonal lines across the general field window, indicating that the object is being updated.

To paint an image of the spreadsheet onto the screen, use the following command:

```
@0,0 SAY tmem.ts_mem
```

FoxPro takes its cue from the general field, determines that it contains a spreadsheet, and paints it on the screen accordingly. Again, the size of the image is under program control. You can use the SIZE clause to delineate the area to be filled with the spreadsheet. If the region is too small, FoxPro clips the image to the size specified. You can use the STRETCH or ISOMETRIC clauses to tell FoxPro how to fill the region. If you use TrueType fonts, the text is scaled accordingly. If you use bitmapped fonts, the image looks worse if it is enlarged or shrunk.

The embedding or linking of a graph generated in Excel is as simple as that of a spreadsheet. While in Excel, create a graph by using the built-in feature. Select only the graph, if that is all you want displayed, and copy it to the Clipboard by pressing the right mouse button, using the Edit menu, or pressing Ctrl+V. Return to FoxPro, open a window to the general field, and select Paste or Paste Special. The graph now becomes an object that you can display by using the previously described syntax. Like a spreadsheet, a graph is scalable.

Displaying a graph is similar to displaying a .BMP file. Like the display of pictures or spreadsheets, the display of graphs is subject to the keywords CENTER, STRETCH, and ISOMETRIC. If you scale the graph up or down, you should use a TrueType font for your legends so that they look as good as possible at any scale. Excel maintains colors, graph type, and default size. Using the code previously described, you can update the data either by using Excel or DDE. If you have a database with 10 groups and run a query to tally results, you can enter them into your graph by using the following code:

```
* query-based update to a graph linked to CVGRAPH2.XLS
USE cvsales
DO cvtally.QPR  && returns with sales tallied in cursor
iChannel = DDEInitiate("Excel","CVGRAPH2.XLS")
FOR iRow = 1 TO 10
  = DDEPoke(iChannel,"R"+LTRIM(STR(iRow,2))+;
      "C2",STR(query.sum_1,8))
ENDFOR
= DDETerminate(iChannel)
```

As long as the OLE graph object is linked, the general field reflects the last time you ran the query. You can run the update process in the background by using another instance of FoxPro. This keeps your graph current without any direct intervention from the foreground program. If you use a combination of OLE and DDE, the possibilities are endless.

Adding a Sound Object (.WAV)

If you have a sound board such as Sound Blaster or the Microsoft Sound Board, or have installed the Microsoft speaker driver, you can play .WAV files by using the Sound Recorder OLE server. You can link or embed sounds in general fields as easily as you can with .BMP files or spreadsheets. However, if you examine the general field after placing a .WAV file in it, you see the icon for the Sound Recorder, which looks like a microphone. Double-clicking the icon does not edit the sound, but plays it. To edit the sound, you must select the Edit option of the Modify Sound Object submenu.

Likewise, if you try to SAY a general field that contains a .WAV file, all you see is the bitmapped image of the microphone. To hear the sound, you must issue the following command:

```
@0,0 SAY tmem.ts_gen VERB 0
```

VERB 0 tells FoxPro to play the sound rather than display the image shown in the general field. If you change the command to VERB 1, FoxPro activates the Sound Recorder for the purpose of editing the .WAV file.

To improve performance, you should have the Sound Recorder already active in the background before you try to play your first sound. You can do this by issuing the following command:

```
RUN /N7 SOUNDREC
```

Adding a Word Document (.DOC)

Inserting a Word document is identical to adding a .WAV file or a .BMP file. You highlight the text you want to embed and copy it to the Clipboard. You then paste it into the general field or use Paste Link. As with a .WAV file, if you examine the general field, you do not see the document. Instead, you see the icon for Microsoft Word. The only way to see the document behind the icon is to double-click the icon or select Edit Word Document Object from the Edit menu.

If you try to print an embedded Word document in a FoxPro report, the only part of the document that is included in the output is the Word icon as a bitmapped image. This result is similar to that of trying to print a .WAV file. If you want to print a Word document that is embedded in a general field, you must invoke DDE to explain to Word what it is supposed to do. For example, suppose that record six of the database has a Word for Windows document. You must issue the following code to print it:

```
USE tmem  && open the database
GO 6      && go to the Word document
@0,0 SAY ts_gen VERB 0  && fire up a copy of Word as OLE server
** initiate conversation with Word

c = DDEInitiate("WinWord","System")
&& tell Word to Print then close
= DDEExecute(c, "[FilePrint][FileClose]")
= DDETerminate(c)  && end the conversation
```

As you can see, this is too much for the Report Writer to handle, so you can't print an embedded Word document as part of a FoxPro report.

Adding Other Objects

When you use the Insert Object... menu, you have many choices. Your list might look something like the following:

Microsoft Drawing

Microsoft Excel Chart

Microsoft Excel Worksheet

Microsoft Graph

MS WordArt

Paintbrush Picture

PowerPoint Slide

Sound

Word Document

This list includes the registered OLE servers and the objects they maintain. The actual list that you see depends on what Windows applications you have installed. You should experiment with linking and embedding each of the types listed.

OLE links are somewhat delicate. Files that are linked cannot be moved. OLE does not have a facility for tracing a new path to the object. However, after you enter an object into a general field, you can convert the object from embedded to linked, or vice versa.

Adding Objects Programmatically

You can append general fields with OLE objects programmatically by using the APPEND GENERAL command. The procedure is similar to adding a file to a memo field. For example, you might issue the following command:

```
APPEND GENERAL ts_gen FROM embedme2.doc
```

FoxPro then looks at the extension and determines from the registration database what the OLE server should be. If there is a problem, you can specify the server explicitly by using the CLASS clause, as follows:

```
APPEND GENERAL ts_gen FROM embedme2.pic CLASS "PBrush"
```

This indicates to FoxPro that you want to embed this object as a Paintbrush Picture Object. If you want to make this a linked object, you must include the keyword LINK, as follows:

```
APPEND GENERAL ts_gen FROM embedme2.pic LINK CLASS "PBrush"
```

Unlike memo fields, you cannot append to an existing general field, you can only overwrite an existing field. If you must concatenate pictures, sounds, or documents, you must do it programmatically by using successive records or return to the OLE server and concatenate the objects.

The Brave New "Docu-Centric" World

Although DDE and OLE are not perfect, they are rather large steps towards a *docu-centric* world. By that I mean a world in which you don't have to worry about running multiple applications to create the ultimate document, but can instead create one document and embed knowledge about required applications within the actual document.

For example, suppose you want to create a document describing profit and loss by product along with an accounting of inventory and pictures of the items within the inventory. In the application-oriented world, you must first create a generic document. You then create a spreadsheet calculating profit and loss. Then you run a report from your database describing the inventory. Finally, you must run a program such as Paintbrush to produce the pictures of the items in the inventory.

In the new docu-centric world, you create only a document—for example, a Word document describing each of the three sections. You link in a spreadsheet, using OLE, in the appropriate section knowing that whenever you change your profit and loss statement, your document reflects those changes. Next, you produce your inventory report by using DDE and FoxPro. Using general fields, you embed picture files of each of the reports in your database for display in the ultimate document.

You can embed sounds if needed, along with Word Art, Graph, and countless other applications. As long as each object is linked, the document becomes a living report that can be consulted on-line, producing the most current information each time it is viewed.

The bottom line is that Windows opens a whole new world of information management and FoxPro for Windows becomes an important part of that world. Good luck and have fun!

CHAPTER 19

Library Routines

You don't need me to tell you that library routines are beneficial. For years, good programmers like you have created programs that are called from many different places in an application.

Therefore, I will not pretend that I invented library routines. I will not pretend that library routines written in the MEI manner constitute Object-Oriented Programs. I won't pretend that MEI style library routines are in any way superior to the library routines that you already use. I won't even pretend that library routines are something new.

I will, however, pretend that I am conscious long enough to:

- Contrast the benefits and the drawbacks of using library routines. (You didn't know there were any drawbacks, did you?)

- Fulfill promises from earlier chapters by explaining the l3msg and l3nextid routines.

- Outline some rules for creating library routines.

- Demonstrate an exceptionally flexible, and programmer-friendly method for passing multiple parameters to a procedure.

- Explain the creation of *Shell* library routines that provide *front-ends* to more sophisticated library routines.

- Explain how to use Shell routines to ensure that the creation of new library routines does not require a rewrite of existing applications.

- Provide you with a word-wrapping routine that supports fonts and styles.

- Provide you with a dialog box that takes full advantage of the Windows environment.

Good News, Bad News

Like most things, library routines have their benefits and drawbacks. Table 19.1 lists a few of the more meaningful ones.

Table 19.1. Benefits and drawbacks of library routines.

Benefits	Drawbacks
Reduce coding by making a single procedure call to execute many lines of code.	Programmers forced to learn the "language" of the library in addition to FoxPro.
Applications share a common look and feel because all dialogs, messages, and so on, are produced by the same library routines.	Programmers become dependent on the library and fail to fully explore the FoxPro language.
Reduced debugging.	Decreased performance.
An enhancement made to a library routine ripples through all the applications that make use of that library routine.	FoxPro enhancements frequently make library routines obsolete.
	Fully developed, fully debugged, well-written library routines can take a long time to write, but a new version of FoxPro can make them obsolete in a hurry!
	Programmers often fall in love with their own library routines. As a result, they write their applications to fit existing library routines, instead of writing applications to fit the user's requirements.

Note: It might seem that including Table 19.1 implies that I do not think library routine usage is a valuable approach to FoxPro programming. This is not the case.

To correct any possible misunderstanding, let me state unequivocally that I use library routines extensively. Further, I suggest that you also use library routines extensively.

However, I also suggest that you *do not* create an overly extensive library of routines! An extensive library of routines takes a long time to develop, and an even longer time to debug and tune.

Keep in mind that, by the time the developer completes the creation of the library, a new version of FoxPro might have been released, making the majority of those library routines obsolete. Unfortunately, after spending so much time writing library routines, the developer is often unwilling to stop using those library routines, even when better, native FoxPro alternatives are available.

You can avoid the pitfalls and drawbacks of using library routines in the following ways:

- To reduce the impact of learning another language in addition to FoxPro, make your library routines follow FoxPro syntax whenever possible. (*Note:* See the section on passing multiple values in a single parameter for more information on creating FoxPro-like UDFs and procedures.) In addition, emphasize the use of native FoxPro code whenever possible.

- To prevent yourself and your staff from becoming too dependent on your library routines, insist that each new release of FoxPro be explored for new ways to accomplish library routine tasks with native FoxPro code.

- To reduce the impact of library routine overhead on system performance, avoid using library routines in computationally intensive loops. Use IIF() and other native FoxPro functions instead of UDFs in connection with Browse windows, index keys, queries, and other *multiple-record* processing commands.

- Because FoxPro is updated frequently, do not create monolithic libraries of routines in anticipation of every conceivable shortcoming in the FoxPro language. Instead, create library routines only as the need arises. Remember, by the time you need a function that reads the CONFIG.SYS file to determine the number of available file handles, for example, FoxPro probably will have included such a function in the new release.

Remember, the best set of functions available for FoxPro is not the Goley library, it's not your library, it's FoxPro's built-in function and command set.

Suggestions for Happy, Healthy Library Routines

Library routines are called different names by different programmers. Some developers call them utilities, others call them reusable code, and still others call them objects. Whatever you call them, good library routines are

1. Flexible

2. Easily called

3. Easy to remember

4. Thoroughly debugged

5. Used throughout the application

6. Well behaved

I cover measures to increase the flexibility and ease of use of library routines in a moment. For now however, I want to address the topic of making your library routines well behaved.

 Caution: Because library routines can be called from any point in an application, extra care must be taken to ensure that library routines do not inadvertently change memory variables, leave the program with the wrong work area selected, change the state of SET commands, modify ON KEY LABEL settings, alter menus, or change the environment they inherited from the calling program.

In other words, before returning to the calling procedure, a library routine should put things back the way it found them.

Here are some of the most valuable techniques for saving and restoring the environment:

```
PROCEDURE demosavemenu
PUSH MENU _msysmenu && Save a copy of the menu
** commands...
POP MENU _msysmenu && Put the menu back the way you found it

PROCEDURE demosavekey
PUSH KEY && save ON KEY LABEL settings
** commands...
POP KEY && Put OKLs back the way you found them
```

```
PROCEDURE demosaveset
** Save current SETtings
l_oldtalk=SET("TALK")
SET TALK OFF
** commands...
SET TALK &l_oldtalk. && Put setting back

PROCEDURE demosaverror
** Save current error trap
l_olderr=ON("ERROR")
ON ERROR kerror=ERROR()
** commands...
ON ERROR &l_olderr. && Put error trap back

PROCEDURE demosavearea
** Save current work area
l_oldsele=SELECT()
SELECT myarea
** commands...
SELECT (l_oldsele)  && Return to original work area
```

In addition to saving and restoring environmental settings, library routines must ensure that they do not inadvertently change the content of memory variables defined in calling programs. FoxPro provides the PRIVATE command for this purpose. If you aren't familiar with FoxPro's variable scoping, run these two programs:

```
* hiding.prg
CLEAR MEMORY
FOR xx=1 TO 10
  ? xx
  DO badidea
ENDFOR

FOR xx=1 TO 10
  ? xx
  DO goodidea
ENDFOR

PROCEDURE badidea
xx=500
DISP MEMO
RETURN
```

continues

```
PROCEDURE goodidea
PRIVATE xx
xx=500
DISP MEMO
RETURN
```

Obviously, library routines must make extensive use of PRIVATE commands to ensure that no "bad idea" scenarios arise. A close examination of the PRIVATE command reveals the following optional implementations:

```
** All variables with names that start with "L_" will be
** declared private automatically.
PRIVATE ALL LIKE l_*

** All variables will be declared private automatically.
PRIVATE ALL

** All variables except those with names starting with
** "K" will be declared private automatically.
PRIVATE ALL EXCEPT K*
```

Passing Multiple Values in the Same Parameter

For library routines to be flexible, they have to receive information from the calling procedure. That information directs the library routine to behave in a prescribed manner. This information is passed to library routines through parameters.

For example, if we had a library routine that prompted the user with a message, and then provided a Yes push button and a No push button, we could call that routine as follows:

```
IF l3yesno("Do you want to quit?")="Yes"
  QUIT
ENDIF
```

In this case however, we need a dialog that enables us to modify the push buttons like so:

```
IF l3yesno("Do you want to quit?","Quit;Resume")="Quit"
  QUIT
ENDIF
```

If this is a commonly used routine, it is reasonable to expect the developer to remember which of the two parameters is the message and which should hold push buttons. Further, developers who are required to maintain this block of code can be expected to determine which parameter is the message and which is the button string.

Our dialog requirements are more demanding, however. We have to be able to pass message, push button, title, row, column, height, width, timeout, bell, justification, and bitmap information. Here is a sample call:

```
IF l3yesno(;
    "Do you want to quit?",;
    "Quit;Resume",;
    "Alert",;
    1,0,5,30,120,3,"C","stop.bmp")="Quit"
    QUIT
ENDIF
```

The original LB*.PRG library routines used at Micro Endeavors looked very much like this. However, we noticed the following difficulties associated with library routines that provided a multitude of parameters:

1. It was difficult to remember which parameter was associated with which behavior. For example, which of the aforementioned parameters is "obviously" the bell setting?

2. New programmers spent way too much time looking up library routine parameter lists. In other words, the learning curve was too steep.

3. When writing courseware, documentation, articles, books, and presentations, we spent too much time explaining which parameter performed which behavior.

4. When we wanted to add or change a parameter in a library routine, all the developers had to be retrained to handle the "new" parameter sequence. As a result, we avoided changing library routine parameters, even when an obvious improvement was possible.

5. When we only wanted to pass the message and the number of times to ring the bell, we ended up with code that was indecipherable, even to common users of the library routines. For example:

```
IF l3yesno(;
    "Do you want to quit?",;
    "Quit;Resume",;
    .f.,,.f.,,.f.,,.f.,,.f.,,.f.,3,.f.,,.f.)="Quit"
    QUIT
ENDIF
```

Creating FoxPro Applications

In contrast to the rigid syntax imposed by the original MEI library routines, FoxPro allows great flexibility in the ordering of arguments for a command. For example, the following commands perform exactly the same task:

```
USE george ALIAS tom ORDER name IN SELECT(1)

USE george IN SELECT(1) ORDER name ALIAS tom

USE george ORDER name IN SELECT(1) ALIAS tom
```

I always admired and enjoyed that aspect of the FoxPro language. So, I set out to create a parameter-passing scheme that allows the MEI developers to pass parameters in any order, and that makes it clear to any reader of the program what parameters were being passed to the library routine. Here are three examples:

```
IF l3msgw(;
   "msg=[Do you want to quit?]"+;
   "butt=[Quit;Resume]"+;
   "titl=[Alert]"+;
   "wlro=[1] wlco=[0] wrow=[5] wcol=[30] "+;
   "bell=[3] just=[C] bmp=[stop.bmp]")="Quit"
   QUIT
ENDIF

IF l3msgw(;
   "bell=[3]"+;
   "butt=[Quit;Resume]"+;
   "msg=[Do you want to quit?]")="Quit"
   QUIT
ENDIF

IF l3msgw(;
   "bmp=[stop.bmp] msg=[Do you want to quit?]"+;
   "butt=[Quit;Resume] wlro=[1] just=[C]"+;
   "wlco=[0] titl=[Alert] "+;
   "bell=[3]")="Quit"
   QUIT
ENDIF
```

As you can see, all options are passed to L3MSGW.PRG in a one-character string parameter. These options, or *messages,* are parsed into memory variables by the L3MSGW.PRG routine, and then processed appropriately. Table 19.2 lists the benefits and drawbacks of the one-character string parameter approach.

Table 19.2. Benefits and drawbacks of the one-parameter approach.

Benefits	Drawbacks
Code is more maintainable, because each parameter is identified in the option string.	More typing required to call a library routine.
Code is more FoxPro-like because each option in the parameter uses the name of a FoxPro function whenever possible.	Slight performance penalty incurred when the library routine parses the options out of the parameter string.
Programmers can submit options to the library routine in any order.	
Programmers can omit options without worrying about unpassed parameters "in the middle."	
Support for new options can be added to the library routine without requiring a resequencing of parameters.	
Default options for a library can be stored in a single memory variable. (See "Shortcuts" section that follows.)	

Shortcuts for One-Parameter Library Routines

"Hey George, that's a great idea, but I usually want to ask a simple Yes/No question. Do I have to type 18 parameters into a string every time I call L3MSGW.PRG?"

Good question—and there is a good answer. Assume that you like the results produced by L3MSGW.PRG, but you also like simple UDF calls like this:

```
IF l3yesno("Do you want to quit?")="Yes"
  QUIT
ENDIF
```

If you create a memory variable like this one:

```
kyesno="titl=[Question]bell=[1]butt=[\!\<Yes;\?\<No]"
```

You can directly call the l3msgw routine like this:

```
IF l3msgw("msg=[Do you want to quit?]"+kyesno)="Yes"
  QUIT
ENDIF
```

Obviously, you can maintain a multitude of k variables for this purpose. However, if that still looks like too much typing, you can rewrite your L3YESNO.PRG like this:

```
* l3yesno.prg
* Standard Yes/No question
PARAMETERS p_msg
RETURN l3msgw("msg=["+p_msg+;
  "]titl=[Question]bell=[1]butt=[\!\<Yes;\?\<No]"
```

Now, your call to l3yesno("Do you want to quit?") utilizes the L3MSGW engine, without requiring the programmer to type all the parameter options. We call this technique (using a library routine strictly as a front-end for another library routine) *creating a shell*.

The Shell Game

When you update your library routines or when you shift to using someone else's library routines, you need a way to let old code utilize new library routines. For example, in the time sheet application that you worked through in the first eight chapters of this book, you made several calls to L3MSG.PRG. For the most part, those calls were in one of these two forms:

```
DO l3msg WITH "Sorry. I can't add a record now."
IF l3msg("Do you want to quit?","Yes;No")="YES"
```

L3MSG.PRG is one of the oldest and most used utilities in the Micro Endeavors library. However, when I created L3MSGW.PRG for use with FoxPro 2.5 for Windows, I decided that a one-parameter calling scheme was in order.

To take full advantage of the new features in L3MSGW.PRG, I can:

1. Rewrite all my existing programs to call L3MSGW.PRG instead of L3MSG.PRG, using the proper calling tree.

2. Enhance L3MSG.PRG instead of creating a new library routine, and continue to use the old parameter passing scheme.

3. Convert L3MSG.PRG into a "shell" for L3MSGW.PRG.

Needless to say, I opted for approach number three. Here is the "hollow" version of L3MSG.PRG:

```
* l3msg.prg
* shell program for l3msgw.prg
PARAMETERS p_msg,p_butt,p_options
RETURN l3msgw("msg=["+p_msg+"]"+;
  IIF(TYPE("p_butt")="C","butt=["+p_butt+"]","")+;
  IIF(TYPE("p_options")="C",p_options,""))
```

Using L3MSGW.PRG

L3MSGW.PRG produces a dialog box that the programmer can fashion with text, bitmap, wall paper, color, title, size, location, and push button information. The length of the message is limited to 65,000 characters, and L3MSGW provides word wrapping as necessary. L3MSG also returns the text of the selected push button. If the push button is a bitmap, the full name of the bitmap file associated with the selected push button is returned.

You can take a look at a sample L3MSGW.PRG dialog shown in Figure 19.1, but you would probably rather look at the code that generated that dialog. After I show you the L3MSGW.PRG code, we discuss:

1. Parsing multiple options from a single parameter string.

2. Default values for unpassed options.

3. Word wrapping in proportional fonts.

Figure 19.1. A sample L3MSGW.PRG dialog.

Here's the code:

```
* l3msgw.prg
* displays message and prompts for action
** p_msgopts = A character string containing one or more of
**          the following options:
**
**     MSG=[Read this] Message to be displayed.
**               USE "¦" for line break.
**     Butt=[\!\<Yes;\?\<No] Buttons for the dialog.
**          "\!", "\?", and "\<" are supported.
**          These options will be preceded with "@*H " as
**          part of the terminating push button.
**          If no options are passed, "\!\?\<Ok" is the default
**          .BMP push buttons are supported.
**     Titl=[Window title] title of message window
**     Wlco=[20] Leftmost column of message window
**     Wlro=[2] Topmost row of message window
**     Wcol=[20] Number of columns in message window
**     Wrow=[20] Number of rows in message window
**     Wall=[marble.bmp] Wall paper
**     BMP=[qmark.bmp] Bitmap to display on left side
**               of dialog box
```

```
**      WAV=[tada.wav] Wave file to play on entry to the msg dialog
**      Just=[L] (L)eft, (C)entered, or (R)right justified message.
**              By default, just=[C] if msg is one line, just=[L]
**              if msg is more than one line.
**      Time=[10] Length of timeout. No timeout by default.
**      Bell=[0] Number of times to ring the bell before selection
**              Default is 1. 0 will produce no rings.
**

PARAMETERS p_msgopts

** Set environment
PRIVATE ALL LIKE l_*
PUSH KEY CLEAR
m.l_oldtalk=SET('talk')
SET TALK OFF
m.l_oldexact=SET('exact')
IF m.l_oldexact#"OFF"
  SET EXACT OFF
ENDIF

m.p_msgopts=IIF(EMPTY(m.p_msgopts),"",m.p_msgopts)


** Look for the message
m.l_parse=ATC("MSG=[",m.p_msgopts)
m.l_msg=IIF(m.l_parse=0,"",SUBSTR(m.p_msgopts,m.l_parse+ 5,;
  AT("]",SUBSTR(m.p_msgopts,m.l_parse+ 5))-1))

** Convert "¦" to chr(13) in msg
m.l_msg = CHRTRAN(m.l_msg,"¦",CHR(13))
m.l_msgwin="l3msg"

** Look for buttons
m.l_parse=ATC("BUTT=[",m.p_msgopts)
m.l_butt=IIF(m.l_parse=0,"\!\?\<Ok",;
  SUBSTR(m.p_msgopts,m.l_parse+ 6,;
  AT("]",SUBSTR(m.p_msgopts,m.l_parse+ 6))-1))
** Handle old versions of lbmsg which used "¦"
** for button separators
m.l_butt=CHRTRAN(m.l_butt,"¦",";")

** Wall paper
m.l_parse=ATC("WALL=[",m.p_msgopts)
```

continues

453

```
    m.l_wall=IIF(m.l_parse=0,"",SUBSTR(m.p_msgopts,m.l_parse+ 6,;
      AT("]",SUBSTR(m.p_msgopts,m.l_parse+ 6))-1))

    ** .WAV file
    m.l_parse=ATC("WAV=[",m.p_msgopts)
    m.l_wav=IIF(m.l_parse=0,"",SUBSTR(m.p_msgopts,m.l_parse+ 5,;
      AT("]",SUBSTR(m.p_msgopts,m.l_parse+ 5))-1))

    ** .BMP file
    m.l_parse=ATC("BMP=[",m.p_msgopts)
    m.l_bmp=IIF(m.l_parse=0,"",SUBSTR(m.p_msgopts,m.l_parse+ 5,;
      AT("]",SUBSTR(m.p_msgopts,m.l_parse+ 5))-1))
    m.l_bmpwide=IIF(EMPTY(m.l_bmp) OR NOT FILE(m.l_bmp),0,10)

    ** How wide are the buttons
    m.l_buttwide=0
    IF ".BMP"$m.l_butt && picture buttons
      m.l_buttwide=(OCCURS(";",m.l_butt)+1)*11
    ELSE TEXT buttons
      l_start=1
      FOR l_xx=1 TO OCCURS(";",m.l_butt)+1
        l_end=AT(";",m.l_butt+";",l_xx)
        l_len=l_end-l_start
        m.l_thisbutt=STRTRAN(SUBSTR(m.l_butt,l_start,l_len),"\!","")
        m.l_thisbutt=STRTRAN(m.l_thisbutt,"\?","")
        m.l_thisbutt=STRTRAN(m.l_thisbutt,"\<","")
        m.l_buttwide=m.l_buttwide+MAX(TXTWIDTH(m.l_thisbutt,;
          "System",10,""),10)+1
        l_start=l_end+1
      ENDFOR all buttons
    ENDIF picture buttons

    ** Look for window width parameter
    m.l_parse=ATC("WCOL=[",m.p_msgopts)
    m.l_wcol=IIF(m.l_parse=0,50,VAL(SUBSTR(m.p_msgopts,m.l_parse+ 6)))
    ** Minimum width is 15, Maximum is width of screen
    m.l_wcol=MIN(SCOLS(),MAX(m.l_wcol,15))
    ** Factor in width of buttons
    m.l_wcol=MAX(m.l_buttwide+2,m.l_wcol)

    ** Determine number of word wrapped lines rows for the message,
    ** and fill the a_msgarr array with those lines.
    DIMENSION a_msgarr(1)
```

```
m.l_memlines=l3wrap("msg=["+m.l_msg+"]cols=["+;
  STR((m.l_wcol-2.5),10,2)+;
  "]font=[System,10]styl=[]arra=[a_msgarr]")

** Look for window height parameter
m.l_parse=ATC("WROW=[",m.p_msgopts)
m.l_wrow=IIF(m.l_parse=0,MIN(SROW()-2,m.l_memlines+4.5),;
  VAL(SUBSTR(m.p_msgopts,m.l_parse+ 6)))
** Minimum number of rows is 7, Max is size of screen
m.l_wrow=MIN(SROWS(),MAX(7,m.l_wrow))

** Starting row for window
m.l_parse=ATC("WLRO=[",m.p_msgopts)
m.l_wlro=IIF(m.l_parse=0,-1,VAL(SUBSTR(m.p_msgopts,m.l_parse+ 6)))

** Starting column for window
m.l_parse=ATC("WLCO=[",m.p_msgopts)
m.l_wlco=IIF(m.l_parse=0,-1,VAL(SUBSTR(m.p_msgopts,m.l_parse+ 6)))

** Title
l_titl=ATC("TITL=[",p_msgopts)
l_titl=IIF(l_titl=0,"",SUBSTR(p_msgopts,l_titl+6,AT("]",;
  SUBSTR(p_msgopts,l_titl+6))-1))

** Color for the window
m.l_parse=ATC("COLO=[",m.p_msgopts)
m.l_colo=IIF(m.l_parse=0,7,SUBSTR(m.p_msgopts,m.l_parse+ 6,;
  AT("]",SUBSTR(m.p_msgopts,m.l_parse+ 6))-1))

** Color
IF TYPE('l_colo')="N"
  l_colo="SCHEME "+STR(IIF(BETWEEN(l_colo,1,24),l_colo,7))
ENDIF  use scheme
l_winopts="COLOR "+l_colo

** Wall paper
IF NOT EMPTY(l_wall)
  l_winopts=l_winopts+" FILL FILE ["+l_wall+"]"
ENDIF

** Define window
DEFINE WINDOW l3msg AT l_wlro,l_wlco ;
  SIZE l_wrow,l_wcol+m.l_bmpwide ;
```

continues

```
      TITLE l_titl FLOAT SHADOW FONT "System",10 SYSTEM ;
      &l_winopts.

 IF l_wlco=-1 OR l_wlro=-1
   MOVE WINDOW l3msg CENTER
   IF l_wlco>0
     MOVE WINDOW l3msg TO WLRO('l3msg'),m.l_wlco
   ENDIF passed us only a column to use
   IF l_wlro>0
     MOVE WINDOW l3msg TO m.l_wlro,WLCO("l3msg")
   ENDIF passed us only a row to use
 ENDIF center the window

 ** Determine number of times to ring bell
 m.l_parse=ATC("BELL=[",m.p_msgopts)
 m.l_bell=IIF(m.l_parse=0,1,VAL(SUBSTR(m.p_msgopts,m.l_parse+ 6)))

 ** Determine timeout clause
 m.l_parse=ATC("TIME=[",m.p_msgopts)
 m.l_time=IIF(m.l_parse=0,0,VAL(SUBSTR(m.p_msgopts,m.l_parse+ 6)))

 ** Activate the window
 ACTIVATE WINDOW (m.l_msgwin)

 ** Find the "starting" button
 IF "\!"$m.l_butt                            && default value
   m.l_start=OCCURS(CHR(59),LEFT(m.l_butt,AT("\!",m.l_butt)))+1
 ELSE
   m.l_start=1
 ENDIF has a default value
 m.l_retopt=""

 ** Get justification for the message
 DO CASE
   CASE "JUST=[C]"$UPPER(m.p_msgopts)
     m.l_just="I"
   CASE "JUST=[L]"$UPPER(m.p_msgopts)
     m.l_just=""
   CASE "JUST=[R]"$UPPER(m.p_msgopts)
     m.l_just="J"
   OTHERWISE
     IF l_memlines>1 or not empty(m.l_bmp)
       m.l_just=""
```

```
      ELSE
        m.l_just="I"
      ENDIF
ENDCASE


l_offset=-0.5
** Display the bitmap if requested
IF NOT EMPTY(m.l_bmp) AND FILE(m.l_bmp)
  @ 0.5,0.5 SAY (m.l_bmp) BITMAP SIZE 3.5,9 STRETCH
  ** Center message relative to bitmap if less than
  ** four lines in the message.
 IF l_memlines<4
   l_offset=(3.5-l_memlines)/2-.5
 ENDIF fewer
ENDIF bitmap was requested, and it exists


** Display the message
IF m.l_memlines<=l_wrow-4
  ** Enough room for the entire message to fit in the window.
  FOR l_xx=1 TO m.l_memlines
    @ l_xx+l_offset,m.l_bmpwide SAY a_msgarr(l_xx) ;
       SIZE 1,l_wcol-2 PICTURE ;
       "@"+m.l_just STYLE "O"
  ENDFOR
ELSE
  ** Insufficient window space for the message, so provide a
  ** scrollable edit region.
  @ 0.5,1+m.l_bmpwide EDIT m.l_msg ;
    SIZE m.l_wrow-2.5,m.l_wcol-2 SCROLL NOMODIFY
ENDIF message fits in the window


** Put the buttons in the dialog.
m.l_retopt=""
l_buttcol=(WCOLS()-l_buttwide)/2
@ l_wrow-1.6,l_buttcol GET m.l_retopt PICTURE "@*H"+;
  IIF(".BMP"$UPPER(m.l_butt),"B","")+" "+m.l_butt ;
  SIZE 1.5,10,1


** Setup for the .WAV file if requested
IF NOT EMPTY(m.l_wav) AND FILE(m.l_wav)
  SET BELL TO (m.l_wav),7
ENDIF wav file requested, and exists
```

continues

457

```
** Ring the bell the requested number of times
FOR m.l_xx=1 TO m.l_bell
  ?? CHR(7)
ENDFOR

** Modal read
READ CYCLE TIMEOUT (l_time) MODAL OBJECT (m.l_start)

** Reset environment
SET BELL TO
RELEASE WINDOW (m.l_msgwin)
IF m.l_oldtalk#"OFF"
  SET TALK ON
ENDIF
IF m.l_oldexact#"OFF"
  SET EXACT ON
ENDIF

POP KEY
RETURN m.l_retopt
```

Parsing Multiple Options from a Single Character String

Every option in a parameter string consists of up to four characters, an equal sign, a left bracket, a value, and a right bracket. For example, `"butt=[Yes;No]"` contains the button option. Our approach for parsing begins by placing the starting position of our string in a variable called `l_parse` as follows:

```
m.l_parse=ATC("BUTT=[",m.p_msgopts)
```

Once we know where the string starts, we can obtain the value associated with the option as follows:

```
m.l_butt=SUBSTR(m.p_msgopts,m.l_parse+ 6,;
  AT("]",SUBSTR(m.p_msgopts,m.l_parse+ 6))-1)
```

However, this only works if the `"butt=["` option exists in the p_msgopts variable. To guard against the possibility that no button options were passed and to provide a default button setting, we use the `IIF()` function as follows:

```
m.l_butt=IIF(m.l_parse=0,"\!\?\<Ok",;
  SUBSTR(m.p_msgopts,m.l_parse+ 6,;
  AT("]",SUBSTR(m.p_msgopts,m.l_parse+ 6))-1))
```

Similar algorithms are available for logical, numeric, and date values to be parsed from a string. I wrote two of these parsing expressions before I decided to automate the parsing of options from a string.

The first, obvious, option was to create a library routine to do the job. However, I was already worried about the performance impact of parsing options, so I wanted to avoid the additional overhead of calling a UDF.

Instead, I wrote L3PARSE. As you can see in Figure 19.2, L3PARSE is a simple dialog that automates the writing of parse expressions. (The source code for L3PARSE.PRG is included on the source code disk.) Here is the code that was pasted into the L3MSGW.PRG as a result of the dialog in Figure 19.2:

```
m.l_parse=ATC("NEWPARM=[",m.p_msgopts)
m.l_newparm=IIF(m.l_parse=0,"Default value",;
  SUBSTR(m.p_msgopts,m.l_parse+ 9,AT("]",;
  SUBSTR(m.p_msgopts,m.l_parse+ 9))-1))
```

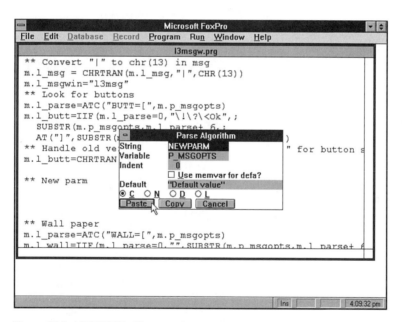

Figure 19.2. L3PARSE facilitates option parsing.

The Value of Default Values

Notice that L3PARSE and all the code it generates provides for default values—in case the option in question was not passed to the library routine. By providing defaults for all the nonessential options of a library routine, we reduce programmer effort and give the library routine a default behavior.

Only when the programmer has to change this default behavior will she or he have to pass an option to the library routine. For example, we almost always want to center messages. So, if no row and column information is passed to L3MSGW, it automatically centers the window.

Word Wrapping with Proportional Fonts

Windows generated by L3MSGW should be large enough to display the entire message, if possible. In order to do that, however, we have to know how many rows the message will consume.

In the DOS product, or whenever we use an unproportional font, we can rely on FoxPro's MEMLINES() function to determine how many word-wrapped lines are contained in a character string. Unfortunately, this method does not work for proportional fonts.

MEMLINES() works by attempting to wrap some number of characters in the number of columns specified by the last SET MEMOWIDTH TO command. MEMLINES() assumes that each character consumes exactly one column.

As you know, characters in a proportional font are of varying widths. As a result, we need to create a replacement for MEMLINES() that can determine how many word-wrapped lines a character string consumed in an unproportional font.

Our L3WRAP.PRG has to work for any type font, size, or style, in a specified number of columns. L3WRAP has to return the number of rows required to display the message in the specified number of columns. In addition, because L3MSGW has to display the content of the word-wrapped message one line at a time, L3WRAP has to optionally store each row of the message in an array. Here is the code for L3WRAP.PRG:

```
* l3wrap.prg
* Wraps words in proportional or unproportional fonts
* p_opts is a string containing one or more of the following:
*   FONT=[FoxFont,7] Font name and size, defaults to current window
*                    settings.
*   STYL=[BI] Style Defaults to current window settings
*   msg=[This is my message] Message to wrap
```

```
*  cols=[20] Number of columns in which to wrap.
*  arra=[myarray] Array to hold output
PARAMETERS p_opts
PRIVATE l_xx,a_3wrap,l_font1,l_font2,l_font,l_parse,l_styl,l_msg,;
  l_arra,l_cols

** Look for the font
m.l_parse=ATC("FONT=[",m.p_opts)
m.l_font=IIF(m.l_parse=0,"",SUBSTR(m.p_opts,m.l_parse+ 6,;
  AT("]",SUBSTR(m.p_opts,m.l_parse+ 6))-1))
** Look for the style
m.l_parse=ATC("STYL=[",m.p_opts)
m.l_styl=IIF(m.l_parse=0,WFONT(3),SUBSTR(m.p_opts,m.l_parse+ 6,;
  AT("]",SUBSTR(m.p_opts,m.l_parse+ 6))-1))
** Look for the message
m.l_parse=ATC("MSG=[",m.p_opts)
m.l_msg=IIF(m.l_parse=0,"",SUBSTR(m.p_opts,m.l_parse+ 5,AT("]",;
  SUBSTR(m.p_opts,m.l_parse+ 5))-1))
** Look for the number of columns
m.l_parse=ATC("COLS=[",m.p_opts)
m.l_cols=IIF(m.l_parse=0,WCOLS(),;
  VAL(SUBSTR(m.p_opts,m.l_parse+ 6)))
** Look for the array
m.l_parse=ATC("ARRA=[",m.p_opts)
m.l_arra=IIF(m.l_parse=0,"",SUBSTR(m.p_opts,m.l_parse+ 6,AT("]",;
  SUBSTR(m.p_opts,m.l_parse+ 6))-1))
IF EMPTY(l_msg)
  RETURN 0
ENDIF Nothing to wrap

** Get the font size
IF NOT EMPTY(l_font)
  l_font1=LEFT(l_font,AT(",",l_font+",")-1)
  IF ","$l_font
    l_font2=VAL(SUBSTR(l_font,AT(",",l_font)+1))
  ELSE
    l_font2=WFONT(2)
  ENDIF no size sent
ELSE
  l_font1=WFONT(1)
  l_font2=WFONT(2)
ENDIF sent us a specific font to work with
```

continues

461

```
l_needarra=NOT EMPTY(l_arra)
IF l_needarra
  DIMENSION a_3wrap(LEN(l_msg))
ENDIF need to fill an array with wrapped lines
l_wrapline=1
** Convert CRLFs and CRs to chr(254) for easier debugging
l_msg=STRTRAN(l_msg,CHR(13)+CHR(10),CHR(254))
l_msg=CHRTRAN(l_msg,CHR(13),CHR(254))
DO WHILE LEN(l_msg)>0
  ** get next paragraph
  l_para=LEFT(l_msg,AT(CHR(254),l_msg+CHR(254))-1)
  ** shorten l_msg appropriately
  l_msg=SUBSTR(l_msg,LEN(l_para)+2)
  IF LEN(l_para)=0
    l_para=" "
  ENDIF consecutive CRs
  ** Word wrap the paragraph
  DO WHILE LEN(l_para)>0
    ** start at the column marker
    l_spot=l_cols
    ** Find the point at which we are too wide
    l_txtwidth=TXTWIDTH(LEFT(l_para,l_spot),l_font1,l_font2,l_styl)
    DO WHILE l_txtwidth<l_cols AND ;
        l_spot<=LEN(l_para)
      l_spot=l_spot+1
      l_txtwidth=TXTWIDTH(LEFT(l_para,l_spot),,;
        l_font1,l_font2,l_styl)
    ENDDO
    ** Now, look for a place to word wrap
    l_line=LEFT(l_para,l_spot)
    IF l_txtwidth>l_cols AND " "$l_line
      ** look for break points
      l_xx=1
      l_bpoints=OCCURS(" ",l_line)
      l_line=LEFT(l_line,RAT(" ",l_line,l_xx)-1)
      DO WHILE TXTWIDTH(l_line,l_font1,l_font2,l_styl)>l_cols AND ;
          l_xx<l_bpoints-1
        l_xx=l_xx+1
        l_line=LEFT(l_line,RAT(" ",l_line))
      ENDDO check break points for a place to wrap the line
    ENDIF there are breakpoints to use
    IF TXTWIDTH(l_line,l_font1,l_font2,l_styl)>l_cols
```

```
      ** there is no breakpoint up to the column width,
      ** so just backup until we find a string that will fit
      l_spot=LEN(l_line)-1
      DO WHILE TXTWIDTH(LEFT(l_line,l_spot),l_font1,l_font2,;
          l_styl)>=l_cols AND l_spot<=LEN(l_para)
        l_spot=l_spot-1
      ENDDO
      l_line=LEFT(l_line,l_spot)
      ** shorten l_para appropriately
      l_para=SUBSTR(l_para,LEN(l_line)+1)
    ELSE && able to use a break point to wrap the line
      ** shorten l_para appropriately
      l_para=SUBSTR(l_para,LEN(l_line)+2)
    ENDIF there is no break point
    IF l_needarra
      ** Load the wrapped line into the array
      a_3wrap(l_wrapline)=l_line
    ENDIF need an array
    l_wrapline=l_wrapline+1
  ENDDO wrap this paragraph
ENDDO get all paragraphs
IF l_needarra
  ** put work array into calling program's designated array
  DIMENSION a_3wrap(l_wrapline-1)
  =ACOPY(a_3wrap,(l_arra))
ENDIF
RETURN l_wrapline-1
```

Exploring *l3nextid* and Passing Procedures to Procedures

In Chapter 13, "Multiuser Discussions," I promised to show you the l3nextid UDF. I try my best to keep my promises, so we'll take a few pages here to explore l3nextid.

As you recall, l3nextid obtains the next available ID number for a table from a system table. This is accomplished by first finding the system record associated with the target table. Then, after locking the system record, l3nextid increments the next available ID number and returns the next ID to the calling program.

Many times, the calling program then attempts to add the new record to the target table. Unfortunately, if that attempt fails, the system record has already been updated, and there is a "hole" in the consecutive numbering of records.

We would like the l3nextid UDF to add our record(s) for us. However, because there are so many different ways to add records, and because we might want to add records to many different tables, and because success depends on a variety of conditions, it is not possible to create parameter options that handle every conceivable new record request.

Of course, we can write a custom procedure that can accomplish the adding of records for a specific situation. The trick is to get l3nextid to run our custom procedure while it has the system record locked.

Our first step is to pass the name of our custom procedure to l3nextid as an option in a parameter string. Next, l3nextid uses the EVAL() function to evaluate our procedure. If our procedure returns .T., signifying that we successfully added all our records, l3nextid increments the system record's next available ID field. If the UDF returns .F., l3nextid does not increment the system record's next available ID field.

Here is a simple implementation of l3nextid:

```
PROCEDURE addone
IF l3nextid("sysd=[tssyst]syst=[sy_tag]sysn=[sy_number]"+;
    "id=[tsclient]udf=[addone2]")
  DO l3msgw WITH "Added new client"
ELSE
  DO l3msgw WITH "Failed to add new client"
ENDIF


PROCEDURE addone2
PARAMETERS p_num
m.cl_clid=STR(p_num,FSIZE("cl_clid","tsclient"))
RETURN l3insert("alia=[tsclient]")
```

Although the l3nextid UDF is very useful in developing applications that use sequentially assigned IDs, the real value of l3nextid in this discussion is how it passes procedures to procedures. In essence, this simple technique enables us to "embed" procedures in other procedures. The actual code involved in accomplishing this trick is trivial—look for it in bold face in the following listing of L3NEXTID.PRG.

```
* l3nextid.prg
* returns the next available id for this system tag

* p_idopts = a character string with the following options:
* sysd=[exsyst] system database
* syst=[sy_tag] system database tag to use for lookup
* sysn=[sy_number] field with next system number in it
*   id=[CHECK] id to lookup in the system database
```

```
*   qty=[1] Qty to increment the value. Defaults to 1.
* retr=[100] Number of times to retry in case the system rec is
*           locked.
* time=[.1] Time to wait between attempts to access locked system
*           record.
*   msg=[Waiting for next check...] Message to be displayed while
*                                   waiting for a lock on the
*                                   system rec.
*   udf=[myudf] Name of a UDF to be evaluated after the
*       system record is updated, but before the system
*       record is unlocked. The next id will be passed as
*       a numeric value to the UDF. The UDF must return
*       .T. to accept the update, or .F. to reverse the
*       increment.
* nocl=[] If l3nextid opens the system database,
*       don't close it when l3nextid() exits.


PARAMETERS p_idopts
PRIVATE ALL LIKE l_*
m.l_idopts=IIF(TYPE('m.idopts')="C",m.idopts,"")
m.l_parse=ATC("SYSD=[",m.l_idopts)
m.l_sysd=IIF(m.l_parse=0,ksysdbf,SUBSTR(m.l_idopts,m.l_parse+ 6,;
  AT("]",SUBSTR(m.l_idopts,m.l_parse+ 6))-1))


m.l_oldsele=SELE()
m.l_thisnext=0
IF NOT USED(m.l_sysd) AND NOT FILE(m.l_sysd+".dbf")
  m.l_thisnext= -1
ELSE
  m.l_wassys=.T.
  IF !USED(m.l_sysd)
    m.l_wassys=.F.
    m.l_newspot=SELE(1)
    USE (m.l_sysd) IN SELE(1) AGAIN
  ENDIF  system file not open
  * Now that we know we are going to need them, get the
  * rest of the parms
  * get an order to use
  m.l_parse=ATC("SYST=[",m.l_idopts)
  m.l_syst=IIF(m.l_parse=0,ORDER(l_sysd),SUBSTR(m.l_idopts,;
    m.l_parse+ 6,AT("]",SUBSTR(m.l_idopts,m.l_parse+ 6))-1))
  * get a field to use
  m.l_parse=ATC("SYSN=[",m.l_idopts)
```

continues

```
        IF m.l_parse>0
          m.l_sysn=SUBSTR(m.l_idopts,m.l_parse+ 6,AT("]",;
            SUBSTR(m.l_idopts,m.l_parse+ 6))-1)
        ELSE
          SELECT (m.l_sysd)
          l_fldq=AFIELD(l_sysnarr)
          FOR l_xx=1 TO l_fldq
            IF l_sysnarr(l_xx,2)="N"
              EXIT
            ENDIF
          ENDFOR
          l_sysn=IIF(l_xx<=l_fldq,l_sysnarr(l_xx,1),"")
          SELECT (m.l_oldsele)
        ENDIF no system number to use
        IF EMPTY(m.l_sysn)
          m.l_thisnext=-2
        ELSE
          * figure out what to look for
          m.l_parse=ATC("ID=[",m.l_idopts)
          m.l_id=IIF(m.l_parse=0,ALIAS(),;
              SUBSTR(m.l_idopts,m.l_parse+ 4,;
            AT("]",SUBSTR(m.l_idopts,m.l_parse+ 4))-1))
          IF !ORDER(m.l_sysd)==UPPER(m.l_syst)
            SET ORDER TO (m.l_syst) IN (m.l_sysd)
          ENDIF wrong or no order set in m.l_sysd

          IF !SEEK(m.l_id,m.l_sysd)
            m.l_thisnext=-3
          ELSE
            * check on locking info
            m.l_parse=ATC("RETR=[",m.l_idopts)
            m.l_retr=IIF(m.l_parse=0,10,VAL(SUBSTR(m.l_idopts,;
              m.l_parse+ 6)))
            m.l_parse=ATC("TIME=[",m.l_idopts)
            m.l_time=IIF(m.l_parse=0,.5,VAL(SUBSTR(m.l_idopts,;
              m.l_parse+ 6)))
            m.l_parse=ATC("MSG=[",m.l_idopts)
            m.l_msg=IIF(m.l_parse=0,"Waiting for next id...",;
              SUBSTR(m.l_idopts,m.l_parse+ 5,AT("]",;
              SUBSTR(m.l_idopts,m.l_parse+ 5))-1))

            IF NOT (RLOCK(m.l_sysd).or.l3rlock("msg=["+m.l_msg+;
               "]retr=["+ALLTRIM(STR(m.l_retr))+"]"))
```

```
          m.l_thisnext=-4
        ELSE
          * how many do we want to add?
          m.l_parse=ATC("QTY=[",m.l_idopts)
          m.l_qty=IIF(m.l_parse=0,1,;
             VAL(SUBSTR(m.l_idopts,m.l_parse+ 5)))
          SELECT (m.l_sysd)
          m.l_thisnext=EVAL(l_sysn)          && get next number
          REPLACE (l_sysn) WITH m.l_thisnext+l_qty
          * see if she sent me a udf to add the target record
          m.l_parse=ATC("UDF=[",m.l_idopts)
          m.l_udf=IIF(m.l_parse=0,"",;
             SUBSTR(m.l_idopts,m.l_parse+ 5,;
            AT("]",SUBSTR(m.l_idopts,m.l_parse+ 5))-1))
          IF NOT EMPTY(m.l_udf)
            IF NOT EVAL(m.l_udf+"("+STR(m.l_thisnext)+")")
              SELECT (m.l_sysd)
              REPLACE (l_sysn) WITH m.l_thisnext-l_qty
            ENDIF his udf returned .f., so back out the update
          ENDIF wants to do a udf
          UNLOCK IN (m.l_sysd)               && unlock system record
          SELECT (m.l_oldsele)
        ENDIF able to lock, update, and unlock tag record
      ENDIF no system record for this add
    ENDIF missing system number field
    * see if they will let us close the system database
    m.l_nocl="NOCL=[]"$UPPER(l_idopts)
    IF NOT m.l_wassys AND NOT m.l_nocl
      USE IN (m.l_sysd)
    ENDIF
    SELECT (m.l_oldsele)
  ENDIF missing system file
  RETURN m.l_thisnext
  *: EOF: l3nextid.PRG
```

Final Thoughts

When I originally designed this chapter, it included 50-75 pages. However, as I wrote Chapter 13, "Multiuser Discussions," I found myself including more and more of the routines that I had intended to discuss in this chapter. So, if you haven't already read Chapter 13, I suggest you give it a look.

There are languages that cannot be used without extensive lists of library routines. C and Clipper are good examples of these types of languages. FoxPro, on the other hand, is not a library-dependent language. It has a robust, high-level programming language that is augmented by power tools. As a result, FoxPro programmers can spend less time developing or learning libraries, and more time developing applications.

For those times when you do need a library routine however, I hope this chapter has provided useful tools for the creation of those library routines. In addition, I hope you find the existing L3*.PRG library routines to be of value.

CHAPTER 20

A Data Dictionary

When I first plotted this chapter, I envisioned a thorough review of every module in the L3DICT data dictionary program. However, a cursory review of that system revealed some 1,500 lines of code, and I started plotting a new course!

Instead of painstakingly exploring each and every line of code in the entire data dictionary program, I decided that I would show you how to use L3DICT.APP. Along the way, I stop to discuss the most important programming concepts behind the creation of a data dictionary.

 Note: Don't worry, the entire L3DICT.APP is on the source code disk. In the rest of this chapter, you can find a variety of tips to help you utilize L3DICT or to help you create your own data dictionary programs.

When you finish this chapter, I hope you discover:

- Several new Browse window techniques.
- The most important considerations in the creation of a passive data dictionary.
- Several tricks for integrating your programs into the native FoxPro environment.
- How to use the L3DICT data dictionary to increase your personal productivity.

Active, Passive, and Supportive Data Dictionaries

An *active data dictionary* is referenced by your application at runtime to validate data, create views, handle cascading deletes, and generally control the maintenance of data. Many database products include such a data dictionary as an integral part of their design. FoxPro is *not* one of these databases.

A *passive data dictionary* is simply a repository for .DBF, field, and tag definitions. It is not used at runtime, and is most useful as a developer's reference.

A *supportive data dictionary* can be used during the generation of screens and reports to provide formatting and validation rules. It can be used also at runtime to rebuild indexes, or to provide descriptive information to the user. It is not however, responsible for validating or maintaining data.

The L3DICT data dictionary that we are about to discuss is a passive data dictionary. Its only function in life is as a developer's reference. Although we occasionally use L3DICT to support the re-creation of indexes, and the generation of user-friendly query builders, the primary purpose of L3DICT is to assist one or more developers in the creation of applications.

Goals

Like most developers, I have used a variety of data dictionaries over the years to keep track of table names, field names, field attributes, index tag names, index tag expressions, and descriptions of all the aforementioned.

Several years ago, I used FoxPro 1.02 to create a data dictionary program that is still in use at Mobil Oil, Georgia Pacific, and several other Micro Endeavors clients around the world. That data dictionary was called L2DICT, and it used three databases to store information for tables, fields, and tags, respectively.

L2DICT was extremely valuable in team programming efforts in which multiple programmers needed constant access to the latest data design of their joint application. However, because of its three table design, I was never able to create an interface that was smooth enough for my taste.

So, I began work on L3DICT. I wanted to keep all the best parts of the previous data dictionaries, but I also wanted to make the data dictionary easier to use. In fact, I wanted a data dictionary that would:

- Remain on the desktop at all times, being instantly available to the developer, especially during the writing of programs, creation of screens, and creation of reports.

- Read existing database structures.

- Write databases to any location using structures defined in L3DICT.

- Support multiple data dictionary files so each application can have its own data dictionary, and so each developer can have her own data dictionary.

- Re-create index tags.

- Print a report of the data dictionary.

- Allow the programmer to quickly move from .DBF to .DBF.

- Allow the programmer to see fields from multiple .DBFs simultaneously.

- Allow the programmer to copy fields and database structures.

- Be distributable in a single .APP file.

- Allow the programmer to easily cut and paste data dictionary information into programs, screens, reports, queries, and menus.

Data Structure

One of the first requirements for L3DICT was that it remain on the desktop at all times. Another requirement was that L3DICT had to simultaneously display fields from multiple databases.

In order to minimize L3DICT's impact on available work areas and file handles, and to facilitate viewing of all fields in the application simultaneously, I decided to put all of the information about .DBFs, fields, and tags into one database. Here is the structure for that database:

```
Structure for table:    c:\book\dbf\tsdict.dbf
Number of data records: 198
Date of last update:    03/05/93
Memo file block size:   64
Field   Field Name   Type        Width   Dec   Index
    1   DD_DBF       Character       8
    2   DD_RECTYPE   Character       1           Asc
    3   DD_NAME      Character      10           Asc
    4   DD_DESC      Character     254
    5   DD_NOTES     Memo           10
    6   DD_KEY       Character     221
    7   DD_TYPE      Character       1
    8   DD_LEN       Numeric         3
    9   DD_DEC       Numeric         2
   10   DD_FOR       Character     221
   11   DD_UNIQUE    Logical         1
** Total **                        733
```

Here are the tags for the data dictionary file:

```
Select area:225, Table in Use: C:\BOOK\DBF\TSDICT.DBF
  Alias: DATADICT
Structural CDX file:   C:\BOOK\DBF\TSDICT.CDX
Master Index tag:    DD       Key: UPPER(DD_DBF+DD_RECTYPE+DD_NAME)
       Index tag:    DD_NAME Key: DD_NAME
       Index tag:    DD_RECTYPE  Key: DD_RECTYPE
       Memo file:    C:\BOOK\DBF\TSDICT.FPT
```

You can probably guess what the various fields contain based on their names. However, it is much better to be able to see a full description of each of the fields and tags, before writing programs to work with this or any other database. As you can see in Figure 20.1, L3DICT provides this information in a Browse window.

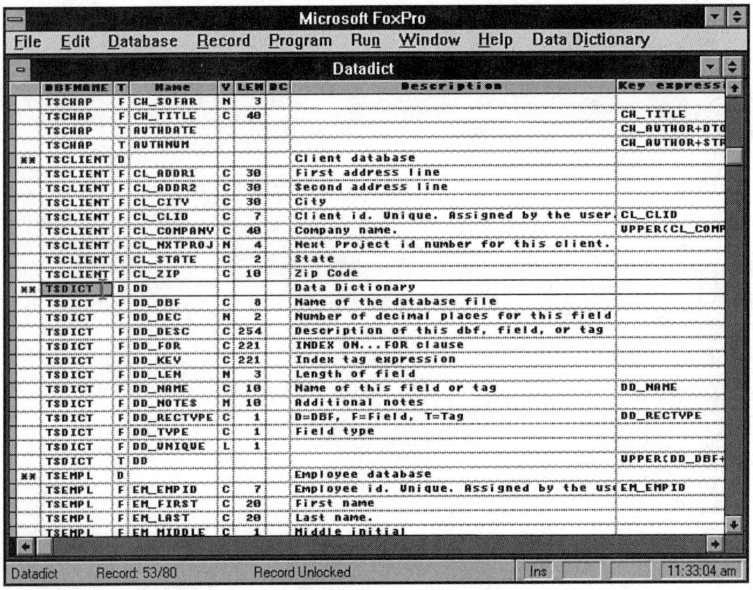

Figure 20.1. The L3DICT data dictionary Browse window.

Notice that the underlying .DBF for the DATADICT alias is TSDICT.DBF. When you DO L3DICT, the application prompts you to create a new data dictionary or use an existing data dictionary. In this way, you can maintain a separate data dictionary for each project.

Keeping the Data Dictionary Active

To keep the data dictionary active at all times, I need a Browse window.

To provide the programmer with a view of all fields in the data dictionary simultaneously, I need a Browse window.

To be able to minimize the data dictionary when desktop real estate becomes precious, I need a Browse window.

In short, I need a Browse window. Here is the code for the Browse window:

```
PROCEDURE l3dictbr
SELECT datadict
IF NOT WEXIST("datadict")
  DO CASE
    CASE _dos
      DEFINE WINDOW datadict01 FROM 1,0 TO SROWS()-2,SCOLS() ;
        FLOAT GROW ZOOM CLOSE MINIMIZE
    CASE _windows
      DEFINE WINDOW datadict01 FROM 0,0 TO SROWS()-2,SCOLS() ;
        FLOAT GROW ZOOM CLOSE MINIMIZE FONT "foxfont",7
  ENDCASE
  BROWSE FIELDS t1=IIF(dd_rectype="D","**",""):2:H="",;
    dd_dbf:p="@!":H="DBFNAME":8,;
    dd_rectype:H='T':1:p="!":v=dd_rectype$"DFIR",;
    dd_name:H="Name":10:p="@!",;
    dd_type:H="Y":1:v=dd_type$"CNFDLMG":p="!";
    :E="Valid types are C,N,F,D,L,M,G":F:W=dd_rectype="F",;
    dd_len:H="LEN":3:p="@KZ",;
    dd_dec:H="DC":2:p="@KZ",;
    dd_desc:H="Description":50,;
    dd_key:H="Key expression":35,;
    dd_for:H="Index For expression":25:W=dd_rectype$"FI" ;
    AND NOT EMPTY(dd_key) ;
    WINDOW datadict01 NOMENU NOAPPEND NODELETE ;
    TITLE "Datadict" NOWAIT ;
    FOR NOT DELETED()
  RELEASE WINDOW datadict01
ELSE
  ZOOM WINDOW datadict NORM
  ACTIVATE WINDOW datadict TOP
ENDIF
RETURN .T.
```

Note: Procedure l3dictbr provides for both DOS and Windows versions of the data dictionary by using FoxPro's _DOS and _WINDOWS system variables to create different windows for each environment.

The power of this procedure lies not in any wizardry on my part, but in the elegance of the BROWSE NOWAIT command. Once the BROWSE NOWAIT is issued, the resultant Browse window stays on the desktop until it is specifically closed. The programmer can modify a screen, modify a program, modify a report, issue commands in the Command window, or even run the application, all while the DATADICT Browse window remains on the screen. Figure 20.2 illustrates a sample development environment using the DATADICT Browse window.

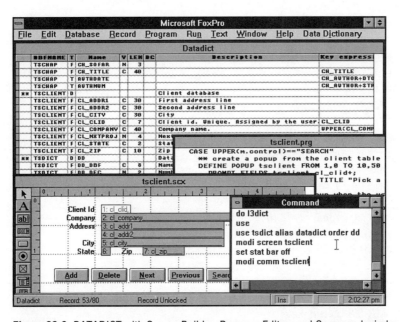

Figure 20.2. DATADICT with Screen Builder, Program Editor, and Command window.

In other words, by using a BROWSE NOWAIT to present the data dictionary to the programmer, we allow the programmer to work in the native FoxPro environment, with all the tools that environment can provide. If we had chosen to implement a data dictionary that ran as a screen set, or as a popup, or as any kind of dialog, the programmer would have to constantly enter and exit the data dictionary system to access table, field, and tag information.

When we have implemented data dictionaries that require the programmer to interrupt development to DO the data dictionary program, we have watched programmers stop using the data dictionary.

In these cases, the programmer might turn to printed data dictionary listings or the programmer might eschew the data dictionary altogether, because the data dictionary is intrusive. The last thing you want to do when you're in a groove writing a complicated data entry screen is stop, find the data dictionary option on a menu, pick the data dictionary file, wait three seconds while the screen is drawn, and then respond to five dialogs to get the information you need.

L3DICT's BROWSE NOWAIT approach avoids the intrusion problems posed by other solutions by providing constant access to the DATADICT Browse window. Therefore, when you use L3DICT, or when you write your own data dictionary application, you want to investigate the use of BROWSE NOWAIT to add tools to your programming environment.

Triggering Data Dictionary Activities

It's one thing to be able to see the data dictionary for your application, but it's another to be able to do something with that data dictionary. Because I decided that a READ CYCLE session is inferior to a BROWSE NOWAIT window, I needed to find a place to identify options for the data dictionary Browse window.

The best place for Browse window options is in a menu popup on the system menu. These options are always available, even when using the screen builder, the Menu Builder, the Report Writer, the program editor, or the Command window. However, there are a few challenges involved, including the following:

- Some menu options should be available only if the programmer is in the data dictionary Browse window.

- Some options should be available only if the data dictionary is open.

- All options must call programs that reside within a single .APP file.

- Hot keys on the data dictionary menu should not interfere with existing hot keys.

- Activities must save any pending Browse window changes before processing.

Figure 20.3 shows the state of the data dictionary menu when a window other than DATADICT is on top of the desktop.

Note: FoxPro does not consider the Command window when determining which window is currently on top of the desktop. Therefore, when the Command window is on top of the desktop, and DATADICT was on the desktop prior to the Command window, the data dictionary menu acts as if DATADICT is still on top of the desktop.

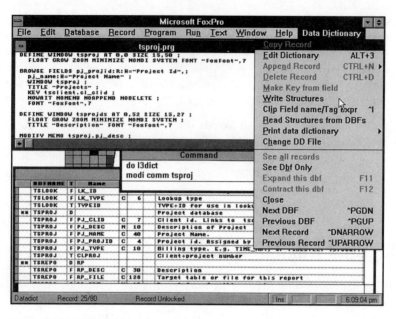

Figure 20.3. Data dictionary menu.

Enabling and disabling a menu prompt is accomplished through the Skip For dialog of the Menu Builder. For example, the Delete Record option should only be available if the programmer is in the DATADICT window. Here is the DEFINE BAR command generated from the L3DICT.MNX:

```
DEFINE BAR 4 OF datadictio PROMPT "\<Delete Record" ;
    KEY CTRL+D, "CTRL+D" ;
    SKIP FOR (not used('datadict')) or not wontop('datadict')
```

On the other hand, the Edit Dictionary option should be available if the DATADICT database is open. Here is the DEFINE BAR command for the Edit Dictionary bar:

```
DEFINE BAR 2 OF datadictio PROMPT "\<Edit Dictionary" ;
    KEY ALT+3, "ALT+3" ;
    SKIP FOR (not used('datadict'))
```

Executing Data Dictionary Activities

We expect to see a command like the following associated with each of the bars on the data dictionary popup:

```
ON SELECTION BAR 8 OF datadictio do l3dictrd   && Read dbfs
```

However, one of the goals for L3DICT was to store the entire application in one .APP file. In other words, I wanted the L3DICT application to run with just the L3DICT.APP file, and one or more data dictionary databases of the programmer's creation.

Building an .APP file from the L3DICT project was not a problem. However, this meant that L3DICTRD.PRG, and all the other programs associated with the data dictionary, were stored in a single .APP file. As a result, when the user selected the eighth bar of the DATADICTIO popup, FoxPro could not find the L3DICTRD.PRG program!

The solution to this dilemma comes in two parts. First, all programs that are called from the menu must be made into procedures and stored in the L3DICT.PRG program—the main program for the L3DICT PROJECT.

Second, all ON SELECTION statements have to be adjusted as follows:

```
ON SELECTION BAR 8 OF datadictio do l3dictrd IN l3dict
```

When the user selects the eighth bar of the DATADICTIO popup now, FoxPro looks in L3DICT.APP's main program for a procedure named l3dictrd. From that point, any procedure or UDF call searches the entire .APP file first.

Saving Pending Browse Window Changes

With all my DO xxx IN l3dict commands in place in the menu system, I thought my worries about triggering Browse vents were over. They weren't.

To see why my worries weren't over, run the following small program:

```
* badbrows.prg
* helps demonstrate the problem with pending browse changes
DEFINE PAD george OF _msysmenu PROMPT "George"
ON SELECTION PAD george OF _msysmenu DO bad2 IN badbrowse
CLOSE DATA
USE tsclient share
BROWSE NOWAIT


PROC bad2
SELECT tsclient
SCATTER MEMVAR MEMO BLANK
cl_addr1="Bad idea"
INSERT INTO tsclient FROM MEMVAR
```

When BADBROWS.PRG finishes, you will be sitting in the first record of the TSCLIENT database. Please type several characters into the cl_addr1 field, *but do not press Enter* or exit the field in any way. Then, click the George pad that you placed in the system menu.

When you do, you are presented with an error message like the one in Figure 20.4. More importantly, the change you started to make in the TSCLIENT record is ignored!

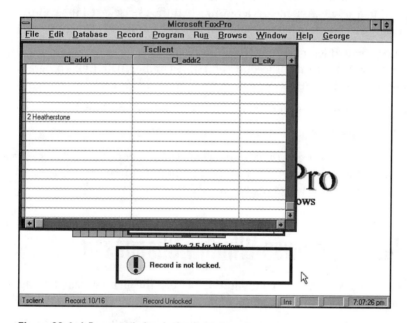

Figure 20.4. A Browse window losing its memory.

There are several potential solutions. First, we can open the data dictionary file for EXCLUSIVE use. Second, we can FLOCK() the data dictionary file when we open it. Third, we can include a WHEN clause on the BROWSE command that locks the current record.

None of these solutions is particularly attractive in a multiuser scenario. So, I came across the following solution: Whenever a menu activity is selected from the data dictionary menu that might cause the record locking problem, we KEYBOARD a {TAB} and a {BACKTAB} key to ensure that any pending changes were saved.

As a result, the ON SELECTION command became:

```
ON SELECTION BAR 8 OF datadictio do l3dictmn ;
  in l3dict with " l3dictrd()"
```

478

Here is the code for the l3dictmn procedure inside the L3DICT program:

```
PROCEDURE l3dictmn
* processes selections from menus after insuring
* that the user's changes to the current field have been
* saved
PARAMETERS p_expr
PRIVATE l_expr
IF UPPER(WONTOP())="DATADICT"
  PUSH KEY CLEAR
  m.l_expr=["]+p_expr+["]
  ON KEY LABEL ctrl+f12 DO l3dictmn2 IN l3dict WITH &l_expr.
  KEYBOARD "{tab}{backtab}{ctrl+f12}"
ELSE
  =EVAL(p_expr)
ENDIF
RETURN


PROCEDURE l3dictmn2
PARAMETERS p_expr
=EVAL(m.p_expr)
POP KEY
RETURN
```

As you can see, we have a timing problem in the evaluation of the expression that is passed to l3dictmn. We need the {Tab} and {Backtab} keys to be processed *before* we evaluate the expression passed to l3dictmn. Our solution was to attach a {Ctrl+F12} key to the {TAB}{BACKTAB} sequence, so that the l3dictmn2 procedure is executed.

This process of "chaining" hot keys to allow our programs to interact with the native FoxPro interface can come in handy in the creation of a variety of programming tools. I'll leave those investigations up to you, however, because we have more data dictionary issues to discuss.

Reading Existing .DBF Structures

I hate typing, and I really hate typing things twice. So, if I have taken the time to type in the file, field, and tag names for a database, I don't want to reenter those names in the data dictionary program. Instead, I want the data dictionary program to be able to read the structures of existing database files into the current datadict database (see Figure 20.5).

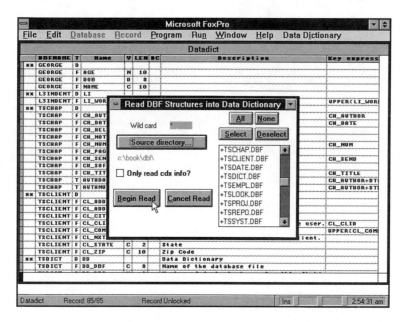

Figure 20.5. The Read .DBF Structures into Data Dictionary dialog box .

Here is the code from the l3dictrd procedure that updates the DATADICT database
with the structures from existing .DBF files:

```
l_thisdbf=UPPER(SUBSTR(l_thisdbf,2))
IF !FILE(l_thisdbf)
  ** couldn't find the dbf
  l3dictrdfi(m.l_rdfile,1)="@"+l_thisdbf
  SHOW GET m.l_rdfile
ELSE
  kerror=0
  SELECT 0
  IF USED('l3dictrd')
    USE IN l3dictrd
  ENDIF
  USE (l_thisdbf) AGAIN ALIAS l3dictrd
  IF kerror<>0
    ** failed to open, probably someone has
    ** it open EXCLUSIVE
    l3dictrdfi(m.l_rdfile,1)="#"+l_thisdbf
    SHOW GET m.l_rdfile
  ELSE
    ** Add the database if it is not already
    **   in the data dictionary
```

```
SELECT datadict
SCATTER MEMVAR MEMO BLANK
m.dd_dbf=PADR(STRTRAN(l_thisdbf,".DBF",""),8)
m.dd_rectype="D"
l_firstfld=FIELD(1,"l3dictrd")
m.dd_name=IIF(SUBSTR(l_firstfld,3,1)="_",LEFT(l_firstfld,2),"")
** L3uniq_a will add the record only if it is unique
DO l3uniq_a WITH m.dd_dbf+m.dd_rectype
IF NOT SEEK(m.dd_dbf+"D")
  ** couldn't add or find the record for some reason
  l3dictrdfi(m.l_rdfile,1)="$"+l_thisdbf
  SHOW GET m.l_rdfile
ELSE
  ** since we were able to find the database
  ** Now get all of the fields for this database
  SELECT l3dictrd
  =AFIELDS(rdstru)
  SELECT datadict
  FOR l_yy=1 TO ALEN(rdstru,1)
    SCATTER MEMVAR MEMO BLANK
    m.dd_dbf=PADR(STRTRAN(l_thisdbf,".DBF",""),8)
    m.dd_rectype="F"
    m.dd_name=PADR(rdstru(l_yy,1),10)
    m.dd_type=rdstru(l_yy,2)
    m.dd_len=rdstru(l_yy,3)
    m.dd_dec=rdstru(l_yy,4)
    IF SEEK(m.dd_dbf+m.dd_rectype+m.dd_name)
      GATHER MEMVAR FIELDS dd_type,dd_len,dd_dec
    ELSE
      INSERT INTO datadict FROM MEMVAR
    ENDIF wasn't new
  ENDFOR get all fields for this database
  ** Now pick up all tags for this database
  l_zz=1
  m.l_tagdbf=PADR(STRTRAN(l_thisdbf,".DBF",""),8)
  DO WHILE NOT EMPTY(KEY(l_zz,"l3dictrd"))
    ** get info about the tag
    m.l_tagname=PADR(TAG(l_zz,"l3dictrd"),10)
    m.l_tagkey=KEY(l_zz,"l3dictrd")
    m.l_tagfor=SYS(2021,l_zz,"l3dictrd")
    ** see if there is a record for this tag
    IF SEEK(m.l_tagdbf+"F"+m.l_tagname) OR ;
        SEEK(m.l_tagdbf+"T"+m.l_tagname)
```

continues

```
        REPLACE dd_key WITH m.l_tagkey,;
          dd_for WITH m.l_tagfor
      ELSE
        INSERT INTO datadict (dd_dbf,dd_rectype,;
          dd_name,dd_key,dd_for) VALUES ;
          (m.l_tagdbf,"T",m.l_tagname,m.l_tagkey,;
          m.l_tagfor)
      ENDIF this is a field name tag
      l_zz=l_zz+1
    ENDDO process all tags
    USE IN l3dictrd
    l3dictrdfi(m.l_rdfile,1)="*"+l_thisdbf
    SHOW GET m.l_rdfile
  ENDIF failed to add the database record to datadict
 ENDIF failed to open the file somehow
ENDIF couldn't find the file
```

Note that the afields() function makes it very easy to obtain the field names for a database. The TAG(), KEY(), and SYS(2021) functions make it possible to determine *almost* everything about an index tag. Unfortunately, there is no native method for determining the existence of a UNIQUE or DESCENDING flag on a given TAG. If this information is crucial to some aspect of your application, you can issue a command like the following to place the needed information, and much more, in a text file:

```
LIST STATUS TO textfile.txt NOCONSOLE
```

This information can then be read with FoxPro's low-level file I/O functions.

Writing .DBF Structures with the Data Dictionary

I hate typing, and I really hate typing things twice. So, when I take the time to enter file names, file descriptions, field names, field attributes, field descriptions tag names, tag expressions, and tag descriptions in the L3DICT application, there had better be some way to write those changes to real databases. That way I don't have to repeat the effort.

In other words, I want L3DICT to be a replacement for MODIFY STRUCTURE. To do this, L3DICT must be able to:

- Create new databases.

- Add new fields to existing database structures.

- Delete fields from existing database structures.

- Move data from old fields to new fields if a field name is "changed."

- Remember which records from the original table were marked for deletion.

- Create .BAK, .CDK, and .TBK files in case of emergency.

- Prevent the creation of invalid database structures.

- Rebuild index tags.

In general, we will write the proposed structure stored in the DATADICT file to a temporary table. Then, we will append the data from the original database into our temporary table. Finally, we will rename our original tables to .BAK/.CDK/.TBK files, and assign the "real" name of our database to our temporary tables.

As you can see in Figure 20.6, the Write Structures option of L3DICT allows the programmer to choose which database structures to write. In addition, the programmer can elect to "only" rebuild .CDX tags from this same dialog.

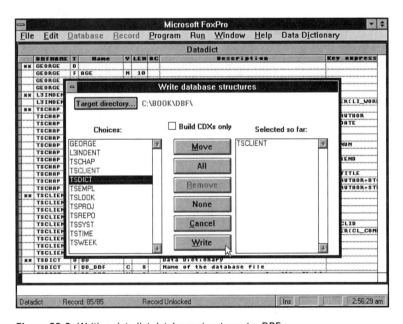

Figure 20.6. Writing datadict database structures to .DBFs.

Once we have determined which database definitions are written in a given session, our next task in creating or updating a .DBF structure is to obtain the field definitions from the DATADICT database. Here is the code:

```
SELECT dd_name,dd_type,dd_len,dd_dec ;
  FROM datadict WHERE ;
  dd_dbf=PADR(l_dbf,8) AND dd_rectype="F" ;
  INTO ARRAY l_dbfstru ORDER BY dd_name
```

483

Now that we have the database structure of a database stored in the l_dbfstru() array, we are ready to check for invalid database structures, as follows:

```
IF _TALLY>0 && at least one field for this database
  ** put field list into an array
  ** check to see whether the structure is ok
  l_badstru=.F.
  IF !BETWEEN(ALEN(l_dbfstru,1),1,254)
    \<<l_dt>>:<<l_dbf>>:Wrong number of fields:
    \\<<alen(l_dbfstru,1)>>
  ENDIF wrong # fields
  FOR l_xx=1 TO ALEN(l_dbfstru,1)
    l_curfname=l_dbfstru(l_xx,1)
    IF ASCAN(l_dbfstru,l_curfname,ASCAN(l_dbfstru,l_curfname)+1)#0
      l_badstru=.T.
      \<<l_dt>>:<<l_dbf>>:Duplicate field name:<<l_curfname>>
    ENDIF
  ENDFOR  duplicate fields
  FOR l_xx=1 TO ALEN(l_dbfstru,1)
    l_flddef=.T.
    DO CASE
      CASE l_dbfstru(l_xx,2)="C" .AND. ;
          (!BETWEEN(l_dbfstru(l_xx,3),1,254).or.;
            l_dbfstru(l_xx,4)#0)
        l_badstru=.T.
        l_flddef=.F.
      CASE l_dbfstru(l_xx,2)="N" .AND. ;
          (!BETWEEN(l_dbfstru(l_xx,3),1,20) .OR. ;
          (!BETWEEN(l_dbfstru(l_xx,4),0,l_dbfstru(l_xx,3)-2);
          .and.l_dbfstru(l_xx,4)#0))
        l_badstru=.T.
        l_flddef=.F.
      CASE l_dbfstru(l_xx,2)="M" .AND. ;
          (l_dbfstru(l_xx,3)#10.or.l_dbfstru(l_xx,4)#0)
        l_badstru=.T.
        l_flddef=.F.
      CASE l_dbfstru(l_xx,2)="D" .AND. ;
          (l_dbfstru(l_xx,3)#8.or.l_dbfstru(l_xx,4)#0)
        l_badstru=.T.
        l_flddef=.F.
      CASE l_dbfstru(l_xx,2)="L" .AND. ;
          (l_dbfstru(l_xx,3)#1.or.l_dbfstru(l_xx,4)#0)
        l_badstru=.T.
```

```
          l_flddef=.F.
       CASE !l_dbfstru(l_xx,2)$"CNLMDGP"
          l_badstru=.T.
          l_flddef=.F.
     ENDCASE
     IF !l_flddef
       \<<l_dt>>:<<l_dbf>>:Invalid field definition:
       \\<<l_dbfstru(l_xx,1)>> <<l_dbfstru(l_xx,2)>>
       \\<<l_dbfstru(l_xx,3)>> <<l_dbfstru(l_xx,4)>>
     ENDIF
   ENDFOR invalid field length or decimal
```

Once we are assured that the proposed data structure is valid, we can determine whether this is a new database. Here is the code:

```
IF !l_badstru
  ** see whether database is in use
  IF USED(l_dbf)
    ** close it!
    USE IN (l_dbf)
  ENDIF database is in use
  ** see whether the database is in use under another alias
  FOR l_xx=1 TO IIF(_WINDOWS OR "(X)"$VERSION(1),225,25)
    IF DBF(l_xx)=l_target+l_dbf+".DBF"
      USE IN (l_xx)
    ENDIF
  ENDFOR dbf in use under another alias
  ** see whether this file exists
  l_existing=FILE(l_target+l_dbf+".dbf")
  SET TALK WINDOW ON
  SET TALK ON
  SET ODOM TO 1000
  IF !l_existing
    ** new file
    CREATE TABLE (l_target+l_dbf) FROM ARRAY l_dbfstru
    USE
  ELSE
```

Now for the hard part. When we use the MODIFY STRUCTURE command to change the name of a field, FoxPro does its best to import the data from the original field to the new field. However, when we change a field name in L3DICT, we don't have access to the original database.

For example, assume that we have used L3DICT to create the following TSCLIENT.DBF:

```
Structure for table:     c:\book\dbf\tsclient.dbf
Number of data records: 23
Date of last update:     03/23/93
Field  Field Name  Type        Width   Dec    Index
    1  CL_ADDR1    Character      30
    2  CL_ADDR2    Character      30
    3  CL_CITY     Character      30
    4  CL_CLID     Character       7            Asc
    5  CL_COMPANY  Character      40            Asc
    6  CL_NXTPROJ  Numeric         4
    7  CL_STATE    Character       2
    8  CL_ZIP      Character      10
** Total **                      154
```

Now, while in the data dictionary, we change the name of the company name field from cl_company to cl_name. When we go to write the data structure of TSCLIENT, the cl_company field does not exist in our temporary table.

As a result, when we append data into our temporary table from the original TSCLIENT.DBF, the information stored in tsclient.cl_company is lost! When the programmer attempts to write the new TSCLIENT definition, however, L3DICT is smart enough to determine that the cl_company field exists in the TSCLIENT.DBF, but not in the new structure.

As you can see in Figure 20.7, L3DICT provides the programmer with three options in this case. First, the programmer can elect to keep the cl_company field even though it is not a part of the new definition. Second, the programmer can elect to remove the cl_company field from the about-to-be-created TSCLIENT.DBF. Third, the programmer can elect to copy the content of the old cl_company field into the cl_name field, as I have done in Figure 20.7.

As L3DICTWR writes structures to .DBF files, errors are trapped and logged to a DATADICT.ERR file, which is automatically edited if any errors occur during the writing of the database structures.

The Next and Previous Database

Even modest applications can require 25 or 30 databases. Applications like Mobil's Mariner system often require several hundred databases. Scrolling through 2,500 fields strewn about 150 databases is no fun whatsoever, even in a cool-looking Browse window like the one created by L3DICT.

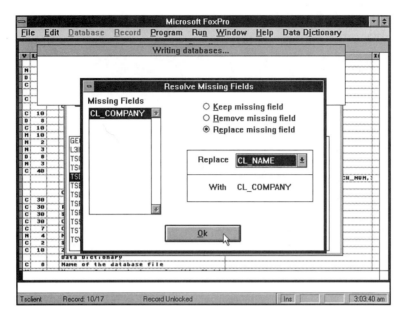

Figure 20.7. Resolving missing fields during database structure writes.

Happily, there is a solution. In L3DICT, by pressing Ctrl+PgUp the programmer can quickly move to the previous database. By pressing Ctrl+PgDn, the programmer can quickly move to the next database. These hot keys are tied to bars in the data dictionary menu, so they are always available. This technique has application in a variety of data entry situations, and the code looks like this:

```
PROCEDURE l3dictmv
* moves forward or back one database file
PARAMETERS p_direction
PRIVATE l_thisdbf,l_oldnear,l_olddele
p_direction=IIF(TYPE('p_direction')#"N",1,p_direction)
l_oldnear=SET('near')
l_olddele=SET("deleted")
SET DELETED ON
SET NEAR ON
l_thisdbf=datadict.dd_dbf
SELECT datadict
IF p_direction>0
  SET ORDER TO dd ASCENDING
  IF .T. OR datadict.dd_rectype="D"
    ** Create a string that is one ASCII value
    ** greater than the current database
```

continues

```
      l_thisdbf=LEFT(l_thisdbf,LEN(l_thisdbf)-1)+;
        CHR(ASC(RIGHT(l_thisdbf,1))+1)
    ENDIF
    SEEK l_thisdbf
    ** Now we are sitting on the next database!
    IF EOF()
      GO TOP
    ENDIF
    l_thisdbf=datadict.dd_dbf
    ** Put us on the database record associated with
    ** the next database.
    SEEK l_thisdbf+"D"
  ELSE
    SET ORDER TO dd DESCENDING
    IF datadict.dd_rectype="D"
      ** Create a character string that is one
      ** ASCII value smaller than the current database
      l_thisdbf=LEFT(l_thisdbf,LEN(l_thisdbf)-1)+;
        CHR(ASC(RIGHT(l_thisdbf,1))-1)
    ENDIF
    SEEK l_thisdbf
    ** Because the tag is descending, we are now sitting
    ** on the previous database in datadict!
    IF EOF()
      GO TOP
    ENDIF
    l_thisdbf=datadict.dd_dbf
    ** Put us on the database record associated with
    ** the next database.
    SEEK l_thisdbf+"D"
    SET ORDER TO dd ASCENDING
  ENDIF
IF l_oldnear<>"ON"
  SET NEAR OFF
ENDIF
IF l_olddele<>"ON"
  SET DELETED OFF
ENDIF
```

Using Find, Cut, and Paste

Because the Browse window supports FoxPro's native text search facility, the programmer can simply press Ctrl+F to look for any character string in any field in the data dictionary. Further, because Browse windows participate in cut and paste activities, programmers can simply mark text of interest, and use Ctrl+C, Ctrl+X, and Ctrl+V to cut and paste that text between records in the Browse or between the Browse window and programs, screens, menus, or reports.

However, I often find a need to copy a field name from the Browse window into a program on which I am working. In those cases, I have to:

1. Find the correct record in the data dictionary.

2. Mark and copy the database name in the DATADICT window.

3. Click my program window.

4. Paste the database name into the program window.

5. Type a period.

6. Click the DATADICT window.

7. Mark and copy the field name.

8. Click my program window again.

9. Paste the field name into the program window.

This is far too much work for such a common activity. So, I added the Clip Field name/ Tag expr bar to the L3DICT menu. Then, I associated this command with that bar:

```
ON SELECTION BAR 7 OF datadictio ;
_cliptext=iif(used('datadict').and.datadict.dd_rectype$"TF",;
IIF(datadict.dd_rectype="T",trim(datadict.dd_key)+" "+;
CHR(38)+chr(38)+" "+datadict.dd_name,;
lower(trim(datadict.dd_dbf)+"."+;
trim(datadict.dd_name))),_cliptext)
```

The purpose of this command is to place the database name, a period, and the field name on the Clipboard. (*Note*: If the current data dictionary record defines an index tag, the index expression is placed on the Clipboard.) Because I have assigned the Ctrl+I hot key to this bar, the programmer can:

1. Find the correct record in the data dictionary.

2. Click the program window of interest.

3. Press Ctrl+I to capture the current DATADICT database and field names.

4. Press Ctrl+V to insert the captured information in his or her program.

In some cases, this is still too much work! After all, if I need the names of several fields from the same database, I have to click back and forth between the DATADICT window and the program window.

Instead, I want to be able to move among records in the DATADICT file while I am editing a program file. I can already move from database to database in the DATADICT file with the Ctrl+PgUp and Ctrl+PgDn keys. So, it should come as no surprise that I enabled the Ctrl+Up-Arrow and Ctrl+Dn-Arrow keys to call the following procedure:

```
PROCEDURE l3dictmr
* Move one record forward or back in the current datadict
PARAMETERS p_direction
l_olddele=SET("deleted")
SET DELETED ON
IF EOF("datadict")
  GOTO BOTTOM IN datadict
ENDIF
IF BOF("datadict")
  GO TOP IN datadict
ENDIF
IF NOT EOF("datadict") AND NOT BOF("datadict")
  IF p_direction>0
    SKIP IN datadict
    IF EOF("datadict")
      GO TOP IN datadict
    ENDIF
  ELSE && backup
    SKIP -1 IN datadict
    IF BOF("datadict")
      GO BOTTOM IN datadict
    ENDIF
  ENDIF forward
  IF NOT WONTOP("datadict")
    WAIT WINDOW datadict.dd_dbf+" "+datadict.dd_rectype+" "+;
      datadict.dd_name+" "+datadict.dd_type+" "+;
      STR(datadict.dd_len,3)+" "+STR(datadict.dd_dec,2)+" "+;
      TRIM(datadict.dd_key)+" "+TRIM(datadict.dd_desc) NOWAIT
  ENDIF data dictionary is not on top of the desktop
ENDIF not eof or bof

IF l_olddele<>"ON"
  SET DELETED OFF
ENDIF
RETURN
```

Notice the use of the WAIT WINDOW NOWAIT command. This allows the programmer to see information about the record to which he or she has just moved. In essence then, the programmer can:

1. Press Ctrl+Dn-Arrow to move to the next field.

2. Press Ctrl+I to capture that field information on the Clipboard.

3. Press Ctrl+V to paste that field information into the current program window.

Showing Only .DBFs

When looking at 1,500 or more records in the data dictionary, it is often difficult to envision the tables that make up the application. Even moving quickly from database to database is no substitute for a simple list of all the databases in the application, with their descriptions.

L3DICT accomplishes this simple feat with the following block of code:

```
PROCEDURE l3dictsee
* change filter
PARAMETERS thissee
PRIVATE ALL LIKE l_*
SELECT datadict
DO CASE
  CASE UPPER(thissee)="DBF"
    SET FILTER TO dd_rectype="D"
  CASE UPPER(thissee)="ALL"
    SET FILTER TO
  CASE UPPER(thissee)="EXPAND"
    SELECT datadict
    IF NOT "¦"+dd_dbf+"¦"$FILTER()
      IF NOT "DD_DBF"$UPPER(FILTER())
        l_newfilt=[dd_rectype="D" OR "¦"+dd_dbf+"¦"$"]+dd_dbf+[¦"]
      ELSE
        l_newfilt=LEFT(FILTER(),LEN(FILTER())-1)+"¦"+dd_dbf+[¦"]
      ENDIF no databases are in the filter
      SET FILTER TO &l_newfilt.
    ENDIF this database is not in the filter
  CASE UPPER(thissee)="CONTRACT"
    IF "¦"+dd_dbf+"¦"$FILTER()
      l_newfilt=STRTRAN(FILTER(),"¦"+dd_dbf+"¦","")
      SET FILTER TO &l_newfilt.
```

continues

491

```
    ENDIF
ENDCASE
SHOW WINDOW datadict REFRESH SAME
RETURN .T.
```

When we choose the See Dbf Only option of the data dictionary menu, L3DICT simply establishes a filter for the current data dictionary. However, L3DICTSEE has a great deal more capability than just establishing a simple filter.

Expanding and Contracting Current .DBF Structure

While I usually want to see as many fields from the database as possible, I often find myself wishing that I could look at just the fields associated with a single database. In that way, I could concentrate on just those fields.

In L3DICT, I have enabled the F11 and F12 keys to help in this endeavor. After choosing to See Dbf Only, the programmer can press F11 to expand an individual database. The programmer can expand or contract a number of database descriptions at the same time. For your reference, I have expanded the TSCLIENT and TSPROJ definitions in Figure 20.8.

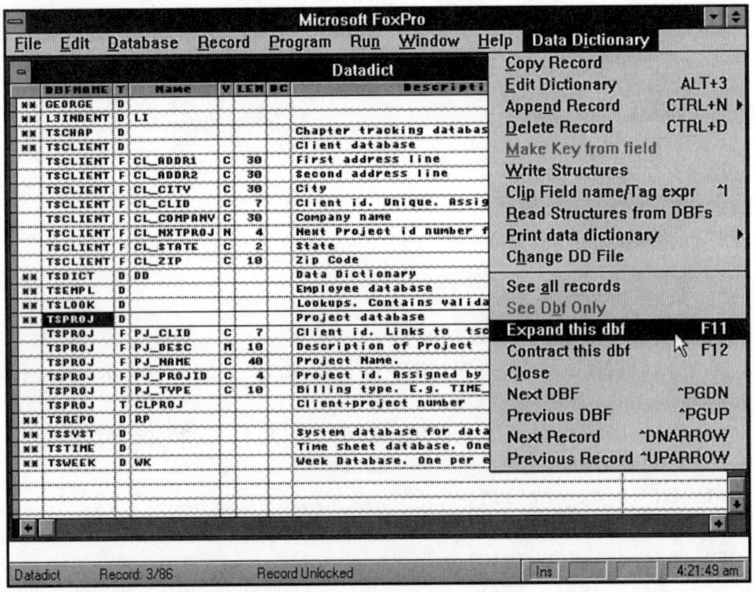

Figure 20.8. Looking at individual database definitions in the DATADICT window.

Adding and Copying Records

Because there is nothing particularly interesting about the way we add or copy records in the L3DICT data dictionary, I'll let you check the source code in L3DICT.PRG if you are interested in such things. In the meantime, I hope you are able to use L3DICT in your development efforts. I also hope that the topics explored in this chapter inspire you to write some of your own programmers' utilities.

CHAPTER

21

Cross-Platform Issues

At one point, *Creating FoxPro Applications* was going to include FoxPro 2.5 for DOS and FoxPro 2.5 for Windows versions of every screen shot, program, and narrative in the book. That idea lasted about two minutes. Instead, I decided that, like MEI's training materials, the book would concentrate on FoxPro 2.5 for Windows, and include a separate chapter that would explain how to integrate the two products.

Because **Melissa Dunn** had just finished the sections on cross-platform issues for Micro Endeavors new training materials, I asked her to contribute the chapter that follows.

A *cross-platform application* is one that runs in more than one operating environment. With FoxPro 2.5, you can create and maintain applications that run in both the Windows and MS-DOS environments. What the application looks like and how it behaves in each environment is up to you.

FoxPro 2.5 offers three cross-platform choices:

- In the Windows environment, you can run the character-based DOS applications *as is*.

- You can use the FoxPro 2.5 Transporter to convert MS-DOS screens, reports, and labels to Windows format without changing the appearance of the user interface.

- You can transport MS-DOS screens, reports, and labels to Windows and then update the user interfaces to include Windows elements and characteristics such as fonts, spinners, and OLE objects.

The purpose of this chapter is to help you make the "cross-platform decision" by presenting information on how FoxPro maintains cross-platform tables, how the Transporter works, how you can have FoxPro create platform-exclusive screens, and how you can use code bracketing for platform differences in your applications.

Moving Cross-Platform

Before beginning this discussion of cross-platform issues, I make the following distinction between the two versions of the FoxPro 2.5 language: I consider FoxPro 2.5 for DOS as the actual FoxPro command set, while FoxPro 2.5 for Windows is a superset of that command language.

In other words, FoxPro 2.5 for DOS is the lowest common denominator. The Windows version contains all the same commands and quite a few more.

Therefore, if you want to write an application that runs in both platforms without any modification, write the application using the DOS platform and then run it *without transporting* on the Windows platform. This doesn't take advantage of the graphical interface, but does work.

In fact, if you run the application as a FoxPro application program (.APP), users must simply run the .APP file in either platform. No further action is necessary. The same is true for uncompiled programs. FoxPro recompiles the programs in either platform, as required.

Visual differences between the two products exist because of the inherent nature of character and graphical environments. For example, MS-DOS uses a monospaced font based on the OEM character set whereas Windows uses an ANSI character set with fonts that can be fixed or proportional. Although FoxPro for Windows provides FoxFont, which closely emulates the DOS OEM character set, finding a match between the two character sets is not always possible.

Therefore, some special characters in an application may not be directly reproducible in Windows, causing that portion of the application to appear odd. FoxPro provides the OEMTOANSI() function to help reduce the effect of the character set differences. However, you might find it necessary to use code bracketing for the differences in the environments. We'll discuss code bracketing later in this chapter.

The appearance of controls is another area in which visual differences are obvious. FoxPro for MS-DOS controls do not match the size of Windows controls. Most MS-DOS controls are one line high. When you run an MS-DOS application in Windows, a special one-line-high control is produced. This control appears "squashed" compared to controls written in, or transported into, Windows.

Finally, all user-defined windows created in FoxPro Windows have a title bar if they include any of the following clauses: TITLE, FLOAT, ZOOM, MINIMIZE, or CLOSE. This is not true for windows created with the MS-DOS product. To reduce visual differences between the two environments, a half-height title bar is used for user-defined windows in Windows, unless you include the SYSTEM keyword or create the windows by using the FONT clause.

FoxPro makes these changes automatically to minimize differences between the two environments. However, if you want to take advantage of the enhancements available in the Windows platform, you must transport the screens, reports, and labels from one environment to the other. To understand how the Transporter works, you must understand how FoxPro constructs the interface tables.

FoxPro Tables and the Transporter

When you first create a screen, FoxPro creates a special database file that has the extension .SCX. This database contains one record for each object on the form, a record for the environment information, and one record to hold Screen Layout options (READ clauses, setup code, and so on). Along with fields describing the properties of the various objects, the .SCX file includes fields that identify the platform, unique ID, and timestamp for each object.

Note: Although we discuss what happens specifically to a transported screen, be aware that the same processes hold true for reports and labels.

As you know, FoxPro stores the information captured in the Screen Builder in a database with an extension of .SCX. As a result, we are able to USE and BROWSE the records in the TSPLAT.SCX database.

As you can see in Figure 21.1, the TSPLAT.SCX screen was originally created in FoxPro for DOS. When we open the TSCLIENT.SCX screen in FoxPro for Windows, FoxPro recognizes that no records in the screen table are for the Windows platform. In response to this situation, FoxPro executes the Transporter program.

As Figure 21.2 shows, when we elect to MODI SCREEN tsplat in FoxPro for Windows, the Transporter program enables us to select the Transport and Open option on the TSPLAT screen. The Transporter then duplicates all the DOS object records, making some changes to accommodate the different platforms and changing the platform field to "WINDOWS". You can see the result of the transport in Figure 21.3.

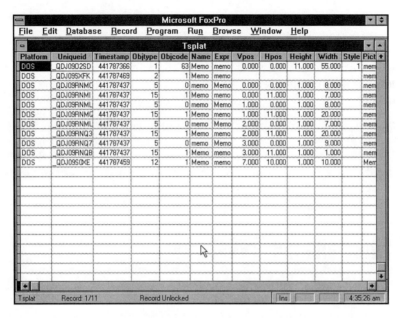

Figure 21.1. The screen for TSPLAT.SCX, which contains only DOS objects.

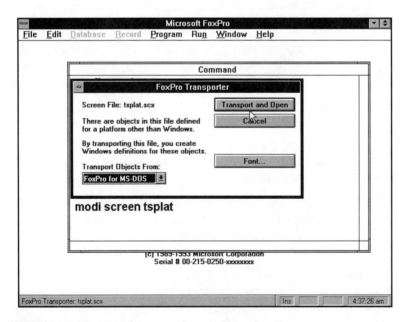

Figure 21.2. The Transporter.

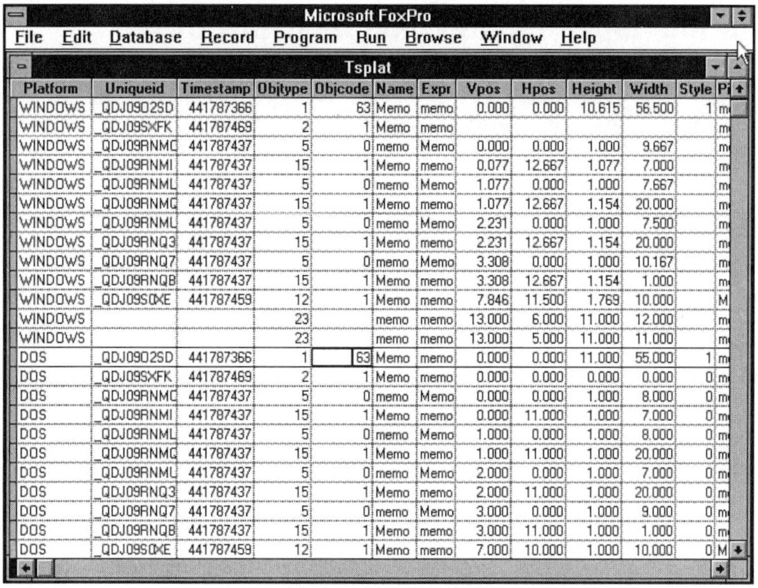

Microsoft FoxPro

File Edit Database Record Program Run Browse Window Help

Tsplat

Platform	Uniqueid	Timestamp	Objtype	Objcode	Name	Expr	Vpos	Hpos	Height	Width	Style	Pi
WINDOWS	_QDJ0902SD	441787366	1	63	Memo	memo	0.000	0.000	10.615	56.500	1	m
WINDOWS	_QDJ09SXFK	441787469	2	1	Memo	memo						m
WINDOWS	_QDJ09RNMC	441787437	5	0	memo	Memo	0.000	0.000	1.000	9.667		m
WINDOWS	_QDJ09RNMI	441787437	15	1	Memo	memo	0.077	12.667	1.077	7.000		m
WINDOWS	_QDJ09RNML	441787437	5	0	memo	Memo	1.077	0.000	1.000	7.667		m
WINDOWS	_QDJ09RNMQ	441787437	15	1	Memo	memo	1.077	12.667	1.154	20.000		m
WINDOWS	_QDJ09RNML	441787437	5	0	memo	Memo	2.231	0.000	1.000	7.500		m
WINDOWS	_QDJ09RNQ3	441787437	15	1	Memo	memo	2.231	12.667	1.154	20.000		m
WINDOWS	_QDJ09RNQ7	441787437	5	0	memo	Memo	3.308	0.000	1.000	10.167		m
WINDOWS	_QDJ09RNQB	441787437	15	1	Memo	memo	3.308	12.667	1.154	1.000		m
WINDOWS	_QDJ09S0XE	441787459	12	1	Memo	memo	7.846	11.500	1.769	10.000		M
WINDOWS			23		memo	memo	13.000	6.000	11.000	12.000		m
WINDOWS			23		memo	memo	13.000	5.000	11.000	11.000		m
DOS	_QDJ0902SD	441787366	1	63	Memo	memo	0.000	0.000	11.000	55.000	1	m
DOS	_QDJ09SXFK	441787469	2	1	Memo	memo	0.000	0.000	0.000	0.000	0	m
DOS	_QDJ09RNMC	441787437	5	0	memo	Memo	0.000	0.000	1.000	8.000	0	m
DOS	_QDJ09RNMI	441787437	15	1	Memo	memo	0.000	11.000	1.000	7.000	0	m
DOS	_QDJ09RNML	441787437	5	0	memo	Memo	1.000	0.000	1.000	8.000	0	m
DOS	_QDJ09RNMQ	441787437	15	1	Memo	memo	1.000	11.000	1.000	20.000	0	m
DOS	_QDJ09RNML	441787437	5	0	memo	Memo	2.000	0.000	1.000	7.000	0	m
DOS	_QDJ09RNQ3	441787437	15	1	Memo	memo	2.000	11.000	1.000	20.000	0	m
DOS	_QDJ09RNQ7	441787437	5	0	memo	Memo	3.000	0.000	1.000	9.000	0	m
DOS	_QDJ09RNQB	441787437	15	1	Memo	memo	3.000	11.000	1.000	1.000	0	m
DOS	_QDJ09S0XE	441787459	12	1	Memo	memo	7.000	10.000	1.000	10.000	0	M

Figure 21.3. Windows records added to TSPLAT.SCX.

In this case, we have transported a simple screen from DOS to Windows. As a result, all the objects were transported more or less without change. Because the Windows version of FoxPro has a greater variety of objects and more flexibility in the display of those objects than does the DOS version, transporting is not always so smooth. The following subsections describe some of the differences between the two products, and how the Transporter attempts to reconcile the differences.

Transporting Reports from MS-DOS to Windows

After we transport a report from MS-DOS to Windows, we find the following differences:

- Grouped objects are no longer grouped.

- Objects marked to FLOAT AS BAND STRETCHES are positioned relative to the *bottom* of the band.

- Objects marked both to STRETCH VERTICALLY and FLOAT AS BAND STRETCHES are positioned relative to the *top* of the band.

Transporting Reports from Windows to MS-DOS

If you create or enhance a report in the Windows platform and then transport it to the MS-DOS platform, the following changes are made:

- Grouped objects are no longer grouped.

- Colors are not transported.

- Fonts, font styles, and font sizes are not transported. In fact, FoxPro removes their attributes and places them on-screen as monospaced character mode text.

- Multiple-line text objects are broken into separate objects in which each line is an object.

- Multiple-line text objects that have $1\frac{1}{2}$-line spacing are transported with single-line spacing.

- Picture fields are not transported.

- Coordinates are changed from their fractional state to whole numbers through the use of an internal algorithm.

- Pen sizes for boxes are transported as follows:

Windows Pen Size	DOS Equivalent
1	Single
2	Double
4	Panel
6	Single

- Multicolumn reports are transported as single-column reports, and the column headers and footers are merged into the page headers and footers.

- Group Header and Footer fields that have been marked to stretch are cut off at the Group Header or Footer band.

- Individual fields in Windows can have the option to suppress blank lines turned on or off. However, the MS-DOS Report Writer applies the option to suppress blank lines throughout the entire report. Therefore, if one field in FoxPro for Windows has this option on, the option is on for the entire report in FoxPro for MS-DOS.

- Options to suppress repeated values are transported to MS-DOS as follows:

FoxPro for Windows	FoxPro for DOS
Page or Column	Page
Group	Group
Group Overflow	Not transported
None	Report

Transporting Screens from MS-DOS to Windows

When you transport a screen from MS-DOS to Windows, all objects are transported without change. The only exception to this is that grouped objects are no longer grouped.

Transporting Screens from Windows to MS-DOS

The complete transport that occurs when you transport screens from DOS does not occur when you transport screens created or enhanced in Windows. Transporting Windows screen objects to MS-DOS has the following effects:

- Picture buttons become regular controls with the bitmap (.BMP) file name as the prompt.

- Rounded rectangles become regular rectangles.

- Spinners become standard numeric GET fields.

- Rectangle, line, and text colors are transported and converted into MS-DOS color pairs.

- Fonts, font styles, and pen sizes are not transported. FoxPro removes their attributes and places the object on-screen as monospaced character mode text.

- Multiple-line text objects are broken into separate objects. Each line becomes its own object.

- Multiple-line text objects that have $1^{1}/_{2}$-line spacing transport to single-line spacing.

- Picture fields are ignored. Nothing is transported.

- Grouped objects are no longer grouped.

- Coordinates in FoxPro for Windows are fractional. The Transporter uses a complex algorithm to convert these fractional coordinates into whole numbers.

- Pen sizes for boxes transport as follows:

Windows Pen Size	DOS Equivalent
1	Single
2	Double
4	Panel
6	Single

As you can see, transporting from the command set to the superset (MS-DOS to Windows) involves very few changes to the form. However, if you take advantage of the Windows superset, providing a smooth user interface after transporting to MS-DOS requires quite a few modifications to the form.

Updating Objects

Now that you have two sets of records in the TSPLAT.SCX, one for the Windows platform and one for the DOS, what happens if you change one of the objects?

When you change objects in a screen, only the records associated with the running version of FoxPro are changed in the underlying .SCX file. For example, if you are running FoxPro for DOS and you change the push button in the TSPLAT screen, only the DOS record for the push button changes in the TSPLAT.SCX database.

To have your changes appear in other platforms, you must reopen the screen of interest in the other platform. In this case, I would now run FoxPro for Windows and modify the TSPLAT screen.

This shouldn't be a problem, because when we open the screen on the new platform, FoxPro executes the Transporter and makes the changes automatically. Right? Well, not exactly.

First, we must understand how the Transporter knows whether or not the table has been changed, and which objects are involved.

Caution: If you change an object or form's (for example, Screen Layout) dialog (that is, clauses, format, and so on), FoxPro updates the object's timestamp. However, if you change the object's appearance (that is, the size, font, color, or location), the object dialog is not affected and the timestamp is not updated.

When you open the table in another platform, FoxPro compares the timestamps on each object's platform records. If the timestamps differ, FoxPro determines which platform has the most recent timestamp. If the record with the most recent timestamp is from a platform other than the current platform, FoxPro executes the Transporter.

In other words, if you are currently running the Windows version of the product and one of the DOS records has a more recent timestamp than its Windows equivalent, the Transporter executes. However, if all the Windows records have a more recent timestamp, the Transporter is not activated.

Tip: If you add a new object to a screen and subsequently modify that screen while running FoxPro on another platform, FoxPro calls the Transporter to handle the new objects.

After the FoxPro Transporter dialog appears, you can choose to update the entire set of records or only those records with newer timestamps. Figures 21.4 and 21.5 show your choices.

Whenever the Transporter appears, you must decide whether to update all objects, only objects that are new to the platform, only objects that have a newer timestamp in another platform, or no other platform records at all.

Which of these options you choose depends on whether you want the object or object changes in all platforms. Remember, however, that if the change is one that does not affect an object dialog or add a new object (for example, changing the field location or size), you must make the change manually in all platforms.

Code Bracketing and FoxPro

We now know that the Transporter creates and modifies records for any platform in which the screen (or report) table is modified. We also know that the records in the table must generate a program (.SPR) before we can use the screen. The next logical question is how does FoxPro know which records to use when generating a screen program?

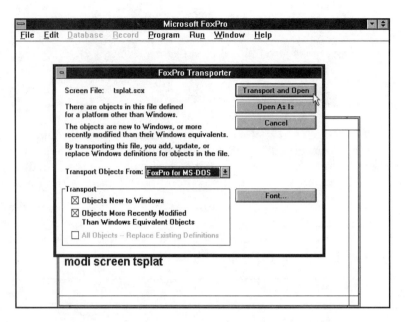

Figure 21.4. Transporting new and updated objects.

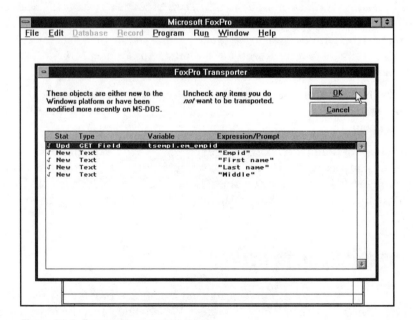

Figure 21.5. Transporting selected objects.

The answer is simple: FoxPro neither knows nor cares. In fact, when you generate the screen program, FoxPro writes the screen code for any platform that has records. Consequently, if you have records for both the MS-DOS and Windows platforms, FoxPro writes a screen program that contains code for both.

Because FoxPro generates only a single program, regardless of how many platforms exist in the table, there must be a way to differentiate between the code generated from the different sets of records. After all, when you are in Windows, you get the screen with the Windows objects, and when you are in MS-DOS, you get the screen designed on the MS-DOS platform.

In fact, the FoxPro screen generator performs *code bracketing* by using two FoxPro system variables, _DOS and _WINDOWS:

```
DO CASE
CASE _WINDOWS
     #REGION 0
     REGIONAL m.currarea, m.talkstat, m.compstat
     IF SET("TALK") = "ON"
       SET TALK OFF
       m.talkstat = "ON"
     ELSE
       m.talkstat = "OFF"
     ENDIF
     m.compstat = SET("COMPATIBLE")
     SET COMPATIBLE FOXPLUS

     m.rborder = SET("READBORDER")
     SET READBORDER ON


     *************************************************
     *         *
     *         *      Windows Window definitions
     *         *
     ******************************************************
     ** remaining code for Windows version of the screen
CASE _DOS
     #REGION 0
     REGIONAL m.currarea, m.talkstat, m.compstat

     IF SET("TALK") = "ON"
       SET TALK OFF
       m.talkstat = "ON"
```

continues

```
ELSE
  m.talkstat = "OFF"
ENDIF
m.compstat = SET("COMPATIBLE")
SET COMPATIBLE FOXPLUS


***************************************************
*         *
*         *         MS-DOS Window definitions
*         *
***************************************************
** remaining code for DOS screen version
```

The platform system variables are true only when you are on the corresponding platform. So, when you run the program on the Windows platform, only the Windows code is executed; when you are on the MS-DOS platform, only the MS-DOS code is executed.

In other words, FoxPro has bracketed the code by platform, ensuring that superset commands and objects won't generate runtime errors on another platform.

Platform-Specific Code

Based on what you have learned so far, it should be obvious that the screen program can become extremely large, depending on the complexity of the screen or screen set. This might be unnecessary overhead if you want the code for one platform exclusively.

Therefore, in both platforms, the Generate Screen dialog provides the capability *not* to produce cross-platform code. When you choose the Windows (or MS-DOS) Objects Only option (as shown in Figure 21.6), the program generator produces a single set of screen building instructions, as if only one set of records were in the table.

Code Bracketing and You

Even when you have platform-specific formats for a screen, you have a single screen program (.SPR). However, because of differences in the actual form design, we might need the control program to behave differently depending on the platform.

For example, suppose we have an inventory maintenance screen that contains a general field picture of the current inventory item, a spinner to indicate the point at which the item should be reordered, and picture push buttons. In other words, our Windows screen uses Windows objects, whereas our MS-DOS screen is set up as nicely as possible for the character-based environment.

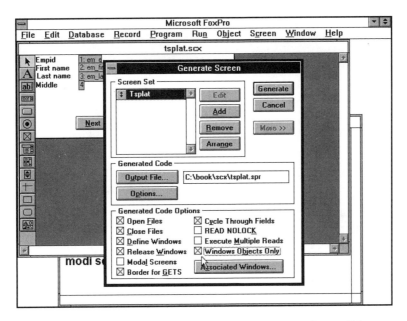

Figure 21.6. Generating only Windows code from the Generate Screen dialog.

As we already know, however, none of the Windows-only objects transport into MS-DOS properly. We therefore have an entirely different set of records for the MS-DOS screen.

In our program, however, we must make sure that MS-DOS does not try to execute Windows commands or we get runtime error messages. To prevent this from happening, we use *bracketed code*.

For example, the procedure that controls the display of items (`controlshow`) can't display the invisible button over the picture object because the MS-DOS version of the screen has no equivalent objects:

```
PROCEDURE controlshow
SHOW GET m.iv_item DISABLED
SHOW GET m.iv_desc DISABLED
SHOW GET m.iv_onhand DISABLED
SHOW GET m.iv_backord DISABLED
SHOW GET m.iv_reorder DISABLED
SHOW GET m.iv_price DISABLED
```

continues

```
IF _WINDOWS
   SHOW GET m.invbutton DISABLED
ENDIF windows invisible button

SHOW GETS OFF
RETURN
```

Because all the other fields are the same—although they may not look the same—we need to bracket only the one field.

Changing and resetting the push buttons requires another bit of code bracketing, because we use picture buttons in Windows and regular prompt buttons in DOS:

```
PROCEDURE showbuttons
SHOW GET delbutton DISABLED
SHOW GET srchbutton DISABLED
SHOW GET nextbutton DISABLED
SHOW GET prevbutton DISABLED
SHOW GET exitbutton DISABLED
DO CASE
  CASE l_addmode     && adding an inventory item
    l_edit = "STOP"
    SHOW GET addbutton ENABLED
    DO CASE
      CASE _DOS
        SHOW GET editbutton,1 PROMPT "\<Stop" ENABLED
      CASE _WINDOWS
        SHOW GET editbutton,1 PROMPT "trffc14.bmp" ENABLED
        SHOW GET m.invbutton ENABLED
    ENDCASE
  CASE l_editmode    && editing an inventory item
    l_add = "SAVE"
    l_edit = "ABORT"
    DO CASE
      CASE _DOS
        SHOW GET addbutton,1 PROMPT "\<Save" ENABLED
          SHOW GET editbutton,1 PROMPT "\<Abort" ENABLED
      CASE _WINDOWS
        SHOW GET addbutton,1 PROMPT "save.bmp" ENABLED
        SHOW GET editbutton,1 ;
          PROMPT "trash02b.bmp" ENABLED
    ENDCASE
ENDCASE
RETURN .T.
```

```
PROCEDURE expbreset
* resets expb push button
l_add = "Add"
l_edit = "Edit"
DO CASE
  CASE _DOS
    SHOW GET addbutton,1 PROMPT "\<Add " ENABLED
    SHOW GET editbutton,1 PROMPT "\<Edit " ENABLED
  CASE _WINDOWS
    SHOW GET addbutton,1 PROMPT "misc18.bmp" ENABLED
    SHOW GET editbutton,1 PROMPT "pencil05.bmp" ENABLED
ENDCASE
SHOW GET delbutton ENABLED
SHOW GET nextbutton ENABLED
SHOW GET prevbutton ENABLED
SHOW GET srchbutton ENABLED
SHOW GET exitbutton ENABLED
RETURN .T.
```

Because of differences in screen layout (proportional fonts versus characters), we also need to use code bracketing when attempting to use relative screen addressing to embed a Browse window:

```
l_bottom=WLROW('exorders')+WROWS('exorders')
l_right=WLCOL('exorder1')
l_left = WLCOL("exorders")
DO CASE
  CASE _DOS
    DEFINE WINDOW exordebr AT l_bottom+2,l_left ;
       SIZE SROWS()-l_bottom-3,l_right-2 ;
      TITLE "Line_Items" ;
       COLOR SCHEME 8 ;
      GROW ZOOM FLOAT
  CASE _WINDOWS
    DEFINE WINDOW exordebr ;
       AT l_bottom+2,l_left;
      SIZE SROWS()-l_bottom-3,l_right-2 ;
       TITLE "Line_items" ;
      FONT "Foxfont", 9 ;
      FLOAT SYSTEM
ENDCASE
```

There might not seem to be much difference in these code-bracketed versions of the DEFINE WINDOW. But if you look closely, you notice that the Windows version uses a FONT clause to ensure that the FoxPro for MS-DOS emulated font "FoxFont",9 is used to DEFINE the window. This minimizes the visual differences between the two platforms.

The *ON SHUTDOWN* Command and the Windows Screen Font

Our cross-platform application should probably contain the following code in the main calling program:

```
DO CASE
   CASE _WINDOWS
      MODIFY WINDOW SCREEN FONT "FoxFont",7
      ON SHUTDOWN DO exquit
ENDCASE
```

Because the user can change the FoxPro window font in Windows, we must ensure (by issuing the command MODIFY WINDOW SCREEN FONT "FoxFont",7) that our application is running in the fixed FoxPro font or our screens might not align properly.

FoxPro for Windows is a well-behaved Windows application. As a result, the user can shut down a running version of FoxPro simply by electing to close the FoxPro window. Further, the user can elect to exit Windows entirely, thereby closing FoxPro for Windows.

The ON SHUTDOWN command gives us an opportunity to intercept these efforts to close FoxPro while our application is running. The program that you identify with the ON SHUTDOWN command is executed whenever someone or something attempts to close FoxPro.

This program can do anything you want it to do, but it usually does one of the following:

- Saves any outstanding changes to databases and issues a QUIT command.

- Presents a dialog that insists that the user exit the application by the normal means, and not issue a QUIT command. (In this case, the user is left in your FoxPro application.)

- Prompts the user to save or abort changes before issuing a QUIT command.

Maintaining Cross-Platform Applications

The bottom-line cost for writing cross-platform applications is extra maintenance. To have a Windows look and feel in Windows and a MS-DOS look and feel in MS-DOS, you must maintain dual-platform records in the screen and report tables.

If the addition and changes are platform-specific, such as changing the field size in Windows to fit a change in font, you don't have to do anything in the MS-DOS environment because nothing changes in MS-DOS. However, if you reposition a field or change the size of a field within the file structure, you must remember to make the change in both environments.

Screens

The Transporter can pick up any changes made to the object's dialog, such as the addition or change of a VALID clause or formatting instructions. But you still must remember to go to the other platform and modify the screen just to activate the Transporter. Sometimes you can transport changes but you don't want them to appear in the other platform. You can discard such changes by using the Transporter dialog, which appears when you choose Transport and Open.

This "selection" dialog appears in both platforms. Unchecking any object that shouldn't be changed in the current platform ensures that the two platform records retain their unique identity.

Reports

Cross-platform reports work in much the same manner as screens. However, unless you have used special fonts or Windows objects in a report, you don't actually have to transport the report to MS-DOS. The same holds true if you have created the report in MS-DOS. Unless you want to add Windows-specific features, don't bother transporting the table.

Menus

I haven't yet mentioned menus in this discussion, even though they can play an integral part in your application. Menus do not require transporting because they do not contain information specific to any one platform.

However, you might need to enable or disable menu options based on the platform. For instance, if you use OLE objects in the Windows version of your application, you might include the FoxPro system menu Edit pad with its options for embedding or linking OLE objects. Because OLE objects exist only in the Windows platform, these menu options should always be disabled when the application is running in MS-DOS.

The same is true for MS-DOS menu options, such as the Color Picker. Although you might want to include this option for the MS-DOS version, there is no need for this option in the Windows version, because the Windows OS color set controls all the color schemes.

To prevent users from choosing nonapplicable menu options, we use code bracketing in the Menu Builder by using the SKIP FOR option associated with the popup options in question.

For example, by placing the following code into the SKIP FOR expression, we disable the PASTE SPECIAL option when the MS-DOS system variable is .T. (that is, when we're in the MS-DOS version of the product):

```
_DOS
```

This creates an expression that translates as "skip this menu option when _DOS is True" after the menu is generated. You can apply the same technique to all platform-specific menu options.

Labels

In FoxPro for Windows, labels are considered to be a columnar report. Because this is different from FoxPro for MS-DOS, which still has the Label Designer, you can transport a label file only once. After that, you must update both platforms to maintain cross-platform similarities.

Unless you must use the Windows fonts or graphical objects, you should simply leave the labels in MS-DOS character mode and run the same label form on both platforms.

Putting Cross-Platform to Work

The best solution for the cross-platform issue is to choose a platform and stick with it. But if you must go cross-platform, the simplest way is to create the MS-DOS versions of the reports and screens first, because the standard command set is the lowest common denominator. Then transport them into the Windows platform.

Note: If you create your application in FoxPro 2.5 for DOS, avoid DOS-specific tricks such as RUN CD or REPORT FORM TO FILE.

After you transport the reports and screens, you must decide whether you want to run MS-DOS screens and reports in Windows, or Windows screens and reports in Windows.

If you want to take full advantage of the Windows environment, you will find yourself modifying tables to include general fields and adding graphical objects such as spinners and pictures to the screens and reports.

However, once you undertake this cross-platform project, you must remember to make any changes on both platforms. This requires a bit more time and effort. You must also be sure that any Windows platform-specific reference inside of programs is bracketed to prevent runtime errors when you run the programs in MS-DOS.

You also must take the time to learn when and when not to transport objects that have been changed. All in all, cross-platform applications take more code and thought than single-platform applications. Is it worth the effort? Only time, and your users, will tell.

Team Programming

When we first talked about including a chapter on team programming, I was determined that the discussion would focus on real solutions MEI has developed for real problems we have encountered over the last 10 years of providing programming services to companies around the world. So, I turned to our most experienced "team programmer" and asked him to come up with a few ideas for the chapter.

Bruce Troutman has worked on team programming projects at companies such as Georgia Pacific, Mobil Oil, and Exxon, so when I asked him for ideas, he had plenty— in fact, he had enough ideas for an entire book.

Because I was nearly finished with this book and would not start another such effort without a full frontal lobotomy, I asked Bruce for a discussion of some of the most important issues involved in starting a team programming project. What follows is an often pointed, always practical, and never dull crystalization of a few of the lessons Bruce Troutman and Micro Endeavors have learned in the last decade. I hope you find them valuable.

Getting the Job Done Together

When two or more people join a team to produce a FoxPro application, many new factors are introduced that can lead to the relative success or failure of the project. Whether you are an employee or a contractor, an understanding of the differences between programming alone and in work groups prepares you for a successful project.

If you are a team leader, you can provide an environment for success by implementing some of the techniques suggested in this chapter.

Working Alone

A programmer who works alone does not usually have to worry about coding standards, version control, testing scripts, or even dress code. The projects usually are of smaller scope and require less complexity. The jobs of shorter duration are measured in weeks, not months or years. Only one level of the customer's management is normally involved. The programmer has total freedom in coding style. She or he is usually involved from inception through installation of the system. He or she performs all maintenance on the work, and if everything works, gets all the glory.

Working in a Group

When a project requires more than one programmer, it is usually of sizable scope and longer duration. It involves more money, equipment, and usually more interest from multiple levels of management. A programmer who joins a FoxPro work group brings a set of skills that is similar to some of her peers' skills and quite different from others. These skills are often self-taught and thus can vary widely. The complexity of the project prevents the programmer from "doing it all—her way." Unlike the solo programmer, the work group programmer must fit in. Her coding style must fit. She must work within more stringent guidelines for version control and testing. She may even have to follow a dress code. Good work group programmers must be disciplined. If everything works, the group gets the glory.

Leading a Group

FoxPro as development tool has many features and few limitations for work group projects. In the hands of motivated and talented programmers, FoxPro can be used to solve almost any significant problem. The success of a FoxPro work group project depends on the ability of the project leader and team leaders to organize the work to be done and to provide moderate control of the programming team. If everything works, the leader gets a promotion.

Description for an Example Project

The following section describes a project that is provided for demonstration purposes in this chapter.

The marketing department of the ABC Paper Company, a multinational paper products firm, has obtained corporate approval for the development of a sales order and inventory tracking system to upgrade and replace two older systems. Because Windows is a corporate standard, the company has chosen FoxPro for Windows as the development tool. The system will be developed and installed on an existing Novell network.

The system will provide sales order takers with information on the current inventory of paper products. As sales are recorded, inventory will be reduced. As products complete the production cycle, inventory will be increased. Various sales and income reports will be required.

The requirements for the system have been established. ABC will manage system development in-house with internal Information Systems personnel. The project is named *STAPS,* for *Sales Tracking and Production System.* This is the first FoxPro project at ABC.

The project leaders and a FoxPro consultant have decided to staff the STAPS project as shown in Figure 22.1.

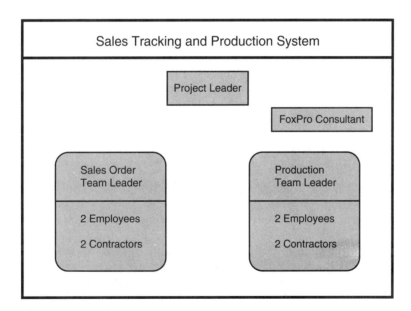

Figure 22.1. Staffing the STAPS project.

Challenges

Every application has its challenges, but multi-programmer applications usually come with their own special set of challenges. I've re-created some of the challenges faced on large team projects for our fictional STAPS project.

The Team Leadership Doesn't Know FoxPro

Because STAPS is the first FoxPro project at ABC, the experienced project and team leaders are not familiar with the language. These leaders must obtain FoxPro training and/or retain a FoxPro consultant to gain insight into the tool. Once they are possessed of this insight, these leaders will be better able to staff the project.

Introductory training courses are effective ways to receive information about the most obvious similarities and differences. For example, FoxPro is often easy to explain to those with COBOL experience. The English-like command names and sentence-like structures are common to both. The differences between code-compile-link cycles and interactive coding are significant and obvious.

An experienced consultant who is familiar with using FoxPro in work groups should be retained on a part-time basis. Such a consultant can explain the not-so-obvious significance of using or not using snippets in screen objects or the proper use of the Project Builder on a network. Team leaders can also use consultants to assist in the staffing interview and selection process.

Staffing with Employees and Outside Consultants

After the STAPS project is completed, ABC personnel will maintain it. Therefore, the development group must include as many ABC employees as possible. Because none have FoxPro experience, they require initial training courses. The best candidates for these positions are experienced programmers, regardless of their background. PC programmers have only a slight advantage over mainframe programmers in understanding the operating system. Those differences disappear quickly.

Experienced consultants should be selected to work with the ABC staff. On the STAPS project, these consultants provide the expertise to make the system work. They teach the new Foxlets how to do FoxPro. You should hire these consultants on a full-time basis to ensure that they will be available throughout the project. Select them not only based on their personal experience and knowledge, but also by their ability and willingness to communicate their knowledge to others, and to receive knowledge from them. Another significant trait is the willingness to adjust individual programming style to that of the group. There is no room for prima donnas on a work group project.

Ownership

The work group must know who owns what in a development project. At the programmer level, one programmer owns each screen set, program, report, and so on. Thus an enhancement or fix can be directed to the owner. Team leaders, analysts, and even users own design concepts, specifications, and requirements. If clarification or confirmation is required, the owner can be readily contacted. Many systems can consist of hundreds or even thousands of owned objects. FoxPro is an appropriate tool to keep track of these ownerships.

Because the project is now a group effort over a longer period of time, a programmer might not see the beginning, middle, and end of a project. He might not be there to see his work praised when it is successful. She might not even work closely with those who are going to use her work. To compensate for this lack of feedback, a good team leader provides programmers with consistent encouragement and recognition.

The Deliverables Approach

The STAPS project should be driven by a series of *deliverables*—milestones to be accomplished in stages. For example, the first pass at the order entry screen is a deliverable. The final user sign-off is one as well. Deliverable schedules and progress provide targets for everyone and can be used by the project and team leaders to encourage and motivate the programmers. The challenge is to keep the schedule within the reach of the talent and expertise of the team.

Standards

It has been said that for every standard there is always one or more reasons to violate it. FoxPro is such a robust language that there are usually two or more ways to do anything. If there were no standards, the STAPS system would likely include every variation, which would create a maintenance nightmare. The team leaders should rely on the FoxPro expert to help establish workable standards for STAPS.

Recommended Standards for a FoxPro Project

- Use a data dictionary (see "The Data Dictionary," later in this chapter).

- Use a version control system (see "The Version Control System," later in this chapter).

- Use Menu Builder, Screen Builder, and Report Generators for the first pass.

- Place program code in program (.PRG) files, not menu (.MNX) or screen (.SCX) files.

- All program code must be programmer tested, FoxDoc'd, compiled, and Project Built successfully before check in.

- Use library routines.

- The programmer and team leader must submit the project jointly.

Communications

ABC is well known for the frequency and length of its meetings. The meetings for the STAPS project will probably be no exception. Most programmers would rather be coding than be in meetings. The "FoxPro Tools for Work Groups" section later in this chapter suggests an issues system that should reduce the frequency of meetings.

One type of meeting that *should* be held, especially for new programmers, is the code walk-through. This is the only method available to ensure that required design logic is being incorporated into the program and that programming standards are being followed.

Team leaders should encourage the sharing of good FoxPro ideas among programmers. There is no advantage in one programmer learning something and not sharing it with the others. One idea is to allow impromptu bull sessions on programming topics. Moderate use of these techniques promotes camaraderie and raises the general knowledge level of the team. Programmers can write their findings in the issues system, described later in this chapter.

You should provide reading materials for the programming team. FoxPro books and periodicals, such as *The FoxPro Advisor, FoxTalk,* and *Data Based Advisor,* can provide ideas that are useful for the project.

Development Environment and Version Control

The FoxPro expert, the network administrator, and the team leaders should agree on a directory structure, for both the network and developer workstations, that enables timely and efficient development and bug-fixing by programmers. This system should also support backup procedures and user testing. Also, the system must be integrated within a version control system that ensures that no more than two copies of a piece of source code ever exist on the network at any time.

A common technique is to require that all development work be kept in a programmer's home directory on the network drive. This facilitates backup and ensures that no development work is lost. Test data can be kept on the workstation drive.

Note: If you are beginning a project on a new network or on a network that experiences significant downtime, you might want to enable your programmers to work on their local workstations. Of course, they will have to upload their local drive activities to their network home directory on a daily basis.

The organization of the network directory structure should be discussed with the network administrator. Drive mappings can provide an almost seamless path from development through testing to production.

As previously mentioned, the programmer's work should be in the home directory. The unit test area should be the next mapping on the path. Thus, when the programmer checks in her code, it is moved to unit test and tested by the team leader. Further up the path is the user test area, which receives the code approved in unit testing. The top mapping is the production area in which currently running code resides.

One suggested pattern follows. It assumes that all development objects—including programs, screen sets, menus reports, and projects—reside in either the production directory or the directory that you are currently using. It also assumes that no .APP or .EXE files are included in these areas.

For example, a new program I am developing is in H:, my home directory. It might call another program that is in P:, production. I don't have to copy the production program to H:, I need only a path to P:. No programming is allowed on local drives, because network backup activities do not pick them up.

The data mapping can always be to one drive letter. The actual data path varies depending on what is being done. For example, in production, T: points to production files, but during testing, T: points to test data. For programmers, T: points to test data, but additional test data can be placed on the local drive.

The administrative area should be mapped so that everyone can access the common project control facilities, such as the dictionary, issues, and version control programs. Table 22.1 shows a typical mapping scheme.

Table 22.1. A typical mapping scheme.

Mapping Area	Drive	Description
Program	H:	The *h*ome directory for each programmer
	M:	The *m*igrate area for new and repaired programs
	L:	The test area for team *l*eaders
	U:	The test area for *u*sers
	P:	*P*roduction programs
Data	T:	The da*t*a area
Administrative	V:	The administrati*v*e area for programs
	X:	The administrative area for data

 Note: Although our example uses a Novell Netware network, FoxPro can take advantage of any NETBIOS-compatible network operating system.

These mappings are established through batch files that are called when FoxPro is loaded. The batch file depends on certain information in the DOS environment, such as USERNAME, which the network log-in script provides. After logging in, the user can execute the following batch file to enter the programmer environment:

```
REM Filename:      PROG.BAT
REM Server Name:   SERVER-1
REM Volume Name:   VOL-2
REM Application:   ACCT  (Accounting)
@ECHO OFF
MAP M: = SERVER-1\VOL2:\ACCT\MIGR\PROG
MAP L: = SERVER-1\VOL2:\ACCT\LEAD\PROG
MAP U: = SERVER-1\VOL2:\ACCT\USER\PROG
MAP P: = SERVER-1\VOL2:\ACCT\PROD\PROG
MAP T: = SERVER-1\VOL2:\ACCT\TESTDATA
MAP H: = SERVER-1\VOL2:\HOME\%USERNAME%\PROG
MAP V: = SERVER-1\VOL2:\ACCT\ADMIN\PROG
MAP X: = SERVER-1\VOL2:\ACCT\ADMIN\DATA
SET FOXPATH=H:.;M:.;L:.;U:.;P:.;T:.;V:.;X:.
```

When FoxPro is loaded, the CONFIG.FPW file executes the following command:

```
COMMAND= SET PATH TO GETENV("FOXPATH")
```

For a programmer with the user name BSTROUTM, the search path looks like this:

```
H:(Server-1\Vol-2\HOME\BSTROUTM\PROG)
M:(Server-1\Vol-2\ACCT\MIGR\PROG)
L:(Server-1\Vol-2\ACCT\LEAD\PROG)
U:(Server-1\Vol-2\ACCT\USER\PROG)
P:(Server-1\Vol-2\ACCT\PROD\PROG)
```

FoxPro Tools for Work Groups

All members of the project team, from programmers to users, can access the administrative area previously mentioned. This provides the communications link. For example, this area can be used to reduce paper work by enabling consultants to file weekly time sheet information, which the project manager can read and print. The tools mentioned in this section were developed for different projects and are intended as examples.

The Data Dictionary

The term *data dictionary* (DD) has many meanings in the Xbase world. I use it in its simplest sense. The purpose of the dictionary is to control the development of data structures and provide information about the system to all team members.

A programming updates the dictionary by building a data structure, testing it with programs, and submitting the structure to the database administrator (DBA). After the DBA obtains the team leader's approval, the name, fields, and indexes are added to the DD.

When changes are needed to update an existing data file, the same process is followed. The test data is updated periodically with the structures from the DD. This forces all programmers to comply.

For example, if a logical field is changed to a character, any program that expects a logical value will crash. The DBA is responsible for informing the programmers of weekly changes. Additionally, the programmers can view the current status of the dictionary and even apply changes to the test data of the local drive.

For more information about building and using a data dictionary, see Chapter 20, "A Data Dictionary." In addition, you can use L3DICT.APP, which is on your source code disk.

The Issues System

Another application useful in the administrative area is one that tracks issues and concerns arising during the development of a project. For example, programmers might be concerned about the valid values for a given field. The team leader might not know the values and have to ask the user. The programmer can accomplish this by creating an issue, addressing it to the team leader. The leader then addresses it to the user for a response. This process can eliminate the need for extra meetings and development discussions.

A side benefit is that the issue is available for all team members to view. Often the impact of an issue reaches beyond those team members who initiate the issue.

The issues system consists of a single, simple, data entry screen, with options for creating, reading, responding to, printing, and filtering messages. The source code for an example issues system, ISSUES.PRG, is included on the source code disk.

The Version Control System

Another significant task that FoxPro can perform is *version control*. Nothing is more destructive to the development process than multiple versions of a program. Programmers are disheartened when others overwrite their changes. Users begin to distrust the system when changes made last week disappear this week.

Many commercial version control products are on the market, so why not use one of them? These products often provide more features than are necessary for a FoxPro project and sometimes are overly restrictive to rapid development techniques.

A successful method for creating your own FoxPro-based version control system begins with the creation of the PROGLOG.DBF. In the PROGLOG.DBF, we store the name of every program, screen, menu, and report in the application, along with the name of the programmer who has checked out the program.

The CHECKOUT.PRG program tests whether a particular file is already "out" before enabling a new programmer to access the object. Thus, if MAINMENU.PRG is checked out to BXTROUTM, no other programmer can place a record in PROGLOG for MAINMENU.PRG until BXTROUTM checks it in.

Note that this does not prevent anyone from copying MAINMENU.PRG into her work area and modifying it. However, the last step is the control. When programmers finish making changes, they must run CHECKIN.PRG. This program compares the programmer ID and the program to be checked in with the log. If they match, the program is moved to M: (the migration area). If not, the program notifies the programmer that another programmer has checked out the program.

The source code disk includes the sample programs CHECKIN.PRG and CHECKOUT.PRG. Both work in an environment similar to the one just described. Paths are hard-coded to reflect such an environment.

Final Thoughts

Hi folks, it's George again. After reading Bruce's chapter, I feel compelled to relate the following truism for the millionth time:

> *The best programs are written by one person. The second best programs are written by two people, and it goes downhill from there.*

This simple truth never fails to wring a laugh from the most conservative IS professionals. Like many simple truths however, it ignores a larger truth:

> *Some projects are too big for one person.*

How then are we to reconcile these seemingly contradictory "truths?" I suggest that we remember the first truth while we accede to the realities of the second.

When we have a project that is too big for one programmer, we break it into smaller projects. Then, we develop or hire programmers who have the skill and talent to start *and* finish a project on their own. After assigning one of these mini-projects to each of our programmers, we direct those programmers to communicate.

Further, we support that communication with version control, issues, and data dictionary tools. Finally, we provide the project team with a leader who has the personal and technical skills to ensure communication among programmers, without reducing the productivity of those programmers.

In short, the lessons of our "conflicting truths" tell us that it is better to let a handful of excellent programmers create several brilliant programs that work together than it is to let a horde of mediocre programmers create a single large program that doesn't work at all.

INDEX

G

M

Complete Computer Coverage

Que's 1993 Computer Buyer's Guide

Que Development Group

This absolute must-have guide
packed with comparisons, recommendations,
and tips for asking all the right questions
familiarizes the reader with terms they
will need to know. This book offers a
complete analysis of both hardware and
software products, and it's loaded
with charts and tables
of product comparisons.

IBM-compatibles, Apple, & Macintosh

$14.95 USA

1-56529-021-6, 450 pp., 8 x 10

Que's Computer User's Dictionary, 3rd Edition

Bryan Pfaffenberger

This compact, practical reference contains
hundreds of definitions, explanations, examples,
and illustrations on topics from programming
to desktop publishing. You can master the
"language" of computers and learn how to make
your personal computer more efficient and more
powerful. Filled with tips and cautions, *Que's
Computer User's Dictionary* is the perfect
resource for anyone who uses a computer.

*IBM, Macintosh, Apple,
& Programming*

$12.95 USA

1-56529-023-2, 600 pp., 4³/₄ x 8

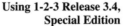

Micro Endeavors, Inc.—The World's Most Successful FoxPro Training and Development Firm

Micro Endeavors trainers have trained more FoxPro programmers than any other firm in the world. We offer FoxPro classes every month at our state-of-the-art facilities in Philadelphia. Each of our students enjoys the individual use of a 486-based PC connected to one of our four local area networks. Between every two desks a special monitor displays the current content of the instructor's screen, enabling all students to clearly follow the instructor's actions.

Our 17,000 square foot facility enables us to hold as many as four FoxPro or Access training classes simultaneously, so there is always enough room for any number of students from the same company. However, we are happy to provide the same high-quality MEI training classes at your site, if you wish.

Micro Endeavors, under exclusive contract with Microsoft University, wrote the course materials that are used in Microsoft University approved FoxPro and Access training courses worldwide. Every student leaves our FoxPro classes with more than 400 pages of detailed documentation, a disk with the sample applications she or he creates in class, and a disk containing Micro Endeavors' own library routines.

Our trainers include George Goley (author of *Creating FoxPro Applications*), Melissa Dunn (co-author of *Creating FoxPro Applications* and author of the Microsoft University FoxPro Courseware), Dr. Michael Brachman (co-author of *Creating FoxPro Applications*), Bruce Troutman (co-author of *Creating FoxPro Applications*), Richard Wolf (author of the Microsoft University Access Courseware), and other distinguished members of the Micro Endeavors training and development team.

Our training clients include Microsoft, AT&T, Sprint, MCI, SBT, The CIA, The Federal Reserve Bank, The FDIC, Sun Oil, Warner Lambert, and hundreds more. In addition, we have developed successful, multiuser, mission-critical applications for clients like Mobil Oil, J.P. Morgan, Marriott, Georgia Pacific, Rhone-Poulenc Rorer, and many others.

Obviously, we'd like to tell you more about Micro Endeavors' classes and services. To obtain more information, you can:

- Call us at 1-800-331-9434.

- Fax us your name, address, phone number, and fax number at 1-215-449-4757.

- Send us your name, address, phone number, and fax number on CompuServe at ID 71140,3527.